Further Stories of Minack

DEREK TANGYE

Further Stories of Minack

Comprising

A Drake at the Door
A Donkey in the Meadow
Sun on the Lintel

Sketches by Jean Tangye

WARNER BOOKS

A *Warner* Book

This omnibus edition first published in Great Britain
by Warner Books in 1997

This edition copyright © Derek Tangye 1997
A Drake at the Door copyright © Derek Tangye 1963
A Donkey in the Meadow copyright © Derek Tangye 1965
Sun on the Lintel copyright © Derek Tangye 1976

A CIP catalogue record for this book
is available from the British Library.

ISBN 0 7515 2040 3

Typeset in Sabon by
Palimpsest Book Production Limited,
Polmont, Stirlingshire
Printed and bound in Great Britain by
Mackays of Chatham plc, Chatham, Kent

Warner Books
A Division of
Little, Brown and Company (UK)
Brettenham House
Lancaster Place
London WC2E 7EN

Contents

A Drake at the Door

1

I heard one day that my neighbour was leaving. We had been neighbours for seven years and, in view of the manner of our coming, conflict between us was perhaps inevitable. The neighbour represented the hard-working peasant, Jeannie and I the up-country interlopers.

Minack and our six acres of land belonged to his farm, although in reality it was not his farm. In the years before the last war, farms in West Cornwall were difficult to let and landowners were thankful to dispose of them under any conditions; and the conditions were sometimes these:

A prosperous farmer would rent an unwanted farm, stock it with cows, put a man of his own choosing called a dairyman into the farm-house, charge him rent for each cow, and then let him run the farm as he wished. My neighbour was a dairyman.

Both of us, then, paid rent to the same absentee farmer; my neighbour for twelve cows, myself for the primitive cottage and the derelict land I was allowed to have with it.

On a practical basis I had the worst of the bargain. It was a whim that led us to Minack; an emotion that made us believe the broken-down cottage edged by a wood and looking out on Mount's Bay between Penzance and Land's End, could become our personal paradise. And after seven years I still did not possess a scrap of paper which proved our legal right to the tenancy.

The reason for this dilatoriness was fear on our part. When in the beginning we pleaded for Minack, the absentee farmer clearly did not mind whether we had it or not. We had to nudge our way into his good humour. We had to be as careful as a ship in a minefield. One false move, a word too thrusting, a suggestion too bold, and we would have been retreating from his presence without a hope of return.

This was an occasion, we both felt, which logic or the legal mind would be a hindrance. It was not the moment to bargain or be too meticulous in wrapping the deal in legal language. We wanted Minack and in order to secure it we had to appear foolish. The result was no lease, all repairs and improvements without prospect of compensation, and six acres of scrubland which most people considered unsuitable for cultivation.

And there were other snags. There was the barn, for instance, within a few yards of the cottage which belonged to my neighbour and not to Minack. Here he used to stable his horses, collecting them in the morning and returning them in the evening; and in wet weather when no outside work could be done he would clear the muck from the floor and pile it beside the lane which led up to his farm-house a quarter of a mile away.

We had made this lane ourselves, opening up again an ancient one by first cutting away the brush which smothered it; for when we first came to Minack the only means of reaching the cottage and the barn was by crossing two fields, waterlogged in winter.

In the autumn my neighbour used to spend days at a

time in the other half of the barn 'shooting' his potatoes for January planting in his section of the cliff; and if it were a period when we were not on speaking terms Jeannie and I found it irksome.

'Did he say anything this morning?' I would ask Jeannie if she had seen him first.

'Not a word.'

Of course there are some who say that the Cornish resent any 'foreigner' who comes to live among them. I am Cornish myself and I do not believe that such resentment, if it exists, is confined to the Cornish alone. Most countrymen if they live far from an urban area are on guard when a stranger appears in their midst. Strangers represent the threat of change, and change is the last thing the true countryman wants. He views the city from afar and is not impressed by its standards; and when in the summer the inhabitants disgorge over the countryside, a leavening of them always confirm the countryman's worst suspicions. The Cornish for the most part heave a sigh of relief when the holiday season is over and Cornwall belongs to them again.

As for individuals, the Cornish have the same basic ingredients as everyone else, the same kindliness or meanness, good humour or jealousy. It is only in obstinacy that the Cornish excel. If a Cornishman senses that he is being driven into taking a step against his freewill nothing, not even a bulldozer, will make him budge.

So our neighbour was leaving. He was forsaking his job as a dairyman to take over a farm of his own. He had won promotion by his hard work, while we now had the chance to take over not only the barn, but also those fields and cliff meadows adjacent to our own which were essential for certain expansionist plans we had in mind. We were delighted. Here was the opportunity to put sense into our life at Minack, to regularise our position by securing a lease, to act indeed in a practical fashion. It was not, however, a question of expressing a desire, and the desire materialising without more ado. We soon discovered there were complications.

The news of my neighbour's coming departure speedily spread through the neighbourhood, and young men began tumbling over each other in efforts to gain the vacant dairymanship for themselves.

The lure, in particular, lay in the cliff meadows which were renowned for the earliness of their potatoes and daffodils. Most of these were as steep as those we had cut in our own cliff, and I did not fancy them very much myself . . . we had enough hand labour already, turning the ground in the autumn, carrying down the seed potatoes, shovelling them in, shovelling them out, carrying the harvest hundredweight after hundredweight up the cliff again. And in any case I sensed the golden days of Cornish new potatoes from the cliff were over.

But there were other meadows cresting my neighbour's cliff that were ideal for our needs, large enough for a small tractor, and accessible to the Land Rover when it was necessary to use it. This was reason enough why we wanted them, but there was another.

These meadows were reached by passing in front of the cottage and taking the track towards the sea which led also to Minack meadows. We had watched our neighbour for seven years using this throughfare and we did not want to see anyone else doing the same. Minack, in substance, was remote from any habitation, breathing peace in its solitude, and we wanted to eliminate any prospect of enduring again the grit of friction.

And there were the fields around us. Had we been able to wave a magic wand we still could not have made use of all of them; but there were four surrounding Minack which, if we possessed them, would provide the twin advantage of isolation with the practical one of giving us the elbow-room vital for development.

In particular we needed flat ground for greenhouses. We already had one small greenhouse tucked in a clearing of the wood and another, a splendid one a hundred feet long and twenty-one feet wide, stretching down in front of the cottage on land that was swamp when we arrived. We felt sure that our future security lay in such factory-like protection; the only way possible to demolish the omnipotence of the weather.

We were aware, then, that we were at a crucial moment of our life at Minack. Here we were poised between stagnation and progress, an irritant and solace; and the success or failure of the action I was about to take would dominate the years to come. I had decided to be bold.

The absentee landlord had by now become a good friend of ours.

'Harry,' I said to him one day, 'how about your giving up the lease and letting me have it instead?'

I knew quite well that by making this overture I was heading for a period of bargaining. He belonged to the breed who prefer this period of bargaining to its culmination; and should it be a horse he was buying, or a motor-car or a load of hay, his ultimate pleasure lay in the skill with which he had conducted the negotiations. I, on the other hand, like to get a deal over as quickly as possible. I have not the nerve of a dealer. If I know what I want, I find no pleasure in protracting negotiations provided the sum is reasonably within the figure I have decided to pay.

Nor had I, as far as these negotiations were concerned, any cards up my sleeve. I was living again the time when I first asked Harry for Minack. I had to have it, and he knew it. I was naked. I was at his mercy.

Inevitably he began to dally; and, as if I were a fish on a hook, he set out to give me plenty of line and himself plenty of play before he landed me neatly on the bank. Out came the excuses . . . he had promised the farm to Mr X . . . it had been for so long in his family that for sentimental reasons he did not wish to give it up . . . if Mr X did not have it, he would use the fields for young cattle . . . and so on. all these proposals were told with such conviction and friendliness that I would come back to Jeannie in despair.

'He won't let us have it,' I would say to Jeannie disconsolately.

It was the mood that Harry wanted to create. He knew that, keen as I was to do a deal, he could titillate me to be still keener. I *had* to buy the lease from him, and each fruitless interview only made me more frantic; a cigarette dangling from his lips, he watched me betraying my anxiety.

Meanwhile a corner of my mind was occupied by another problem. When, and if, Harry and I came to terms I would find myself a tenant not only of Minack but also of the hundred-acre farm to which it belonged.

This was absurd. I had been consumed to such an extent by the desire for self-preservation that I had ignored the implications the success of my endeavour might entail. And anyhow, would the landlord accept me as a tenant?

The landlord was a remote person who owned large estates in Cornwall and who, as is customary, employed a land agent as a buffer between himself and his tenants. He was an enlightened landowner and he possessed a zeal to preserve the countryside, not to exploit it; in particular he felt a special trust for the wild, desolate coastline where Minack was situated. His tenants were of course carefully chosen and his farms well managed but, and this was the key to the situation as far as I was concerned, the Minack farm was the only one on his estates which was now leased to an absentee farmer.

I now found myself in the process of conducting two negotiations instead of one, and in both I was sure to be the financial loser. I did not care. I had the same irrational, dynamic instinct which pushes a man up a mountain, the urge for conquest without a material value, to reach a halo which rewards the individual but never the onlooker. Security at Minack meant to us a way of life we loved. How do you price such an acquisition?

I outlined the situation to the land agent who needed no persuading to appreciate the chance I was giving him. I was offering, in fact, to buy the lease of a farm, and return it without charge to the landlord. It had never happened before in the land agent's experience; and yet fortunately, he had enough subtlety of mind to realise there was guile behind my offer.

I was expecting payment, but the payment was not to be made in pounds, shillings and pence. I was asking for the fulfilment of my plan to secure a direct lease for Minack together with the extra land I required; and I was also asking to propose my own nominee for the farm proper.

Such an arrangement would enable the landlord once again to have direct control of Minack and the farm; and we would have the peace we sought. A secure lease for ourselves, a co-operative neighbour of our own choosing.

As it happened I already knew whom I wanted to have the farm. I had stopped the Land Rover by the milk stand which corners our long lane and the main road a week or two previously when a young farm worker called Jack Cockram came up to me. He had heard the farm was vacant and could I put in a good word for him?

At the time, of course, I could be of no help. I had neither the ear of Harry nor of the land agent, and so there was nothing I could do. But I knew the occasion was important. I had always liked Jack. He had been a wartime evacuee on the farm where he was now a skilled farmworker. He had married Alice Grenfell, niece of Jim Grenfell who kept the inn at St Buryan, and they lived in a council house in the village with their one little girl and were soon to have another.

He was plainly a type who could become a good farmer and yet, because of lack of opportunity, he would be more likely to remain a farmworker for the rest of his life. Both

Jeannie and I now began to experience great pleasure that not only was there the prospect of benefiting ourselves but also the possibility of launching this couple into a new life. And so, as soon as the land agent had given tacit approval to my suggestions, I determined to complete my negotiations with Harry.

I had no need to force the issue. The evening I saw him he too had decided the time of dithering was over. I thought his proposals were perfectly fair, and I promptly accepted them. He had gained from the sale of the lease the amount he would, in any case, have received in due course from the rents of myself and my neighbour. But there was one aspect of the deal from which he could claim a victory. It was indeed a handsome victory; and when I returned from the meeting to Jeannie my elation was tempered by this subsidiary problem which now faced us.

'Jeannie,' I said, 'we are now the owners of twelve useless cows.'

My concern was due to these particular cows being classified as reactors which meant they had failed to pass the tubercular test examination. Up to a year or so before this would not have mattered as there were scores of farms in Cornwall with reactor cows to be tested, and those which failed had to be destroyed and sold only for meat consumption. The deadline for this edict was at the end of this particular year.

The result had been that the value of such cows had nose-dived; yet I had contracted with Harry to pay him the price of eight years before, the same valuation of the twelve cows with which he had stocked Minack when my neighbour, the dairyman, was installed.

I was further hampered by my inability to set about selling the cows until Michaelmas Day when my neighbour departed. The only thing I could do was to study the cattle markets of various centres in Cornwall, and to stare at the cows themselves as they munched in the fields around us.

As they were not entities in my life, I inevitably began to feel sorry for them; but I also discovered the streak of the businessman was becoming alive in me. I was paying £35 for each of these cows and according to the markets they were not worth £15 apiece; and already the flush of my triumph in securing the lease had started to dissolve into an unhappy feeling that I was wasting a great deal of money. I waited for Michaelmas Day.

At midday the cows became ours. Twelve cows peacefully grazing in a meadow – £420 worth. They looked so content and handsome chewing the grass, the Guernsey buff against the green, the dark Minack wood behind them and in the distance the sea, that Jeannie and I found ourselves marvelling at the toughness of people who can deal in animals as merchandise. The first and last time we were ever to sell an animal. And the sooner it was done the better.

Jack Cockram, now installed at the farm, had agreed to look after them but he too urged speed although for a different reason. The cows might get ill and then I would be worse off than ever; Thursday was market day at Penzance and the best thing I could do would be to arrange for a haulier to collect them. But I had observed that the prices at this market had been lower than anywhere else. It was Monday and I had two days to decide.

Meanwhile I had a most unexpected piece of good fortune. As the new owner I received the cow dossier, a document containing the history of each cow, and to my delight I found that one of them was not a reactor after all. It had passed the test. It was the equivalent of a thoroughbred. In a matter of seconds this particular cow had shot up in value from £15 to over £70. And there was more good fortune soon to come.

On Tuesday afternoon around four o'clock, at a moment when I was pacing the sitting-room discussing with Jeannie what we should do, a car arrived; and when I looked out of the window to see who it could be, there was Harry getting out of one door and another man, in a faded tweed suit and a weather-worn trilby, getting out of another. This was the first occasion that Harry had arrived at Minack without being the boss. I wondered why.

It was an endearing reason. Having completed the deal with me, having tasted his victory, he had an unsophisticated wish to soften the difficulties in which he knew I would be involved. He had brought me a cattle dealer. Here was a man who, if I agreed to his offer, would carry the cows away and I would never have to see them again. It was an idea which had a special appeal to Jeannie.

I found myself, then, with Harry sitting on one side of me on the sofa and the cattle dealer on the other, while Jeannie, after a hurried instruction from me, was in charge of dispensing the beginnings of a bottle of whisky.

Harry, because that had always been his intention, performed the task of breaking the ice and he did so by extolling the virtues of the cattle dealer. He was an old man, and I felt that he carried with him the sniff of cattle on the move from one place to another; and, although he belonged to a world of human beings with whom I had no common denominator, I had enough zest for opportunism to listen and not to contradict.

The price discussion began. Out of the corner of my eye I admired the polish with which Jeannie removed one empty glass, refilled it, then watched again as that too became empty. Harry meanwhile, having unloaded his charm, slipped quietly into a corner, listening but taking no part.

I found a wonderful toughness within me that I had expected to be smothered by the threat of failing to complete a deal. Why does one have to wait for an emergency to be aware of the secret self? I can cope with the emergencies of my old life, the instant quick adjustments when countering the moves of those on similar wavelengths; but I fumble when faced by those with whom, except in the matter of the moment, I have nothing in common.

So there I was discussing the price of these cows when I saw Jeannie disappear out of the front door. One does not embark upon the kind of life I was leading unless one's wife is so part of it that one never for one second has to consider her as one of its problems. Never begin if there is doubt on either side. This is an adventure which is doomed unless it is shared . . . and there was Jeannie disappearing out of the front door.

I had now become increasingly confident, a wave of unreality had taken charge of me and I was talking about cows to this cattle dealer as if I had myself been a dealer all my life. I did not believe my voice . . . 'Give me £25 each for the lot and it's a deal.'

I learned in due course that this was the moment when Jeannie felt she could do nothing more. She felt I was among wolves. Her affection was tested not by offering any practical help, but by releasing me from her presence; as if she, because of her familiarity, might bring doubt to me as to whether or not I was capable of standing up against so strange a creature as a cattle dealer.

She took a walk to the cliffs, and looked down on the sea of Mount's Bay. It is a sea which is always reassuring. It has the familiarity of the street outside other people's homes. For Jeannie, at that moment, it had the reassurance to bring her back to the cottage with the certainty that all was well.

And all *was* well. As she came up the path from the cliff, the cattle dealer was signing a cheque using the bonnet of his car as a desk . . . and the price for each reactor cow was £23.

Harry was looking for a cigarette and I gave him one.

Now we were ready for the next stage of our life at Minack.

2

Jane was with us now. She had knocked at the door of the cottage one August evening the year before while Jeannie and I were having supper. She wore jeans, sandals, and a dark blue fisherman's jersey. Hair, like a pageboy's, fell the colour of corn to her shoulders; she was tiny, and yet there was about her a certain air of assurance, a hint of worldly confidence which belied her child-like appearance. She was fourteen years old.

'I'm Jane Wyllie,' she announced, 'I want to work for you.'

There was no sound of the soil in her voice. It was a bell, a softly pitched bell and her words came pealing out in a rush; as if they had been rehearsed, as if a pause would break the spell of childish enthusiasm with which she was flooding the cottage. Neither Jeannie nor I dared interrupt. We had to wait until her role had been played, watching blue eyes that seemed to lurk with laughter, paying proper attention to an intense performance designed to prove her services would be invaluable.

Her mother said later that a relation had declared that Jane was deadly; meaning that Jane, once she had made up her mind on the course to take, was never to be deterred. She overcame obstacles by smothering them with her tenacity. She did not, like some, leap over them in the zest of temporary emotion, landing on the other side only to find the thrill had disappeared. She crawled to her goal and, once there, blossomed her achievement by being content.

Her plot, in this particular instance, was a simple one; for Jeannie and I were to be the means by which she would be able to leave school. We were the pivot of her future. If she could win us, total strangers as we were, over to her side she would be able to defeat an array of schoolmistresses, relations and friends who were urging her to pursue a scholastic career. We were, therefore, unsuspectingly the ace up her sleeve. We sat in innocence and listened.

She was at a boarding school near Salisbury and as she would be fifteen that November she would be old enough to leave at the end of the winter term. Her headmistress looked upon the prospect with displeasure; because, it seemed she possessed the kind of brains which could be moulded into the pursuit of a conventional career. At this point, unknowingly of course, she had struck a chord of sympathy in both Jeannie and myself. Both of us carried the memory of youthful rebellion, and neither of us had ever regretted it. Jane had begun to seep into our affection.

Her home life, we learned, had been haphazard; and when she began to tell us about it she lost her tension, bubbling a tale of the nomadic adventures of her family as if there had never been any sadness in their substance. A farm in the New Forest, another on Bodmin Moor, another at Wadebridge . . . there were so many homes that I lost count and yet the theme, as she told of them, was one of happiness despite the plain fact that the story was one of a family struggling financially to survive.

I realised as I listened that here was a girl, young as she was, who appraised the values of life by the events she experienced rather than by what she was told. She was off the main road of convention rambling in the scrubland discovering pleasures that were hidden to others; and as she talked it became clear that she had a remarkable mother.

It was the impetus of her mother's new job that had pushed her to Minack. The family, for practical reasons, had now split up. One older sister had married, another had become a groom in a riding stables, her father had entered the hotel business, and her mother had now become herdswoman at the neighbouring farm of Pentewan. She had arrived at the end of July from her previous job at Wadebridge together with Jane, Jeremy who was nine, Acid a brindle bull terrier, Eva a griffon, Sim a Siamese cat, Val a white Persian, Polly the parrot who had belonged to Jane's grandmother, and Lamb. Lamb was now a sheep.

The farmer, a quiet fellow, from whom it happened I rented two acres of cliff land, had viewed the arrival of the Wyllie gang with surprise. He had expected only the herdswoman whom he had interviewed in a Truro hotel; but the caravanserai had arrived in a van with an *élan* which drove him into silence.

He greeted them doubtfully at the farm, then sent them on down the cobbled lane to the cottage which was to be their home.

It was the centre one of three that were strung together, posted above a high cliff, a cliff which plunged in stages to a sea that was restless even when the wind was light. And when the storms raged, spray drifted over the cottages, windows were filmed with salt, and sometimes the gales in their fury punched open the doors spewing like a jet inside.

Gulls swept above the rocks below, and cormorants speeded over the waves, and on the inaccessible cliff to the left a colony of jackdaws spent the day long in endless chatter. At places below the cottages, wondrous to a stranger, were shadows of once cultivated meadows lodged in the cliff like crevices. Who thought they were worth creating? Jane was to find them and to this day there is one where the daffodils she planted still bloom in the spring. There was no electric light in the cottages, no indoor sanitation, and water, except for a trickle of a well, was drained from the roof. The main road and the bus stop were a mile away.

Each cottage had a small garden with a gate that opened on to a narrow field which broadened as it went eastwards until it met another, a huge one leaning towards the panorama of Mount's Bay like a giant carpet of green. At the distant end was a low stone wall. Over this into another field, and half way across the tip of Minack chimney comes into view, then its massive width, then the roof. So many countless times was Jane to come this way; and when the gales blew she either had to fight head down for every yard she covered or had to race across the ground like a feather in the wind.

I looked at her now as she sat neatly on the edge of a chair. She was dainty, small hands and feet, and although her figure was sturdy she did not suggest the stamina for a landgirl.

'What does your mother say?'

'Mum's not quite certain, but if I get a job . . .'

Her mother was in the quandary of all mothers. The age of breaking away, the taut arguments which swing this way and that, the rampaging emotions of love and responsibility, so anxious to act for the best, not to be selfish, not to yield to the temptation of keeping a child at home when the horizons await.

'Mum wants me to do what I feel I want to do, and I want to work on a flower farm.'

No wonder we were the ace up her sleeve. Five minutes' walk over the fields and she would be home. A job, in fact, on her doorstep. A home where her mother would be with her and her animals around her. We were her only chance. There was no other market garden in the neighbourhood who would need her; and neither did we.

'Jane,' I said gently, 'you see we don't need anyone like you. I've a man helping me and I don't want any-one else.'

She flushed, and her eyes wandered away from mine; and there was a silence except for Hubert the gull who chose this moment to cry for his dinner from the roof.

'That's Hubert,' I said, grateful for the distraction, 'he's very old and I don't think he'll be with us much longer.' Jeannie had gone outside and thrown him up a slice of homemade bread, and the silence had returned. I did not doubt that Jane would be useful but another wage, however small, only added to our expenses. And yet . . . enthusiasm cannot be priced.

'Perhaps,' I said, 'when you get back next term you'll find you want to stay on after all.' And then, yielding a lit-tle, I added, 'If the winter flowers do well we *might* be able to give you a couple of days a week after Christmas.'

We did not see her again until the first of January. I had almost forgotten her. Unaware of her character I imagined her visit had been a passing whim and some other excitement was now occupying her mind. Suddenly, however, I looked out of the window at eight o'clock on New Year's Day morning, and there was Jane coming up the path to the cottage.

'Heavens,' I said to Jeannie, 'the girl's here. What on earth am I going to say?'

There was no need for me to worry. Within a fortnight she had nudged her way into our life. Within a month we had engaged her permanently.

Geoffrey was our mainstay at the time. His home was in our village of St Buryan where generations of his family had lived. He was in his early thirties, strong as an ox, and the fastest picker of daffodils I have ever seen. He raced through a bed of daffodils as if he were some special machine devised to do the work automatically. The art of such picking lies in turning your hand backwards, burying it in the foliage, then moving forward, breaking the stems off at the base until your hand can hold no more; each handful is dropped on the path and collected into the basket when the length of the bed has been completed. As always the final skill lay in instinct. Geoffrey had an uncanny knack of inevitably picking the right stem; for myself, if I tried to go too fast, I would curse myself for picking a daffodil still green in bud.

He was a good shovel man. This is an outworn phrase today but when we launched our ambitions at Minack, a man who was so described by his fellow villagers was among the labouring *élite*. The area was greatly dependent on cliff meadows and such meadows could not be dealt with by machine. The long Cornish shovel was the master. It turned the ground in the autumn, it planted the potatoes, it dug them out, and in August it was at work again planting the daffodil bulbs.

'He's a good shovel man,' therefore became a testimony as powerful as one given to a Rolls-Royce engine.

I have spent many hours of my life behind Geoffrey and his shovel. I felt humble as I watched him for there was a polish about his actions which I could never hope to emulate. Just as he picked daffodils with style, so did he use his long-handled shovel.

And there was Shelagh.

We first met her in the square outside St Buryan Church and we left her on that occasion without knowing her name or having any idea that she was to become for ever a part of Minack. We had A. P. Herbert staying with us at the time and one morning when we had gone up the village a cluster of people had gathered around us, autograph books in hand, pressing A.P.H. for his signature.

Sometimes at such moments autograph hunters are like moths round a candle; they see one of their number collecting a signature, and they press forward themselves without knowing the identity of the celebrity whose signature they are seeking. Something is up, they realise, and they must not be left out.

Among this particular cluster were a number of children who, because of their age, had no real reason to know of A.P.H's distinction; and one of them was a young girl about twelve years old with mousey-coloured hair and pink cheeks who hovered shyly in the background, notebook in hand, until everyone else having received their autograph, she moved forward.

By this time it was perfectly clear that none of the children had the faintest idea who A.P.H. could be. He had gently asked each one, and each one had only been able to reply in a mumble. He, of course, was not upset at all by this. He only asked the question to bring life to a situation which might otherwise have been embarrassingly silent. Then up came Shelagh.

'I'll give you a shilling if you can tell me who I am,' smiled A.P.H. taking her notebook and beginning to scribble. Shelagh blushed confusedly and looked down at the ground.

'Sir Hubert . . . or something,' she blurted out.

Even then, unknowingly, she had become a part of Minack. For a gull that summer had begun to haunt our cottage, sweeping inland every day from the cliffs, perching on the roof, watching us as we went about our business, splendidly emphasising a sense of community with the wild.

'An old gull it'll be,' someone had explained to us, 'it won't be with you long. They often start coming to a habitation when their time is near.'

For that reason we had given it no name. If it were soon to die it was better for it to remain anonymous. So when it sailed to us out of the sky, one would call to the other: 'The gull's here!' Just a nameless gull out of the hundreds which passed daily over Minack. And yet, as week after week passed by, and it became as familiar to us as the chimney beside which it strutted, we began to realise that sooner or later it must have a name. The gull had character. We found ourselves accepting its company in the same natural way as the sight of Monty our cat, stretched on a wall in the sun.

It was up there on the roof that morning we returned from St Buryan. We drove up the lane in the Land Rover, pulled up outside the cottage, and as I switched off the engine, the gull suddenly put back its head pointing its beak to the sky, and began to bellow the noise of a bird-like hyena.

'That,' said A.P.H. in mock solemnity, 'is a protest against my being called Sir Hubert . . . or something.'

From then on the gull had its name. For no other reason than this he was known to the end of his days as Hubert. He had a long time to go; and, as I will tell, Shelagh was with us when one day years later he came to us dying, shot through the foot by an airgun.

But at the time of Hubert's christening, we of course did not know the name of the girl who had inspired it and we did not see her again for a year or more. Then her mother by adoption who had a house in the village came to help Jeannie in the cottage once a week, and when she was not at school Shelagh came too.

She was very shy. Some who grow up without ever knowing the love of their true parents develop a grudge against society; and who is to blame them? Unwanted from birth they have reason to punch at life like a boxer hitting his opponent in the ring. They carry with them an unremovable scar. Their creation was a careless indulgence yet they, not their true parents, pay the penalty. I do not think it would be easy at times to be calm if one was one of them.

But there are others, and Shelagh was one, who suffer

the hell of no confidence, who pursue their lives in a secret world in which kicks are expected; who, though yearning for affection, cannot believe it can be gained without hurt. They are suspicious without being cynical. They seek for ever to give and find the love their sweet natures were born to receive.

Shelagh came from St Buryan parish but spent the first few years of her life in the north country with the couple who had adopted her. When they retired they came to live at St Buryan; and inevitably everyone in the village knew of Shelagh's secret. In a village where people were not so kind this might have been a bitter experience but no one, not even the children, ever made her deliberately aware that they knew of it. Yet she must have known that she was pointed at. She certainly knew she was pitied.

She blushed easily and was very silent; and when she did say a few words she mumbled them so that they were difficult to hear. She was, however, extraordinarily intelligent. We never had to tell her twice how to carry out a task, even in those first days when she was still at school; and if we praised her she greeted it with surprise.

She was learning to be a seamstress, and was already an excellent one; and so Jeannie used to give her socks to darn, zips to put in, the hem of a skirt to be altered, curtains to make, and so on. She used to take whatever it was home with her, and when she returned she would timidly ask for some tiny charge which Jeannie used immediately to treble. Jeannie, because they were of the same size, used to give her clothes she no longer needed herself; and I remember a tweed suit which Gertrude Lawrence had given Jeannie when she was playing in *The King and I* on Broadway. Shelagh was wearing it one Saturday afternoon when I saw her gaily sauntering down Market Jew Street in Penzance. The mark of Fifth Avenue on a waif.

When her mother by adoption stopped working for us, Shelagh continued to come on Saturday or Sunday mornings. We did not specifically ask her to do so, but she would arrive and start doing something useful like cleaning the shoes or, during the season, washing out the jam jars and galvanised pails. And there was one occasion, the first in which she played a vital part in the pattern of our life, when her presence seemed to us to be beyond value.

Jeannie and I had developed an idea in which we believed lay our flower farm fortune. It was one of those ideas which come to you in the middle of the night and, to your surprise and delight, appear still just as bright in the middle of the following afternoon. The idea was to exploit the urge of holiday visitors to acquire mementoes by offering them a neat pack of daffodil bulbs. Instead of the factory-made lighthouses, ashtrays and other ornaments, I would offer them something which was genuinely Cornish. They would look at their daffodils the following spring and happily remember their holidays of the previous year; and as daffodil bulbs need not necessarily deteriorate, each future spring would give them the same pleasure. Something alive to take back from Cornwall, instead of a tasteless inanimate object from a gift shop.

Nor did we have any competitors. Pre-packs at the time had not yet entered the bloodstream of the public, and certainly no one had thought of pre-packed Cornish bulbs. They were to do so, of course, the following year; but Jeannie and I were the pioneers, and the pathfinders for the big growers who thought our idea such a good one.

We now had to put our plan into effect; and there was a brush between Jeannie and myself. It was January, and though the holiday season was six months away we had immediately to begin our preparations. The fundamentals were clear. We would use for the packs the bulbs of those daffodils which we had found commercially uneconomical. We would begin digging them up when the foliage had died back in the middle of May or the

beginning of June; and we would distribute the bulbs
in one-pound packs to any gift shop in Cornwall which
would take them. My difference with Jeannie was that I
wanted to begin cautiously with a plain polythene pack
and a suitable label attached, while she insisted the secret
of our success would lie in an attractively designed pack
which caught the eye.

I compromised by agreeing to seek the advice of an
expert, and in due course the gentleman arrived at the
cottage. He represented a huge company. He was a merchandise expert dealing with a vast variety of pre-pack
designs throughout the country. He was smoothly self
important. He crushed me with facts, figures and theories
until inevitably I realised he had his noose around my
neck. I had to surrender unconditionally to such a man.
He *knew* how to sell a product whether nylon stockings,
washed carrots or bulbs. He possessed the magic link
between the idea and the tick of the cash register. We
were lucky indeed to have found him.

We had, therefore, an elaborate design for our pack.
It was in three colours, red, yellow and green. There
was the map of Cornwall in yellow with certain holiday
centres such as Newquay and Falmouth marked in black,
a gay sketch of daffodils in bloom backed by a sheaf of
green foliage; and in bold red letters at the bottom of the
polythene bag the words, Bulbs From Cornwall. It was
very effective. And it was crowned by a splendid idea of
the expert. Balancing the design in large red letters were
the two words, Lamorna Pack, and underneath in tiny
letters, Packed by Tangye. Thus we had skilfully imposed
upon the public a trade name. Throughout the land the
public would be asking for *our* pack.

For by this time, and after several visits, the imagination
of the expert had taken wings. We were now close friends.
I looked forward to his visits with excitement for he
conjured up prospects of our future prosperity so lush
that I began to wonder where the bulbs were going to

come from with which to fill our packs. Our sales would
not be limited to Cornwall. We would compete with the
imported Dutch bulbs. We would make use of the magic
name of Cornwall and sell our packs throughout the
country. The potential sales were enormous. My friend
knew of city stores who would queue up for our supplies.
I even began to worry that the object of our escape to
Minack might be defeated. Supposing we ended up by
having a factory?

We now had to decide how many packs to order. Before
the expert had become my friend I had been thinking in
terms of a couple of thousand but now the picture had
become so rosy that I had to think in the role of an
imaginative business man. After all, as the man pointed
out, his firm would not be able to replenish our supplies
at a moment's notice; it would take at least six weeks and
might we not lose in that time the flush of our sales?
And there was another point, a very old point as far
as salesmen are concerned. The more we bought, the
cheaper per thousand they would be. It was a tempting
situation.

We were being encouraged, meanwhile, by our friends
and those with gift shops who would stock the packs. We
were flattered by their applause and delightfully deceived
by their enthusiasm. Ours was a gimmick which could not
fail. A small fortune lay ahead of us. We would be fools
not to prepare for such success with verve. We ordered
twenty thousand. And it was their arrival which gave me
my first apprehension.

Ours is a long lane, narrow and twisting, and the
turning space in front of the cottage is confined. It is a
major task for a lorry to turn. The prospect of one trying
to do so is always disquieting. And on this occasion on
a peaceful Friday in the first week of June when Jeannie
caught sight of the lorry lumbering slowly down the lane
and shouted: 'British Railways are coming!' . . . I suddenly
found my confidence ebbing swiftly away from me. I had

had good ideas before in my life so why should this one succeed when others had failed?

The threat from the lorry did not materialise. It turned without mishap and as it bumped away, Jeannie and I were staring at a huge cardboard packing case it had left behind. Again I had a sense of foreboding.

'£120 worth of polythene,' I murmured as I stuck a knife into the edge of the case. I tore the top off, and there were our Packs. A vast concourse of Packs, sandwiched together, thousand upon thousand of them, the map of Cornwall a shining yellow, the clarion call of Bulbs From Cornwall a gleaming red. It was immensely impressive. My friend, true to his word, had done an expert's job.

'They're marvellous,' said Jeannie happily.

My morale had many times been boosted by Jeannie's buoyancy. She attacks a problem without burrowing too closely underneath it and thus balances my sense of realism which I so often find depressing.

'Perhaps they look marvellous,' I said lugubriously, 'but we have to fill them *and* sell them.'

It was her luck, however, that at this very moment a car arrived and out of it stepped a handsome young man who explained he had a gift shop at Land's End. He had heard, he said, that we had packed bulbs to sell and could we let him have a hundred Packs as soon as possible?

Land's End! The prospect of having an outlet in this memento paradise seemed equal to winning a football pool. I was instantly at the other end of my personal see-saw. I was more excited than Jeannie. I visualised the hordes disgorging from their coaches and cars, posing beside the Last House in Britain, and returning from whence they came with our Pack in their bags.

'We must get Shelagh tomorrow to help us,' I said urgently to Jeannie, 'this is our great chance.'

The three of us worked throughout Saturday and it was the charm of Shelagh that, young as she was, her enthusiasm was as great as ours. It was always to be thus. Some days, of course, she was to have her moods like everyone else and I would say to Jeannie: 'What's wrong with Shelagh today?' I would ask sometimes the same question about Jane. But neither, when later the two of them were the backbone of our work at Minack, ever failed to give us the enthusiasm we hoped for.

Shelagh had quick hands. In front of us on the bench of the packing shed we had cardboard boxes in which were heaped the various kinds of bulbs. Hospodar and Lucifer and Bernardino, Sunrise and Laurens Koster and Croesus. We had bought these bulbs when first we had come to Minack, because they were very cheap and we did not know the blooms were no longer wanted in the markets. To us they were beautiful to look at; but daffodils have fashions, and these to the salesmen of Covent Garden were as incongruous as the costumes of the 'twenties. They consumed, however, the same time and expense in picking, bunching and sending away, as daffodils which fetched three times their price.

But now at last they were rewarding us. A few of each in every Pack, then on the scales and off, a wire clip around the neck of the Pack, and it was ready to join the others. Jeannie at one end of the bench, I in the middle, Shelagh at the other; and for every Pack that I filled, Jeannie and Shelagh filled two. It was tiring. We had to concentrate. But never throughout that Saturday did Shelagh pause. She was only fourteen.

In the late afternoon Jeannie and I set out for Land's End, the Packs grouped in boxes in the well of the Land Rover. It was a moment of high expectation; and when we joined the line of cars heading for the conglomeration of buildings, higgledy-piggledy like litter, which lay lumped at the end of the road, we were blind this time to the ugliness of the crowds. Land's End, for us, had only been a place to visit in winter; when the seas were lashing the Longships, and the sun was setting angrily, and mysterious cargo boats struggled on their course, and we were alone except for the seagulls. But on this afternoon the crowds were our friends. The jammed car-park was a delectable sight. The coaches, spilling out vast quantities of the human race, presented us with notions which would have even excited the manager of Marks and Spencer's. What potential sales! Six packs per coach and this first supply would be gone in a morning. And there were still all the other holiday centres of Cornwall.

'Jeannie,' I said, as we arrived at the Gift Shop, my voice firm with conviction, '*this* is the moment we have fought for.'

I do not know, even now, what went wrong. I think perhaps our idea was ahead of its time. More likely we did not possess the flair to exploit our opportunities. The art of salesmanship requires a toughness that is not part of our characters. Neither of us can bargain, and we are too easily bruised if a stranger by his manner makes us feel we are living the role of a petitioner.

That summer we roamed Cornwall with our Packs. True we covered our expenses but the prairie fire we expected never materialised; and without the urge of instant success our enthusiasm flagged. The holiday-makers preferred Midland-made hardware to our bulbs, and not even the eye-appealing, cunningly designed front of our Pack could persuade them differently. Our friend the merchandise expert had been proved wrong.

We never saw or heard of him again. He had proved himself an excellent salesman and he had left us something to remember him by. It is still there in the packing shed. A huge cardboard packing case. Nineteen thousand empty Packs inside.

Shelagh left school the following year and went to work as a domestic help on a farm. We seldom saw her. A year or so later she left to join a number of girls on a large flower farm near Penzance; and, in order to save her money on the bus fare, she used to bicycle to and fro from St Buryan, up and down the hills underterred however bad the weather.

One day, as she was leaving work, her bicycle skidded and she fell off, so injuring her head that she was for ten days on the danger list. It was, of course, some weeks before she was fit again to work and by this time she had lost her job. One morning she arrived white-faced at our door. She looked as if a long period of convalescence was essential.

But I knew without her speaking why she had come. Jobs are difficult to find for girls in West Cornwall and so it was inevitable that she should think of us. She had walked the three miles from St Buryan; and if during this walk she had been reciting to herself the phrases she planned to use, all she now could blurt out was: 'Have you got a job for me?'

There was no job. She was just too late.

'You see,' I explained, before driving her back to St Buryan in the Land Rover, 'we have just taken on a young girl. Jane . . . Jane Wyllie.'

I wish I had known at that moment that these two were to become such close friends. The lost look on Shelagh's face would not have been necessary.

3

The first task we gave Jane was looking after the sweet peas in the long greenhouse in front of the cottage. We had sown the seeds in September and transplanted the sturdy little plants in October. Now in January they were speedily climbing their supporting strings, and requiring the same persistent attention as painters give to the Forth Bridge.

They were scheduled to flower early in April; and we had chosen this crop, after earnest discussions with our horticultural advisers, because the greenhouse was unheated and sweet peas were certain to withstand the limited cold that might be expected in our area. We had not, however, foreseen the labour they would involve.

The shoots had endlessly to be pinched out, and when you have two thousand plants the extent of this mammoth task can become a nightmare. Not for Jane. She used to disappear into the greenhouse at eight o'clock in the morning and still be there at five in the evening, day after day. And when periodically I used to open the door and call for her, an answer would come from somewhere in the jungle of green like the squeak of a rabbit.

'Yes?'

'Are you all right?'

'Yes, thank you.'

I met her mother one day after a month of this and asked her how she thought Jane was enjoying herself. I felt sorry that her first task was proving so dull. It was very useful but dull.

'Oh,' said her mother, 'you don't have to worry. Do you know what she said to me yesterday? She said: "Mum, while I was among the sweet peas today I thought how lucky I was to be doing what I've wanted to do all my life."'

I believe one of the salutary first lessons I had was when I discovered that a task painstakingly performed did not inevitably result in achievement. It was a depressing discovery. Even as a boy I felt that the years were too short; and so when I learned one can often work arduously without at the end having anything to show, I was deeply affected. Ever since I have been impatient for quick results.

I wonder, then, if Jane was affected by what happened to the sweet peas. I do not expect so. The first disappointment does not do any harm. Only a scratch on the hand. It is hardly to be noticed. One is safe if there is no quick repetition; and then, when this happens, a girl like Jane will remorselessly struggle on to the next time. No doubts for her. Or, if there are, they are quelled.

Not a single sweet pea flowered. Not a bud. Not even the prospect of a bloom, had we decided to continue nurturing the plants until Domesday. The leaves were a fine green and the stems thick as my little finger. No sign of disease. And Jane had attended to their wants, pinching the side shoots and performing the awkward, time consuming, patience testing task of layering . . . she had cared for them with the same diligence as she would

have cared for pampered children in a kindergarten. And
now only foliage to gaze upon. Why?

I have had many inquests at Minack and doubtless will
have many more. There is a macabre comfort in gathering
together the specialists to stare at the doomed crop. One is
paying court to the principle of learning from failure, and
seeking reassurance that the catastrophe is not of one's
own making.

And yet it can be a sterile experience. The specialists,
spared of any financial interest, sometimes have a sadistic
relish in declaring that if such and such had been done at
such and such a time, all would have been well. It is their
dogmatism that irks me. It is their forgetfulness. I have
often been guided by specialists along paths which, after
failure, they have forgotten were their idea.

So here we were staring gloomily at the sweet peas
with a specialist. The curriculum began, as usual, with
a few moments' silence, standing at the entrance of the
greenhouse, the long lines of green offenders stretching
in front of us. There followed a sudden movement, a
few steps taken swiftly forward, a hand outstretched, a
leaf rubbed between the fingers, a stem caressed, a finger
poking at the soil around the roots; it was a ritual of
cultural investigation I have witnessed many times before
and since.

'What do you think?'

I maintain always a note of optimism in this question.
Perhaps it springs from some primitive belief in the power
of the witch-doctor; more likely it is a left-over hope from
my youth in which the magic of the expert was daily
drummed into me.

'Get an expert's advice,' some relation would say to me
comfortably. It is always a comfort to push a decision on
to somebody else. It is pleasant to believe that there is
someone who can answer your conundrum. It is security
in an insecure world. It is the twentieth-century version
of an aborigine's faith in an idol.

But there was, of course, nothing we could do about the sweet peas. Everyone agreed they were magnificent plants. Never before had it been known for such healthy specimens to be without flowers. It was extraordinary. It was worth making a special report. It was an example of what makes a specialist's life so interesting, a crop failure which defies interpretation. A crop failure. It happened to be the first crop we had grown in our splendid new greenhouse. And therein lay the clue to what had happened.

The site of the greenhouse was in the dip of the land in front of the cottage, and we had chosen it because we had no alternative. Our neighbour was still in possession of the flat fields which were more suitable; and we had no idea he was soon to leave and that we were to gain control of them. The site of the greenhouse had been a bog.

The bog had provided us with our first challenge at Minack. It had coaxed us into action because of the closely growing elm trees on three sides and the willow hedge, bordering the lane, on the other. Here was a haven for flowers, once we had succeeded in draining the water away.

It took three seasons to achieve. We began, in our foolishness, with a broken cup and a trowel, cutting little channels which had no effect on the bog whatsoever; and we ended up with hundreds of feet of earthenware drainpipes in three foot deep trenches and a deep gulley to rush the water away to the sea. Our reward was a good crop of violets one year, of anemones the next, of potatoes the third. And then we set our hearts on the greenhouse.

We were prompted, of course, by material reasons. We could not afford the capital expenditure, but we also could not afford to do without the income such capital expenditure might bring in. An old story. The lure that carefully planned extravagance reimburses the sacrifice it demands. The sheer necessity of adding to one's commitments in order to survive. The urge to lasso a future that only has optimism to guarantee success. Surely we are right to spend the money. Surely a greenhouse will be a fine investment.

We had drained the ground of surface water, but there was still the obstacle of three huge elms standing exactly in the middle of where the greenhouse would be. Why not a smaller greenhouse which would not interfere with the trees? Even the greenhouse salesman suggested it might be wiser if we were not so ambitious. It was chilling to hear him trying to persuade us not to be so bold. We did not want to be bold ourselves. We would have preferred to change our minds; and yet there persisted a relentless gnawing inside us that we were on the right road. The rest of our lives was to be spent at Minack and nothing mattered, nothing at all, so long as we had the foundations which enabled us to exist. A small greenhouse demanded the same emotion to erect as a big one. The same worry. And as we could not even afford a small greenhouse, we would lose nothing by having a big one; irrational reasoning perhaps, but to use it made sense. For at least a big one would earn more money.

So instead of a fifty-foot house only ten foot wide, we ordered a hundred-foot house which was twenty foot wide; and the elms had to be removed.

I find it a little awesome when one puts in motion a large plan from which there is no turning back, and I was in this mood when I watched the end of the elms. It made me sensitive to the sadness of losing the trees. They had welcomed us when we first came to Minack, and I was now their executioner. I could not treat them briskly as inanimate objects which happened to bar my progress. They were entities of our life. I could not watch their end without sentiment. They had received our fresh eyes of enthusiasm and now were the victims of inescapable reality.

They were reluctant to go. I had engaged a young man to do the job who had arrived one day with a very old tractor and a saw. First the main branches were cut off each tree, then the main trunk just above the base; and it was now that the elms became obstinate. A wire rope was lashed around the remains of the trunk and hitched to the tractor; and then the tractor was driven in short, quick bursts, so that the violence of its motion loosened the roots clinging deep to the soil. They were slow to loosen. I watched from the cottage window and was aware that any profit to the young man from the arrangement we had made together was likely to be dissipated by the break-up of his tractor.

'Listen,' I said to him, while he was having a particularly obstinate session with the last of the elms, 'let me find someone with a bulldozer.'

Such a foolish suggestion. The young man was a Cornishman who had intense belief in the value of being independent. Nobody was going to suggest he could not do a job. This was the kind of insult which reared angrily in a Cornishman's mind and remained there simmering long after everyone else had forgotten it. I had made a mistake and knew it as soon as I had spoken.

He and his tractor again attacked the old elm with venom, successfully removed it, and then he came politely to inform me that his activities had unearthed four large rocks exactly where the foundations of the new greenhouse would be.

'I'll remove them for you,' he said, looking at me carefully, 'if you want me to.'

I could not possibly say no; and as I gave him the go-ahead I had the coward's thought of wishing I had never embarked on the enterprise. I had started a chain of events which would carry me steadily forward, relentlessly as if I were an object on a conveyor belt. This greenhouse would be only a beginning. I would want more greenhouses. I was a man whose personal freedom depended upon twining more and more responsibilities around himself. I could not avoid them. If I were to maintain the momentum of our happiness at Minack, the fear of material failure had to accompany me and I had to learn to accept it. It was obvious I would be frightened when it was my nature to do nothing; but Jeannie and I were not a rich couple in their South of France villa lolling on the terrace wondering how to fill the day. We were escapists, but we were not escapists to idleness. We had to earn a living out of our personal endeavours; and I had to be prepared to brace myself against such fleeting fears as beset me that morning when I waited for the rocks to be jerked out of the places where they had been since the beginning of time.

I was helped by the attitude of the young man. I have often found that individuals who formed no part of my life have influenced me at crucial moments. I do not mean they have been aware that they have done so, nor that their influence has been on matters of much importance. But something they say or do reflects, it seems to me at the time, a part of me that I am searching for. I suddenly realise what it is I need.

For as I expected, the tractor broke down; but instead of bemoaning the fact, using it as an excuse to cease his task, the young man cheerfully said he would go off to find a spare part and would be back as quickly as possible. He had already snapped a wire rope, a rope which to this day lies on the hedge as a rusty memento of his efforts; and there were still two rocks to move. But back he came, and the tractor began roaring again, lunging angrily, anchored by the rock which moved only an inch at a time. I know now he was foolhardy and that the strain he imposed on the tractor was quite unnecessary; for a stone cutter would have split the rocks and they could have been dragged away easily in pieces. But at the time there was for me a shine in his obstinacy. I had someone to share my own.

The greenhouse, except for the foundations of cement and breeze blocks, arrived all together on a lorry that edged down the lane with its cargo peering high above the hedge, the glass in vast packing cases, the cedarwood structure in numerous bundles. It was a terrifying sight. The lorry crept down the hill stopping every few yards halted by boulders on the edge of the lane which caught the wide wheels. It would back, the driver would twist his steering wheel, and then forward again, bumping and slithering towards Minack. It turned the last corner, straightened up for the last two hundred yards, and then I knew the really dangerous moment had arrived. A stretch lay ahead like a miniature causeway with a ditch on either side. Was it wide enough? Had we made a mistake when we built this part of the lane?

For this lorry, in a fashion, was making a maiden voyage. Only a few weeks before, the lane had been changed from the appearance of the dried up bed of a turbulent river, into a surface fit for a limousine. Up until then we had called it our chastity belt. It had been impassable for private cars and rough enough for the Land Rover to make us hesitate to go out on trivial errands. We had been contained in a world of our own choosing, voluntary prisoners whose object was to be screened from the kind of life we had left.

The idea of building the lane did not mean our attitude had changed. We were as immune from gregariousness as when we first arrived. We saw no gain in transferring ourselves from a city social life of which we had grown tired into a countrified version with its added drawbacks. At least in a city your attendance at a party is mitigated by the probable proximity of your hosts; in the country you have to develop the habit of driving forty miles there and back. Our life was too full for such waste of time. We were content in each other's company.

We decided to build the lane because we realised it was necessary for our business. We could hardly expect to be treated seriously by salesmen who had to leave their cars a quarter of a mile away from us. We could sense in their manner on arrival at the cottage that they labelled us as amateurs; which we were, of course, but not in the way that they inferred. We were not playing at growing as they hinted. We were so painfully serious that we were touchy.

This touchiness came to boiling point one day when an official called on behalf of the Ministry of Agriculture to investigate our qualifications for a road building grant. This grant, which meant that fifty per cent of the cost would be paid for by the Ministry, was obviously vital to our plans; and when, through the sitting-room window, I saw the official arrive, I determined to be on my best behaviour. Here was an occasion when I must not display my allergy to officialdom.

He wore a smart tweed cap, a check flannel shirt, a bow tie, and a loosely cut country suit, the uniform of a prosperous farmer on market day. He was indeed a farmer, one who was engaged by the Mininstry to serve on Agricultural Committees that watched over the affairs of fellow farmers. An unpaid job. An overworked one. But one which carried with it the pleasures of prestige.

I came out of the cottage and down the sloping path to where he was standing, a smile on my face and my hand outstretched.

'Good afternoon,' I said warmly. 'It's very nice of you to come.'

I had scarcely uttered these words when I sensed he did not wish to notice my arrival. He was gazing round at the broken down walls, the shells of disused buildings of long ago. He threw a glance at the cottage. He stared across the untidy moorland to the sea. He looked at some boulders heaped on one side of the path. It was obvious he was performing an act for my benefit.

'Gosh,' he suddenly said, 'what a place!' And had I looked close enough I would have seen him shudder.

I knew at once what he was up to. The Ministry quite rightly had to guard against unwarranted claims as there were, in any case, enough genuine claims to soak up the grant allocations. Hence it was perhaps inevitable that people like ourselves were looked upon with suspicion; for we might be pretending to have a market garden in order to gain the advantage of the grant.

'Good afternoon,' I repeated. But I no longer offered my hand. Whatever his suspicions he had no need to be tough.

'Don't tell me you live here all the year round?'

He had addressed me for the first time, looking me up and down as he did so, as if he were judging the points of a steer. I felt uncomfortable.

'Yes, indeed,' I said, keeping my voice calm. 'It is the most wonderful place in the world.'

I was rather like a father whose child has been unfairly criticised. Here was our beloved Minack receiving the scorn of a stranger. Our life was being questioned. Someone who did not know anything about us was daring to suggest to my face that Minack was not a fit place to live in. My touchiness was awake. His attitude could not have been better calculated to make me lose my temper.

'You had better show me round,' he said.

It was February and in Minack fields the green shoots of the early potatoes were breaking through the ground. Down the cliff the haulms were already beginning to cover the rows; and over at Pentewan the two acres of meadows we rented were a picture of possible prosperity. Facing due south and earlier than Minack they had long rows of youthful potato tops, a foot apart, lines of healthy, dark green; and we were very proud of them.

'I don't see how you can expect to get a potato crop from *this* meadow.'

The tour, I had expected, would prove to the official that we were after all serious growers. We had seven tons of seed potatoes. We were one of the largest growers of cliff potatoes west of Penzance. And I confidently felt, as we set out, that the official would quench his asperity as soon as he took stock of our efforts. Now he was criticising the condition of a meadow; and the maddening thing was he was right. We had happened to pass the one meadow at Pentewan of which I was not proud. It was patchy. It needed weeding. But what was it to do with him?

I am one of those who have never felt comfortable in the possession of power over a fellow human being. It is my weakness of character that I can never give an order or attempt to impose my will without a wavering doubt. I do not want to hurt. I do not want to exploit the weakness of another because I am aware of the weakness in myself. I could never become a tin god because I have never believed that the pursuit of power is an end in itself.

Such an attitude, however, breeds on occasion a violent reaction. The easy way out of letting things slide, the lack of courage or conviction to state your views clearly suddenly comes up against a brick wall; for suddenly some incident, on top of all those others you have failed to face up to, stings you into fury. You explode, and the victim is surprised. He has underestimated you.

The official, of course, was surprised when I exploded. I put up for an hour with his taunts and then could not restrain myself any longer. My politeness suddenly turned into rage. The anger which I had felt as soon as I first saw him had simmered into an outburst in which my words tumbled out so fast that they stumbled over each other. I finished by saying:

'And anyway, what damn right have you got to speak to me like this? I'm asking for a grant, not a lecture!'

He was amazed. It was as if a gale had blown him flat. He grinned at me sheepishly. He fingered the peak of his cap and shuffled his foot round an imaginary stone. I was amused to see how suddenly he had become deflated.

'Now, now, now,' he said soothingly, 'I didn't mean to sound rude. I've a difficult job to do. I can't recommend grants for everybody. I must make sure . . . I promise I will do my best in your case.'

We shook hands after that.

And we secured our grant.

The lorry was now advancing on the trickiest part of the lane. The miniature causeway covered the section which was filled with quickthorn and elm tree saplings when we first came to Minack; and in the winter it used to become a swamp, collecting the water which drained down the valley. Hence the contractor whom we employed to build the lane raised up this section, leaving ditches on either side to act as drains. There was not an inch to spare. The driver had to keep the wheels plumb straight or else the lorry with its enormous load, a load of such high hopes for Jeannie and myself, would topple over.

Slowly, slowly . . . it was now half-way across and I could see the driver in the cabin grimly holding the steering wheel. Never had a greenhouse been delivered in such dangerous circumstances. Why on earth was I courting disaster? This was only the beginning. Had not somebody warned me that a greenhouse would never stand up to the gales that lashed Minack?

'Come on, come on.'

I was standing a few yards in front of the bonnet. I could see the fat tyres of the back wheels riding the lane's edges as if on two tight-ropes. Another three feet . . .

The lorry was safe.

It took a fortnight to erect the greenhouse; and when it was completed Jeannie and I used to stand inside for an hour on end, gazing in wonderment. It was our personal Crystal Palace. The expanse of it, the heat of the sunshine despite the cold winds outside, the prospect of now being able to grow crops without the endless threat of the elements, produced such excitement that we bought a bottle of champagne and christened it.

'To the greenhouse and its crops!' And we stood in the middle with glasses raised.

It was a pity, therefore, that the sweet peas behaved as they did. With such a beginning they might have responded by flowering. Even a few flowers.

But we did not know that sweet pea plants become sterile if the roots are in wet soil; because that winter, while we proudly watched the lush green climbing up the strings, the roots had found their way to the drainpipes.

And so our first crop had been doomed before it started to grow.

4

In the summer Jane once again disappeared into the greenhouse, tending the tomatoes.

We had seven hundred plants of a variety called Money-maker in eight long rows. Each had a string attached, like the sweet peas, around which the stem had to be twisted as the plant grew; and each had to have their shoots continually pinched out so that the main stem was left to grow on its own. Then at a later stage the plants were defoliated.

It was easy to teach Jane what to do. As with Shelagh, Jeannie or I had only to show her something once for her to grasp the idea, and probably improve on it. She watched plants, any plants she was looking after, as if they were individuals; and so if a tomato plant, for instance, showed signs of a fault, she was quick to notice it.

'Mr Tangye?'

'Yes, Jane?'

I would be standing at the greenhouse door and from

somewhere in the green foliage in front of me piped her small voice.

'The thirty-first plant in the third row from the right shows signs of botrytis on its stem.'

Sometimes I have noticed among people who work on market gardens a certain pleasure in reporting some disease or other misfortune to a crop. Not so Jane. I always found she was as upset as myself that something was wrong.

When it was fine she worked barefooted, looking like a child peasant, blue jeans and loose shirt, with the summer sun bleaching her hair fairer and fairer. There was something of a pagan about her. She was unlike Shelagh who was to be as tidy at the end of the day as at the beginning, however dirty the work she had been doing. Instead Jane, within an hour of arriving, would have smudges on her face which would remain there until she went home. She was quite unconcerned.

It was particularly dirty among the tomato plants, and so Jane was an inevitable victim. Tomato plants ooze a green stain-like dye. I had only to walk the length of the greenhouse between two rows for my shirt to be touched with green. And so Jane, who spent the whole day there, would finish up with green hands, a green face and, for that matter, green hair.

She had an unreliable sense of time. Both her mother and herself had a strange effect on watches. I believe this sometimes happens when people have a surfeit of electricity in their bodies; but whatever the reason no watch would keep correct time for these two. Hence Jane would occasionally arrive for work at unconventional hours. Sometimes very early, sometimes very late.

Of course, it did not matter her being late because she could make up the time at the end of the day. Indeed, she was never a clock-watcher. She always stayed on until the job was finished. But in the beginning, when she was late, when she did not know what our reaction might be, she used to creep along like a Red Indian, keeping out of sight behind hedges, reaching Minack by a roundabout route; and hoping that she could begin work without her absence having been noted. She did out of adventure, not out of guile. She always told us in the end.

At first we used to water the tomato plants in the old-fashioned way with a hose; and it was Jane's job to spend hour after hour dragging the length of the hose down the path behind her, thrusting the nozzle towards the base of the plants on either side. Jane performed the boring task without complaint but when I, at week-ends, took her place, I soon found myself wondering why I should waste my time in such a way. My time, and Jane's, could be better employed doing something else.

So here was the old evergreen problem. Money had to be spent to save money. Sense seemed to be on the side of extravagance for if the watering was made automatic not only would hours be saved, but also it would be distributed more accurately. The arguments seemed wonderfully convincing. My only hesitation sprang from my impatience that the price of efficiency should be a bottomless pit.

I always hesitate. I have never bought a piece of horti-cultural equipment with the *élan* that others, for instance, buy a car they cannot afford. I never enjoy that feeling of wild abandon that comes to people who have had a burst of extravagance. I have been extravagant, I have spent money I cannot spare, but the equipment which is the result gives me no joy. Its only attraction is its necessity.

Salesmen are quickly aware of my lack of enthusiasm so they tempt me by the hook of sound sense. As I am not buying for pleasure, as I look as if I am the gloomiest buyer imaginable, they set out to pierce my resistance by likening the piece of offered equipment to someone I might be employing. It is a persuasive trick.

'Now if you pay £12 a month for this tractor you can't say that's an agricultural wage,' a salesman will say to me, 'and yet you'll have a machine doing five times an ordinary man's work in a week. Five times . . . I should have said twenty times!

'And the money paid to a workman is gone . . . you'll never see it again. Look at it this way . . . you pay the hire-purchase as if it's a wage. Then . . .' and this was always the telling moment in the sales talk . . . 'then in twelve months you've got a workman for free!'

I have fallen so often for this patter. It subtly appeals to my progressive ambitions. It even suggests that I am getting something for nothing. So I yield. And as a result I have had many an inanimate workman at Minack on hire-purchase pay rolls. The automatic irrigation was to be another.

It consisted of rubber tubing, the thickness of my forefinger, which ran the length of the greenhouse alongside the base of each row of plants. Opposite each plant was a nozzle and, when the tap was turned on, all the plants began to receive by drips an equal amount of water.

It had a still further advantage. The top end of the tubes was connected to a larger tube which, in turn, was hitched to the water tap; but, and this was the cunning part, the tube on its way to the tap was fastened to a contraption in a two-gallon glass jar. In this jar was tomato feed concentrate, and by turning the dial on the contraption, one could control the feed for the plants as soon as the tap was turned on. It could be a strong feed or a weak feed, and all the plants got the same.

Such standardised feeding naturally contains certain snags. Not all the plants have the same appetites, nor do they desire identical meals; some want more nitrogen than others, some more potash. But I have learned now to forget the odd men out. If the bulk are all right, and I now grow thousands of plants, I am only too thankful that I have an inanimate workman to look after them.

The water came from the well up the lane, a surface well that now belonged to us. This water was unsuitable, as far as we were concerned, for human consumption; and so we continued to use the well above the cottage, which we sank ourselves, for domestic purposes.

This well remains a shining example of how expensive it can be if you set out to do a thing cheaply. I had been assured that the spring lay so near the surface that it would cost only £30 to reach it. I watched the £30 disappear, and saw no sign that the hole was even damp. I should, of course, have cut my losses and fetched the firm who find water by boring a hole. But their charges at the time seemed enormous. I was not impressed by their guarantee of a huge column of water. I could not afford to be.

Instead I urged the two miners I had engaged from the mines at St Just to dig on. And on and on they dug. It was a beautiful hole, if a hole in the ground can be beautiful, the sides plumb straight, the granite sliced like a knife by their skilful hand-drilling and dynamiting; but never a sign of water. The hole was so deep that I dared not stop. So much of my money was now down the hole that it was too late to seek the help of the others. Perhaps another foot, or another, or another . . .

My persistency never gained its true reward. The miners got thirty feet down then a man with a compressor and special drilling equipment tried drilling twenty-foot holes. Water was found in the end; but it was a lazy trickle of water taking its time to fill the bottom of the well. It still takes its time. And in October, when springs fall low, it can only pump seventy gallons before it is dry.

Our tomatoes, therefore, were dependent on the well up the lane; and we were lucky to secure the water without the expense of pumping for it. The reason was simple, though, to my kind of mind, it was difficult to understand. It was a question of gravity. The well up the lane was so much higher than the level of the greenhouse that, having dropped a copper pipe with perforated holes in the well and then, patiently filled the alkathene pipe between the well and the greenhouse with water, a stream came out of the tap by the greenhouse like a main.

It was not, however, always as clean as a main. This did not matter because part of the equipment for the automatic irrigation was a filter and this prevented even the smallest build-up of dirt from blocking the nozzles attending each plant. But the filter, of course, had periodically to be cleaned.

I noticed, however, in late June of this particular summer, that Jane was spending an inordinate amount of time attending to this filter. I could not feel such attention was justified; I liked Jane very much but I could not allow her to dally. I was particularly irked when I saw she was emptying the dirt from the filter into a pail. This was really foolish. I could not understand how she could justify her time in doing this. The filter need only be rinsed. There was nothing more to it than that.

It was not so important that I had to make a fuss. Indeed it was only when I was in a worrying mood that I thought anything about it. She worked hard enough. If she slipped up by being slow on the filter, it balanced all the other good work she did. It was trivial. It was one of those small situations which only erupt when a boss seeks a quarrel.

'What are you doing, Jane?'

It was just before the lunch hour, and I happened to pass Jane as she, barefooted, was bending earnestly over both filter and pail. She looked up at me so freshly, having noticed no note in my voice to suggest that, in reality, I was vexed with her, and said:

'I'm rescuing the tadpoles.'

Then, of course, I saw what was happening. The suction of the pipe in the well up the lane was sucking the tadpoles, which abounded at that time of the year in the well, into the pipe which led to the greenhouse; and quickly, they were blocking the filter. Jane, having discovered what was happening, served both the tomato plants by cleaning the filter and the tadpoles by returning them to the well.

'I take them up in my lunch hour back to the well,' she said timidly, yet with a tiny note of defiance, 'or at the end of the day.' She had put them, of course, in the pail. That was how she was spending her time when she prompted my doubt about her. What could I say?

I was down on my knees beside her before I spoke. A tadpole, still alive, was clutched to the face of the filter, and Jane, with a stalk of couch grass, was easing it away. It was flabby. A tiny piece of flabbiness that, to rescue, would make all the clever people laugh. It was a thing alive, but why help it? What a strange waste of time to find pleasure in an object so unproductive. And yet this was the kind of pleasure that was the pulse of mankind, the creed of those who prefer to face the present rather than scurry away.

'My dear Jane,' I said in a very practical manner, 'I'm all in favour of you helping the tadpoles . . . but they'll only come back again through the pipe.'

She glanced up at me, just a flash, as if I were an ignorant man.

'Only a few,' she said, 'the others will be safe.' Then she grinned, looking up at me as if she had known all the time what I had been thinking, making me feel foolish, 'I'll be working an extra half-hour today!'

We had a wonderful crop of tomatoes that summer, and Jeannie and I were quick to realise that the success was a signpost to the future. We still grew potatoes on a large scale, but here was an alternative for a summer income which did not suffer the everlasting threat of obliteration by the elements. I saw too another particular advantage. Tomatoes and potatoes are of the same family, and if our district was noted for the earliness of the potatoes, it could also be noted for the earliness of the tomatoes; and earliness, of course, meant a chance of higher prices. Furthermore there was not the expense of sending the crop to distant markets. We could sell every tomato we picked in Penzance.

The vast influx of holiday-makers were waiting to eat them.

We put in the plants, that first year, in the beginning of April, and by the middle of June they were a festoon of ripening fruit. We began to have visitors. Word had got around among neighbouring farmers of our good fortune and, although they would never grow a tomato themselves, they could not forbear to investigate the extent of our success. It was a relief to us that we had something so pleasant to show them. It was a change. Instead of insecurely seeking their advice I was able to talk to them on a subject they knew nothing about. Of course, I knew little myself, and I am not much wiser even now; but I have learned certain principles which now set the pace of our growing at Minack.

It is no use growing our own plants from seed because too much time and labour are involved. Seedlings require the art of the expert and in my case, as far as we were concerned, they take up space in a greenhouse just at the period when we need that space for the winter flower crop. It is more profitable, therefore, to collect cash for the flowers and pay out cash for the plants.

But this policy is not as straightforward as it sounds. If we grew our own plants they would be there on the premises to plant out in their permanent positions whenever it happened to suit us. We could delay or hasten the planting out according to the progress of the winter flowers; if the flowers, freesias, for instance, were still blooming and fetching a good price, we could hold back the tomatoes for a week or so. If, because of a warm spring, flowers finished early, the tomatoes could be planted early. We would, in fact, be independent.

As it is we are at the mercy of whoever it is we have asked to supply us. We order the plants before Christmas, state a guesswork of a date when we will want them, then are ready to accept the panic which is sure to beset us. It is not only the progress of our flowers that we have to worry about; we can also expect the supplier suddenly to disrupt our carefully laid plans by saying he is delivering the plants a week early, or for that matter, it could equally be a week later.

Thus from the middle of March to the beginning of April every year I am generally in a state of high excitement. I am not alone. Tomato growers all over the country are also yelping cries of distress. Shall we scrap the flowers which are still earning us money? If we don't where can we put the tomatoes in the meantime? Don't you realise they'll get leggy if we put the soil blocks too close? Surely it's wiser to look after the tomatoes from the beginning?

When the turmoil is over and the plants are in the ground, there begins a pleasant period of observation. The period in which the little plants create pleasure by the sturdy way they show they accept their new quarters. It is now that Jeannie and I will waste time together in the greenhouse, staring fixedly at the plants and making remarks to each other such as:

'They're an awfully good colour.'

'That one over there has a flower already.'

'Hello, there's one with stem rot.'

'Don't tell me that's a Moneymaker. It's a rogue.'

As they develop, as they progress from the innocent stage of lining the greenhouse in straight rows like guardsmen on parade, both Jeannie and I become more suspicious.

'Am I imagining it? But some look like missing their first truss.'

'Why is it that every year that patch on the left, halfway down, has such a pale green?'

'I don't know, Jeannie, but some of these stems seem a little thin. I'll start feeding.'

It is wonderful the various ways that one can be advised how to grow a good crop of tomatoes. So many experts, never lacking assurance, pronounce what the grower ought to do. Some, for example, say you should begin feeding as soon as the plants have been planted. Others, that you must let a plant struggle to establish itself; a kind of test of character suggesting that plants are like students. The diet is equally perplexing.

As a matter of convenience we fed the tomatoes that first year with a concoction having the title of Orange Ring. We read, however, in an article in the trade press, that this was a lazy way of feeding; and as we were amateurs desperately anxious to grow the right way we duly took note of what we ought to have done. At successive stages of growth we should have given them Red Ring, Orange Ring, Blue Ring, and finished up with Green Ring; and technically speaking this meant that they began with a high amount of potash and ended with a high amount of nitrogen. Can you imagine our confusion then, when the following year the pontification was reversed? And that we were right in the first place? That Orange Ring fed all the way through the season had now been proved to give the best results?

But now it is the end of June and we are beginning to pick; and Jane has emerged from the green forest with a basket of tomatoes in either hand and with the news that she has only picked a single row.

'There are masses in there,' she says excitedly, 'absolutely masses.'

It is a sweet moment when a long awaited harvest awakes. It shares the common denominator of pleasure which embraces all endeavours that have taken a long time to plan, to nurture, and then suddenly bursts before your eyes in achievement. You are no longer an onlooker waiting impatiently. The harvest is there to give you your reward; the fact of it destroys your worries and galvanises you into action. I know of few things so evergreen sweet as the first picking of a new crop.

But mine, as far as the tomatoes were concerned, was only a token picking. It was Jeannie and Jane who disappeared into the greenhouse twice a week; and then

Shelagh too when she came to work for us and we had the additional greenhouses. I was considered too clumsy. It was alleged that I carelessly knocked the trusses as I passed down the rows, knocking off tomatoes before they were ripe, stepping on and squashing them as they lay on the soil. It was pleasant for them to have a butt.

'He's an elephant, isn't he, Mrs Tangye?'

'Elephants should be more careful.'

A pause for a few moments as the picking continued. Then a small voice and a giggle.

'Oh, well, some jobs men will never do as well as women.'

I was, therefore, in charge of taking the tomatoes to the packing shed, grading and packing them, then driving the chips to Penzance. Each full chip, of course, weighed twelve pounds and I separated them into two grades; normal-sized tomatoes, then misshapen and small ones together. Such straightforward grading is however, considered a sin. The cry is for perfect uniformity. The perfect chip of tomatoes, in the opinion of the leaders of the industry, is one that contains fruit of exactly the same shape, as if the contents have been churned out of a machine.

Flavour, it seems, does not matter; the tomato can taste of nothing at all and still win the laurels. Perfect shape, perfect size, but it can taste of soap; and this campaign of artificial standards is considered essential if the needs of the housewife are to be met. Who is this palateless housewife? No doubt, a computer-produced automaton.

Thus I continue to grade on the basis that people still want tasty tomatoes and therefore, within reason, the shape and size are unimportant. And yet how much longer will I be able to do this? I grow a tomato variety which is bred to have flavour. The thousands and thousands of tons of tomatoes which are shipped into this country every year have only shape as their merit. These varieties produce more tomatoes per plant and can be sold cheaper.

It therefore may be only a question of time before I, too, sell tasteless tomatoes.

When you have a crop such as tomatoes which you sell locally, it is tempting to by-pass the wholesaler and court the retailers and hotels instead. In theory it is a splendid idea. You will obviously get a better price. But there are snags in the theory which Jeannie and I soon found out when we tried this method of sales ourselves.

To begin with we had the wrong temperaments. We could not bargain. We could not say to a retailer: 'The price is so much.' Instead we would arrive at the shop and timidly ask what price they could give us which would allow them a profit. We were not in command. We were supplicants. And if indeed they expressed a desire for so many chips on the following Friday, on the preceding Thursday we would take so much time selecting the tomatoes that it would have been more profitable from a man-hour point of view to have sold them at half the price elsewhere.

As for hotels, they provided us with a subtle danger. If I were leaning against a bar having a pint, and the landlord asked for three chips next Saturday morning, I would of course have to say I would deliver them. The landlord would infer he was doing me a favour by helping me to dispose of my produce.

But Saturday would come, and being in a peaceful mood, the last thing I then wanted was to drive to Penzance. The chips of tomatoes, however, were promised. I had to take them. I was in business, and I would be collecting sixpence a pound more than I would have done at a wholesaler. Eighteen shillings, in fact, for the three chips.

The cost of the Land Rover at a shilling a mile was ten shillings; and so, from an accountant's point of view, I now had eight shillings left as a profit.

That, unfortunately, was not the end of my expenses. Having come into Penzance with the tomatoes in a mood of duty instead of pleasure, it did not take much persuasion to stay a little longer than I had planned. A little longer than both of us had planned.

Because Jeannie and I always went together unless there was a specific reason not to do so. Neither of us has ever developed the habit of going out on our own. Jeannie had never shown any inclination to take part in gatherings of her sex, while I have never discoverd the advantage of spending a session in men's company at the expense of leaving her at home. And so when tomatoes were to be delivered at a hotel I would always hope that Jeannie would come with me.

We would arrive and the landlord would offer us a drink. A little later, when he had paid me, I would offer him one in return. And now would begin the rising of our *alter egos*, the egos which were occasionally waiting to beckon us back to the life we used to know. We began to enjoy ourselves. We became careless and forgetful. And so it was not until we returned to Minack, bumping down the lane to the cottage, that we remembered our tomato profit had been dissipated. Nothing had been gained except the anger of time wasted, nothing achieved except a limpid imitation of a life of which we had grown tired. The tomatoes embroiled us. It would be safer to deal through a wholesaler.

I first met my wholesaler when I was walking down Market Jew Street and a voice shouted at me, aggressive, but friendly:

'When are we going to do business?'

The voice, in fact, belonged to half my wholesaler, to George, the Jackson brother with a handlebar moustache. He and his brother Harold had built up from a five pound note a chain of retail greengrocery shops in West Cornwall, apart from a wholesale business in the area served by lorries.

So I began sending them potatoes, then crates of lettuce, and in due course, they began receiving all our tomatoes.

We committed our produce entirely to them. We neither sought other outlets nor argued about the price. It was, as if having endured the stresses of growing, we had no energy left to cosset the produce on its final stage. Thus as time went by they became a barometer of our progress. They were always fair.

'Easing up on potatoes, aren't you? Wise, old man, you're wise.'

'Been a good lettuce year for you. I've been looking at the figures.'

'Take my tip, get your tomatoes *early*.'

Periodically, as growers always do with their wholesalers, I would have a token row with them. I would find the dark, handsome Harold, who looked like a Guards officer, standing at the entrance of the warehouse that was close to the harbour. I would fume at him for some low price I had received, and he would reply by blinding me with figures as to why I was lucky to get any price at all. And if I were in the mood to be dispassionate I would see the truth of what he said.

'Absolute glut of tomatoes, old man. Turning them away. What can one do when Jerseys are selling at sixpence a pound?'

It is at such moments that I have a despair that seems to freeze me with fear. There has to be behind any endeavour a façade of confidence which the individual concerned is aware is pretence. This make-believe confidence is the propulsion which drives you to the success you aim for. But it is a frail thing. If you talk loud enough, if nobody contradicts you so vehemently that you have to listen, if you meet with no unfair disaster, then you can nose this confidence until you reach a harbour.

But I was a long way from harbour. I could not fall back, shrugging my shoulders and saying to Jeannie, 'Oh, well, it's just one of those seasons.'

Because when Harold Jackson told me that day there was a glut, it happened to be our first summer of tomatoes.

The greenhouse had been erected almost a year. First we had the failure of the sweet peas; and now the superb crop of tomatoes, clustering like huge grapes from the stems, had met a glut.

I was frightened at that moment in a base way. I wanted to give up. I felt that if after all the thought we had given to our future, if after all the strain of raising the money for our plans, if after all the denial of personal pleasures in order to consolidate our present, we were to be defeated again by circumstances beyond our control, surely it would be wisest to surrender.

This was an occasion when, if a partner of an enterprise snares the other into sharing his weakness, the brave hopes dissolve. I tried to ensnare Jeannie.

She would not allow me to.

5

I wonder sometimes which of the Walter Mittys in me
I was looking for. It is easy to become so immersed
in day-to-day events that you lose sight of yourself. It
is a chronic disease. A disease. A daze of living. The
twentieth century speeds faster and faster and the pace
only allows you to live in perpetual disguise.

But I had time of my own. In the matter of motion
it would seem I belonged to another age. I had the
sumptuous daily experience of getting up in the morning
when I wanted to get up, not because I feared a factory
hooter or the punishing look of an office doorkeeper. I
could lie on the rocks on a sunny winter's day staring
at the sea, while others could only peruse a brochure
for next summer's fortnight. I seemed to be as free as
anyone can be in a brittle society; and yet I was looking
for a Walter Mitty.

I still do not know which one it was I wanted to be. I
do not believe it was ever clear in my mind. I had only
the wish to survive, to preserve our way of life at Minack

at any cost; and if this meant behaving in a manner utterly opposite to the intentions with which we began, it had to be accepted as the penalty of personal freedom.

Perhaps in my subconscious I have always wanted to be a tycoon, and a tycoon was my Walter Mitty. Certainly in my limited way I behaved like one. Within the next two years I had bought a tractor, a large number of daffodil bulbs, and four more greenhouses.

I was consumed by the conviction that our business could only be made successful by capital expenditure; and as that capital, like the capital of most businesses, could only be borrowed, the noose was tightening around my neck. The more I extended my plans, the more committed I became to responsibilities I wanted to avoid. I was pursuing the age-old formula of sacrificing the present for the ephemeral future. I had to spend in order to earn the turnover which would give us security.

Our fourteen acres stretched along the rim of Mount's Bay, glorious meadows tilting towards the sea where we could stand and marvel at the beauty of the fishing boats below us as they hurried busily east to Newlyn and west towards Land's End. And beyond were the cargo boats and Atlantic liners sailing aslant across the horizon from the Wolf Rock to the Lizard.

The gannets dived a half-mile out, sometimes singly, sometimes by the score, plummeting from the sky, hitting the water with a spit of a bullet. The gulls fluttered low, watching as if enviously. Cormorants sped on their mysterious missions. Curlews called their wistful cries. And sometimes as we stood there the sea looked so meek that it seemed there never would be a storm again; and sometimes its rage was so terrible that we held each other and were scared.

In olden days most of this land was cared for by hand labour. The meadows were too confined and steep for a plough, and so the shovels used to lurch through the soil. They were being used on this land when we first came to Minack, but I, thinking of myself as forward-looking, decided I could do the work both more cheaply and more efficiently by using machines. Hence I began using a rotovator.

It was a punishing instrument; and after three or four hours of hurtling up and down the meadows clutching its handlebars, I used to return to the cottage and lie down exhausted on the sofa. Nor did my muscles ever learn to accept the punishment, and for days following a rotovating session I would ache with muscular pains.

It was never a friendly machine. It was obstinate to start, drawing the fire of my temper even before the real task had begun. It broke down with frequency, as if it were a recalcitrant workman who pursued a policy of lightning strikes whenever he considered the work was too tough for him. It was dangerous. Once it turned over, a tine hooking my foot as it did so, and putting me to bed for a fortnight. I hated it, and although there would always be periods when it would be useful, I had to face up to the fact that it was too small for the job we now had in hand; and in any case, having suffered so much myself I could hardly expect Geoffrey, who now worked for me, to suffer as well.

We set about, therefore, searching for a tractor. It had to be small and easily manoeuvrable, and it most certainly had to be well balanced. Tractors are inclined to topple over on any hilly ground, but at Minack a tractor would face tests like those of a motor-bike scramble. We perused the catalogues, Geoffrey and I, and decided that two might meet our requirements; and we asked for a demonstration. Each tractor came from rival firms. Both arrived at the same time.

It was a cold November afternoon and an east wind from the sea was chilling our fields. A cheerless day and its mood fitted that of the demonstrators. They were irritated they had chosen the same hour to show off their paces. They eyed each other, coat collars buttoned high, as if they were rival centurions waiting for the off in their chariots.

I sensed that both were apprehensive. This was no ordinary demonstration in which the trial tractor patrolled an inoffensive field, careering up and down like a new car on a highway. It was like the course for an obstacle race. Steep slopes, hidden rocks just below the surface of the ground, tablecloth spaces to turn upon . . . all these lay ahead. It amused me to observe Geoffrey, who had planned the course, wryly smiling in the background as the first tractor set out for the start.

It was a crawler. A small track-propelled tractor, based on a tank. It was also, as far as Geoffrey and I had secretly decided, the favourite. There was something secure about a tractor without wheels, crawling along with its whole body on the ground. A sudden bump could not upset it as a rock might upset a wheel. It moved relentlessly clasping the soil so that, if the chance was there, it would climb up a mountain. We had read these things in the catalogue. We watched it set off.

The demonstrator, perched in the seat, was accompanied by two city-dressed colleagues. The presence of these two served, perhaps, as a moral support; but they looked cold, and unsure of their duties, and I could not help feeling that within minutes of arriving at Minack they fervently wished they had never come.

It so happened that Jeannie, without my having to say anything, felt exactly the same; and she arrived just as the demonstration was about to begin with a jug of tea. I wonder how many jugs of tea Jeannie has brewed for no other reason than that she hoped to give somebody confidence. Anyhow, after the tea, the crawler set off on the first test set by Geoffrey, and the two city-dressed gentlemen walked along by its side offering directions.

Unfortunately these directions were necessary. I was aware within a few minutes of the operation beginning that the crawler had never been designed for such deceit of the earth as awaited it at Minack. The first test was a level piece of ground called from time immemorial the stable field; and Geoffrey had chosen it as a limber-up. It appeared so simple that he had considered it a kindness that the first trip of both machines should plough such a level surface.

After five yards the crawler came suddenly to a stop, as if it had been a yacht in full sail which had been jerked immovable by an anchor. The two gentlemen gathered round the demonstration; and I observed that the other, the rival demonstrator, showed his good manners by turning his back on them and walking away. There was a flurry of instructions and counter instructions, then the two gentlemen, their faces pink with cold, backed away as if they were the seconds of a boxer in the ring; and the crawler started off again. Another jerk. Another full stop.

As I watched, Goeffrey beside me, I had a strange premonition that it was I, not the tractor, who was running into trouble. I found myself thinking, affected no doubt by the bleakness of the afternoon, that it was unreal that the people present were dependent in some form on my patronage; the demonstrators who would have their reports to make, success or failure to explain; Geoffrey who would be passing on his observations over high tea at home; and even Jane, though not directly concerned, would go back across the fields at five and discuss the events of the afternoon with her mother. None of these people would have been at Minack were it not for Jeannie and me, and the dreams we had. And now they were leading me, almost dragging me along a route which frightened me.

For I could not pretend I had any lilt in deciding which tractor to buy. The acquisition would be a burden. There would be no prospect of some light-hearted compensation. It was not a foolish venture of frivolous intent. It was utilitarian. A lump of metal which would remind me day after day of the penalties of expansion. I was standing there, the wind sharp against my face, being courted by an object I did not want; which would prove irresistible. I was at a beginning that had no banners to welcome me. I had no feeling of faith, as I watched, that what I was doing, what I was prepared to gamble, what indeed were my secret hopes . . . that any of these things were justified. I was being driven by a force that did not belong to me, which I distrusted, yet obeyed.

I watched the crawler fail, and had this stupid, maddening premonition that it was the symbol of my own failure. I was trying to be too big, entering a realm in which my nature did not belong; as if I were thrusting myself on a social scene which did not intend to receive me. I was taking on the outward appearance of a go-getter without possessing the inward equipment, the standard of ruthlessness, the lack of sentiment, the greed masquerading in the guise of efficiency. I was trying to play a role for which I had no heart and to adopt characteristics which I had escaped to Minack to avoid. I felt frightened of myself on that unfriendly November afternoon. Yet I had to make a decision.

I bought the second tractor; and Geoffrey was as pleased as I was doubtful. It was an odd-looking machine, the diesel engine was behind the driving seat and the instruments were placed in the centre between the four wheels. These instruments, the plough, for instance, were controlled by hydraulic lifts with levers fixed to the steering-wheel column for the use of the driver. Thus, if you were ploughing, you unhitched a lever and the plough dropped to the ground and off it went turning its furrow as soon as you put the tractor in gear. Then you pulled the lever in the opposite direction and up came the plough clear of the ground. This system had for us great advantages. The driver could watch the plough at work below him, and so had an admirable chance to nose the plough without mishap over the numerous rocks which

hid just beneath the surface of the soil. But there were
rocks above the ground, and the steepness of the meadows;
and from the beginning I was scared by the devil-may-care
attitude that Geoffrey adopted to these hazards.

'For heaven's sake, Jeannie,' I would shout, 'look at
Geoffrey!' And Geoffrey would be careering over one of
the larger meadows as if the tractor were a racing car.

Indeed from the beginning Geoffrey behaved to the
tractor as if it were his own. He was for ever polishing,
oiling, greasing, testing the tyres, and taking it out of the
shelter where it was kept on any pretext he could devise.
It was his toy, and I was not allowed to interfere.

'What are you doing this morning, Geoffrey?'

'Ploughing the skol meadow.'

I was stimulated to find him so keen. I was also
apprehensive.

'Be careful.'

I was apprehensive not only because he drove the
tractor fast, but also because he seemed to have no fear
in its handling. He would, for instance, be ready to plough
a steep meadow *uphill*; and the engine being at the rear,
the tractor was then poised to turn turtle. I used often
to help balance the tractor on these occasions by sitting
above the front wheels, thus countering the weight of the
engine. But if I were not there Geoffrey would still pursue
his self-appointed task; and then I would catch him by
surprise, the noise of the engine hiding my arrival, and I
would find him reaching the top of a meadow, clutching
the steering wheel, and the front wheels of the tractor
an inch or so free of the ground they were travelling
over. Daylight between wheels and soil. Plough still in
its furrow. A sight which suggested that at any instant
there could be a tragedy.

'Geoffrey!' I would shout above the rumble of the
diesel. 'Don't you realise the risk you're taking?'

He did not want to realise. He was having fun out of
the challenge he was creating; he was covering with a

tractor the same kind of ground which he used to dig with a shovel, so had he not got something to prove? He was securing a victory over tradition. He would have something to boast about.

'You should have seen me,' he yelled back at me, grinning, 'when I was ploughing that piece above the obs where the badgers are.'

I had already observed the result. He had ploughed a previously unproductive bracken-covered piece of land part of which was a badgers' playground. He had done it when I was out for the day, and it was so steep that I would have thought twice before driving the Land Rover over it. It was a neat example of ploughing. But Geoffrey had driven the tractor and plough across the hill, as if he were inviting it to upset; and the last furrow was within a couple of feet of a bank which dropped three feet to the meadow where the obs bloomed in the spring, the miniature King Alfred daffodils with an ugly name, yet so exquisite to look at.

'I'll have to get Emily to talk to you,' I said, Emily being his fiancée, 'perhaps she'll make you see sense.'

It is my weakness that I prefer to carry someone with me instead of imposing my wishes. I find it easier to appeal rather than to order. And if you have a concern like ours, so small and intimate, it is more essential than ever to have a spirit of co-operation. In my anxiety to achieve this co-operation I find I usually expect too much. I so desire to skirt the prospect of a mood on the part of someone I am employing, that I fall into the trap of failing to give clear orders. I prefer to rely on a kind of telepathy. I state the position as I see it, then expect the individual concerned to react in the same way, wishfully and foolishly thinking that my tedious process of thought has been shared by the other. I forget that I was alone when I assessed the future; that I alone endure the strains of raising finance, of carrying the burden of a crop disaster, of hoping to see daylight in another year.

I should not expect the wage-earner to feel and think as I do.

Geoffrey, for instance, used the tractor more as a sport, while for me it was a weapon in a campaign. It was a fine weapon but within a year I knew that it would not alone solve our problems. I was forced to realise that, although we were now able to cultivate so much more of our land and thus increase the scope of our crops, prosperity did not follow. We were too dependent on the weather. We were unbalanced. We were also at the tail-end of an era and this we had yet to wake up to.

We had come to Minack when any amateur could make a living out of flowers and new potatoes in our part of Cornwall provided he had decent land and worked hard enough. The mildness of the winter and the earliness of the spring meant that West Cornwall followed the Scilly Isles with daffodils. There was a leap-frog of daffodil harvests that went on all the way up the country from the Scillies to Lincolnshire; and because the Scillies and the Land's End area were the earliest we naturally had the best prices. In those days the Channel Islands did not grow the vast quantities they grow now. Nor were there precooled bulbs housed in acres of greenhouses throughout the country, producing artificial daffodil harvests all through the period when we used to have the markets to ourselves.

So, too, with potatoes. The new potatoes dug from the cliffs along the edge of Mount's Bay were considered both as a delicacy and a necessity. The grind of carrying the seed down the steep paths to the meadows, the planting, the weeks of caring for the plants, the shovelling out of the crop, the wearisome climb back up the cliff with the harvest . . . all this effort was repaid with a fair price. In those days the harvests of other countries were not being shipped into the country at the same time. In our part of Cornwall one could risk the spite of the weather because one year's profit would cover another year's losses. Our laborious efforts faced no competition.

There were the other flowers, the violets, anemones, stocks, wallflowers, calendulas, forget-me-nots – all these would earn their living. Wages were low and so was the cost of transport; and there were no jets speeding flowers to Covent Garden from all parts of the world. The cities needed our flowers and were ready to pay for them.

Thus when Jeannie and I began our life at Minack our course appeared to be straightforward. We had to absorb the tradition of the area, and the best way to do so was to ferret out the old hands seeking their advice and following it. In our innocence we thought this method would be foolproof. We had no clue that science and the cost of living were on the verge of destroying the old standards. We held the simple belief that we had only to master the technicalities of growing the crops which everyone else grew in the area, for us to earn a living. For the climate was an unshakeable ally. It would overcome our inexperience. All we had to do was to listen and learn and work.

We used, therefore, to hang on to the words of the old growers as attentively as we used to listen to prominent politicians at times of crisis. We would fuss over an old chap in a pub about the merits of wallflowers with the same zest as we once sat in the Savoy's Grill Bar hearing the confidential views of some editor.

'Mark my words,' the old chap would say, sipping his beer, 'wallflowers are a proper crop. Cheap seed, can treat 'em rough, quick to pick, and a shilling a bunch.'

This was the kind of remark we loved to hear. A high priest was talking. He was passing us on information as valuable as a bar of gold. We used to go back home to the cottage, take pencil and paper, and calculate; and the calculation used to make us dizzy with excitement. It was simple. If we grew several thousand wallflowers we really would not have to grow anything else.

And there was another line of talk which warmed our

hearts. It happened whenever someone praised Minack and hinted at its golden future. I remember meeting a taciturn farmer who charmed me by describing the land around Minack as the best in the district. Such flattery coming from one who was noted for his lack of good humour impressed me greatly; and I hastened to ask him why he thought so and what he would grow in my place. He was recognised as a very good farmer and his family had lived in the district for generations.

His eyes lit up.

'Taties along those cliffs,' he said, his voice coming to life, 'have fetched ten shillings a pound . . . and princeps eight shillings a bunch!'

He had no cliffs on his farm. He had had no opportunity to share the exploitation of the war and post-war years. It had rankled ever since. It had so seared into his mind that the cliffs had become to him a golden mirage. He was envious of me. He jealously saw a glorious future for me as a grower of potatoes and a picker of princeps, the hedgerow daffodil the most common of all. Greed had pushed him to praise the land around Minack.

But this I did not realise at the time. Nor did I appreciate that many of the others who made us happy by their remarks were only reflecting frustration. We had the chance which they wished for themselves, although in fact the value of the chance was wildly inflated. Their envy sprang from an extinct El Dorado. A memory which had no relation to the present or the future.

The aura of their attention, however, had its effect on Jeannie and me. It blinded us. We never for an instant saw that progress would be our danger and there would come a time when the system of our kind of market garden would have to change. The cliffs, we thought, were immune. The softness of West Cornwall everlasting. The only challenge that had to be met lay in ourselves. We had to emulate the peasant. We had to bring ourselves so close to the earth that we knew by instinct how to tend our crops. This, and patience and an endless capacity to accept hard labour was all we required to achieve prosperity at Minack.

Then as the years passed, we began to realise that this formula did not measure up to its simplicity. The realisation came slowly, like the drip of water on a stone. We had found our perfect environment but we were losing the material battle. We had considered ourselves isolated from the penalties of progress. We had freed ourselves from the entanglements of conformism. No electricity, no telephone, no television. We were peasants. We were spared the impact of an industrial society. We had no need to look over our shoulders, catching sight of those who wished for our jobs. We were independent. Hard labour our pleasure. And yet, like a creeping paralysis, we were being embraced again by the fears we had left behind.

What ought we to do? It was in April that I most often used to pose this question. April was our month of assessment. We were between harvests. It was the month in which we measured the results of the flower season just ended and began preparing for the next. One winter merged with another, meadows of discarded plants alongside others of rich, bare soil, awaiting seeds.

Where once bloomed the daffodils were carpets of green foliage. Here and there were flickers of yellow, heads which were damaged or had come too late for market. There was desolation under the April sky; the daffodils had erupted in their glory, smiled their loveliness in a thousand, thousand homes, and were now forgotten. I would wander amidst the green waste remembering that the Magnificence had had a poor year or the King Alfred's a good one, or that by some curious chance the once despised California had brought us the most money.

I would stare at the winter-flowering wallflowers, shorn of their primrose, and stained orange, and deep red blooms, sticking up from the ground like cabbage stalks. I would remember the seeds last April, the weeding, the transplanting in June, the weeding again, the wonderful moment in November when enough stems were plucked from the plants for the first box to be sent on the flower train from Penzance. A year of caressing and battering gales, and sweet scents, and heavy baskets lugged to the packing shed; and now they awaited obliteration from the rotovator and the plough.

Sporadic flowers peered from beds of anemones, stocks and violets; and, maddeningly, the beds of calendula were a riot of orange. I would look at them thinking of the frost which crushed their buds into pulp, delaying them for weeks until, the season ended, they were no longer wanted. The violet plants, plump green cushions, were reaching to each other across the rows, perfume from the leaves touching the air; row upon row of them ready for dismemberment, a dozen runners from each, to be pushed into the ground in May, to fatten in the summer, to bloom again in the autumn. It was always thus in April; we ended and we began.

What ought we to do? I do not make wise decisions when I try to be logical. My arguments, on either side of the problem involved, cancel each other out with such effect that I am left hanging in mid-air; and I do nothing. I like, therefore, to act out of emotion. I find that what successes I have had in my life have been born out of flashes of insight, the seizure of an opportunity which would have died a sudden death had I stopped to reason. And I have usually found that a most inconsequential event promotes the opportunity I need.

One April afternoon a few months after the tractor had been bought, Jeannie and I had gone into the packing shed with the idea of cleaning it up. The odd dried daffodil stalk lay on the floor in the corner, a few withered leaves of wallflowers under the table, cardboard boxes, bottoms and tops, were strewn on a shelf, address labels and contents labels were higgledy-piggledy on the window-sill like a spilt pack of cards. Jam jars, galvanised flower pails, some still undrained; and at random on shelves and table were the clippers which trimmed the daffodil stems, a much thumbed invoice book, rubber bands small enough for the violets and big enough for the wallflowers, a stapling machine to fix the labels, a half used ream of white paper, and flower sticks with their metal sharp ends which secure the bunches in the boxes after they have been packed. We began to put order into this chaos when Geoffrey suddenly appeared at the door.

'What's up, Geoffrey?'

He looked at me shamefaced, a smile trying to hover.

'Tractor's upset.'

I had been expecting this to happen for so long that at first I accepted his news as calmly as if he had been reporting that his shovel had broken. Then I had wonderment and thankfulness that he was unhurt. It was incredible.

It had happened in our big field which slopes unevenly down to the top of the cliff and which is locally known as the cemetery field ... so called because from time immemorial the old cattle and horses used to be buried at the bottom where the hedge crests the cliff. He had been charging across it when a rear wheel hit a rock, he was flung out, and the tractor somersaulted down the hill and came to rest with its wheels in the air.

I could not, of course, refrain from pointing out to him the number of times I had warned him what would happen if he continued to drive so fast; but I could not be angry. For one thing he was so ashamed, for another, the tractor had miraculously suffered only superficial damage. Indeed, having inspected it and, with Geoffrey, pushed it back on to its wheels, I had a curious feeling of elation. A magic had saved us from tragedy. I had such a sense of happiness and gratitude that I wanted to burst into song. It was in this mood I returned to the cottage and found a stranger awaiting me.

He was a salesman of greenhouses. He seemed surprised

by the enthusiasm with which I greeted him. He was accustomed to make the patter of sales talk, but here was I bubbling with excitement.

I suddenly knew what we had to do. One greenhouse was not enough. We had to have more. And I was not going to listen to the logic that we could not afford them.

6

I launched my grandiose plan before I had time for second thoughts. It was flamboyant. It had no relation to our financial resources but it projected an image of such likely security that the cost could look after itself.

I ordered two mobile greenhouses each seventy feet long and eighteen feet wide, and provisionally ordered two more.

This fling at the fates so intoxicated our imaginations that we drew up a blueprint for the coming year so vast in its scope that if it came off our material problems would be solved for ever. It was also sensible. We were not allowing our enthusiasm to interfere with our judgement. And yet, in retrospect I wonder if our gesture was not prompted by an emotion similar to that of a losing boxer in the closing rounds of a fight . . . fists flying in a desperate bid for a win. We had lost patience with caution. It was time to take a gamble.

We planned a two-pronged attack, outdoors and under cover. We would, for instance, make use of every piece of land we had, and because of the tractor there would be no delay in preparing it. We would grow all the usual flowers but on a far bigger scale. A quarter of an acre of calendula, an acre of anemones, three quarters of an acre of wallflowers, thousands of violets, tons of daffodils, beds and beds of winter-flowering stock, and a mass of Blue Bird forget-me-nots.

The physical problem of planting all these was, of course, formidable. But by the end of the summer the land was filled with our potential income; and most important of all, the two mobile greenhouses were erected. These were our pride.

They looked like miniature glass aircraft hangars on wheels, small wheels which rested on rails that enabled them, in our particular case, to be moved over two sites; and this meant we were able to grow two crops at the same time, one already covered, one waiting to be covered.

They appeared perilously exposed to the weather. They stood in the field bordering the lane and although to the west they had the protection of the wood, they were certain to be hit by the northerly and easterly and the terrible fierceness of the southerly. I do not believe I would have ordered them if I had thought twice, if I had not been flushed by the mood of abandon which struck me after the tractor overturned. I would have been too frightened. I would have seen disaster ahead. The gales were waiting. The hands of the wind would find the gaps by the wheels and lift them up. How could I expect such a greenhouse to stand up to a fury which could obliterate an outside crop in a night? After all, even our hundred-foot greenhouse, firmly based on foundations, shivered when the gales blew.

We were, however, so stimulated by the pattern that lay ahead that we were able to dispense with such anticipatory fears. We at last were upsetting the much-used curriculum of growing potatoes. For year after year we had grown potatoes and the luck was always against us.

Gales had blasted them, droughts had hit them, frosts had turned them into pulp, gluts had ruined the price. There never was a year when Jeannie and I lolled in the pleasure of a great success. The early potato harvest from the cliffs was economically dead. We had been trying to live on a dying tradition.

Instead we would now become big tomato growers. The tedious labour of the cliffs would be replaced by the more gentle task of tending the tomato plants in the greenhouses. We had already proved we had a market on the doorstep and so there was no expense of transport. Our summer income seemed assured.

We then had to decide what flowers we should grow in the greenhouses during the winter; and we received the usual bewildering assortment of advice. Every bulb and flower in the catalogue was deemed suitable for our attention; and we pored over the lists, paper and pencil in hand, calculating possible financial returns based on the figures of the previous year's market reports.

Jeannie was very earnest. She drew diagrams, for instance, of pre-cooled daffodil bulbs represented by dots, hundreds of little dots representing the bulbs in a bed, then a blank space for a path, and more hundreds of little dots. And she finally added them all up and divided by twelve, and announced how many bunches there would be to pick. There were simpler ways of calculating, but Jeannie obstinately preferred this visual method.

At last we decided that in one of the mobiles we would have a slow-moving harvest, forget-me-nots which would bring us an income January onwards; and in the other we would have a quick, all in one week, harvest of Wedgewood iris, which would rush into readiness at the end of March. And in the big static house we would grow the Giant Pacific polyanthus.

Thus our plans were laid for the distant spring and the summer to follow. The money was there in the growing crops, but meanwhile we had to live. We also had to cope with the vast amount of work without employing extra labour, extra labour which was needed, but which we could not afford. In time, if all went well and the crops mastered the winter, we would have to find someone to help with the harvests. It would be pleasant to do so. The money would be coming in so that it would not hurt paying out. The hurt was now during the long wait.

There was a struggle every week to pay Geoffrey's and Jane's wages. Saturday morning would arrive and I would count the notes and hand them over; and then I would return to Jeannie and say that I envied them as wage earners. Jeannie and I had aimed at the splendours of individualism without computing what such freedom demands. Personal freedom is a word, not a fact. Personal freedom creates its own chains. We were expanding but the expansion had burdened us with more commitments; expansion was inescapable if we were to keep on Geoffrey and Jane and lift our own lives above those of peasants. We had to spend in order to remain free.

But the wonder of our life was that we never wished to shift its base. There in the lonely cottage where the sea murmured through the windows, we had the exquisite knowledge that if the map of the world had been open to us and we could go where we chose, money no object, we would have lived nowhere else. We were the lucky ones. We had an environment which cushioned us against the worries which burrow and sap confidence. We were living the life of our choice and Minack was our armour. We were not looking out at the horizon like others, searching for a life that is beyond reach. We did not have to say we would find happiness if we did this or did that, having to brighten the greyness of the passing years by praying that one day a dream would be fulfilled. We had our dream around us; and if there were times when the conventional stresses of living jabbed at us, challenging the sincerity of our happiness, we could not for long remain depressed. For we only had the trouble in hand to face.

We had a particular crisis that summer which required all our resources to defeat. It was a prolonged crisis which went on for week after week. Every day we waited anxiously for the postman to come across the fields; and when the expected letter arrived I would have to spend hours writing convincing answers to the questions the letter contained. I replied to a score of such letters that summer; and when in the end the crisis was over, when on a glorious August morning a letter arrived to tell us we could have a measure of financial help until the promised harvest came next spring, I rushed out to Geoffrey and Jane to give them the good news.

This gesture was, of course, only a reflex of my own relief. As each week we struggled to pay their wages, I had identified them in my mind as part of our struggle. This is what happens in a small business. I, for instance, faced with my anxiety to pay the wages, had become so consumed with my efforts to do so, that I found myself believing that Geoffrey and Jane had shared my anxiety. Hence, now that Jeannie and I had won a reprieve, I had an irresistible desire that they should share our delight. It was an indulgence. It was also a thankfulness that now I would be able to look at them on a Saturday morning without grudging the wage they deserved.

First I saw Geoffrey who was digging a ditch in the wood, and when I shouted to him that everything was now all right, he paused for a moment resting on his shovel. Geoffrey has a kind face. He has blue eyes. He is very strong, and he is perhaps the best handyman I have ever known. He could be a plumber or a mason, and memories of his art remain tangible at Minack to this day. He looked at me, half-smiling, and he obviously could not understand what it was I was so excited about. I passed on to Jane.

She was thinning lettuce plants in the stable meadow.

As usual she was bare-footed, looking like some Continental peasant child, uncomplicated, utterly free, the wonderful fair hair touching her shoulders.

'Jane!' I shouted. 'We're all right!'

It was such conceit on my part that I could believe she should understand my enthusiasm. Why did I expect so? She was only sixteen and a half. And yet she had that kind of enthusiasm which flared such sincerity that both Jeannie and I felt its benefit. Jane, both Jeannie and I felt, was part of us. And Jeannie and Jane talked to each other as if there was no difference in their ages. For both, life was a gay excitement; and for me who saw them together, it was wondrous to see two different generations together as if passing time did not exist.

'Jane! Isn't it wonderful?'

Her response to good news, even if she did not know its significance, was usually effervescent. If I had a letter containing some pleasant information and I told her, I could rely on her to react happily despite the fact that I had not given her the details of its contents. She was by nature an enthusiast. She would, for instance, appear as pleased as we were when we received news that prices for our flowers had gone up. It was part of the fun to tell her. She never failed to add to it.

And yet on this particular day she was disappointing me. She did not look me in the face, and to my surprise there was no smile to show she was glad. She stared at the ground, scratching the soil with the hoe within an inch or two of her bare feet. Of course she did not know the extent of the tremendous relief in my mind, and so I was plainly expecting too much from her. But always before there had been the telepathy conveying the mood of our excitement. It was obviously not working on this occasion.

Suddenly she looked up, but instead of meeting my eyes she looked to one side. Something was wrong. Whenever Jane was confused her cheeks became like red berries and her eyes wandered in every direction except straight in front of her.

'I've been meaning to tell you, Mr Tangye,' and in a flash I knew my high excitement was about to disappear, 'I'm leaving.'

I have sensed sometimes that someone who is working for me is thinking of going. There is a look about them, a slight casualness, a confidence towards me that they did not previously display. I am aware they are saying to themselves: 'I've been here long enough. It's time to move on.' It's a dying relationship between us, a product of *ennui*, the job has become dulled by the routine. I am therefore prepared.

But I was not by Jane.

'Say that again.' It was I who had now become flushed. I was thinking purely of myself. The thrill of overcoming our problem, the moment of celebration, was to be dissipated. Instead of relaxing for the first day in weeks, the weariness of the burden we had carried clear of our shoulders, here quickly was another to take its place.

'You see, Mr Tangye,' she said, and she had suddenly become animated, a bubbling enthusiasm which certainly had nothing to do with Minack, 'Mum and I are going to Turkey.'

This was a surprise.

'Yes,' she said, and because I was showing interest her confidence was returning. 'We're going in a van with two friends, and camping all the way, and when we get to Turkey we're going to live near Ankara, and grow our own vegetables, and spend our time digging for buried treasure.'

The programme was rushed out breathlessly and I would have laughed had it not been Jane who had spoken. True she used to have wild enthusiams, but she was also so sensible. I respected her opinions. If she told me that a certain section of our work could be improved this way or that, I would generally have reason to agree with her. She thought out her work. She had a sense of responsibility. Had we gone away at any time and left her in charge I would never have worried. She was deliciously reliable.

'I really don't see how you can live on vegetables,' I said, and there was a note of condescension in my voice, 'after all they take time to grow and what do you do in the meantime?'

My condescension was not as real as it sounded. I had a certain understanding for such a crazy idea. I had had so many myself which had been laughed at by outsiders. I was once fired as a columnist of a daily newspaper on a Wednesday, only to announce on the Thursday that I had resigned in order to go round the world. My friends at the time thought it was a complicated alibi to explain my dismissal. I knew better. I had an excuse to force myself into doing what I had always wanted to do.

Jane's mind would always range widely. She could not always thin lettuces or pinch out tomatoes or enjoy the leisurely pleasure of a peasant girl. She was too intelligent ever to be cushioned against conflict. And her mother felt the same; she was alert to the knowledge that Jane looked for adventure however small might be its canvas. Why not give her a chance for a real adventure?

'Oh, we've planned how to live in the meantime.' She was returning my condescension in a way I had learned to associate with her. When in doubt she was most superior. She set out to swipe her opponent out of the arena by the sheer force of her character. She *knew*. The opponent didn't.

'I won't be going immediately,' she said encouragingly, 'but I wanted you to know in good time. I'm awfully sorry . . .'

I returned to the cottage and told Jeannie the news. At first she laughed at my solemn face and said the whole idea was absurd and that it would never materialise.

'You know Jane!'

But when I described the way Jane had told me, how

it seemed to be different from her other enthusiasms which had melted away, she began to share my concern. After all Jane had given in her notice. That was final enough; and she had too cool an intellect to do that unless she and her mother had made their final decision. And as we discussed it, both Jeannie and I became vexed. The day's pleasure was being side-tracked. Instead of celebrating our personal achievement, we were talking about Jane. Who should we get to take her place? Did we want a girl or should we have a boy to help Geoffrey? The tedious worries of an employer, bitty and sterile. Round and round the same subject and going nowhere. She won't leave, she will. Jane, Jane, Jane . . .

Then we asked ourselves why we were so concerned whether Jane stayed or left. She was certainly thorough but she had not the knowledge to make her indispensable. We could easily find someone to take her place. So why waste time talking about her?

It was her attitude to life that we wanted to keep. Young as she was, she was in tune with us. An essence of happiness is to wake up in the morning and look forward to seeing the people with whom you are going to work. If you are at ease with them, if they are friends and not robots, if they do not irritate you, if they are not envious, then another dimension enters your life. Time does not drag. Evenings are not wasted worrying about the mishaps of the day. And if you are small employers the weight of responsibility is lightened, the enthusiasm of co-operation becoming as important as the technical ability to do the job.

There was the basic fact that Jane possessed the same wild love for the coast along which we lived as we did ourselves. It is no ordinary coast. The stretch where Minack lies and where Jane's cottage still stands gaunt, staring out at the ocean, is not the kind of country which appeals to the conformist. The splendour of the cliffs does not lead to beaches where people can crowd together, transistors beside them.

The cliffs fall to rocks black and grey where the sea ceaselessly churns, splashing its foam, clutching a rock then releasing it, smothering it suddenly in bad temper, caressing it, slapping it as if in play, sometimes kind with the sun shining on the white ribbon of a wave, a laughing sea throwing spray like confetti, sometimes grey and sullen, then suddenly again a sea of ungovernable fury lashing the cliffs; enraged that for ever and for ever the cliffs look down.

And among the rocks are the pools; some that tempt yet are vicious, beckoning innocently then in a flash a cauldron of currents, pools that are shallow so that the minnow fish ripple the surface as they dash from view, pools so deep that seaweed looks like a forest far below, inaccessible pools, pools which hide from everyone except those who belong to them.

High above, the little meadows dodge the boulders, and where the land is too rough for cultivation the bracken, the hawthorn, the brambles, the gorse which sparks its yellow the year round, reign supreme. This is no place for interlopers. The walkers, tamed by pavements, faced by the struggling undergrowth, turn back or become angry, their standardised minds piqued that they have to race a way through; and it is left to the few, the odd man or woman, to marvel that there is a corner of England still free from the dead hand of the busybody.

The badgers show the way. Their paths criss-cross, twist, turn, pound the soil flat, a foot wide, high roads of centuries, and when the bracken greens or coppers the land, the way is still there, underneath, so that if you have a feel for the countryside the undergrowth does not halt you. The badgers lead you. As you walk, feet firm and safe, you part the bracken to either side and after you have passed, it folds back again, leaving no sign of your passage.

Here, on our stretch of the coast, man has not yet brought his conceit. It is as it always has been. Gulls sweeping on their way, a buzzard sailing in the sky, foxes safe from the Hunt, birds arriving tired after a long journey, others ready to leave, swallows, white-throats, chiff chaffs, fieldfare, snipe, the long list which we welcome and to which we say good-bye. Our stretch of the cliff has a savagery that frightens the faint-hearted.

'Why isn't there a decent path cut out along the cliff top? Absolutely disgraceful.'

'All right in the summer, I suppose?'

'I wouldn't live here if it was given me.'

'How wonderful if uranium was discovered!'

'There's going to be a coastal path. You can't escape it, you know!'

'This is marvellous. An August day in Cornwall and no one to be seen.'

There they are, the philistines and the individual they would like to destroy. Mass enjoyment, mass organised walks, mass anything if it can score a victory over the sensitive; thus the philistines, barren of feeling, plod their dreary way, earnest, dull, conscientious, honest, misguided – I pity them. So did Jane. But Jane, like ourselves, was infuriated by their conceit.

Every day of our lives was spent in unison with this coast, the rage of the gales, salt smearing our faces as we walked, east winds, south winds, calm summer early mornings, the first cubs, a badger in the moonlight, wild violets, the glory of the first daffodil, the blustering madness of making a living on land that faced the roar of the ages. These were the passages of our year. Glorious, hurting, awakening us to the splendour of living. But the philistines. They nose. They want to disturb. Yet they are blind to beauty. They glance at our coast as they rush by. They want to see a path on the map. That is their object. Everything must conform. No time to pause. Hurry, hurry, hurry . . . we have another two miles to go.

Once there was an uncommunicative young man who spent a month on behalf of some Ministry, mysteriously hammering on the rocks of our cliff, making a map and taking samples from the results of his hammering. His presence immediately alerted us to the possible dangers of his activity. Was he looking for uranium? Or tin? Or some other metal vital for industrial progress?

And only a few weeks afterwards, on a hot June day while we were digging potatoes, an aeroplane had droned to and fro all day long over our heads, towing a box-like contraption several plane lengths behind. It angered us. And while Geoffrey and I plunged our shovels up the rows, and Jeannie and Jane knelt picking up the potatoes and putting them in the baskets, our conversation buzzed over the possible threat the box might represent. It also, of course, provided a diversion from our monotonous task. Jane seized my shovel, at one stage, stood in the middle of a meadow and with the mock fury of a native who had seen a white man for the first time, pretended to hurtle the shovel at the plane like a spear.

Her response, however, to the young man with the hammer had been mischievous. He was shy and desperately earnest and although both Jane and ourselves tried to get him into conversation as he went to and fro to his rocks every day, all we were able to extract from him was a 'Good morning' and a 'Good evening.'

It was Easter and on the Sunday the young man arrived to perform his hammering, on some lonely rock beneath the cliffs. It was beneath Jane's section of the cliff and before climbing below, he had dumped his haversack in a meadow that sloped steeply from Jane's cottage. He was, however, unaware that he had dumped it exactly in the middle of the area in which a regular Easter game was about to be played; for in Jane's family there was a tradition to hide each other's Easter presents outside in a chosen area of ground. In the garden, or, as on this occasion, somewhere in the meadows in front of the cottage. Jane, her mother and young Jeremy, played their game, and then Jane decided to play another.

She took two small chocolate eggs wrapped in silver paper, stole down to the haversack and placed them neatly so that the young man would see them as soon as he returned from his duties. Later that day she saw him clamber up the cliff and arrive at his haversack; then she waited for his reaction. None. He hesitated for a moment, then strapped up the haversack and hoisted it on his back, and marched off. But what delighted Jane was that he kept the Easter eggs, he made no gesture of throwing them away. And so, because she was fanciful and because next day he made no mention of his find, she came to a happy conclusion. The young man had believed a pixie had put them there.

Jane had no fear of climbing the cliffs and sometimes I called her foolhardy. There was one section the marine commandos used to use for climbing practice. They came in their boats from Newlyn, then nosed inshore, and one by one they sprang on a sea-lashed rock; or they fell in the water. I have seen a dozen in the sea swimming in their life-jackets.

Their attempts would be watched by Jane who, after they had gone, would clamber to the spot they had chosen and begin to climb herself. She had the good sense not to go very far but she felt forced to make the attempt; it was a challenge and she was always looking for a challenge.

Heaven knows how she ever reached her secret bathing pool which could not be seen from anywhere above; and then climbed back afterwards. Jeremy, her brother, never dared do it, and he was adventurous enough. It lay in a zone below the cottage, first a steep grass slope, then a sheer drop of a hundred feet, except for a narrow grassy ledge which fell like an almost perpendicular toboggan run on one side.

I do not know how anyone could stay on the ledge without slithering to the rocks at high speed unless there was a rope to hold. Jane never had a rope. And she thought so lightly of the risk, that on hot summer days she would rush back from Minack at lunch time so that she could spend the greater part of her hour splashing in her pool and sunbathing beside it.

High above and eastwards towards Minack was the meadow she called her own. It was cradled in a cliff called Carn Silver, fifty feet above the sea and facing south to the Wolf. She reached it by a tortuous path which could never have been found by a stranger, and that, of course, was part of her fun. It was her own meadow and, she once told me, it seemed to welcome her as if it were alive, as if it were an animal. It was edged by man-placed stones, but it had been neglected for scores of years, and so it was perhaps possible that the spirits were glad Jane had become their chatelaine. She suited them. Her ways belonged to them.

It was here in this meadow of about thirty feet square that she carried out her market garden activities. They were not, of course, of the scope which merited the name market garden, but she had a game which she enjoyed and this was to pretend that it was indeed a market garden. Hence she used to write to various horticultural suppliers heading her notepaper after the name by which the three cottages were known. The Pentewan Nurseries, she called herself and her meadow.

She liked digging the meadow by moonlight. I wonder what the badgers and foxes said to themselves as this mid-twentieth-century teenager, long fair hair over her shoulders, sturdy, utterly content, jabbed the spade into the turf; for at first it was hard going, the ground had to be turned and the result waited upon, before it became soil. There she was, poised above the restless sea, the moonlight giving the Carn behind her its name, watched by the wild, sensed by the spirits, echoing the ageless effort of the peasant.

'How did you get on?' I would ask her next day.

'I think I'll finish it in another two nights.' Her voice, as always, piped. Voices that are high can irritate. They can provide the effect of a false note. One feels sometimes that the person behind such a voice is shallow and that their behaviour is designed for effect. Jane pretended, she wrapped herself in illusions, but hers was always a true part in a glorious game.

In due course Pentewan Nurseries began to have callers or, to be exact, callers tried to find out where to call. A representative of a famous seed establishment, another on behalf of a world-renowned fertiliser company, another who had special lightweight flower boxes to sell, another who had a rotovator to demonstrate, these people wandered the district looking for Jane's meadow.

On one occasion a Dutchman who had come to see me at Minack told me his next call was at Pentewan Nurseries and solemnly asked me to direct him. We have a number of Dutchmen who visit us during the year selling bulbs. They are an earnest, persistent lot. They have a silver-tongued patter which is persuasive and it was particularly persuasive in the years after the war when daffodil prices were high.

The farmers, envious of their horticultural neighbours, set out to plant bulbs as if they were turnips. They were also fascinated, since many of them had never left their own parishes, by the charming broken accent of the Dutchmen. It was a hint of the great world beyond, of naughty Europe, of sophistication they only read about. The Dutchmen played upon this weakness with such effect that West Cornwall was swamped with bulbs, and where cattle should peacefully have grazed, there were acres of daffodils. The honeymoon did not last very long. The farmers defeated themselves. They bought so many bulbs that they were incapable of looking after the daffodils. They had neither the time to grade and pack to professional standards, nor the wish to do so. They were only interested in the cream of the market and a quick return; and so when prices began to fall and daffodils were no longer easy money, they gave them up. And the charming Dutchmen had to be glib elsewhere.

They came often down the lane to Minack, in small cars with a left-hand drive, so easily recognisable that if one of us saw a flashing glimpse of the car through a gap far up the lane we would shout: 'Look out, a Dutchman's coming!'

We were a little malicious towards them. Jane, in particular liked to tease them although they had no notion that the teasing was in progress. She hatched a plot, for instance, to deal with those Dutchmen to whom I owed money.

It was easy to owe them money because part of their salesmanship was to offer credit until the flowers were in bloom. The fact that a glut had occurred, the prices been low, and we had made a loss on the deal did not, of course matter. The bulbs had proved their virility. And inevitably in the spring the Dutchmen would be coming down the lane to collect their cheque.

It was for this reason that Jane devised a series of compost heaps each of which bore the name of a creditor. She got the idea from a story Jeannie told her from a thriller she had read. A gentleman, famed for his prize vegetables, had murdered his wife and buried her under the compost heap which was the envy of his neighbours. The story titillated Jane.

Her theory was that anyone who was so bold as to come to lonely Minack asking for money should be attacked, then buried in the compost heap allocated to him. Hence, when one of these people arrived, I would catch sight of her in the background making elaborate, fanciful signs denoting the method of his disposal. Sometimes, as I solemnly talked, I would see her aiming at the back of a creditor as if she possessed a bow and arrow, and the arrow was about to fly. I have also seen her, when looking over the shoulder of my visitor, performing blood-curdling gestures with a knife; the creditor's throat was being symbolically cut.

On one occasion there was an especially tough creditor, a man so dominated by his mission that he failed to praise the glory of the coastline. Such a failure vexed Jane as much as it did ourselves. We judged people by the degree of enthusiasm they displayed for our coast. Those who said how awful it must be in winter, as if the isolation could only be tolerated in summer, were placed by Jane and ourselves at the bottom of the dustbin. This particular creditor seemed to think that Minack was an appalling place in which to live a twentieth-century pattern, winter and summer.

Jeannie, nevertheless, because it was tea-time was prepared to offer him a cup of tea. The creditor and I were on a white seat outside the cottage and I saw Jeannie, as I sat there, hand Jane a cup, then Jane disappeared for a moment.

When she appeared again she came up to the gentleman with a low bow and handed him his cup. There was a glint in her eye.

'Thank you very much,' said the man.

'I *hope* you'll enjoy it,' said Jane.

She had, in her fanciful fashion, allocated him his compost and, equally fancifully, had contrived a method of getting him there. It consisted of a potion, now emptied into the cup, of stewed stinging nettles, chickweed and heliotrope. She had planned the potion as soon as I told her, a few days before, that this particular gentleman was coming to visit me. He was very polite. He drank his tea without complaint. And, of course, he does not know to this day that in theory he is part of a compost.

After this episode we called Jane a witch. 'Cast a spell, Jane,' we would say whenever there was something we particularly desired.

But here was a Dutchman asking me the whereabouts of Pentewan Nurseries; and obviously I could not betray

Jane by describing it as a meadow thirty feet square poised on an inaccessible cliff. It was my duty to support her. The matter had to be treated seriously. So I said:

'The proprietor of Pentewan Nurseries *helps* here. I'll introduce you.'

My introduction was enough to speed Jane's idea of fun to such an extent that the Dutchman, innocent, was talking in terms of tons of bulbs for Pentewan Nurseries. I felt, as I listened, that he was aware that something might be wrong but the prospect of his commission confused him. This was an opportunity. A new customer. And the girl was obviously knowledgeable.

It is an art to know at what moment to end a joke, and Jane never persevered too long. She disengaged quietly. She did not close the session of joking with a guffaw, forcing her victim into blustering embarrassment. She slid out of the joke. She left a question-mark in the victim's mind. And the Dutchman departed, a suspicion of a smile on his face, wondering whether she would indeed write to him about the order she promised to consider.

So was she joking about going to Turkey? Was it a whim or a jest to say that she was leaving us? Perhaps the mood we were in had deprived Jeannie and me of a sense of humour. We had no laughter to spare. We had been drained by the weary struggle for survival, our senses had been deadened by the pitiless monotony of pretence; the pretence to be prosperous, the pretence to be gay, the pretence to have hope when none seemed to exist. Far from the cities, ensconced in the home of our dreams, we could not escape the twentieth-century malady. The sordid routine pursued us. And now on the day that we had momentarily rejoiced in a reprieve, here was Jane telling us she was going.

'It's no use worrying about it any more,' said Jeannie, 'it's just a pity she didn't choose another day to tell us.'

Weeks passed and nothing happened. The winter came and still the trek to Turkey was never mentioned. Then one windy, rainy November afternoon, Jeannie broached the question again at a moment when Jane had lugged a couple of baskets of wallflowers into the packing shed.

'Oh, Jane,' she said casually, 'what's happened to your Turkey trip?'

Jane heaped a pile of the wallflowers on to the table and started to strip off the leaves. She still wore her oilskin. It was huge, black, and three times too big for her; and her sou'wester, also black, buried her head so that all you could see was a nose and a few strands of fair hair.

'We've decided not to go just yet,' she said. A firm little voice, a note of slight irritation in it which comes when one is asked about a plan which has miscarried.

'Not *yet*, at any rate,' she added.

The answer was all that Jeannie required. She knew her Jane.

The Turkey visit had been permanently postponed.

7

The spring came early the following year. In February there were gentle west winds, balmy days which sent the larks into the sky to sing a month before their time. The green woodpecker in the elms below the cottage clung to the bark tapping his note of joy, unperturbed that the splendour of his crimson crown among the bare branches was there for all to see. The sunshine was his safety.

There was a rush of wings in Minack woods. Exultant songs from the willows, blackbirds courting, and thrushes rivalling them with glorious notes. Harsh warbles from the chaffinches, and the trills of the wrens, fluffing their tiny bodies, then bellowing their happiness. Magpies coarsely cried. The two ravens from the cliff flew overhead coughing their comments on what they could see below. Robins were careless in hiding their nests, no time for danger for spring was here. Owls hooted in the daylight. The wintering flocks of starlings gathered in the sky like black confetti wondering whether to leave. Too soon for the chiff chaffs or the warblers or the white-throats. They did not know we had an early spring. Minack woods still belonged to those who lived there.

The sea rippled in innocence, and when the *Scillonian* sailed by to and from the Islands we could hear in the cottage the pounding of her engines; for the wind and the surf were silent. Fishermen were tempted to drop their lobster pots, and one of them every day had a string across our tiny bay. There were others feathering for mackerel. Cockelshell white boats with men in yellow oilskins, engines chattering until the moment came to switch off and to drift with the tide. Gulls aimlessly dotted the water, like lazy holidaymakers. Cormorants on the edge of rocks held out their wings to dry like huge, motionless bats. The first primroses clustered on the cliff's edge and the white blooms of the blackthorn spattered the waste land above. A beautiful spring, only the task was to be part of it; but to us it held a threat. There was danger in the lovely days. There was menace in the soft breezes and warm nights. For our livelihood depended on cold. We required brisk weather and frosts up-a-long. How could we sell our flowers if flowers from everywhere were flooding the markets?

This was our first spring at Minack without Monty. He had died the previous May and lay buried beside the little stream that crossed the lane at the entrance to Minack, and which was for ever to be known as Monty's Leap. His shadow seemed always to be with us. And although, when one loses a loved one it is necessary to be practical and not to mope or to be indulgently sentimental, we yearned for the soft fur curled at the bottom of our bed at night, the sudden purrs, the wonderful comfort of his greetings on our returns, the splendour of his person – the colour of autumn bracken – poised ready to pounce on a mouse rustling in the grass.

He had been part of our lives for so long. He had been a friend in the sense that he had always been there to cope with our disappointments, ready to be picked up

and hugged or to bring calm with a game or to soothe by
sitting on my lap and being gently stroked. He had been
an anchor in our life. He was only a cat, but he had shared
the years; and thus he would always be part of us.

I said to him on his last day that I would never have
another cat. I felt, in saying this, that I was in some strange
way repaying his love. I was giving him his identity. I was
proving to him that he was not to me just one of a breed
who could be replaced, like replacing a broken cup with
one of the same pattern. He was Monty, and there would
never be another. It would be no use some well-meaning
person arriving at the door with a kitten, curbing grief by
offering a substitute. I was telling him that I would always
be loyal to him. The only cat I had ever known.

And then I made a remark that in retrospect was to
prove so extraordinary. I found myself saying that I would
make one exception . . . if a black cat whose previous
home could never be discovered came crying to the door
of the cottage on a storm. I was so astonished by my own
words that I went and told Jeannie. I was ashamed by
what I had said. At the very moment I was trying to prove
my devotion, I had hedged. I had not meant what I had
been saying to Monty. My emotion had deceived me and
my subconscious had come out with the truth. I would,
in fact, accept a successor. True, I was able to console
myself by realising I had made an apparently impossible
condition.

And now it was February, a wonderful summer-like
February, nine months after he died, and there had been
no sign of a black cat crying at the door. There had been
no sign of any stray cat coming to Minack; and cats,
except for Monty's memory, had been dismissed from
my mind. We had other companions.

Old Hubert, the gull on the roof, continued to waddle
along the ridge, staring down at us as we went about
our business, sitting sometimes with feathers fluffed out
at the top of the massive stone chimney, strutting in the

garden, alighting on the cedar-wood covering of the coal shed waiting for Jeannie to feed him.

He had been with us for six years, since that day we came up from the cliff aware that we had lost the rewards of our potato harvest to the weather, all our hopes gone. Tommy – who then worked for us – told to leave because we had no money for his wages, a moment of despair; and then we came up the path to the cottage and saw the gull on the roof.

He was to us the symbol we needed. The sight of him reassured us in the sense that at this moment of material defeat, the wild had suddenly accepted us as it had accepted the generations who had toiled at Minack before us. The gull had watched and now was prepared to trust. We had never attempted to lure him. We had never noticed him before. He was one of hundreds who flew every day in the sky above Minack, and he had chosen this moment of distress to adopt us. It was from that time that we felt we belonged to Minack, that we were no longer interlopers from the city imposing ourselves on the countryside, pretending in fact to be country people. We had passed the test. We were no longer looking on from the outside, armchair escapists who believe that dreams are real. We had been defeated, and there would be no soft way out for victory. We had joined the ghosts of Minack in the endless struggle against the seasons and, in doing so, we had embraced all the things they had seen and heard and done. We had become part of the ageless continuity of Minack; and the gull on the roof was its symbol.

And then there were Charlie the chaffinch and Tim the robin. Monty had treated these two with indifference, as indeed he did all birds. Yet both Charlie and Tim often gave him reasons to be justifiably irritated. Charlie, who was so gaily beautiful in the spring and summer and so drab in winter, used to hop around him as he lay somnolent in the garden as if he were playing a game of dare. And Tim used to tempt him by coming into the cottage and perching on the back of the chair upon which he was lying; then start to warble, softly, almost a gurgle.

We had not sought the friendship of Charlie or Tim. They each pushed their personalities into our lives. We had not set out to bribe them by the customary method of crumbs. It was just that we became gradually aware day after day, week after week, that a particular chaffinch and a particular robin took far more notice of us than any of the other birds in the neighbourhood.

Indeed their behaviour exactly suited our personal attitude to wild life. It should come to man and not man to it. Some people like to try to conquer the natural instincts of a wild bird or animal, and then boast they have an unusual pet. True it has required great patience on their part to score the victory but it always seems to me to be a hollow one. It makes me feel that vanity is the motive of the conquest, for it certainly cannot be of any benefit to the wild creature concerned. Its instincts will strive to be free again and, if it escapes, it will probably go to its doom by trusting other animals and men who are normally its enemy.

Jeannie was brought a fox cub once by a trapper who had found it in one of his snares. It was surprising that he had not killed it, for it was trapped in sheep country and foxes had been worrying the sheep in the neighbourhood; but it was so pitifully young, not a month old and perhaps caught on his first venture out from the earth, that he had not the heart to do so. He had made a special trip to Minack, for the snare had badly cut its right foot and it needed attention; and the trapper felt that Jeannie was the one to help.

He took it out of a basket and handed it to her and it immediately snuggled into her arms like a puppy. It looked so safe and harmless that I put out a finger to stroke it. I just touched it, and was nipped; but it never nipped Jeannie for the whole six weeks she looked after it. It was a male cub, and she called him Sammy.

For the first few days she kept him in a wire-covered box near the stove in the sitting-room, teaching him to lap bread and milk from a saucer. Three or four times a day she bathed the foot and although it must have hurt him, he showed no resentment towards her. He obviously had complete trust.

We were about to plant tomatoes in our small greenhouse, a hundred and twenty plants direct into the soil. The ground was ready. The plants were waiting. A small number in proportion to those we grew in the other greenhouses, but still a useful one. It was, therefore, financially unfortunate that Sammy had arrived at this particular moment, for Sammy could not stay for long in the sitting-room and what better place could he go than to the greenhouse?

So we surrendered the tomato plants, filled a chicken coop with hay, half-covering it with a rug to give the darkness of an earth, and introduced Sammy to his new home. He was very timid, and as soon as Jeannie released him he scurried to the coop and hid himself in the hay. I do not know what else I expected him to do. He had every reason to be frightened and yet, as he hid that first time, I had a fleeting understanding of what it is that makes the unwise try to tame the wild.

I was irked by the instinct that Sammy would never be my friend. It was an affront to my goodwill. My vanity was hurt. I had a sudden anger making me wish to impel him to like me; and this, I thought, was the same unsavoury compulsion I despised in others. I should like to force Sammy to be so dependent on me that I could pretend he was fond of me. I had to surrender little. He had to surrender his life.

Jeannie patiently nursed his foot until it was well again; and when darkness fell, and there was a moon, we used to watch him running about through the panes of the greenhouse. She still fed him by hand, pushing a saucer up to him as he lay in his coop; and slowly she began to wean him from bread and milk to dog biscuits, and then to slugs. We spent a great deal of time collecting succulent slugs, but in order at first to persuade him to eat them we had to be harsh. Jeannie withheld the dog biscuits for a day so that he became so hungry that he had to taste the dish which would be one of his stand-bys when he was out on his own.

Naturally enough we had plenty of advice as to what to do with him. We should look after him for three months. We should let him go immediately. And there were the unsophisticated countrymen who, untrammelled by complications of thought, innocently proposed we should keep him for good. No subtle emotion behind the proposal. Just the plain fact that if we kept him, he would become like a dog.

What was so odd was that these blunt minds, no conscious cruelty in their stories, would proceed to tell us what had happened to other foxes which had been treated like dogs. One farmer kept a fox for three years, locking it in a pen when the Hunt was around. But one day the Hunt came on his land unexpectedly and before he had time to hide his fox, it rushed out with the other farm dogs to see what was happening; and came face to face with the hounds.

There was another fox which was happy enough with the farmer who had adopted him, which sauntered one day gaily through the front door of a neighbouring farm. He had no sense of danger. He was only doing what he had always done, being friendly. But they locked him in a room until a gun was brought.

Jeannie, who does not like to read or hear unhappy stories, would walk away and worry about what would happen to her Sammy. For he belonged to her. He would never have anything to do with me; but Jeannie could pick him up or play with him as if he was indeed a puppy.

He had no fear of her, and he seemed grateful that she had nursed him back to health and strength. So it was Jeannie who was the saddest on the evening we decided to let him go.

We knew, however, that he was ready because he had been trying to dig his way under the door on the previous few nights. His foot was healed and he was big enough to look after himself, but there was the doubt as to whether he would know how to do so. Would his instinct be enough? Or would he try homing the ten miles to the earth where he came from? Or would another vixen, and there was one with cubs near by, be ready to adopt him?

We said good-bye to Sammy, watched him slip out of the greenhouse door into the long grass, then to the side of the hedge and over the bank into the wood. And as he went Jeannie suddenly had an idea. Supposing he stayed in the wood enjoying his freedom but relying on her to feed him until he felt big and bold enough to start on his journeys? It was the kind of practical thought which softened the parting; and that night dog biscuits soaked in milk awaited Sammy's return in a saucer in the open doorway of the greenhouse.

It was gone the next morning, not a crumb left; and Jeannie was naturally elated. Sammy was being helped. Sammy had the good sense to know that he could rely on her. So dog biscuits soaked in milk were put out every night, and every morning the saucer was clean. This programme continued for ten days until one early morning, soon after dawn, Jeannie got up with the idea she might see Sammy having his meal. She didn't of course. Sammy had never been back. He was far away by now. It was only our wishful thinking that made us believe the food had gone to him; for Jeannie that early morning saw who were enjoying their breakfast, dipping their tiny beaks into the saucer.

A family of bluetits.

It was in that early spring that Shelagh returned to

Minack. She had been laid off for a few weeks by the shop in Penzance where she worked, and she came to us for a temporary job; and this time we were able to give it to her. We welcomed her with delight. For the summer-like weather had brought on the flowers in profusion, and Minack was ablaze with daffodils, wallflowers, anemones, violets, calendulas and stocks. Here was the harvest of last year's planning and within the space of six weeks we had to win the reward.

Six weeks. There can be no neat production line on a flower farm. The results of a period of over-production cannot be stored in a warehouse, waiting the moment when the demand is there again. Flowers do not pause in their blooming for our convenience, nor do they hasten. Jeannie and I are at their mercy. Nor can we plan with any exactitude; for this week may be warm and the next bitterly cold, holding back the flowers instead of forcing them on. Only one thing is certain, we have to clear our harvest by the end of March whatever the weather is like, for by then the great flower farms in the centre of England are storming the markets with their produce.

It was part of the charm of Shelagh that she fitted into our ways as if she had been working regularly for us as long as Jane had done. We did not have to explain to her what was at stake. She had not come to do a job of work just in order to collect a wage at the end of the week. She seemed to show that she wanted to be part of something, as if the nature of her background provided her with a vacuum which she was searching to fill.

Such a mood was understandable. She had been well brought up in a comfortable home but, however comfortable it might have been, there was no possibility of her sensing the natural love she saw others of her own age enjoying. She was illegitimate and, in a small village, there was no way of hiding the fact. Who was my father? Who was my mother? The questions must have tormented her over the years. The secret battle within her that no one could share. Perhaps the outsiders could have given her the answers. Perhaps they knew as they whispered and pitied. Shelagh on one side of the frontier, the rest on the other.

It was inevitable that Shelagh and Jane should like each other. Neither of them suffered from any pretensions and both were incapable of being jealous. Both were quiet and so neither of them would churn the friendship away by endless chatter. Indeed they were so quiet sometimes in each other's company that Jeannie and I at first thought their silences represented disagreements. It was a foolish mistake. They were, in fact, sufficiently at ease with each other to dispense with unnecessary talk. Jane was now sixteen, Shelagh was seventeen.

But Shelagh looked younger than Jane, and Jane did not look sixteen. Shelagh was a little taller but she took away the inches of height by hunching her shoulders and walking head bent downwards. We used to tease her about it, the tease which is meant to improve a habit, 'What are you looking for, Shelagh?'

She had a little hart-shaped face with a perfect complexion, a slow smile, mischievous, a smile that she used as a manifest of her affection. Jeannie or I used to surprise her sometimes suffused by this smile as she watched a mouse sitting on her knee, sharing her lunch-time sandwiches.

She had soft light brown hair and she took much pride in it. While she worked she protected it with a grey and blue woolly skull cap with a red tassel; and on Saturday mornings before her weekly visit to Penzance she carefully set her hair and added a scarf to hide the curlers.

Her eyes were grey-blue and since her accident, when she fell off her bicycle and was on the danger list, she had to wear glasses. They were the conventional, ugly glasses and they spoilt her prettiness; and the first thing she saved up for after the flower season was over and it was decided that she should stay with us permanently, was an elegant black pair.

She had a flair for dress and, if she had wanted to do so, could have earned her living as a dressmaker. She was dainty and very appealing. When Jeannie and I saw her off-duty in Penzance, we used to say to each other that it would not be long before Shelagh was married.

She loved giving presents. She used this giving as a backbone to her life, as if here was something she could grasp firmly. It gave her sense of security because the dates of birthdays, Christmas and Easter were on the calendar. They gave her opportunity for being appreciated and they gave her something to look forward to. All her presents were thought out well in advance.

And so were Jane's. There was one Christmas before Shelagh came when Jeremy, Jane's brother, arrived at the door on Christmas morning with a large brown-paper parcel. Jeremy, aged ten, often complained of living in a house of women, Jane and his mother; and about this time he had been helping us on Saturday mornings by washing jam jars. He had broken one or two and Jane had ticked him off when I, out of fun, said to him that I thought women were awful the way they nagged. Jeremy stopped his work, looked at me and heaved a great sigh:

'You're telling me!'

But on this Christmas morning he was at the door with a parcel. And when he brought it into the cottage, unwrapped the brown paper and then the tissue paper, we found a beautiful blue velvet cushion, piped in gold braid with a tassel in one corner; and in another, woven in red and gold, was a crown and under the crown was the letter M. As Jeremy handed it to us he bowed solemnly like a medieval page boy.

M, of course, was the initial for Monty, and he had many a pleasant sleep on this cushion. And for Jeannie and me, the cushion remains as evidence of the happiness we shared with Jane. She had no need to spend the time, or the money, making that gift for 'His Lordship' as she always called Monty. It was a gesture of her enthusiasm and her affection.

March was a busy time for Shelagh's spirit of giving. There were two friends who had birthdays and there were Jeannie and myself; myself at the beginning and Jeannie in the middle. Even when she was in the casual contact with us she used to send us birthday cards, but now she was working at Minack, and she would see us on THE day, she had to contrive to give us something that measured up to her standard of giving.

At the beginning of March, I received a box of cats' tongues chocolates. And Jane gave me something which to this day gives me pleasure. There is in the smaller of the flower packing sheds a beam which stretches across at the height of my forehead. Day after day, month after month, year after year, I used to forget that beam and walk down the packing shed, and bang my forehead against this beam. It cut me. It bruised me. It made me angry that I always forgot. And so Jane decided to do something about it for this particular birthday.

She bought a bath mat from Woolworths of a spongy plastic material, and cut it up in strips so that she was able to cover the whole beam, making it a cushion instead of an edge. On my birthday the flower shed was jammed with daffodils waiting for me to bunch, and as usual I went into it without thinking and as usual I hit the beam. But so softly! It will always be one of my pleasantest memories of Minack when I remember the sight of Jane and Shelagh laughing at me. They had seen me through the window. They had been out picking early and in each hand they held a basket of crimson wallflowers until they were laughing so much that they dropped the baskets to the ground.

'Happy birthday!' I heard them call.

My cats' tongues chocolates were only a preliminary. Shelagh was waiting for Jeannie's birthday before she gave us our real joint present, and it must have taken her many spare evenings to complete it. I remember when I first saw it that I had a nervous reaction. It is always the same when someone gives you something which is meant to be displayed in the home, and the someone is a regular visitor. You cannot put the object away, optimistically hoping to bring it out at the right moment. Sooner or later you forget.

Shelagh had sewn and embroidered a pyjama case of black silk with pink silk lining. It was decorated with stars stitched in gold surrounding the words 'Good night' and the words 'His' and 'Hers'. And even if we had not liked it, which we did, we would still have had to keep it on our bed. For Shelagh was working in the cottage as well as outside.

In fact, I gave Shelagh to Jeannie as a birthday present. In the few weeks she had been at Minack she had proved herself invaluable. Jane hated housework. Shelagh enjoyed it; and so no wonder Jeannie wanted to keep her. And as for myself, instead of being irritated by someone dusting and sweeping in our sitting-room, I did not mind at all. I felt always at ease with Shelagh whatever I was doing. I did not notice when I was sitting at my desk that she was on her knees brushing the carpet, or at the sink doing the washing-up. Jeannie who had done all the work herself for years was astounded that I should be so docile. None of that: 'I've got work to do. I don't want someone in here disturbing me,' kind of attitude. I was tamed. I was the meek husband who not only was delighted that his wife was spared housework, but also made no fuss over the presence of the substitute.

One of Shelagh's tasks which gave Jeannie particular pleasure was the preparation of tea. A small task, it might seem, but in reality the drudgery of it had grown to mountain size in her mind. The custom in these parts is for the staff to bring their own tea for croust, the mid-morning break, and have a cup from the farmer's pot at lunch-time. In the afternoon they work right through to five o'clock without any break at all.

Jeannie and I, on the other hand, kind perhaps but unwise, chose to be more liberal and set a new pattern. We gave Geoffrey (Jane went back to her cottage) a jug of tea and cake for lunch, and also filled a Thermos for his tea and another for Jane's with more cake for both. If we had casual labour or workmen at the cottage they received the same treatment, and cascades of tea were carried out to wherever those concerned might be.

A gesture such as this is inclined to become a habit which is taken for granted; but for Jeannie it remained a tedious chore around which the day revolved.

'Oh dear, I've run out of tea.'

'Will you fetch Geoffrey's Thermos?'

'Be careful with the milk or there won't be enough.'

'I wish this kettle would boil. They're waiting.'

'I had better make a cake.'

'Will these biscuits be all right for them?'

'I must get home because I haven't done the tea.'

It was this conscientiousness of Jeannie's that Shelagh was now able to take over. She used to come into the cottage from whatever she was doing outside about an hour before lunch-time, do her cleaning, then depart with that tea. It was a merciful relief for Jeannie.

The flower season, once it starts, proceeds at such a pace that the days mingle into each other leaving one vague to the passing of time. The clock and the calendar are represented by the end of picking one variety of flower and the beginning of picking another. Thus when the meadows of Magnificence, our earliest yellow trumpet daffodil, are thinned of blooms, and then the Sulphur and then the dainty Obvallaris, I know without ticking off the days that, by being in the middle of the California and the King Alfred, we are nearing the end of our harvest, and that a month has gone by, and that in the month we have succeeded or failed in our effort to earn a living.

There are, of course, the soft flowers; and by these were meant, in the particular season that Shelagh started with us, the anemones and wallflowers, violets and calendulas, Beauty of Nice stocks, forget-me-nots, freesias and poly-anthus. The sun shone down day after day hurrying the flowers into bloom. Picking, bunching, packing, rushing the boxes to Penzance station, the volume of the work was enormous. We had no time to enjoy the loveliness of the weather. We were blind to the burstng beauty of the spring.

And these flowers also served as hour hands of passing time. First, the stained orange and yellow wallflowers disappeared into the markets leaving a miniature petrified forest where they once sweetened the air; then the Vulcan, and the dazzling crimson of Fireking.

The anemones, greedy for warmth, burst their flowers too soon, looking like pansies; and the heavy dews left moisture on the petals browning the tips, so that we would pick a basket, set them out in jars, then next morning find them unbunchable.

The stocks, side-shoots plucked day after day from the main stems, began to look like a meadow of sticks. The freesias and the polyanthus sheltered by the glass, thus cosseted in normal times from the cold, rewarded our care by resenting the blazing sun; the flowers wilted and lost their colour, the petals were soft and tired even before their journey had begun.

The violets and the calendulas gloried in the warmth; but, because they were so generous they were not wanted. There was a glut everywhere.

Then, as the flowers were consumed, as our consign-ments to the market became fewer, as our patience and hard work and pride were expended, we slowly began to realise our great plans of a year ago were close to failure. We had succeeded to the extent that we had a vista of flowers, no fault here in the art of growing; only the sun had defeated us. The warmest spring in many years.

Even our Cornish posies had failed us. Jeannie had started these a few years before, while I had given them their name. She had begun by using short and twisted flowers of different kinds which were unsuitable for despatch on their own; and she had gathered them into a bunch, so mingling the varieties and the colours that they became posies of delicious design. The idea was such a success, each posy was such wonderful value, that the markets began asking for more. Thus we grew flowers with the deliberate intention of including them in the posies. Wallflowers gave them body, calendulas a splash of vivid colour, anemones variety, stocks a spring-like scent, forget-me-nots a breathless blue, freesias and polyanthus another reminder to those in distant cities that spring had come to Cornwall.

The snag of these posies was the time they took to prepare. It was an art requiring patience and artistry, a careful mingling of colours and arrangement of shape. I could not do them. My efforts ended, however hard I tried, in an untidy bunch like that of a child holding a random-picked collection of wild flowers. Hence Jeannie was their creator, then under Jeannie's tuition Jane, and now Shelagh. One could go into the flower-house at the end of a day in which they had been posy making, and the eye marvelled at the patchwork of colours that filled the jars on the shelves.

We were all in this flower-house one day, the three of them working on the posies, myself tying up the boxes prior to taking them to the station when the postman arrived at the door. As usual I quickly opened those envelopes I recognised came from our flower salesman and to my horror I saw the posies had only fetched threepence each. I was enraged, of course, because we calculated that we lost on a posy if we went below a shilling; but I was also very sad. Here around me were Jeannie and the two girls working so hard, and in my hand was the evidence that all their work was a waste of time and money. I was wondering whether to tell them when Shelagh, who had been looking out of the window, suddenly said:

'The black cat is in the stable meadow.'

At the far end, at the entrance of the gap which opens into the big field, was a spot. It was moving cautiously. It reached a patch of bare ground, hurried, then disappeared into a forest of Cromwell daffodils.

'I wonder where it comes from?' said Jane. She was clasping a half-completed posy in one hand, picking a dark red wallflower from a jar with the other.

'Poor thing,' said Jeannie.

It had first been seen a fortnight previously by Jeannie's mother who had been staying with us. Jeannie's mother, who had given us Monty as a kitten, was out for a walk with Angus, her Scottie, when he suddenly dashed into the undergrowth barking madly. She thought he had found a rabbit. Instead, a second later, he was back on the path and ahead of him, like a streak of black lightning, was a cat. It was across a field, over a hedge and down the cliff before Angus had gone fifty yards.

The incident had no significance in my mind whatsoever. Nor, for that matter, did the occasion when I first saw the cat for myself. I had gone out early one morning, long before breakfast time, to make an inspection of the flowers which would be ready to pick that day; and I was passing the calendula meadow when I saw right in the middle, surrounded by the blazing orange of the flowers, a tiny black head and two ears, and a pair of yellow slit eyes. The eyes watched me as I passed, the head moving imperceptibly. I was so occupied by my thoughts that I forgot to mention it to Jeannie until some time afterwards.

'By the way,' I said, 'I saw that cat this morning. It looks a bit young.'

It was perhaps natural that Jeannie should be more interested in these incidents than myself. She had always been a cat lover. Cats held a fascination for her to such an extent that any cat, however casual its acquaintance, would receive her fondling and her affection. I had had only one cat; and in any case at this particular time my mind was filled with anxiety. The flower year was ending, and the bulging enthusiasm with which I planned it was fading away into a great disappointment.

There were, however, still the Wedgewood iris in the mobile greenhouse, twenty thousand bulbs in four beds, climbing stiffly like a multitude of green spires. Here could be a lush harvest, a failure redeemed; and I remember the expert who called one day and saw them, saying to us as if he were gauging the form of a racehorse in the parade ring; 'If you can beat the Channel Islands by three days you're on a winner.'

We did not beat the Channel Islands. Indeed we did not beat anybody. The summer-like spring beat us. For the first time in the memory of iris growers, the outside crop of iris coincided with the indoor. And we had hardly begun to pick our harvest when a telegram arrived from our Covent Garden salesman:

'Send no more. Iris up to warehouse ceiling.'

8

The next time I saw the black cat it was in the chicken-run. We kept half a dozen elderly hens in a clearing in the wood, protected from foxes and badgers by high wire netting, the bottom of which was buried in the ground. Nothing could jump over or dig under. But a cat could claw up a tree, leap on to the roof of the chicken-house, then drop into the run below.

At one period we kept over forty hens, and the chicken-house was spacious and specially designed for such a number. Jeannie had believed they would bring in some useful pin money, and they were, in fact, her responsibility. The eggs also helped, since we lived so far from the shop, to make the daily catering easier for her.

We found however, as others before us, that the pin money was an illusion and that so much was paid out every week on expensive laying pellets that it was cheaper to buy the eggs. Thus gradually the flock was thinned out until these six old pensioners were left. Very occasionally one of them would lay an egg; but the real justification of their existence was based on sentiment. They each had an identity of their own. The prospect of killing them was out of the question.

I had gone along one morning to open them up when I saw the little black cat inside the run by the chicken-house door. For a second it stared at me, motionless, then it ran, racing across the run in panic, until it hit the wire netting at the far side. Foolishly I went after it. I do not know what my intentions might have been but my approach increased the cat's terror and it began clawing at the wire and attempting to thrust its head through the mesh. I suddenly realised it might strangle itself. The head might just possibly get through a hole, but its body, thin though it was, never. For an instant I put out my hands as if to pick it up. The threat of such help from me made it instinctively recoil from the netting; and the next moment I saw it take a flying leap on to the chicken-house roof, up the tree, and down again on to the ground outside the run. It disappeared into the wood behind.

From now on one of us saw the cat almost every day. Sometimes one of the girls saw it when they were picking wallflowers in the skol meadow at the top of the cliff. Another day Shelagh found it in the lane as she was bicycling to work. Jane once frightened it on the path leading to her cottage. And there were numerous times when Jeannie or I spotted it in one of our fields or in our wood. Indeed one of the strange things about its activities was that it was always on *our* land; and yet our land dovetailed into that of my neighbours in most complicated patterns. It kept within Minack boundaries and spurned the others.

But none of us could get anywhere near it. It ran away at the sight of us, although on occasions it sat on a hedge on the far side of a field, watching; a little black spot in the distance. And there were other occasions when it chose to sit in the lane about a hundred yards from the flower packing shed, the other side of Monty's

Leap, as if it were trying to make up its mind to come nearer.

I was still too busy to take much notice of it. I was worried. The income from the flowers was far below expectations. The reserve I hoped for did not exist; the work had been done, the wages paid out, the bills incurred, and here Jeannie and I were at the flower year's end without a penny available for our own endeavours. We had both worked for nothing.

Defeat, or danger, is easy to face when it is met suddenly for the first time. One feels elated that the secret self is being challenged. Here is the chance to bring out the hero, the somnolent section of one's being that longs to justify itself in the dramatic. But I always feel that the very nature of the courage that is required on such occasions is deceptive. It looks like courage while in fact it is an emotional outburst. It can be, indeed, a form of showmanship. In times of sudden danger or defeat one can be so intoxicated by excitement that one is scarcely aware of one's actions.

The aftermath of such courage is when real courage is needed. The gesture has been made but the danger has remained, and a hangover has taken the place of exultation. One now slips into a remorseless delaying action, a tedious clinging to hope; and one is forced to realise that factors have to be faced which provide no stimulus. They are the factors of repetition, the further defeats, the further dangers, leading one on and on until suddenly comes the day one discovers that despair has replaced the struggle for victory as the enemy.

In the kind of life we had chosen it was Jeannie who was tested when promise was unfulfilled. She had left behind in London so much that earned the envy of others. As the Public Relations Officer of the Savoy Hotel Group she was at the top of her profession. She had a large salary and expense account. She was able to mingle with the famous and live a life that had the trappings of a film star. Her office, as she described in her book *Meet me at the Savoy*, was the meeting place of household names. It was used as a club. At any time you might find there Danny Kaye or James Mason or A. P. Herbert or any of the top newspaper correspondents; and she was described by an American magazine as 'the prettiest public relations officer in the world.'

She thus had standards by which to judge the value of her present life that were not ordinary. Moreover she knew that if she so wished she could return to London and live again the sophistication she had surrendered. At any moment of doubt the glamour was beckoning. The gaiety was waiting. She could forget the water which had to be pumped from the well, the paraffin lamps, the endless cooking, the long hours of bunching, the cold wet days picking the flowers, the naked simplicity of her existence. She could leave all this behind. She could look back and call it a time of folly. She would not be the only one who wanted to escape, then found escapism too tough, and returned.

Yet she never did consider such an alternative. I never had to listen to her telling me how wonderful things once had been, or could be again. Nor did she put doubt into my mind that I might be demanding too much of her. Instead it was she who gave me the courage. I count myself tenacious but I do not enjoy taking risks. I foresee trouble before it arises and so I can argue myself out of taking bold action. Jeannie on the other hand, acting by instinct, will stride into a situation undeterred by reason; and once embroiled she does not retreat.

Here we were then at the end of March and our only aid was tenacity. It was, as I have said, something I understood; but both of us were weary. Every problem, however simple, was therefore huge. And any solution required the melancholy prospect of starting again the same pattern of growing as the previous year when our hopes had been high. We had, in fact, gambled and lost.

We had also, as the result of our gambling, become more involved in the mechanics of living from which we had set out to free ourselves. We could consider ourselves no longer as escapists. We now had responsibilities of a parallel nature to those we had left. We had created dependants. The lives of Jane, Shelagh and Geoffrey were bound up with ours.

It was now that the little black cat became a pleasant diversion. It haunted Minack to such an extent that Jeannie and the girls began to taunt me for taking so little notice of it. I was accused by them of all the anti-cat inclinations I possessed before Monty came into my life. I was being obstinate and cruel. Here was a little black cat that was so obviously seeking affection, but I was not even offering to help it overcome its terror of human beings. Here was an example, they said mockingly, of anti-cat brutality.

'He's heartless, isn't he, Mrs Tangye?'

'The poor little thing is starving.'

'Let's wait until he's gone to town and then we'll feed it.'

It was pleasant to be laughed at in this way. It relieved the tension. It helped me to see my problems in perspective. It was foolish to let myself indulge in depression just because I had been disappointed, and was tired, and because I suffered from the sickness of wanting success quickly. I was meeting again my old failing, the belief that endeavour on its own is sufficient to gain material triumph. I was ignoring, as I had done before, the rewards I had won. My eyes were staring at a pedestal so far in the distance that I was blind to what was close to me, the small pleasures which sparkled at me, the glory of awakening every day to an environment I loved. I had no right to demand more than this. The beat of my life was within the truth that men can look for all their lives; and fail to have the luck to find.

Easter was early that year. At the beginning of the week

I saw my friend Walter Grose walking through Minack on his way to hoe potatoes in his part of the cliff. Walter for many years had worked one of the three farms whose buildings straddled the top of the hill and through which we passed on the way to the main road. He had now amalgamated his farm with that of Jack Cockram, the young man I had been able to introduce to my landlord. Walter and Jack made a good combination.

'How are you today, Walter?' I asked. And he replied in his usual way with his warm smile;

'Poor but happy.'

But I had a reason other than pleasantries in talking to him that day. Walter had a large assortment of farmhouse cats which roamed his outbuildings and it occurred to me that the little black cat might be one of them. It wasn't. He had seen it himself down at Minack, but he had no idea whence it came. Why didn't I ask the travelling fish salesman?

I had the luck to see this gentleman in his van later on in the day when I was going into Penzance. Once a week he visited every farm in the district and the cats always hastened from their hideouts whenever he appeared. At each farm they grouped themselves round the open van doors as he displayed his wares to the farmer's wife; handsome toms, battle-scarred ladies, cats of every colour and description. He was the most popular visitor of the week. He was the cats' friend. He knew them all. No one was better placed than he to tell me whether anyone had lost a little black cat. But he could not help. I saw him a week later and he still could not help; and by then he had made special enquiries at every house on his round.

Meanwhile Jeannie, Jane and Shelagh had been active. They waited until I was out of the way, then put down a saucer of milk a hundred yards up the lane; it was just at the spot where the little black cat was in the habit of watching us. An hour or so later the saucer was empty.

The next time they did this I caught them red-handed.

They believed I had gone down the cliff to look at the potatoes, and so I had, but I returned quicker than they expected; and I found Shelagh, followed by Jeannie and Jane carrying a saucer of bread and milk into the old barn where Monty used to hide when he first came to Minack. It was the Saturday morning of the Easter week-end.

'I know very well what you're up to,' I said, and I felt angry, 'you're trying to make that cat stay here. I won't have it!'

I was repeating myself. I had said the same thing about Monty. Here was the simmering again of my pro-dog and anti-cat childhood. True I had loved Monty but there were exceptional reasons why I should have done so. He had been with us in a turbulent period of our lives and he had reflected to me the comfort of security. I had never become a slave to his species as Jeannie had done. I remained suspicious of cats in the mass and I was not going to have another one just because a stray seemed to be in need of some milk. Yet, and this was lurking at the back of my mind, what were my last words to Monty? Did I not talk about a black cat?

The little black cat lapped up the bread and milk though it waited until there was no one about. Jeannie looked in the barn during the afternoon, found the saucer empty and promptly refilled it.

'Look Jeannie,' I said after she had done so, 'I appreciate your feelings but you must try and appreciate mine. I don't want another cat. For one thing we can never expect to have a cat again which doesn't catch birds, and for another I want to keep my independence. After all even with Monty we were pretty tied down looking after him.'

I was aware that my words sounded hollow to her. Indeed I don't think she even listened. She had ideas of her own so she thought it more convenient to let me ramble on.

'I'm thinking of Charlie and Tim,' I said, 'and all the

other birds which now trust us. Are you really prepared
to risk their lives by pandering to this stray cat? I can't
understand it. And you know perfectly well that if you go
on feeding it, it will want to stay?'

I was particularly concerned about Tim. He spent so
many hours of every day on my desk or on the back of a
chair or perched high on the top half of the stable-shaped
front door. He would warble a song, or go to sleep on one
leg, or just observe. And when we went outside and we
wanted to show him off to a visitor we would shout for
him at the top of our voices; and within a few minutes he
would wing his way to us, and I would hold out my hand
for him to perch on. He was unperturbed by strangers. He
was so trustful that it was dangerous; and, having trusted
Monty, would he not trust any cat?

Charlie, I felt, could probably look after himself. He
was a forceful character, always on the move and, in the
spring and summer, a very noisy one. He would endlessly
cheep at us and sometimes he got on my nerves and I
would yell to him to shut up. Indeed this noisiness was to
prove his undoing. He never had the good sense to know
when to stop; and there was to be one day when he went
on too long. But I did not foresee this on that day when
I was telling Jeannie I wanted nothing to do with the little
black cat. Nothing at all.

I do not know how long I would have maintained this
tough attitude; but the following day, Easter Sunday,
something happened which bewildered me. The condition
which I fancifully made when Monty was dying was
fulfilled. It happened in this way.

About eleven o'clock in the morning Jeannie was sitting
in the chair opposite the fire, reading to me her diary of
the year before in which she described her earnest efforts
to help Monty in his illness. It was a wild day, and
perhaps this influenced her to become somewhat upset.
I felt distressed for her because she had always secretly
believed that she might have been able to have done more

than she actually did. This was untrue of course. Nothing could have saved him.

A tremendous storm was blowing and as I often do when this happens, I switched on the trawler waveband to hear what the ships thought of the weather. The unknown voices came over the air from ships I would never know, and yet so frank, so intimate were these voices that I felt I could have taken part in their conversations. Suddenly I heard a cry at the door.

'Did you hear that, Jeannie?'

One can imagine cries in a storm, or cars arriving, or planes overhead. When the gales blow I am always saying that I hear someone shouting, or Jeannie believes someone has roared down the lane in his car, or I am imagining an airliner in trouble. This is what happens when you live in isolation and there are no standardised sounds of civilisation to measure against unreality.

'I thought it was a miaow,' said Jeannie.

And it was.

I opened the door and there was the little black cat huddled outside in the rain. It did not wait for me to invite it in. It rushed past my feet into the room, and sat itself down at the foot of the bookshelf which hides the sink; and waited there, as Monty had always done, yellow eyes looking up at Jeannie for the saucer she was only too ready to give it.

What was I to do? It had acted according to plan. It had fulfilled the conditions. I had put up a resistance, as indeed I had done when Monty was produced to me at the Savoy as a kitten, but the situation was beyond my control. How could I deny a home to a cat which had come to Minack in such a remarkable way?

It was a female. The vet who dealt with her said she was about three months old. He took her away, performed the necessary operation, and when we collected her she purred all the way home. A dainty little cat, totally black except for a wisp of heart-shaped white on her chest, and with a pretty little head fit for a chocolate box. We never knew where she came from. We made exhaustive enquiries within a radius of ten miles in case she had indeed been loved by someone, and then lost; but not a soul knew anything about her.

We were warned that she would not stay with us. A cat born out in the wild, and this must have been the explanation, always returns to the wild. A wild cat, in fact, always a wild cat. That is what we were told.

But she is still with us today, three years later, and she is over there now curled in the corner of the sofa, plump and as glossy as a ripe blackberry. I cannot believe she is the same little black cat which hurled itself against the wire netting of the chicken run.

And her name? She is called Lama, after the Dalai Lama who was at the time escaping from Tibet.

Geoffrey, meanwhile, had accepted the sparring which preceded her arrival with solid calm. He had tolerated the interest shown in the cat, but his mind was on his work. He lived in his own world. And I do not think he really approved that girls were working alongside him. He had spent his life making use of his brawn; always on the cliffs, always turning ground or shovelling potatoes in or shovelling them out, or digging up bulbs or planting them again. His was a world of muscle and long established traditions. It was a fading world and he had, as it happens, the intelligence to know it. The shovel was a dying instrument and the shovel man was going the way of the horse. The reign of the cliffs was over. Science was replacing brawn. All of us who depended on the little meadows that stared out at the sun and the sea, that for generations had rewarded those who toiled in them, were trying to adjust themselves. Jeannie and I were intellectually aware of this. Geoffrey sensed it. That was the only difference between us.

He was away for seven weeks that spring, first in hospital and then convalescence; and I was on my own again as far as the heavy work was concerned. It was the time of tomato planting, of soil preparation and seeding, and then of potato lifting. Most of my waking hours were spent driving the big tractor, ploughing and cultivating the ground, or using the lurching rotovator or, when May came, stabbing my shovel under the potato plants with the girls and Jeannie picking up behind me.

We only had a half-ton of seed that year; and it was the last year we ever grew potatoes. We had planted them in the meadows of Minack cliff which we had cut ourselves when we first came, a patchwork of meadows of deep soil and high hedges, secret meadows so small that you might wonder why they were there. Each one tilting towards the sea, each one so designed to receive the greatest possible protection from the anger of the wind, from the clammy poison of the spray. That was the idea and the hope.

I remember the first of those meadows. We still lived in London but Minack had become tentatively ours in the sense that our friend Harry Laity allowed us to be his tenants. We travelled down whenever we could for a few days; and on one of the earliest visits Jeannie and I became childishly excited because we found a pocket of ground which obviously, long ago, had been a cultivated meadow.

It was right at the bottom of the cliff, edging the last drop to the sea; so when we stood in the shadow of its once-cared-for cultivation, we could look down on the waves when the tide was high, or on rocks and shallow pools when it was low. One side there was an ancient stone wall, on another a high elderberry hedge; and in the centre was the meadow itself, chest high in undergrowth yet seemingly shouting at us to recognise it. Ghosts were there. Old men with sickles, blazing sunshine, parched soil, gulls' cries, tempests raging, forgotten harvests, a wren's song, badgers playing, the scent of primroses on soft spring mornings. We saw this hint of a meadow, and for a glorious two days Jeannie and I with the insane urge of enthusiasm ripped the undergrowth away, broke up the roots, and before we hurried back to civilisation, stared at the sweet earth, thankful for its reality.

Jane loved the potato season, though heaven knows why. Doubtless it was because she was unencumbered by the financial considerations by which Jeannie and I were always judging its progress. We were always worrying whether this meadow or that had had a good yield; or raging because the morning's post had brought news of a bad drop in prices. My aches brought on by the digging became worse on such occasions, and the half-hundred-weight bags when I carried them up to the top of the cliff felt as if they weighed half a ton.

Jane said she liked the sensation of the soil running through her fingers as she searched for the potatoes. She would be on her knees, barefooted as usual, scratching away at the ground like a badger, then call out that she didn't think much of my digging. It was an old joke of the potato season.

'You'd better catch some fish, Mr Tangye. We've got plenty of chips!'

And by this she meant I had been careless, that I hadn't dug deep enough under the plant, and the shovel had cut the potatoes in half. Then, a few minutes later, I would get my own back. I would thrust my shovel into the soil a few yards behind her, and find a potato or two which she had failed to find and pick up.

'Has the picker-up gone home?' I would ask.

An endearing feature of both Jane and Shelagh was the loyalty they had for the crop. Thus, even when we had a poor day's digging, they would report in the evening that we had had an exceptionally good one. There was, of course, fun in doing this. At potato time the parish used to seethe with rumours about the quantities, quality and price of the crop on the various stretches of the cliff. Jane and Shelagh liked to stimulate the belief that Minack cliff was doing particularly well. Jane, for instance, had a malicious pleasure in teasing her mother's boss.

This farmer had grown early potatoes for years on the cliff not far away, and he prided himself on always being the first to send them to market. He was a taciturn chap who took life very seriously; and it was easy for Jane to spread in his mind alarm and despondency. Thus she would naughtily tell him at a stage when he had not sent away anything, that I had sent away a twelve pound chip basket; when, in fact, Jeannie and I had only eaten our first plateful of new potatoes. And then, as soon as the season got under way and he regularly asked her how we were doing, she used to double, even treble, the amount of the day's digging. She would also add salt to the wound by exaggerating the price.

'We dug twenty-two bags yesterday,' she would tell him cheerfully.

'You did?'

'Yes, and we're getting a shilling a pound.'

'You are?'

The farmer would lugubriously look at her, fumbling in his pocket for a packet of cigarettes. Then he would turn away, ruefully wondering whether she was speaking the truth; and next morning she would tell me gleefully what had happened.

Shelagh was too shy ever to be so bold; and in any case as she was a new hand at picking up potatoes on the cliff she was not conversant with our brand of potato wit. She would hurry on with her work, never pausing, and if she talked it would be about her previous evening's bicycle ride, or Russ Conway; she was mad about Russ Conway.

Her bicycle rides were phenomenal journeys in view of the fact she had already done a day's work; and at week-ends she would go on marathon trips with her girl friend Pat, who worked in Penzance. Twenty miles in an evening, forty miles on a Sunday. And on Saturday afternoons she always had a long session at the cinema, two complete shows for the price of one ticket was her aim, and it did not matter how fine was the weather. This, in fact, became a joke.

'Well, Shelagh,' one of us would say on a Saturday morning when the sun was burning us all, 'a really wonderful day for the pictures!'

'Yes,' she would reply, grinning, and delighted we had made a joke of it, 'a really hot day to spend in the dark.'

All through the time we were digging the potatoes it was blazing hot. Jane's hair got fairer and fairer and her skin browner and browner. When a meadow was too small for the three of them to be behind me picking up, Shelagh and Jeannie would stay with me while Jane went off on her own to another meadow. She took the spare shovel which was as tall as herself, and then would vigorously plunge it under the plants. She would get very hot and dirty, smudges of soil all over her face, and then at lunch-time she would suggest to Shelagh that they go down to the rocks to bathe. But Shelagh, who incidentally was always as spruce at the end of the day as she was at the beginning, would be shy at the prospect.

'Isn't it funny,' said Jane to Jeannie the first time, 'Shelagh was quite shocked when I took off my clothes to bathe.' Jane, I do not suppose, had ever owned a bathing suit in her life.

The wonder of these two, each in a different way, was that they were untamed; and they belonged to the cliffs as the badgers and foxes and the birds belonged. They had no edges carved by sophistication, they had no brittle rainbow ideas to lead them away from their happiness. Their eyes and minds were alert for pleasures which, one might say, did not belong to their time.

I remember the delight with which they heard my story, during that May, of how I saw a fox running along the rocks within a few feet of a lazy, lapping sea. I had gone down the cliff to bring up a few potato bags which we had left there the evening before, when I saw a fox stalking a gull at a spot a hundred yards away where the grey rocks met the green landscape. I had shouted soon enough to warn the gull, and it flew off, but the fox without hesitation dashed towards the sea and then, as I watched from above, skipped like a ballet dancer from rock to rock until it disappeared from my view behind a turn of the cliff.

There were also that May two litters of fox cubs all of us were able to watch grow up. One litter had an earth at the top of the cliff in a bank that sloped from the big field to the meadow where our Soleil d'or bloomed in the early spring. There were three cubs and they used the sol meadow as their playground, flattening the dying leaves in their gambols. They were not easy to watch. A hedge hid them from the field side, and a stone wall from another. The only convenient point was to peer through the elderberry trees that divided the sol meadow from the one in which we grew Rembrandt daffodils. From here we used to watch their antics; and it was here that Shelagh used to come in her lunch hour, then tell us of the laughter they had given her.

The other litter salted our pleasure with constant concern. They were not on our land and so they were not safe from a gun like the others down the cliff. The earth was in the corner of a field across the shallow valley from the cottage, so placed that we could lie in bed and see it through the open window. There were five cubs and their parents had been obstinately foolish to dig the earth where they did. For they had been warned in previous years that their presence was not required. They would open up the earth and then, a few weeks later, the farmer would stop it. He quite rightly could not allow a valuable field to be used as a playground.

But this year the farmer had done nothing; and there were the cubs every day chasing each other all over the field while the proud parents sat side by side and watched. They could, of course, see us plainly and hear our voices, but they seemed to think there was some kind of magic to protect them from danger. I could shout at them and all they would do was to prick their ears and stare in my direction. Fear did not exist; and the parents who in normal times lived with fear daily, were so dazed by the happiness of possessing such cubs that they forgot to teach them the wisdom of fear. We had it instead, on their behalf.

The farmer kept a large number of chickens and he naturally had to keep guard over them. He had already taken steps to control the badgers, and one of our worries was that he might take the same kind of steps with our foxes. He had engaged the pest control officer to block up the holes of a large badger sett, and the badgers had thereupon been gassed. Such a method is perhaps merciful, though most countrymen will tell you that only rogue badgers kill chickens.

We now were concerned that the reason why this year the farmer had failed to stop up the earth was because he had decided to wipe out the litter. If he stopped the earth he knew about, they would only go to another he might not know about. So perhaps his idea was to let them be for a while, and then either gas them or shoot them one by one.

Thus every day we expected the wonderous sight of the cubs at play to end; and I was scared what Jeannie might do if she saw the slaughter taking place. She was certain to see it if it did. The cubs, as we watched them from the cottage, had become like pets. We had names for each, and each so clearly had a character of its own; as happens whenever you watch animals for long.

We began to fear every early morning and every early evening, for then it was that the shots would most likely ring out. And so we found ourselves looking at the gambolling cubs, while watching the undergrowth cover which surrounded the field . . . in case we saw a man with a gun.

Our anxiety became absurdly out of hand. We began to worry so much for the cubs that we forgot to enjoy the pleasure of watching them. And yet was our anxiety so absurd? Farmers are unpredictable because they act for the most part according to mood; and adjoining moods can be gentleness and violence. Farmers, in distant parts, can possess the sly instincts of a cornered animal; and thus their actions cannot be trusted. One moment they murmur good wishes, the next howl in distress, or perhaps what is more unsettling, they will nurse a grievance without giving you a clue what the grievance is about.

It was Jane who decided what we ought to do. It was unwise, we all agreed, to ask the farmer what his intentions might possibly be; for it would draw attention to what was happening, and there was still a chance, since the field was distant from his farm, that he did not know. So Jane decreed that we should subject the cubs, and their parents for that matter, to our particular brand of danger. If we took the right measures they would all shake off their halcyon confidence, and yet be saved.

And that is what happened. We imposed fear on them. When they came out of the earth to play we banged dustbin lids together; and when they got used to this noise one of us used to run up to the gate of the field and clap our hands together. Slowly, by these methods, the cubs became aware of fear; and their parents remembered it.

It was during this period that I realised that Hubert, the gull on the roof, was ending his reign as king of the roof. He could no longer squawk for all other gulls to fly away. He, instead, would fly away himself at the screaming demand of an insolent stranger. I was perturbed.

And then one afternoon, an afternoon when we had a particularly good crop of potatoes, Jeannie came calling for me in anguish.

'Hubert's been shot . . . been shot.'

9

I found Hubert on the cedar-wood top of the coal shed where Jeannie always fed him. He was standing on one leg. The other was hanging limply, and blood covered the webbing of the foot. Every few seconds he staggered, hopping an inch or two, his wings unfurling and flapping, trying to keep his balance. He still looked as regal as ever and he was glaring at us; as if he were in the mood of one who was cursing himself for the mess he was in, like an old man who had at last lost his independence.

'What have you done, old chap?' I asked. 'What's happened?'

'He's been shot, I tell you,' Jeannie answered for him angrily. 'I was standing here when he came down and I saw quite clearly a bullet hole through the webbing of his foot.'

He had always been more Jeannie's bird than mine. He tolerated me, he squawked at me when he saw me and when he was hungry, he had even come for walks with me gliding up and down above and around me with the grace of a swallow, but he never awarded me the honour of feeding him by hand. He shied away when I proffered him a morsel. He was nervous of me.

But he was at ease with Jeannie. She used at first to feed him on the roof of the cottage and she soon learned that he required bacon rinds or her own home-made bread. So she would throw whatever it was up on the roof and if it fell short of him, he would slide down to it, using his feathered posterior as a toboggan. This was a comical sight.

Then, as his confidence grew, he decided that the coal shed with a top like a table and situated a few feet from the door, would be more convenient. It was here that Jeannie fed him by hand. She would come out of the cottage calling him, and he would swoop from the roof or the top of the great stone chimney where he had been ruminating, and seize what she was offering him. And when he had gobbled it, he would strut the small space, imperious, impelling his personality upon her so that she weakened, saying: 'Hubert, you've had enough . . . but here's one more small piece.'

Sometimes he was in such a hurry to come to her that, if the wind was blowing, he made an error of judgement in his landing. He hated it when he made such a fool of himself and, after recovering he would sail into the sky like a flying god, majestic wings outstretched, with a symmetry of body that made our hearts beat in excitement. Here was the wild that linked the centuries, noble, remote, free and yet gloriously tempting us to believe we shared something with him. Here was a thing wiser than man, luckier perhaps because he was not fooled by greed. It was content with the splendour of living. It embraced the sky and the sea and the rocks, struggled with the storms and gloried in hot summer days; it was a speck against blue and a crying, swerving, rebellious being that pointed black clouds, shining them by its white, uttering far distant calls, telling us who were ready to listen that the gale was coming again; the same gale, the same gull, the same human beings since the beginning of time.

Yet Hubert also provided the moments of absurdity. There was one occasion when Jane was with us and Hubert got blown by a gust of wind so that he was poised for a second just above Jeannie's head. It was a ludicrous sight. I was beside Jane and I knew why she burst into laughter. Jeannie, for that second, looked like a lady who had searched hard for an original hat; Jeannie who never wore hats.

'You must go to a fete with Hubert as your hat, Mrs Tangye,' laughed Jane, 'you would be a sensation!'

There may have been another reason why he chose the coal shed as his dining-room table beside his growing confidence; and that reason was Gregory, the one-legged gull. I always presumed that Gregory had lost his leg in a trap. In the terrible days of the gins, gulls – when storms blew and they settled for the night inland instead of on the rocks – would guilelessly choose a field which was ringed with traps; and the inevitable would happen. I do not see how else he could have lost his leg.

We called him Gregory after Gregory Peck, who at the time was making the film of Moby Dick and playing the one-legged captain. We had no particular reason to do so, it was just that the name seemed to fit. And so whenever one of us saw him sail down on to the apex of the roof we would call out that Gregory was here; and quickly tend to his wants.

We had to be quick because Hubert did not like him, nor did our other occasional gull visitors. The hate was so strong and Gregory's fear so great, that we used to see him in the field across the valley, a speck against the green, watching, waiting until the roof was clear and he could safely visit us.

He would arrive usually at twilight, and when we had appeared and seen him, he would flutter down to the coal shed and hop about like a man with one leg but no

crutches. But only for a minute. Then, having gained his
sense of balance, he would wait there motionless except
for his head which would follow us as we came out of the
door with the delicacy we had chosen for him.

'Here you are, Gregory,' and we would toss him a piece
of meat.

Then, having got it in front of him, he would look up
into the sky. He was always on guard. He was always
expecting attack. He was always frightened that the hindrance of one leg which made it so slow for him to take
off, would result one day in his being caught unawares.

And it did. I do not know when or where it happened
but there came a day when he did not appear, then
another; then a week, then a month. We never saw
Gregory again.

There had been occasions, however, when Hubert had
caught him on the roof or on the top of the coal shed
having a meal. Hubert was enraged. He had no doubt been
somnolently basking on a rock when the idea occurred to
him that a snack at Minack would be pleasant; and he
would sweep in from the sea and find Gregory already
enjoying one.

Hubert would scream his fury, diving at Gregory who
would desperately try to escape; and always did. But
Hubert on these occasions behaved like a bully and
we obviously gave him no sympathy. He was jealous.
Minack was his kingdom. And we had the effrontery to
feed someone else. And in a different place. It was from
the moment when he first caught us in the act of feeding
Gregory on top of the coal shed that he decided to use it
himself.

Poor Hubert. For months we had observed how he
had been ageing, how he himself was often attacked and
then chased over moorland towards the sea by one of the
harsh young gulls who wanted to usurp his place on the
roof. The old tale of the wild destroying the old. The
inevitable conquest of youth. And there was nothing we

could do except watch and be sad. Hubert was receiving the treatment he used to give to others. And now, like his old enemy Gregory, he was standing on one leg on top of the coal shed. Who had shot him?

I could see the hole quite clearly, an airgun pellet I guessed. It was a neat opening and it appeared that the pellet had gone right through the foot. There was blood, but no swelling as far as I could see; and Jeannie pointed out hopefully that when she first saw him he had, in the effort to keep his balance, momentarily put the foot down. The bones of his leg, therefore, were certainly not damaged. We were staring at him anxiously when he suddenly decided that he had had enough of our attention. He gave us one more glare, then heaved himself into the air and flew off, seemingly as independent as ever. We watched his flight, and it was so powerful that we found ourselves thinking we might be worrying unnecessarily. We ought to be thankful that he had escaped with his life. A miracle, in fact, that he had done so; but we felt enraged at the thought of the person who had aimed his rifle at him as he peacefully stood on a rock by the sea.

The next morning Jeannie and I were up early waiting to tell Shelagh and Jane. Something so pleasant about these two was the prospect of seeing them every day. They were usually sleepy for the first hour or so, silently pursuing their duties in a daze, but by ten o'clock they woke up. They began to talk. And if there were subjects of mutual interest to discuss, I used to wait until that hour to discuss them.

On this particular morning, however, our news shocked them into immediate wakefulness. They loved old Hubert, and they would always be telling me something they had seen him do; chasing another gull or himself being chased, or telling me as if I hadn't known it already that Hubert was squawking his head off, and asking if one of them should go and feed him. Hubert was as much part of their lives as he was of ours.

They too were of course enraged; but Jane had also some important information to impart. Jeremy, her young brother, apparently had an indignant row with some boys who had been walking along the cliffs the previous day. And the reason for the row was because they carried airguns and were taking pot shots at any gull they could see on the cliffs. It seemed to be plain that Hubert had been one of their victims.

Why is it that airguns and .22 rifles can be used without licences by anyone of any age? Why are parents so callous as to allow their children to have them? It is a streak of stupidity and brutality that I will never understand. No doubt it is due to lack of imagination; and as a result birds and animals are killed in the name of pleasure, a pleasure which masquerades as sport.

We next saw Hubert at lunch-time. He flew around above the cottage for a few minutes as if he were wondering how best to make his landing; and as he did so I called the girls so that they too could see his wound and make their comments. He hovered for a moment or so above the roof, then came down gently, and made a perfect landing on the coal shed. As he did so he put out his foot as if he had forgotten it was hurt, then immediately retracted it; so there he was glaring at us on one leg.

He was otherwise unperturbed that the four of us were close to him; and in any case he was far more interested in the juicy pieces of chopped roast beef that Jeannie had kept for him. He began to gobble so quickly that he had to pause and stick up his head, so that we watched the meat bulging down his neck and throat. He certainly had not lost his appetite.

'What do you think?' I said. 'What shall we do?'

I was appealing to their instinct which I felt would be surer than mine. My intellect, in times of distress, becomes mixed up with my emotions creating a confusion in my mind which flusters my ability to make decisions. Jeannie knew this, and the girls guessed it, so my request for their opinions was not really necessary. They had already, without intent to offend me, decided to ignore my views; not, as it happened, that I had any to offer.

The questions to answer were these: how serious was Hubert's injury? Should we try to catch him and keep him somewhere until he was fully recovered? Should we catch him and take him to the Mousehole Bird Hospital? Should we take the chance of letting him live on among the rocks and seas he knew so well, feeding him with special delicacies in the meantime, trusting that he would best stage a recovery in these natural surroundings?

The speed with which Hubert had devoured his meat influenced the girls and Jeannie into believing the injury might not be so bad. There had been time for the reaction of shock. He could have been listless. If it had been really serious, he would not have wished for any food at all. Hence they decided to let him be for the while; and, needless to say, to keep a special watch out for him.

He came regularly for the next four days, and he seemed neither better nor worse. Jeannie had made a special visit both to the butchers and the fishmonger, and had also doubled our weekly order for bacon from the St Buryan grocer. Hubert, even if he lacked an appetite, was to be tempted to have one.

It was on the fifth day that he made a foolish mistake. In a moment of overconfidence, or perhaps it was touching evidence of the trust he had in us, he settled on the apex of the roof as if he were roosting. He was up there like a pigeon having a sleep on a branch. I had never seen him do it before, his habit had been to strut on the roof, up and down, up and down, like a sentry. But there he was, white chest puffed out, enjoying a rest in the sun; and I felt afraid that it would only be a matter of a few minutes before one of his rivals would see him.

Sure enough from the direction of the Carn which stands upright like a monolith above Mount's Bay, a half-mile away, I saw a speck speeding towards us in the sky. Nearer and nearer it came across the moorland with the inevitability of an express train. I guessed it was Knocker, Hubert's particular enemy; and so named by us because whenever it wanted attention it would bang its beak on the roof with the rat-tat-tat of a woodpecker. A few seconds and it was over the stables and poised for its dive of attack.

'Hubert!' I shouted, clapping my hands. 'Look out!'

The old bird looked round just at the instant that Knocker, screaming his war cry, swept past him within a few inches of his head. I picked up a stone and threw it at Knocker who was now high in the sky again, wheeling, a beautiful murderous savage, ready, ready to dive again.

I saw Hubert gathering himself together, like an old man trying to rise from his chair; but instead of standing he slipped, then slid down the roof to the gutter which halted him for a second before he overbalanced, and fell like a half opened parachute into the garden. Up above Knocker cried out his triumph.

Jeannie arrived at this moment. She had been somewhere in the wood and heard the noise, and guessed what was happening; and as she rushed past me Hubert staggered a few feet down the path, then managed to collect himself, heaving himself into the air, so that we were able to watch him together struggling to keep airborne, skimming the stable roof by a few feet, then over the may tree that borders Monty's Leap, towards the moorland and the sea. And all the while Knocker was sweeping round him, twisting and turning above and beneath him, escorting him like a triumphant fighter pilot beside a crippled bomber, taking him further and further from the safety we could have given him.

'I should have caught him when he fell,' I said angrily. I was cursing myself for failing to react instantly. I had gaped like an onlooker at an accident. Had my mind not been so ponderously dull, I could have held him in my arms within a few seconds of his falling; and we could have looked at his wound, and nursed him, or taken him to the Bird Hospital. It was a failure I would always remember.

'Next time he comes,' I said determinedly, as if words would compensate me for my feelings, 'we will catch him and . . .' I added, doubts about my ability to do so brimming again, 'you Jeannie or one of the girls had better try and do the catching.'

But Hubert never did come again. A gale blew up that night and raged across the sea from the south, surging the waves on the rocks where Hubert used to shelter, tearing with the sound of tube trains round the cottage, doom in the noise, so that Jeannie and I lay awake talking and wondering and afraid; and in the morning the gale still blew, and it was so fierce that even if Hubert had been well he would have stayed away from the cottage. He always used to stay away in a storm; and then, when we saw him again, swooping down from the sky to perch on the roof, we used to say a prayer of thanks. Rage had been expended, peace had returned. Normality had replaced cruelty.

Jane said it was lucky I had not caught him. She believed that as he had lived along this stretch of the cliffs all his life, it was better that he should die at some point along them. He would have died in any case cooped up in a cage.

'He died free,' she said. And there was wisdom as well as comfort in her words.

It was the middle of May and a sizzling summer lay ahead; and as the sun beat down parching the soil, denying germination of seeds, drying up the wells, killing transplanted plants, burning us all as brown as South Sea natives, I found no peace in what the holidaymakers called a wonderful summer. Once again we were laying the foundations of another flower season, yet we were being hindered from the beginning. There was threat in the sun and the blue skies. We could not have another year of failure and still hope to keep Geoffrey and the girls. We wanted rain as those in the desert want rain; and it never came.

The anemone corms which in normal times would peep green shoots within ten days, were as hard and dry as nuts six weeks after sowing; fifty thousand corms lying dormant which had to puff out sturdy plants by late September if they were to stand a chance of blooming through the winter. And ten thousand corms which I had failed to lure into growing by soaking them first in water, were dead. The root tendrils, deceived by my cleverness, had pushed out into the dusty soil and, finding no moisture to sustain them, had withered away into nothingness.

But it was the wallflowers which tested our patience the most. We succeeded in germinating them, in nursing them through the stage when weevils and flea beetles attack them in dry weather, in growing them to hand-high plants ready to bed out in their winter quarters; and then the trouble began. Poor Jane and Shelagh. I admired and pitied and was grateful for their endeavours, but I rebelled against helping them. I preferred more congenial tasks. I spent endless hours watering the freesias, for instance, dangling a hose from my hands vacuously watching the spout of water darkening one section of soil, then another. But I refused to help Jane and Shelagh, although Jeannie did occasionally when she could spare time from the tomatoes. The desperate slowness of their task, the vast number of inevitable casualties, the apparent threat that the wallflower crop had already failed before even it had begun to flower, depressed me into inaction. I did not want to see what was happening. I preferred to believe the problem did not exist. Let Jane and Shelagh get on with it. I could trust them to do their best.

And perhaps the wonder of their loyalty and their enthusiasm, was the way they struggled on day after day with this transplanting of twenty thousand seedlings. So many have a task and give up when the task challenges their tenacity. It is easy to be excited about a job which is new, or when the end gives quick reward. Here they were faced by a huge field of hot dry soil, so hot that even Jane complained on some days that her bare feet were walking on hot cinders; and into this hot field they had to bring alive again, after digging them from the seed beds, the early-flowering wallflower upon the success of which so much of the flower season depended.

Each had a pail in which they mixed soil and water until it was a muddy mess, and each seedling was dipped into it. They wrapped the mud around the roots so that there was a cocoon of moist mud. A monotonous job. Hour after hour, day after day; and in the evening Jane would report to me the number that had been planted.

'A record, Mr Tangye,' she would say, proud that they had indeed planted more than ever before, 'we've done twelve hundred today!'

Twelve hundred, it wasn't much. But they had first to dig up the seedlings from the seed bed and this, using a trowel, was a tedious business. The ground was hard like cement, and their hands blistered, and their wrists ached from the jab of the trowel as it scooped out the long tap roots. They were always so meticulous. They never made a show of doing a job. Slipshod did not belong to their vocabulary, and so if progress was slow it was never time wasted. They both aimed for success in everything they were ever asked to do, not for some flamboyant gain; just for the sheer personal pleasure they gained from doing their best.

They were lucky, I suppose, in that they both had a feel for flowers, and a love of the earth, and a communion with blazing suns and roaring winds; and they had minds which found excitement in small things, the sight of a bird they could not identify, or an insect, or a wild plant they had found in the wood. They were always on the edge of laughter, of pagan intuition, of generosity of spirit. They were not cursed by the sense of meanness, of jealousy of others, of defiance. They wanted to love. There was so much in life to be exultant about and I never knew either of them, even in fun, say a harsh thing about anyone.

And yet Shelagh, I feel, suspected the identity of her mother. Indeed she may have met her once, although as a stranger, when she delivered a note to a house in the village where visitors were staying. And there was another time when Shelagh, looking for somewhere to live was given the address of her mother, inadvertently by someone; and Shelagh wrote innocently asking if there was a room to spare. There was not.

These incidents, for all I know, may have happened while she was at Minack, and others as painful as well; and this would explain why there were days on which she appeared silently to sulk and be moody, days on which Jane, Jeannie and I would work hard to win from her that delicious grin.

'What's wrong, Shelagh? Cheer up!'

'I'm all right.'

Jeannie and I were not so foolish as to pry into these moods ourselves. We left it to Jane. And Jane was too subtle ever to bring the mood to bursting point by asking too many questions or by appearing self-consciously aware that something was wrong. If the first approach was turned down by Shelagh, she did not persist. They would work alongside each other in long silences, comfortable silences, and then I would look again and see them chatting to each other, and I would know that Shelagh's mood had passed.

'What was wrong?' I would ask Jane later.

'She didn't say.'

Both of them were secretive and why not? It is impertinence, I think, for those with experience to question the young. The young are a race apart with magical values and standards, with mysterious frustrations and victories, free from repeated defeats, fresh, maturing, bouncing into danger, propelled by opposites, frightened, confused by what is told them. And their lecturers, I believe, are those who, having failed in the conduct of their own lives, recoil to the hopes of their youth, reliving ambitions by pontificating, hurting the sensitive young and being laughed at by the others. Experience should be listened to by the young. It should never be inflicted on them.

Even in high summer Shelagh would be thinking of Christmas, and if one of us wanted to enliven a moment of the day, Shelagh would be asked:

'How many days to Christmas?'

'One hundred and twenty-seven.'

'Did you hear that, Jane?'

'Yes, and I bet she knows what presents she'll give already!'

Shelagh spent the year planning these presents but this coming Christmas was a special one for her. It was the first year that she had earned a wage above subsistence level, and she confided to Jeannie one August morning when she was busy dusting the house: 'I've always promised myself that I would give the most wonderful presents possible to all those I love at the first Christmas I had the money to do so.'

One of our presents from her that coming Christmas was a picture of Lama sitting on the white seat by the verbena tree. Lama, because she is all black, is a most difficult subject to photograph; she dissolves into all normal backgrounds. But Shelagh, noting this, waited one day until Jeannie and I had gone out and lured Lama to sit on this particular white seat and took the photograph with her box camera. The photograph was taken in August and she did not tell even Jane; and the secret was hers until we undid the coloured wrapping and found Lama, eyeing us, in a neat frame.

Lama loved her. Lama, because she had been born wild, did not know how to play and Shelagh set out to teach her. It was extraordinary how, in those first months, we could dangle anything in front of Lama, or tease her with a twig, or play the games associated with cats, and receive no response whatsoever. She just didn't understand what we were trying to do.

But every lunch hour, if Shelagh's pet mouse had not arrived before her, Lama would sit on her lap as Shelagh munched her sandwiches, taking any portion which was offered her and then, as if paying her bill, would tolerate the efforts of Shelagh to make her play; a piece of raffia tickling her nose or a pencil pushed between her paws. In time, with our help as well, Lama woke up to the pleasure that cats are able to give human beings.

Shelagh was phlegmatic towards animals and birds, and yet touchingly loving. If, for instance, I expressed concern at the prospect of Lama coming face to face with her pet mouse, Shelagh would appear quite unperturbed.

'My mouse would hide in my shirt.' And she said it as if it was the most ordinary thing in the world that a mouse should hide in a girl's shirt.

And yet I sometimes saw a ghoulish side to her, a macabre sense of humour which relished an unsavoury situation. I remember once coming into the flower-house and finding the mouse on her shoulder while Lama had entered the door ahead of me.

'Look out, Shelagh,' I said.

She gave me a wide grin, showing no anxiety whatsoever.

'Just think,' she said lasciviously, 'if Lama *did* catch Patsy how wonderful her crunches would sound!'

She delighted in murder stories and the more gruesome the better. And so sometimes, when work progressed and we felt in the doldrums, one of us would sparkle a minute by telling Shelagh that we had read a particularly brutal death in the papers; and her eyes would light up in mock excitement.

'Tell me more!'

And then, if the facts themselves were not horrific

enough for her, we would invent some that were; and we would all end up sharing the same ghoulish laughter.

This apparent callousness was, of course, superficial, though I suspect it was also a form of armament. She was afraid of her own gentleness, and she needed to bolster herself sometimes by pretending she was tough. She had to prove to herself that she was independent. She was not a rebel in the sense that she had a chip on her shoulder; she was just tired of always being under an obligation to others, and she wanted to have her own personality and be free.

She had a wonderful way with sick birds, a fearless, uncomplicated tenderness towards them. There was one morning when she arrived half an hour late and instead of bicycling she had walked.

'Had a puncture, Shelagh?' I called, as I saw her coming up the lane. Then I noticed she was holding something under her coat, and when she came up to me she showed me a wood pigeon. She had found it lying on the side of the road a few minutes after she had started out for work; and she had gathered it up and, because it would be difficult to carry if she bicycled, she had left the bicycle behind.

We took the pigeon straight away to the Bird Hospital at Mousehole. Its wing was broken after being shot, and a pellet had to be extracted. In due course, however, the wing began to heal and the pigeon regained its strength; and there came a day when Shelagh received a note from the hospital that the pigeon had been set free. She was brimming over with happiness, and from then on whenever a pigeon passed overhead she used jokingly to call out:

'There's my pigeon!'

She once had the extraordinary experience of working in one of the greenhouses when a merlin hawk dived through a half-opened ventilator, landed at her feet, and knocked himself out. Heaven knows how he managed to do it or what he was after, but there was Shelagh peacefully weeding the tomatoes when she suddenly felt a rush of air, heard a plomp, and saw on the ground beside her an inert bundle of feathers.

It so happens that birds seldom fly straight into the panes of a greenhouse from the outside. They swerve away in time. Indeed I have only known the gloriously coloured bullfinches appear blind to glass; but they, thank heavens, are migrants in this part of the world. I do not often have to pick up their beautiful bodies.

The trouble starts when a bird goes into a greenhouse and does not know how to get out and in its panic hurtles itself against the glass until it is senseless. Oddly enough it is usually the yellowhammers which are the victims. Time and again I have found a dead or dazed yellow-hammer. A wren is far too nimble-minded ever to hurt itself and although wrens seem permanently to haunt the greenhouses both in winter and summer, I have never seen an injured one. Robins usually ignore our greenhouses and I never saw our Tim in one although he was happy in the cottage. Thrushes, too, do not venture inside. But the blackbirds have a glorious time when the tomatoes are red and ripe. They gorge on the fruit, earning our curses, but we are ready to give them a tomato in return for a song.

Shelagh treated the merlin in the same way she and Jane always treated the dazed yellowhammers. She filled the cup of her hand with water, and in it she dipped the merlin's beak, opening the beak with her fingers so that the water trickled down its throat.

It is an astonishingly quick way to stage a bird's recovery. There it is resting in your hand seemingly helpless . . . and you have the sweet pleasure of watching it slowly come to life. You are alone with it. It is quiet. You feel the tiny claws tickling, then touching then clutching your hand. And then suddenly when all kindness has matured, it is away . . . towards the wood, up into the blue sky, or down along the moorland valley. Here is triumph. Here is truth.

And because the merlin fell by Shelagh he did not have to wait to be helped. Had he chosen a moment to perform his miracle of escape when the greenhouse had been empty, hot, dry, unfriendly to anyone or anything which was injured, he would have died. But Shelagh was there to save it. And she could not keep the victory to herself. So when the merlin began to show life again, and Shelagh knew the danger of moving it was over, she brought it to us in the cottage.

'Look at this,' she said with her delicious grin, and the merlin clasping her hand with his claws. He was awake now. He knew he was alive. He would go soon.

But he stayed long enough for me to get one of the bird books so that I could read out its identification: 'Upperparts are slate blue, the nape and underparts warm, often rufous, buff, the latter with dark streaks.'

It is such a moment which quells worry, and in a wondrous flash transforms depression into exultation. There I saw before me not only the majesty of a bird returning to the wild but the stream, the clear, sparkling stream, the dawning stream of a girl's happiness. If only it could have remained for ever . . .

Both of them had the same stature, Jane, like Shelagh, had the mind which instinctively helped the helpless. Here were these two at Minack, sustaining Jeannie and me with the glory of enthusiasm. In this place we loved so much were these two who shared the pleasures we, so much older, felt ourselves. The young voices calling for their hopes amongst the gales and the rain and the heat. So far to go. So passionately willing to give the present.

Jane was always more sure of herself than Shelagh because she had been loved for herself, since she could remember. And yet, in her way, Jane was as vulnerable. She loved the weak; but when she demonstrated this love she liked to dispense an atmosphere of drama. It was fun to do so. And so it was in this mood she arrived at her work one summer's morning and disclosed an exciting piece of news.

'Mr Tangye,' she said breathlessly, 'a Muscovy drake spent the night in my bedroom. We want to find a home for him. Can he come to you?'

10

The Muscovy drake had arrived in a sack brought in the back of a car by a young farmer who aimed to make himself popular with the Wyllie family. He could not have created a worse impression. Jane, Jeremy and their mother would have starved rather than eat it.

It was magnificent. It was a large white bird, the size of a goose, with dark green feathers on its back, a powerful pink beak with a red bobble on it bridged by two holes like nostrils, huge yellow webbed feet, an angry red skin beneath the white feathers of its neck and head, piercing, intelligent eyes, and the ability to raise the crest of feathers on its head when annoyed, like the fur of a furious cat. It could also hiss like a steam engine.

Jane brought it across the fields from her cottage in her arms, unperturbed by its apparent ferocity, and she arrived at our door as if she were holding a Ming vase. I looked at it apprehensively.

'And what, Jane,' I asked, 'is the procedure for looking after a Muscovy drake?'

She was grinning at me. She knew I had felt a little irked by being forced to agree to accept it. I had not been in the mood to collect any further responsibilities. I had dallied when she offered it to us. I foresaw difficulties. What about foxes? What about it flying away and all the hours we would have to spend searching for it? I saw it becoming a tedious tie, not because I would dislike the bird; on the contrary, I knew I would grow too fond of it. And I felt at the time that I did not relish such a worry.

'Oh, it's quite simple,' said Jane, talking to me as if I were a backward small boy, 'it'll be quite all right in the chicken run with Hetty.' Hetty was our one remaining chicken. She lived in a large chicken-house by herself, and occupied the day pecking in the extensive wired-in run in the wood.

'Surely Hetty won't like being chased by a drake?'

'You're quite wrong,' said Jane with a sweet smile, 'the drake won't show any interest in Hetty at all.'

Here Jane, in due course, was herself proved to be wrong. The drake and Hetty developed a strong platonic attachment and when Hetty, due to old age, began to fade away, the attention of the drake was touching to watch. For the last two days of her life he never left her side. They remained together in the chicken-house refusing to come out. Nor could he be tempted to eat anything.

Jeannie, naturally enough, did not share my hesitant views. The prospect of helping another creature delighted her. She is one of those people who would fill the fields with old horses, the house with stray cats, and leave a legacy to provide grain for the birds on the bird table.

'We must have a pond for him,' she said within twenty-four hours of his arrival at Minack, and I observed that 'it' had already become 'him.' 'The postman,' she added, 'told me this morning he was certain to fly away to look for a pond if we do not do something about it.'

There happened to be a drought. Springs were so low that we had scarcely enough water for domestic use from one well, nor enough for our tomato or freesia seedlings from the other well. The idea of making a pond was an impossible one.

'It's up to you,' said Jeannie in that tone of voice which I knew would mean she would get her way in the end, 'if you want him to fly away . . .'

The idea of his flying away was a threat that hung over us for a long time. People seemed to have a malicious pleasure in telling us this would happen. Cut his wings they said, or you'll lose him for certain. But we did not want to cut his wings for fear of frightening him. We did not want to upset him. We wanted him to feel at home and to trust us. In the end he never did fly away, that is for any distance. He flew, a magnificent beating of his wings, but only round and about the cottage. The prospect of touring the district in search of him never materialised.

I suppose it was the pond which restrained him, although the pond in the end was only an old tin bath just large enough for him to splash in. And he owed it not to Jeannie or me or the girls, but to Julius. We were at our wits' end how to make his pond when Julius found the tin bath thrown away in the undergrowth near the cottage.

Julius was one of those sixteen-year-olds who seem to mature before their time. He was on holiday from his school in Switzerland and staying not far away. We had known him off and on since he was a child, and one day this particular summer he had suddenly appeared at the cottage. He was good-looking, erudite even for an adult, and effortless as far as Jeannie and I were concerned. He had a restless wish to be alone on the cliff, and he would come to us, have a meal and then go off down to the rocks by himself; and later I would find him there staring out to sea.

'What are you thinking about, Julius?'

And in reply I would have a penetrating commentary on world affairs, or a more personal outlook on life. One did not think of him as younger than oneself. One had with him a standard of conversation like playing tennis on the centre court at Wimbledon. The ideas bounced back at one another with speed.

As soon as he found the tin bath he dug a hole in the chicken-run, the exact size, so the rim of the bath was on a level with the surrounding soil; and then he carried water to it until it was filled. We waited expectantly for the drake's reaction and in due course he waddled towards it, dipped his beak into the water, and a minute later was sitting in it looking like a battleship in a small lagoon.

'Well done, Boris,' said Julius.

'Why Boris?' asked Jeannie.

'Well he must have a name and as he is a Muscovy he ought to have a name which sounds like a Russian.'

The Muscovy breed does in fact come from America but Boris sounded good. We all agreed upon that. It had a solid quality about it, tinged by the mysterious, which suited his personality. We had already seen enough of him to realise he was a determined bird who would develop set ways with strong likes and dislikes. He also obviously had intelligence. He would stare at us, not with the vacant expression of a chicken, but as if he were summing us up. It amused us.

'What are you wanting, Boris?'

'He likes being talked to,' Jane would answer for him.

After Hetty died we thought he might be lonely. We considered finding him a mate and some people said he would go off and find one himself unless we did something about it. But a mate would mean eggs and eggs would mean baby Muscovy ducklings and as there would never be any question of killing them we decided to risk him going on an amorous quest. He has never done so. He has remained a bachelor and never given a hint he would like it otherwise.

He lives alone in the big chicken-house, a house that was built for fifty hens. Every evening as dusk falls he waddles off to bed, a flat-footed walk with his whole feathered body wagging from side to side, a measured walk of habit, the same route every day, the soil packed hard by his webbed feet; we have given up trying to grow anything on his route to the chicken-house. And when he arrives he roosts on the perch like a chicken, and waits for one of us to lock the door.

'Have you put Boris to bed?'

'Not yet.'

'Well I'll do it.'

Most evenings there is this scrap of conversation at Minack; for we are on guard about Boris. He is a tempting target for a fox or a badger. We hurry home to put him to bed, plans revolve around him. We do not feel at peace wherever we are if we know the chicken-house door is still open.

And in the morning we act in reverse.

'Get up. It's time Boris was let out.'

I envy those who are able to treat pets casually as if they exist only to titillate man's boredom. I envy them their harshness. They can pursue their relationship with birds and animals on a metallic basis, a scientist's standard. Emotion in their eyes is a vulgar thing. The heart of a bird or an animal does not exist and so they can treat them like a new toy, gloriously loved on its arrival then simmering into being a nuisance, then back again at intervals to being loved again.

Love for an animal is no less than love for a human being. It is indeed more vulnerable. One can compose oneself by the assurance that a human being can evict disillusion by contact with his friends. But an animal yields trust with the abandon of a child and if it is betrayed, shoved here and there, treated as baggage or merchandise, bargained over like a slave of olden days, everyone except the cynic can understand the hurt in its eyes. But the cynic grouses that we who see this hurt are suffering from a surfeit of sentiment, the word which the cynic parades so often as if it were his fortress.

I prefer, therefore, to behave indulgently to those who depend on me and who, for that matter, respond to my attention without deceit. Hence Boris seemed to us from the beginning worthy of our minor sacrifices. He gave us pleasure and so we were glad to repay him.

He was puzzled by Lama. Lama had shed her wild disposition with remarkable speed, and she was now a homely cat, a cat who liked to sit on my knee wasting my time as Monty had done. She showed no wish to go out at night and instead chose to lie curled at the bottom of our bed, not taking up much space for she was a little cat. She had become very trusting, perhaps foolishly so. She appeared to be bewildered by the love that had suddenly come her way. She worried us, for instance, by her careless attitude towards the danger of cars. She always hurried to hide under any which were parked outside, and when we returned home in the Land Rover she would plant herself in the middle of the lane and refuse to budge. She was also insensitive to the threat of Boris's fierce beak.

I think it understandable that Boris should have been jealous. We may have fussed over Boris but Lama, in comparison, was pampered. Boris used to eye us picking her up and hugging her, and although Boris would come for walks with us he did not like to travel far from the cottage; then he would stop and crossly watch Lama continue at our heels, a cat which had more enterprise than a drake.

Thus, whenever the opportunity arose, he liked to show his displeasure. He used to make feint atacks on her if she came near him, outstretching his neck, waving his head like an angry snake, hissing, waddling menacingly towards her. And because Lama in her wonderment believed no one could dislike her she would remain still, watching him come nearer and nearer, and only sidle away at the moment when I was about to shout her a warning.

Boris was always particularly vexed when he was having

a meal outside the door of the cottage and Lama was wanting to come in or go out. We fed him on scraps and more especially Jeannie's home-made bread, though his favourite was the left-over dough with which she had made the bread; like the gulls he would have nothing to do with shop bread. He had, of course, the grass and undergrowth to sift for insects, the freedom, in fact, to go where he wanted, but anything he found on these searches was considered by him to be either an *hors d'oeuvre* or a savoury. He insisted on the square meal that we were able to provide for him and every so often during the day he would pad up the steep path to the cottage.

As we threw him the scraps he would wag his tail feathers in pleasure, and gasp a strange noise like an out-of-breath man. This display of contentment would continue unless he caught sight of Lama poking her black head round the door or coming up the path from behind him; and then he became alert and angry and instead of soft gasps there were hisses.

Lama, on these occasions, responded with caution; a sensible cat who appreciated the rage she had engendered. She was sorry about it and she looked at Boris as if she were telling him so. There was certainly never any sign that she wanted to meet anger with anger. She was meek and mild. She just stared at him, waiting for the moment to slip by when there was the minimum chance of a peck from his beak. Perhaps she considered herself a superior being, a being that could sleep on a bed, not perch in a hen-house. A different social level. A snob. Perhaps she thought it beneath her dignity to take any notice of such raw ill-manners. And yet I doubt that this was so. I am sure she was fond of Boris and enjoyed his companionship. Why otherwise, as I often saw, should she turn on her back in the way she invited us to play with her?

Jeannie and I felt towards Lama the same kind of affection we felt towards Shelagh. Both were waifs. Lama came into our lives from the unknown, a lost wild kitten of the Cornish cliffs while Shelagh, yearning for love, came from the barren land of no true parents. They had this forgotten quality in common and it helped no doubt to create the affection they showed each other. And I was glad, therefore, that Shelagh was there on the one occasion when Lama was in trouble.

Charlie the chaffinch had been with us so long that we knew his appearance with the same detail as one knows the Union Jack. And we had observed during the previous few months that he had developed a bump on his head just above his eye; and then after a little while we noticed the eye begin to close until in due course Charlie was making his monotonous call as a one-eyed chaffinch. We were of course very upset but there was nothing we could do. He was impossible to catch. He also continued to be as gay and thrusting as usual. He was the dominant figure of the bird table. He was the echo which followed us around. And yet we realised he was nearing his time. A healthy chaffinch, a young one, would not have a blind eye. And after all, had not Charlie been with us for eight years?

He used to annoy Monty as the wrens used to annoy him, chirping around his head from a bush as he lay somnolent underneath. He did the same with Lama. I can understand this annoyance, because if you are suddenly awakened from a deep sleep by a noise that flushes you into momentary bewilderment, you are usually for an instant bad tempered. You say something which you afterwards regret. I have never hit anyone, though I have cursed them.

Lama was sleeping under the stunted apple tree just opposite the cottage when Charlie chose to perch on a tiny branch just above her, and began yelling his monotonous call. I was fifty yards away at the time but Jeannie was lying on the grass near by, reading a magazine when, for an instant, she put it down, and saw to her horror that

Lama had leapt at the branch and swiped Charlie into the grass.

She cried out: 'Derek! Derek!'

I had a sick feeling of disaster, and I rushed to her, murmuring those phrases which are aimed to quell distress; 'All right, all right, I'm coming!'

Charlie had recovered from the blow of Lama's paw sufficiently to fly to a branch of a near-by elderberry. It was soothing to see he could fly.

'Now don't worry,' I said to Jeannie, trying to give myself confidence, 'Lama could not have hurt him. He flew perfectly well to that branch.'

I could see him half-hidden by the green leaves, chest puffed out, absolutely still, facing towards us and I could sense his astonishment that after all these years of haunting us, of bellowing his harsh tuneless cry into our ears, that we should have turned on him. I suddenly felt angry.

'What did I say?' I said, taking it out on Jeannie. 'What did I say would happen if we let Lama stay?'

Mine was an outburst which was foolish and unfair. It was nobody's fault, and yet I was ludicrously, selfishly lashing about for a scapegoat. How could I dare blame Jeannie? Or Lama for that matter? It had been one of the miracles of Lama's time at Minack that she, like Monty, showed not the slightest interest in birds. The initial suspense as to how she would behave had disappeared from our minds. I had seen her many times sitting in the garden, dozing or washing herself, while Charlie or Tim or the others bobbed around the flowers looking for grubs. She was a gentle little cat. Only mice stirred her hunting desires.

I was ashamed, a moment later, of my outburst but this was no time for apologies. We had to find out how badly Charlie was hurt. He was sitting there on the branch as if he were frightened to subject his wings to the test of flying away. I had never seen him remain still for so long.

'We'd better try to catch him,' I said.

I believe, in retrospect, that my real intention was to assure myself that he was all right. I was wanting to catch him not so much to help him as to prove to myself that help was not needed. I wanted to see him move. I wanted to create the belief that our fears were false. I wanted to advance on him and relish in the glory of his escape from me, seeing him beat his little wings as he always had done.

Yet I knew he would be frightened of me. He was not like Tim. He had never become domesticated. He had never dared come indoors or stand on my hand as Tim did. And yet, remote as he might have been in comparison, he belonged to Jeannie and me. We could call for him, and he would come. We could go a mile away from the cottage and suddenly find him beside us. He had attached himself to us as a mascot, always friendly, but always elusive.

One autumn he disappeared and after a month or two we gave up hope of ever seeing him again. It was natural to think he was dead and as the winter passed and there was still no sign of him we forgot about him. And then one morning in early spring Jeannie went into the wood to feed the chickens when suddenly she was startled by a familiar monotonous cheep just above her head. There was Charlie on a branch. Charlie in magnificent spring plumage. As boisterous as ever. And Jeannie was so excited that she rushed to tell me, forgetting to feed the chickens. He never went away again.

'You stay this side of the elderberry,' I said to Jeannie, 'and I'll go the other. Then we can converge on him together.'

My intention, if he stayed still, was to let Jeannie catch him. When she was a child she wanted to be a vet, and she had the compassion and gentle touch of those whose ambition is to relieve suffering. She had the courage too, to grasp firmly and not to dither at the instant when calm is the key to success. We advanced.

As soon as we moved I knew we had made a mistake. For he took fright, and tried to fly, but instead of flying this time he fluttered like a falling leaf in a breeze, over a stone wall and down on to the lane which led to Monty's Leap and the stream. It was a mistake in that we now knew he was badly hurt; we could no longer watch him and hope.

'I'll try again,' said Jeannie. And she went carefully forward calling him.

We now knew that it was vital to catch him if he were to be saved; and yet each time Jeannie came near to him he fluttered away from her again. He would rise a couple of feet from the ground, then struggle a flight of a few yards and down again, spreadeagling his tiny body in a tussock of grass. He was treating us as his enemies. He had no trust in us. We who had received such joy from him over the years were being refused the chance to repay him. The long familiarity of his perky presence, the countless times we had, in mock anger, told him to shut up, the delight of his sudden appearance on a walk, all these memories were dissolving into the climax of his life, a climax in which he was doing all he could to evade our help.

He was now three-quarters of the way down the lane; and the stream, and Monty's Leap, were only a few yards from him. We suddenly thought there might be method in his fear of us, and that he was seeking water for the same reason we gave water to dazed and injured birds of the greenhouses. We stood still. Three minutes went by. Five. Then Charlie fluttered again, and with an immense effort, half-flying, half-running, he dumped himself at the stream's edge on the side of the lane where it dashed on through undergrowth and moor to the waterfall which splashed to the sea.

'Look,' said Jeannie, 'he's drinking.'

He was dipping his little beak into the water, so alertly, with such an air of brisk sense that both of us had a wave of thankfulness. Impossible, it seemed to us at that moment, that a bird which was really ill would behave in such a manner.

'Somehow,' Jeannie said, 'we *must* pick him up. As he is he won't last the night – an owl will get him or a rat.'

It was afternoon. Indeed a Sunday afternoon. And we both found ourselves wishing it was an ordinary day. Then the girls would have been with us and we could have discussed the next moves, and we could all have shared the understanding; the understanding which is so absurd to some, the understanding which gives reason to the determination to save a bird's life.

'There are two people coming down the lane.'

I said this as I have often done with a note of apprehension. There is no right of way through Minack but we seldom mind people passing by. In an age when transistors and cars anchor the holiday makers in car parks and packed beaches, it is refreshing to see those who have the initiative to walk. Nine times out of ten the walkers are delightful, and how strange it is that they are so often foreign students and teachers. It puzzles me how it is that, looking at the brochures and preparing their holiday plans, they come to the decision of walking this lonely coast. It pleases me. It is only the map-makers who distress me; only the neat minded folk who look for trouble, badgering farmers who in the process of earning a living block up a gap to stop the cattle escaping; and then are ordered to open it again to allow rare crocodiles of organised walkers to scurry on their way. Even in this untamed land there are those who wish to spoil it. The busybodies. Those who will never be able to understand solitude. For it is the solitude, I have found, the total freedom from signposts and selfconscious man-made paths which attracts the visitors who pass Minack. In this crowded, over-organised world they have found peace in this stretch of Cornwall which has been spared the planners.

'Who are they?'

It was essential that we should not be interrupted in our vigil. If two brash walkers came by, ignorant and insensitive to our task, Charlie would become more frightened than even we had made him.

And then suddenly we saw it was Shelagh. Shelagh and Pat, her girl friend who lived in Newlyn. No purpose in their visit. Just the inclination for a Sunday afternoon walk along Minack cliffs. A lucky coincidence that led them to us at the exact moment we needed Shelagh most. Jeannie and I were so pleased to see her that she was startled by the reception we gave her.

'Why do you think I can help?'

Yet she knew. We did not have to answer her. This was one of the occasions which she would look back upon, revelling in it, rejoicing in the proof that she was needed. She knew she could catch Charlie. There was this primitive uncomplicated kindliness about her which would permit her to go straight to him. There would be no doubts in her mind to make her hesitate. She would go forward, bend down, and pick him up. As easy as that. And that is what happened.

We put him in a small box of dried grass in a warm corner of the greenhouse. He was very weak and both his eyes were now closed. There was nothing we could do to help him and in a few hours he was dead. A silent bundle of feathers.

The next day Jeannie wrote a rhyme:

Dear Charlie, we teased you much about your voice
That sharp, shrill cry.
But how today we would rejoice
To hear you call against the sky.

And having buried him at the foot of the same tree on which he had greeted Jeannie that spring after he had been away, we went down to the cliff meadows. We wanted to be on our own for a little while. We went into a meadow which lies directly above the sea guarded by a low old stone wall. We sat on the grass, the sea before us blue as the Mediterranean and behind, hedging the opposite side, the blazing yellow of the gorse bushes. We had been there for a few minutes when suddenly we were startled by a familiar cry. A monotonous cry. And there, just above us, was a chaffinch perched on a gorse bush.

'This is unreal,' I said to Jeannie.

But it wasn't. It never left us for the half-hour we sat in the meadow, and when we returned to the cottage it came with us, chirping all the way like the yap of a small dog. From then on it took Charlie's place and although it did not possess his boisterous nature, was more timid and not nearly so thrusting on the bird table, we felt that the uncanny way it had replied to Jeannie's rhyme had earned him a worthy name. He became known to us therefore as Charlie-son.

Jane, at this time, was enjoying a passion for music and one day she proudly announced that she had become the owner of a house-sized Wurlitzer organ.

'Now, Jane,' I asked, 'what does that mean?'

One of her charms was that she skated between the serious and the comic; and so when she made this announcement I was a little on guard whether or not she was strictly speaking the truth. She was such a glorious enthusiast that she deserved to be given a leeway in her remarks; for I know myself if I am exulting over some idea I may have had, flushing its prospects with exaggeration, that I resent a listener quelling the sense of it by logic. It is wise to be foolish sometimes, to experiment, to court mistakes; for one cannot embroider personal achievement in any other way. One remains sterile if one always plays safe. It is essential to be mad on occasions.

'I ought to call it a harmonium,' she said, looking at me and smiling, 'but a Wurlitzer organ sounds better.'

Heaven knows what prompted her to buy it. She couldn't even play the piano, or any other musical instrument for that matter. I think perhaps the idea began with a romantic picture of her sitting in the cottage, the window open, answering the roar of the sea and the cries of the gulls with the volume of her music; and mingling all the sounds together in a hymn to her happiness. Whatever the reason it was not a practical one.

The harmonium had spent many years in a Wesleyan Chapel near Camborne until, worn out, it was bought by a dealer who repaired it, then sold it to Jane for nine pounds. It was a bargain price, and he topped it by offering to deliver it free. Poor chap, he did not know the problems ahead because after travelling the long lane to the cottage he found the door too small for the harmonium; and he had to take it to pieces, carry them into the cottage and put them together again.

'And now,' said the man, his task completed, wanting a musical reward for his pains, 'let me hear you play.'

Jane sat down, pounded the pedals with her feet, and crashed out some most unharmonious chords. She did this, apparently, with *élan*; indeed she behaved according to character. She could not play a note but she wasn't going to admit it. She possessed, in fact, courage.

We were given the account of this incident early the following morning when we were cutting lettuces. It was a solemn period of the day. The lettuces had to be delivered at Jacksons, our wholesalers in Penzance, by half-past eight in the morning; and as Jane lived nearest she used to come in early to help us cut and pack them. She was usually three-quarters asleep.

'Jane, you dormouse, wake up!'

There was a routine in which Jane could play her part automatically, in a daze. I used to go up and down the rows pinching the hearts of the lettuces and cutting those which were full. Jane would follow along after me picking up those I had cut and carrying them back on a tray to Jeannie who was on her knees, surrounded by lettuce crates, cleaning each lettuce of its dirty leaves, then packing them twenty-four to a crate.

The sight, in a small way, was impressive when ten crates were full and Geoffrey, who had arrived by this time, was loading them in the Land Rover. But were they worth the trouble? In an age when time and motion experts reduce the prospects of reward for most endeavours to decimal points of profit, I hesitate to believe that our lettuces rewarded us.

Look what had to happen before the housewife bought one. The ground had to be prepared, the fertilisers scattered, the seeds sown, the seedlings thinned out, watering going on all the time, hoeing, probably a battle against greenfly, and then the climax when they were ready for harvesting.

'I've a fine crop of lettuces,' I would say to Jacksons, 'how many would you like?'

Having pursued the struggle of growing them and having poured out the cost, a grower when asking this question is in the same mood as a *prima donna* before an opera peformance. He is tensed.

'How many?'

'Oh well,' comes the answer, 'the public are not buying lettuce. Say ten dozen.'

Jeannie and I have spent many hours of our lives standing in the forecourt of Jacksons store on the front at Penzance discussing lettuces with Fred the foreman or one of the Jackson brothers.

'Surely you can take more than ten dozen?'

'We can't sell what we've got, old man. Honest we can't.'

'I've run out of crates, Fred.'

'Hang on a moment, I'll get you some.'

'When shall I come in again?'

'Make it Friday, early as possible, old man.'

This is the tedious part of growing. The part I do not envisage when the seeds are sown; then all my hopes and concern and endeavour dwell on the struggle to produce the crop. I am blind to the time when I have to sell, when the results of all the hard work depend on the unpredictable whim of the public. My cocoon of pleasure that is wrapped around the achievement of growing a fine crop is now torn to shreds. I am back again in the metallic world from which I sought to escape. I must be a businessman, and bargain and argue and flatter; and I must be prepared to face the fact that what has been produced is not wanted.

And then, perhaps the day after I have returned to Jeannie in gloom, I get a message from Jacksons: 'Bring in as many lettuces as you can.' The public, overnight, have acquired a taste for lettuce. A miraculous force has gathered them together and marched them to the greengrocers. Nothing rational about it. Nothing that even the most experienced could foresee. Just a whim.

Sometimes on these summer mornings when the Jacksons order was a big one, Shelagh would come in early too. And there were occasions when Julius would also proudly arrive.

'A record walk this morning. Clipped a minute off my time.'

His was a wonderful walk. He was sleeping in a caravan in the woods of an estate a couple of miles away; and the route to Minack was across green fields that were raised like a plateau above the sea, then down into a valley where a stream rushed in haste, leaping the boulders, sheltered by a wood where foxes hid, bordered by lush vegetation in summer, and in winter welcoming snipe and woodcock giving them a home safe from the guns. Julius loved this walk. He crossed the valley, then up past Jane's cottage and over the stone hedges to Minack.

'Heavens, Julius, I didn't expect to see you today.'

'I thought I might be able to help.'

He would always quickly go and have a look at Boris because, I believe, he was proud that he had named him.

There was, for always, a link between the two. It may not have been very important, but then I sometimes wonder how to gauge the degrees of importance. I have remembered many things, which at the time outsiders would have considered insignificant.

Julius was one of those people who, youthful though they may be, instinctively wish to help others. It is not just the question of practical help. It is the art of conversation, or of silence; the intuition when to continue a line of thought, or when to stop. There are no lessons to be given about these things; the sense of embarrassment which for a second may be hinted, or the flicker in eyes which give a clue to secret hurt, or the flavour of a moment which insists on a change of subject, none of these occasions can be dealt with by rule of thumb. Instinct is the king.

Thus Jeannie and I would be there with these three who had the promise of the years before them, each helping us, each so full of secret thoughts and hopes, puzzled, contradictory, timid and brave, obstinate and imaginative. I understood why Jeannie said to me one day that she was grateful for the necessity of cutting lettuces; a humble task, perhaps, but there was more to gain than the price received.

The promise of the years . . . how strange it was, in view of what was to happen, that it should be Shelagh living now in the same caravan a year later, who told us that Julius had died in a motor accident.

11

A year later Geoffrey had left Minack and I had not replaced him.

The high hopes we had once possessed that our extra land and bold plans would materialise into productive success had not become fact. I sold the big tractor, decided to do the heavy work myself and to concentrate mainly on crops in the greenhouses.

Jeannie and I were sad about this apparently backward step. We would, of course, have preferred to have seen our production gathering momentum, but the weather had been consistently against us. In the old days growers used to rely on one good year in four, and that one year compensated them for the three bad ones. Such an attitude is out of the question today. High costs have defeated it.

We were prepared to face this step, however, because we were utterly content in our environment. We never had to wake up in the morning and say to each other that we wished to be somewhere else. We never had to daydream about the perfect home. We were in it.

In London we had known many people who displayed the outward pageantry of success; the power to demand homage from others, the money and its claim to buy pleasure, the headlines to flatter them, the gush of friends who were not friends, the illusion that to hurry was to go somewhere. We had seen all this, and known its emptiness. Thus, when we surveyed our disappointments we took courage from our belief that they were trivial compared with the gain.

During April there had been a crisis in Shelagh's life. Her mother by adoption had sold her house in St Buryan and had gone to live in Penzance. In Shelagh's opinion, at that time, Penzance was too far from her work and she set about looking for somewhere else to live. It was a bad time to look. Those who had rooms to let were close to their summer harvest, and they did not relish a permanent guest even if it were Shelagh. By luck, however, we heard that the caravan where Julius had stayed was empty; and the owners, instead of grasping holiday visitors, offered it to Shelagh at a special rent.

How bright was her smile that day she heard the news!

She was grown up. She was going to live on her own. She was trusted. And the very next day she brought Jeannie a present, a little cream jug. When she handed it to Jeannie she was blushing, a moment of great shyness, just a quiver of a smile, then a murmur: 'Thank you.'

There were many ways in which Shelagh showed her affection for Jeannie. When she lived in the house at St Buryan she tended the small garden and was very earnest in her efforts. She and Jeannie used to discuss gardens at great length as they worked together, and periodically Shelagh would bring results from her efforts. She brought mint and parsley roots, and one day when Jeannie had expressed a liking for London Pride, Shelagh brought her some the following morning. Another time Jeannie was complaining of the way the west wind roared through a gap into the tiny front garden, and Shelagh replied she knew just the answer. She dug up a veronica bush from her own garden and planted it herself in the offending space. There was another occasion which was specially endearing. She had read in a magazine article how to make a miniature garden. She took great trouble to give it the semblance of Minack and one morning arrived with it in a box, waited until lunch-time and then presented it to Jeannie. It was tragic. The journey from St Buryan had knocked it to pieces and instead of a miniature garden, it was a jumble of tiny debris.

Shelagh had been brought up to be particularly house-proud and there was endless chatter between her and Jeannie on household matters; whether this detergent was better than the other, whether a new furniture polish was as good as it claimed to be; and endless discussions as to the best way to get a shiny black top to the stove. There was also much talk about recipes. Shelagh was constantly producing new ones from magazines and Jeannie would try them out while Shelagh would taste the result. Once, several months before her birthday, she had shown Jeannie a particularly luscious cake recipe and Jeannie, thinking ahead, said to herself that she would do nothing about it until the birthday was due. She told Jane of her plan, baked the cake, and Jane's mother iced it expertly in two shades of blue. Then they gave it to her. For Shelagh it was a moment of sheer enchantment.

She had been trained to perform any house-decorating task with the efficiency of a professional. When Jeannie mentioned she thought it time the walls were painted and the ceiling papered, Shelagh quickly said she would do it. She had the gift too of being able to share Jeannie's enthusiasm and they discussed together the colour of the paint and the pattern of the paper as if she too were living in the cottage.

Thus her arrival in the caravan did not only provide the delicious sense of the first freedom from continuous contact with older people, but also the chance to put her house-proud instinct and training into practical effect.

The caravan, fifteen minutes on a bicycle from Minack, was a cream utility one. It had long ago lost its wheels and it was raised above the ground by big blocks at its corners. There was an airy space underneath. When I saw this I thought that a westerly gale could pick the caravan up and blow it away with Shelagh inside. I said so.

'Just think of the excitement,' grinned Shelagh. As usual she was enjoying the prospect of drama.

I decided, however, to do something about it, so I got two wire ropes and threw them over the caravan roof, then lashed them to stakes I drove into the ground. Even so, when the westerlies blew, the caravan rocked. It amused Shelagh.

'How did you get on last night?' I would ask, in view of a particularly vicious gale.

'Not bad. Might have been in a dinghy out at sea.'

The caravan did, however, have some special advantages. It had, for instance, a few yards away, a small outhouse in which there was running water, a wash-basin and separate lavatory. These were advantages which did not belong to many farm cottages.

Then there was the site. One might not expect many girls to be thrilled about a caravan which was a mile away from a tarmac road; it was more suitable, perhaps, for an eccentric romantic. For the caravan was poised on a small plateau of a field which fell steeply to a wood and a sparkling stream; and this wood and stream shared a companionship until they fell together into the sea. You could see the spot where this happened when you sat in the caravan, down below you perhaps four hundred yards, at the beginning of the sweep of the wild bay with the big boulders lining the shore. No sand. It had the tradition of being a beckoning bay which meant that without apparent reason it lured ships to their doom.

Such a notion delighted Shelagh. It appealed to her

Grand Guignol romancing. It added spice to her excitement of living alone in such a place; and she ghoulishly suggested that she would play her own part in attracting the doomed ships. She laughingly described how, when the storms were raging, she would dangle a lamp outside her caravan in the tradition of Cornish wreckers.

Within a week of her arrival the utility aura of the caravan had been turned into the cosy atmosphere of a home. Jeannie gave her the blue gingham curtains, and Shelagh made covers for the settee and chair to match. She chose a pink, flower patterned curtain to separate the little kitchen, where she had a Calor gas stove, from the bedroom. And on the dining-table, as one would expect of Shelagh, there would be a bowl of flowers standing on a gaily coloured mat. All the time she was there she kept fresh flowers in that bowl, and if there were none to take back from Minack, she collected wild flowers from the wood in the valley.

The caravan was wired off from the rest of the field so that it was enclosed, together with the outhouse, in a sizeable compound. She promptly cleared up the debris which was lying around and set about turning a section into a kitchen garden. Shelagh was always practical. Behind the shyness, she was a determined person; she now had to buy her own food so she was sensibly taking the opportunity to save money on vegetables.

But this good sense was soon to be countered by an impulsive act which seemed to me to be endearing though foolish. I believed that as she had taken on the responsibility of running her own home for the first time, she ought to settle down and appreciate the problems involved. My attitude, of course, was patronising. It had nothing to do with me how she led her life, and I was reacting, perhaps in the same way that a puzzled father is confused by the antics of a teenage daughter. He is near enough in mind to think he understands, but far enough in years to be ignorant.

On a Monday morning, a week after she had become a tenant, she announced to us that on the previous Saturday afternoon she had bought a mongrel puppy and two kittens from a pet shop.

She was so animated and joyous when she told us the news that I afterwards regretted that I was so cool. My intellect answered her. No emotion. A polite reaction, as if she had told me that she had bought geraniums to decorate her garden. And yet what she had done was what I admired, no sense in it, no logic, not waiting to listen to advice which would have deadened the excitement. She had seen a puppy and two kittens in a window, and she had money in her pocket to buy them and somewhere of her own to give them a home. What she had done possessed the irrational enthusiasm which I had always felt, whatever a person's age, was the beat of life. Here was an act for me to admire, and yet I was frigid.

Jeannie did not react to her in the same way. Jeannie saw quickly that Shelagh was gathering in her arms the lost ones who, like herself, had no permanent home. She could not bear to see their faces looking at her through the shop window. For the first time in her life she had the power to help, and she was not going to make the mistake of letting the moment slip by. Jeannie, because of the nature of her character, was emotionally involved. She agreed with Shelagh on the grounds that a puppy and two kittens had been rescued. Three more animals who had a home. My own coolness was due to my doubt as to what kind of a home Shelagh would give them.

I knew, of course, that Shelagh would give them her love, but how could she look after them when she was away from the caravan every day? Shelagh, even if she had felt emotionally empty, always had lived in a home where the details of her life had been cared for. She never had to bother about the tedious routine which makes the day go round. She did not have to make unwelcome decisions, or make up her mind whether or not to make a self-sacrifice.

She was ordered to do something, may have resented it, but she never had to make the mental effort to give the order. She was still a child, and until now she had enjoyed the child's privilege of rebellion without responsibility. Two cats and a dog would certainly test her sense of responsibility.

But I realise now that my doubts were caused by my own personal attitude towards animals. I had developed over the years from a person who treated an animal as a four-legged creature which was pleasant to have around, to a person who was foolish in his devotion. I had become spoilt by the fact that where I worked and where I lived were one and the same place, and so there was no daily break in my relationship with the animal. There were no morning goodbyes and evening reunions. I had become immersed in a continuous relationship. And so it was absurd that I should judge Shelagh or anyone else by the same standard. If an animal receives devotion that is enough, and periods of separation should be considered as a normal hazard in its life.

The kittens were black and white, and she called them Sooty and Spotty. The puppy was a sandy-haired mongrel with a fluffy face like a Yorkshire terrier. She called him Bingo.

The kittens, as one might expect from the self-reliance of their breed, soon settled down. At first, with the floor of the caravan covered by newspapers. Shelagh kept them indoors while she was away; but as they grew older, the knowledge that the caravan was their home and the source of their food being firmly implanted in their minds, she left a window open. They could come and go as they wished, but they always were there to sleep on her bed at night.

Sooty, in particular, was especially fond of her. When she went into Penzance she used to catch the bus at a place called Boskenna Cross, ten minutes' walk away from the caravan along a lane which was edged by tall trees for part of the way and which passed between farm buildings.

Jeannie and I were in the Land Rover one dark evening when the headlights lit up the figure of Shelagh standing by the bus stop and beside her, to our astonishment was Sooty. We drew up and asked her what he was doing there.

'Oh,' she said, undisguisedly pleased that we had discovered Sooty's affection, 'he often comes with me when I go into town.'

'Yes,' I answered, 'but what happens when you get in the bus and leave him on his own?'

Shelagh, in the bright yellow light, smiled triumphantly.

'He waits,' she said, 'until the nine twenty-five drops me back here.'

It was different with Bingo. A dog is not equipped to provide itself with solitary entertainment. A cat can amuse itself for many quiet hours stalking real or imaginary mice. Any rustle is a challenge. But a dog likes to share its enjoyments. It is extrovert. If a particular pleasure comes its way it wants to tell the whole world how happy it is. A cat is secretive. A dog is generous. A cat can look after itself. A dog is dependent.

The caravan, isolated as it was, still was within barking distance of other isolated homes. Bingo, as it happens, proved to be a remarkably silent dog; but there were times when the cliffs echoed with his noise. Poor Bingo, he was bored. He did not know of the pleasure of hunting imaginary mice.

Shelagh had arranged an elaborate paraphernalia for his happiness. It had been prompted, as most of Shelagh's ideas, by a magazine article. What do you do with a dog, she had read, if you have to be out all day yet possess a small patch where it could be free?

The answer was a long wire fixed at the dog's height between two points, and the dog was attached to this wire from its collar by a hook. Thus, when left on its own, it had the freedom to run up and down; and in

Bingo's case he could either stay in the outhouse where he had his basket, food and water, or have a good run outside in the compound.

It was not long, however, before I was saying to myself that we ought to let her bring Bingo to Minack. It was an awkward decision to make, because on our flower farm unless a dog is well controlled it can do a great deal of damage. We had already experienced a dog rushing through daffodil beds in bloom, and another who thought that young tomato plants in the greenhouse were ideal for rolling on.

And yet, of course, we had known some very well-mannered dogs. My cousin, for instance, who lived near St Just, had a beautiful show champion Alsatian named Tara who used to tour the flower farm with the care of a dowager inspecting her garden.

There was another doubt about Bingo. How would he behave towards Boris and Lama? Minack was an oasis where they could wander without danger. It would be unfair to them if they were frightened by a dog. We decided, however, to give Bingo a chance, and so one evening I told Shelagh she could bring him the following day.

She arrived on her bicycle with Bingo on a long lead running beside her. He was an ebullient little dog, and as soon as he saw Jeannie and me he made a dash sideways towards us, nearly pulling Shelagh off the bicycle. And when I saw him do this, a smile on his face as if he were telling me how happy he was to be allowed to stay at Minack, I found myself thinking how pleasant it would be if indeed Shelagh was able to bring him every day. There was the most appealing unity between the two. It is always, of course, to be seen when the years have let flourish a companionship between a man or woman and a dog or a cat; it is to be expected. But there was something special about the look Shelagh gave Bingo as she got off her bicycle. She was pleased with him because he had made a fuss of us; and she was silently telling him so.

Lama was asleep at that particular moment on the bed in the spare room so there was no prospect of trouble as far as she was concerned. The only one we had to worry about was Boris, and yet so endearingly happy was Bingo, rushing about and following Shelagh as she started her work, that I forgot about him. Boris was so independent, so lordly, that I felt sure he could look after himself. And anyhow I was watching Shelagh's face.

I wonder why it was that I was thinking she had a face that would never grow old? As I watched her I knew she was earnestly hoping Bingo would behave with absolute decorum. The picture of a mother who wanted, beyond price of desire for her child to shine. Every move was judged by the hope of acclamation. Every thought was wishing that Bingo would behave in such a way that he would be accepted.

It is so easy, later, to say that you saw a look in somebody's eye that did not belong to those who will live. Yet, that day Shelagh brought Bingo I sensed that look. There was a fleeting compassion that gave me a chill; for Shelagh yielded the impression that she was trying to put a cloak round Bingo. She wanted him to be loved by someone other than herself. She wanted desperately for us to say that he was a dog we loved, and would look after. All her hopes were dependent on how he behaved on this first day at Minack.

After breakfast I went up to the well to turn on the pump. The engine was in an obstinate mood. I had to take out the plug and clean it, then, as this did not help, adjust the carburettor. I once again vigorously turned the starting-handle and this time the engine fired. Water came spurting out of the thirty-foot pipe and into the tank, and I returned to the cottage with a sense of satisfaction that the water supply was now assured for twenty-four hours. And then, as I came down the path,

I heard the most frightful cacophony going on below the cottage.

I ran round the side past the tractor shelter and the greenhouse, and down in front of the flower-house. This was the route that Boris took to and fro from the chicken-house; and as I ran I already knew what had happened. Bingo had attacked Boris.

As I arrived Shelagh was taking Bingo, barking hysterically, away, and he looked to me to be so mad with frustration that Shelagh herself was in danger of being bitten. Jeannie meanwhile, had her hands on Boris who was lying, white wings spread out, on the ground. He was quite still.

'Did you see it happen, Jeannie?'

She had been grading and weighing tomatoes, when she heard the commotion and rushed out to find Bingo pinning Boris to the ground. It was Jeannie, in fact, who first pulled him away, and then Shelagh, realising what had happened, raced from her work to help. When she passed me, she was taking him to the flower-house I had just passed. She was crying.

'Is Boris badly hurt?' I asked Jeannie this question hopefully, because he looked dead to me. He was limp. He was lying with a lifeless abandon. I had seen the same look when, in my youth, I had shot ducks as they came innocently over the Norfolk Broads at dusk.

But as I asked this question Boris began to move, then to struggle free of Jeannie's gentle hands, and to start padding away from us. One wing trailed the ground beside him.

'Thank God,' I said, 'all he's got is a broken wing.'

Here again I was being over-pessimistic. There was no wing broken. Boris had only been behaving in the tradition of wild creatures in a moment of danger. He had been pretending; and as soon as he was a few yards from us, he started to waddle, wings tight to his body, as he had always done. The sudden change in his behaviour made us both laugh. And then I realised that Shelagh had not returned.

'I expect she's soothing Bingo,' Jeannie said.

I now did a stupid thing. I heard Bingo whimpering in the flower-house and I imagined that Shelagh was with him. She had, in fact, gone into the cottage to fetch a jug of warm water and bandages for Boris; but, believing she was with Bingo and wanting to tell her not to be upset, I opened the top half of the stable-type door of the flower-house.

In a second, Bingo whining like a hyena, was over the top of the lower half of the door, and racing towards Boris again. He was on Boris's back and savaging his neck before Jeannie, very bravely, took him by the scruff of the neck and threw him away; and at that moment Shelagh rushed up, as he was about to take another flying leap at Boris, and picked him up, hugging him to her.

What does one do in such circumstances? Here it was well before lunch-time and Bingo had already twice attacked Boris; and Lama might too have been a victim if she had not been out of the way in the cottage, and sleeping.

But there was Shelagh. Both Jeannie and I knew what was passing through her mind. Something which she wanted beyond ordinary understanding had failed totally to materialise. She had willed so hard for it to succeed. It was a corner-stone of the new life she was building on her own that those she loved, loved each other. And here, so soon, she was faced with failure. She realised we could not possibly live a life at Minack in which, at any moment, Bingo was poised for the attack. She could not possibly bring him again. And yet, Jeannie and I thought, perhaps if we gave him another chance, for instance, of becoming acclimatised to other beings, he would accept them.

So we compromised by suggesting that she should bring him every day for a week, keeping him on a lead. She could tie him up to a post near by when she was working in the fields, and if she were indoors or in one of the greenhouses she could leave him in the hut we called the potato-house. It would mean he could get used to us all, and have the comfort of knowing his mistress was with him.

It was no use. Bingo was only quiet when Shelagh was actually beside him. If he saw her from the post to which he was tied or knew she was near when he was shut in the potato-house, the wail of a banshee echoed round Minack.

We had to tell her that she could not bring him.

It was fortunate that shortly afterwards A.P. Herbert came to stay with us. It was particularly fortunate as far as Shelagh was concerned because A.P.H. was co-operating with Russ Conway, who was writing the music, on a version of *A Christmas Carol*. The looks, character, and personality of Russ Conway provided Shelagh with an ideal. He could do no wrong. He provided her with all the sweetness of first love without the heartbreaks of reality. A photograph, scissored from a magazine, was in her caravan. The only picture of a star she had. And now here was someone actually staying with us who was in regular contact with him.

We did not tell Shelagh what we planned. And when the envelope arrived addressed to her in which, we knew, was a personal letter from Russ Conway and a signed photograph, we handed it to her as casually as if it were a circular.

Half an hour later I called into the flower-house where she was having her lunch. She was sitting with Lama on her lap, the photograph propped against a jam jar beside her, a sandwich in one hand, the letter in the other.

I did not have to ask her whether she was pleased. Nor did she have to say anything. She had the smile of the happiest girl in the world.

12

Alan Herbert, during his stay, played an absurd game with Jane and Shelagh when they arrived in the morning. He pretended to take it seriously, and they did too. The game was to check their punctuality not by the normal means of a watch, but by two sundials which he had painstakingly and accurately created.

He called them the Minack Sundials; and one was made from a cocktail tray, the other from the top of a small white table the legs of which he had sawn off.

They had, of course, technical names. The cocktail tray was a Horizontal Sundial, and was allocated to Shelagh because its site was on the arm of the white garden seat which she passed when she arrived in the morning. The table top was an Equatorial Sundial, and so placed that Jane came face to face with it as soon as she jumped over the hedge from her hurried journey across the fields.

I have no idea how A.P.H. made his calculations, but they continued over a period of days and whatever was happening, wherever we might be, we always had to hurry back to the sundials at one o'clock. The purpose was to compare the shadow on the dial he had drawn with the pips of the Greenwich time signal. When at last he was satisfied that accuracy had been assured, he issued the Minack Sundial Instructions; a copy for Jane, a copy for Shelagh.

Unfortunately as his handwriting is very difficult to decipher without the help of a magnifying glass, the girls looked at the instructions in wonderment but without comprehension.

'The Cocktail Tray Sundial,' Shelagh could have read, 'should be dead level, but is warped already.'

'The Table Top Sundial,' Jane may have seen, 'has hour spaces which should be exactly equal . . . but one or two, I fear, are not.'

Jane was also informed in these instructions, 'the dial, believe it or not, is parallel with the Equator which will, I am sure, be a great source of satisfaction.'

Neat diagrams accompanied the instructions and there was an extra page on which was listed the Equation of Time. This was to prove confusing in judging the girls' punctuality because, as sundials owners will know, dials do not coincide with the clock. In August the dial can be as much as six minutes ahead, and in September nine minutes behind. So when the girls arrived for work it was not just a question of looking at the dial. There had to be a mathematical calculation as well.

However, this did not deter A.P.H. He was up every morning at a quarter to eight, waiting. It was a ritual he would not miss, and he was only thwarted when a cloud hid the sun.

'Get away you cloud!' he would shout to the heavens. And if it did, the sun shining once again on his cocktail tray and his table top, he would greet with mock solemnity first Shelagh: 'You're early by two minutes' . . . and then Jane: 'Jane! By your Equatorial Sundial you are three and a half minutes late.'

One morning A.P.H. was still waiting for Jane three-quarters of an hour after she was due to arrive. He was standing by the Equatorial Sundial calling out the minutes: 'Forty-four, forty-five . . .' when she came panting apologetically over the hedge to say that Lamb had disappeared. Lamb, the sheep, which Jane and her mother had taken pity on when it was a few weeks old.

'She was on the grass outside the cottage when we went to bed last night,' she said, 'but there is no sign of her anywhere this morning.'

Lamb led an unusual life for a sheep. She was favoured as if she were a dog. She could come in and out of the cottage as she wished, and when she was in the mood she would join Eva and Acid the dogs, Polly the parrot, Sim and Val the cats, for a share of the food at meal-times. She was part of the household. And at night she either slept in the garden, in a small hut when the weather was bad, or in the grass field on the other side of the garden wall.

'Perhaps someone has stolen her for her fleece,' I said. She had a fine fleece which was about ready to be sheared. 'Anyhow, Jane,' I added, 'you go straight back to get on with your search, and we'll follow you.'

It was a strange coincidence that Lamb should have chosen this moment to disappear. She had been looked after and loved by Jane's family for over five years. They were her life. I used to pass by their cottage and see her lying in the doorway, reminding me of a Newfoundland dog. She would never be able to get used to other people. Nobody would treat her in the same kind way that Jane and her mother and Jeremy had done. It was a coincidence because, only a few days before, Jane had broken the news to us that they had to give up the cottage. The farm had been sold. Her mother was leaving to take a job on Tresco in the Isles of Scilly; and on Tresco island no dogs were allowed or, one might expect, a pet sheep. Thus a new home would have to be found for Lamb.

'And what are you yourself going to do, Jane?' I had asked.

'Oh, I'm going to stay here. I'll find somewhere to live.'

I loved her assurance. I realised that sooner or later she would go to join her mother but she would not leave us suddenly. She was loyal to Jeannie and me. She had that blessed quality which enhanced the stature of those with whom she associated. Jeannie and I felt the better when she was with us. She had the gift of infecting us with her enthusiasm, and she exuded a sense of honesty.

'You can come and stay with me,' Shelagh said, who was in the flower-house at the time, 'there's the outhouse to store your things in, and there's plenty of room in the caravan for you.'

'But there'll be the dogs,' said Jane.

'Oh, Bingo won't mind.'

I took no part in this conversation. It was nothing to do with me. But I wondered what on earth would happen if Bingo, Eva, Acid, and now Acid's pup, should all be left together for the day long.

We searched the cliffs all morning for Lamb, and clambered down on to the rocks in case she had fallen over. We called at neighbouring farms in case she had wandered to them. Nobody had seen her. And we were beginning to think that she might indeed have been stolen, when Jane suddenly discovered her. She had meandered away from the cottage, down a steep path to the wooded valley where a stream rushes to the sea. When she reached the stream she must have slipped and fallen over. For she was lying in the rushes upside down. She was dead.

This incident developed my feeling of impending sadness. I was influenced, no doubt, by its reminder that a period was ending, the usual sentimental sense of loss which pervades the finish of a chapter of one's life.

It seemed the wink of an eyelid since we first saw Jeremy playing with Acid outside their cottage on the grass, throwing a ball at her, Acid retrieving it, on and on, hour after hour. Or the first time we saw Jeremy with a fishing rod taller than himself, and holding a tiny rock fish in his hand. 'A very menacing looking fish, don't you think?' he had suggested. Or when we first met Jane's mother, tall and young looking, coming up the path from the little well they used, and telling us that if we employed Jane we would find her 'very painstaking.' Or that day Jane first came to Minack; and the way she was determined to get the job. Their cottage had seemed without character when we first saw it; but now it would always be alive. We would never be able to pass it without remembering the happiness of the Wyllie family.

At the end of September I loaded the back of the Land Rover with Jane's belongings and drove them over to Shelagh's caravan. A carrier had already taken an advance load which included Jane's harmonium; and when I arrived I found it almost completely filled Shelagh's outhouse. Jane was determined to keep it at all costs. And indeed, when in due course she left to join her mother on Tresco, the harmonium went too; the last part of its journey being in a motor boat from the main island of St Mary's. By this time Acid and her pup had been sent to Jane's married sister; and an exception was made for Eva on Tresco because of her old age and minute size.

Jane's attitude to a car she and her mother had bought had to be different. It was a little saloon car which they had proudly bought second-hand. It was, however, an unfortunate bargain for they seldom were able to persuade the engine to start. It remained immovable in the backyard of the cottage for month after month, and its only virtue was to provide sleeping quarters for the cats. After her mother left, Jane set out to sell it; and the best offer she received was five pounds for the tyres.

I remember Jane's fury. It was an insult; and although she was now living in Shelagh's caravan, her mother in the Scillies, the cottage belonging to a stranger, she indignantly turned down the offer. The car was left where it always had been. A year later it was still there.

She stayed with Shelagh for a month, and then had the luck to be offered a small cottage close by which was let to holiday visitors in the summer. It was still not certain when she would join her mother, and so the routine at Minack went on as usual. She would arrive with Shelagh, both on their bicycles, in the morning and because it was November and the gales were often blowing and rain whipped the land, Jeannie or I would drive them home in the evening, bicycles in the back of the Land Rover. It was part of the charm of their natures that, the journey ended, they thanked us always so freshly.

The routine revolved mostly around work in the greenhouses where we were growing freesias, spray chrysanthemums, and forget-me-nots; while outside we had wallflowers, anemones and a few stocks and violets. We were no longer growing on a massive scale in the open. We had daffodils, of course, but these would not be beginning to bloom until the end of January.

Jeannie and I were, in fact, conducting a rearguard action. We had been bruised in recent seasons. We had lost a little of our confidence. We were no longer ebullient optimists. We were aiming to play safe; and the cornerstone of the safety had been Jane and Shelagh. They knew our ways, and spurred us on when we were doubtful.

I do not believe age determines whether or not you can be on the same wavelength as another. There is simply a meeting of minds of whatever age which instantly feel at ease, just as there are other times when people, hard as they may try to prevent it, find they resent each other, or are bored. Thus a child can find that his thoughts are fluent, so too the means to express them with one teacher, while an hour later, in another class, he finds himself dumb. All he has done has been to be with one teacher who was on his wavelength, another who was not.

There was the incident of the chrysanthemums when,

as I was the boss and the mistake was entirely my fault, both Jane and Shelagh could, perhaps, have been justified in reacting with lofty superiority.

There was frost at the beginning of December and it was my job to light the paraffin heaters in the greenhouses. The one in the chrysanthemum house was an elaborate affair, and one night when I lit it, I forgot to replace an important section of the apparatus. It was the vital section which turned the paraffin from smoke into heat. Thus when next morning I arrived at the greenhouse the chrysanthemums resembled the uninhibited dream of a chimney sweep. The leaves and buds of our precious flowers were covered with soot. I felt very ashamed.

'There's been an accident,' I said, after the girls had come swishing over the gravel on their bicycles in the morning, 'and,' I added, as if I were relieved at the confession, 'it is entirely my fault . . . believe it or not!'

They, of course, made their comments. I was prepared for that. I knew I was destined for a day of being chided, but then I deserved it.

'Don't you think, Mrs Tangye, that we ought to give him a chimney sweep's outfit for Christmas?'

'Soap powder and scrubbing brush would be better!' said Shelagh.

The four of us spent half the morning blowing and puffing the soot off the plants. It was hard work, and if a stranger had seen us I am sure he would have thought we had gone mad. We looked like four people blowing out an endless supply of candles; and we were so slow that I began to wonder whether we could complete the job in the day. Then Shelagh had a bright idea.

'Why don't we use our bicycle pumps?'

'Shelagh,' I said, 'you're a genius. Of course that's the answer!'

And it was. Thanks to the bicycle pumps the chrysanthemums in due course were successfully disposed of in Covent Garden.

It is strange, in retrospect, that none of us ever had a warning about Shelagh. Neither Jane or Jeannie or I, or Pat, the girl she saw most evenings and every week-end, none of us can look back and remember some incident that might have given us a clue. She loved her long bicycle rides with Pat, never showing any signs of tiredness; and never once at Minack did Jeannie or I have to say: 'Shelagh doesn't look very well today.' She never complained. She was never lethargic. And I do not believe she missed one day's work in all the time she was with us.

And yet I wonder sometimes whether I had an intuition there was danger ahead, and which I did not recognise except in my subconscious. Jeannie, too, feels that she had this intuition. Certainly the two of us acted in a strangely protective way towards her, a way which was not inspired by any awareness that something might be wrong.

I, for instance, found myself steering her away from work which tested her strength. She had, of course, baskets of flowers to carry, but I found myself always turning to Jane when I was needing help with my manual labour. My choice was not deliberately made. I just knew instinctively that Jane was the stronger.

Thus it was Jane who used to accompany me as I struggled with trimming hedges and cutting the grass of the daffodil meadows. I had two instruments which I used, a hedge cutter and a motor scythe; and both of them, while leaving me exhausted after an hour or two of using them, also required considerable stamina on the part of my helper. I also required Jane's patience and humour; for both hedge cutter and scythe were my enemies.

The hedge cutter, as long as a fishing rod and as heavy as a sack of potatoes, was fastened to me by a strap across my shoulders; and I used to advance along the chosen hedge, my hands clasping the handles of the hedge cutter, my arms bringing the fast moving blade in a downward sweep, while Jane with a fork speedily swept the cuttings away. It was her speed which eased my labour. If my downward sweep was checked so that the blade was blocked by the debris it had cut, there would be a splutter and the engine would stop.

I would then swear. Jane, on the other hand, because she had grown accustomed to the inevitability that the engine would sometimes stop, appeared not to listen but continued to collect cuttings into heaps. She also knew that a period of swearing was scheduled because the hedge cutter's engine would almost certainly prove difficult to restart.

The performance was repeated with the motor scythe. I would lunge with a thin cord to get it started, and then career through a meadow, cutting a path while Jane pulled the grass quickly to one side. If she was not quick enough, the motor scythe would also get blocked and the engine stall; and my swearing would begin as before.

It is odd, but engines seldom have operated at Minack in a normal fashion. Engineers called to make them go again, have repeatedly remarked that the engine fault has never been known before. One firm lightheartedly suggested they should put up a tent so that their engineer could regularly be on the premises to mend one particular rotovator. On another occasion, after a brand new rotovator specially delivered, remained obstinately silent, the sales manager made the journey from the Midlands to see what was wrong. And as usual his comment was: 'Never known it before.'

Jane maintained that the pixies were at work. They resent the noise, she alleged, and so at night silenced the engines. It was all wrong, and futile, that mechanisation should reign on these ancient cliffs, the ghosts were angry for their values were being challenged; the values which had stood for a horizon of time. Challenged by instruments impervious to loyalty.

There was one tractor, the big one which we sold, that excelled in obstinacy while at Minack; yet as soon as it

was taken away and put to work somewhere else, it
behaved with perfection. While we had it, for instance,
the hydraulic system which lifted the plough would only
operate when it was in the mood; and this was seldom.
Thus we were always asking for mechanics, and the
mechanics were always saying, after two or three hours'
hard work, that they had never known the fault before. I
used to become distraught.

'Jeannie,' I would cry, after a mechanic's visit, 'you
won't believe what he said . . .' Jeannie did not have to
pause; 'I know I know . . .'

When the day came that I sold this particularly large
tractor, the purchaser explained that he would send a
lorry to collect it on the following day. I told Jane.

'Well,' she said, rubbing her hands together and answering me as if she were a conspirator, 'what about getting up
very early and ploughing that piece above the greenhouse
we want?'

Her idea was an excellent one. It was a piece of ground
bordered by ditches which had been dug by me because
of the clinging wetness of the land. If I ploughed it
myself I would not only save the expense of a contractor,
but I would also speed the opportunity to begin using
the land.

The lorry was expected at ten in the morning, so I got
up at six; and by eight, when Jane arrived, I had almost
completed the job. There is a clean, powerful sense of
ambition achieved if you are ploughing a piece of land;
and it is a beautiful morning, woodpeckers laughing,
blackbirds singing, indeed all the birds you live with
throughout the year, are exulting in a blue sky and
a warm sun. Gulls were following my furrow, so too
jackdaws that came from Pentewan cliffs opposite Jane's
cottage, and robins and chaffinches. As I went up and
down the field I rejoiced I had sold the tractor. It was no
longer a hulk of metal to worry about. By the evening I
would have forgotten its existence.

And then, on this lovely morning with Jane now walking up and down behind the plough, turning over the furrows with her foot, the furrows which the plough itself had failed to turn over, I backed the tractor, and a wheel fell into one of my ditches.

'Jane!' I cried out in anguish, 'I'm stuck. I can't get out!'

It was the front right-hand wheel, a small wheel compared with one of the rear wheels; and it was lodged two feet in the ditch, tilting the tractor so that it looked from where Jane was standing as though it might turn over.

She was laughing at me, fair hair against rich brown earth, eight in the morning and a pagan rejoicing in a joke that might have been of her own making. The tractor stuck, me in a panic, the purchaser on his way with a lorry.

'All right, all right, all right,' I said, 'it's all jolly funny, but what are we going to do about it?'

I knew better than she did, that it might be a major performance to get that wheel out of the ditch.

'I'll push.'

She pushed while I revved the engine, but the rear wheels which the engine powered, revolved without any wish to grip the earth.

'Push harder.'

Jane, in rubber boots for a change, was shoving at the tractor, a shoulder pressed to the mudguard, as if she were a female Hercules.

'Give it a little bit more,' and as I said this my foot was on the accelerator, the engine was roaring, and the time was nearing nine o'clock, 'you look as if you can move a mountain . . . so do it!'

And she did.

The tractor suddenly gave a lurch, the wheel cleared the ditch, and I was out on the level ground again.

'Jane, dear,' I said, 'well done!'

'Yes, sir,' she replied with mannered and humorous

politeness, 'but, if I may say so, you don't put a tractor in the ditch two hours before the purchaser collects it!'

Jeannie's intuition about Shelagh concerned her bicycle journeys. She was always saying to her that she should not embark on these marathon rides. And Shelagh just smiled and did not take any notice.

'Oh, I'm all right,' Shelagh would say, 'you don't have to worry about me.'

But Jeannie still worried, and as the winter grew fiercer, she continued to drive Shelagh home. Then in January it became obvious that life in a caravan on a Cornish hillside with gales rocking the caravan every night, torrential storms damping the inside, was scarcely suitable for a girl by herself who was not yet twenty. And so Shelagh decided to move into Penzance and live with her mother by adoption.

Again Jeannie experienced an intuitive sense of apprehension.

'Now, Shelagh,' she said, though of course it was not her duty to impose her views, 'mind you use the bus and not your bicycle. It's too far by bike.'

Shelagh smiled at her. The delicious smile we knew so well.

'I'll see,' she said. And then, reminding us of what we already knew. 'I always biked to and from St Buryan when I was working in Penzance.'

For a while she did as Jeannie had asked her, and at the day's end we would drive her up the long lane to the bus stop. It was a sensible arrangement, and we were glad that she had agreed with us.

But one morning she arrived again by bicycle, and the next, and the next, spring was in the air, she explained, and she loved to feel the soft air in her face.

She never came by bus again.

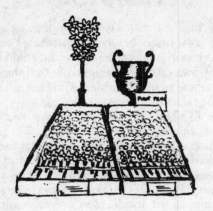

13

When the three of them, Shelagh, Jane and Jeannie were
in the flower-house bunching, Boris would waddle at
intervals to the open door.

He would stick out his long white neck, waggle his tail
feathers, and peer at them with a beady eye.

'Here you are, Boris.'

And one of them would throw him a broken biscuit.

There was always a supply of broken biscuits, cake and
bread crumbs on the flower-bench table. Jane and Shelagh
made it their business to see that this larder was kept full,
because it was not only Boris who expected to be fed.
There was a constant coming and going of chaffinches,
robins, bluetits, and tomtits, a whirring of wings as the
flowers were bunched.

There were, of course, favourites among them. Shelagh
favoured the lady chaffinch which seemed to be Charlie's
wife, and Jeannie preferred Charlie who was not just
as noisy as the first Charlie, and we all loved Tim,
the robin.

'Where's Tim?'

'He's in deep thought . . . up there on that jar of anemones.'

He would perch for an hour on end, quite still looking down on the work in progress. Then suddenly he would treat us to a warble. A whispered warble. A warble so muted that we had to smile.

'A little louder, please,' would come Jane's own quiet little voice. But Tim would continue to warble as softly as before.

He especially enjoyed standing on one leg on a thick black painted beam which stretched across the flower-house; and it was here that I last saw him. It was a beam on which we used to staple the prize cards we had won at the Penzance Flower Shows; and this gave us an opportunity to make idle jokes about him.

'Tim's in a first prize mood today' . . . because he was perched directly above that card. Or at another time: 'Tim feels only like a third prize this morning.'

We never knew what happened. He just disappeared. For a few days we were unperturbed by his absence because there had been previous times when he had gone off; and then returned. On one occasion he even vanished for a month or two, and then to my joy I found him once again in the flower-house. This time four, six, eight, ten weeks passed by, and there was no sign of him. We were still hoping for his return when, just before Christmas, Jane at last left to join her mother in the Scilly Isles. Tim never came back, but Jane did.

She came back for the Penzance Flower show.

This show, the Western Commercial Horticultural Spring Show to give it its full title, is the first mainland flower show of the year, and it takes place on two days in the first week or two of March. It is a beautiful show, for here you see daffodils and so many other kinds of flowers which provide the true herald of spring. They are not unnatural, forced flowers. They are flowers from the Cornish cliffs and the Scilly Isles. Flowers that last longer in the home, because they are not sickened by man-made efforts to bring them into bloom before their time.

As the date of each Show approached there used to be much excitement at Minack. We would be in the middle of the flower harvest, a hectic period of rush in which there was paramount necessity to send away to market as many flowers as possible, as quickly as possible. I was consumed by my urge to do this; and as a result I was placed in mild conflict with Jeannie, Jane and Shelagh. True enough they pursued their work as diligently as ever, but there was a hint in their manner that suggested that their minds were on the following week.

Their talk in the flower-house would dwell on our entries in the various classes. Instead of concentrating their attention to picking and bunching as quickly as possible, I would realise they were keeping a constant look-out for prospective prize-winning blooms. I would find, for instance, superb wallflowers or forget-me-nots or violets hidden away in jam jars in dark corners.

'Jeannie,' I would exclaim in exasperation, 'we simply cannot afford to go into the Show this year. You must tell the girls to forget about it. They must be made to realise their wages depend on the speed we get our flowers away.'

No notice was taken of me. Every year I reacted in the same way. Every year I relented. Every year I was as delighted as the rest to see our entries displayed. Thus they tolerated my initial poor humour.

'Don't take any notice of him,' said Jeannie good-naturedly, after I had raged over a glorious collection of freesias I had found in the dark of the stables. Jane had thought I would never find them.

Both Jane and Shelagh adored this pre-excitement to the Show. It added spice to their day. My attitude made them feel conspirators; and I, looking from the out-side, aware that I was displaying tantrums which were not really tantrums, was touched by the intangible love and understanding between them and Jeannie. They all mocked me.

Up there on the beam were the prize cards Minack flowers had won. First for wallflowers, first in successive years for freesias, first for lettuces; and there were the firsts for one of the gems of the Show, the packed box of mixed commercial flowers grown by the exhibitor. Jeannie won this two years running, and then it was decided to allow bought flowers to be included in the box. Yet Jeannie, despite the bought flowers, again won first prize and the cup with Minack grown flowers.

Jane was always an ardent exhibitor, and she did so from the sheer joy she derived from placing on show something as near perfect as she could make it. When she was only sixteen she won the first prize in the Floral Art class.

Her exhibit was a small sandwich tin in which was placed a little nest of dried grass lined with gleanings of Monty's fur. In the nest there were three tiny blue Easter eggs which she had bought at Woolworths. Around the nest she had built up a mossy bank in which were primroses, violets, forget-me-nots and behind these, miniature daffodils. It was beautiful.

Now when she came back, a year later, in reply to our invitation to stay at Minack for the Show, she brought with her the entries from the famous Tresco Gardens where she now worked. She was in sole charge of these entries. She had chosen the blooms herself and it was her job to prepare, then arrange them on the stands. Five years after she first came to Minack, she was competing on her own with the best growers in Cornwall.

Jeannie met her in the Land Rover when the *Scillonian* docked at Penzance. It was a calm day of blue sky and innocence, and when Jane greeted Jeannie she described the trip across as the best she had ever made. So too had been her trip in the launch from Tresco to St Mary's; and thus her boxes, several boxes of various daffodils and flowering shrubs, had received no buffeting. They now awaited Jane's care and discretion as to how they would be presented in Penzance's St John's Hall, the following day; for the exhibits, Jeannie's also, of course, had to be staged by the exhibitors by ten o'clock on the Wednesday evening.

Jeannie welcomed Jane as an ally, for as usual my anxiety for material results was clashing with my desire to help the Show by exhibiting.

'He's just the same, Jane.'

Jane smiled.

'Well, we've learned not to listen to him!'

It was, of course, imperative that Jane's flowers should be put in water as quickly as possible; but there was also an added apprehension as far as flower show exhibitors are concerned. Would the blooms be in their full glory at the instant the judges passed by?

Jane had erred, if this is erring, in picking her blooms when they were truly fresh, when the buds were just bursting. Yet if the buds did not come into their perfection within thirty-six hours, her efforts would be ignored.

For the prize she was really aiming for, quite apart from the other entries she had planned, was the top accolade of Cornish and Scilly Isle grower, the Prince of Wales Cup.

Only the most illustrious names of growers had been inscribed as the winners. What were her chances?

'The best thing to do, Jane,' I said, 'is to put them in the big greenhouse. The tomatoes we've planted are being kept at a temperature of fifty degrees, and that will bring out your daffodils at just the right speed. No forcing, just naturally.'

So the daffodils, on the Tuesday afternoon, were put there, carefully placed in pails by Jane. They were called Carbineer. An elegant yellow daffodil with a red cup, an aristocrat among the many others striving for the public's attention.

That evening Jeannie, Jane and I went down to see Tommy and Hilda Bailey at the Lamorna Inn. These two, ever since we first came to Minack, had given us encouragement and advice; and if we had a gardening problem we usually sought Tommy's opinion. He was an expert flower grower.

'Fifty degrees is the right temperature for Jane's daffs, don't you think, Tommy?'

'Certainly. We always reckoned that temperature in the old days.'

Tommy looked at Jane. He had often come to Minack, and worked with Jane and ourselves. And he sensed her excitement.

'Jane, my love,' he said, 'don't you worry . . . you're going to win.'

When we left Lamorna a wind was rushing up the valley, and as the headlight of the Land Rover stretched along the road, lighting up the swaying trees on either side, I felt concerned.

'A gale's blowing up,' I said, as I turned the corner to Minack, 'it'll play havoc with the California unless it eases by morning.'

I went to bed and slept well, but I was awakened at six o'clock by Lama jumping on to the bed, and miaowing.

'Shut up, Lama,' I murmured, 'you can't go out yet.'

Then suddenly I was savaged from the comfort of my sleepiness by the roar of the wind. It was a sea wind, tearing in across Mount's Bay.

'Wake up, Jeannie! We must get the California in as quickly as possible. I'll go ahead and start picking.'

How often we had raced against a gale to gather our daffodils before they were so bruised and damaged that they were fit only for the compost heap! How often I had bent down between the beds, blown sometimes off my balance, desperately clutching in one hand the stems I had struggled to pick with the other! Yet it was a task which provided much satisfaction once the basket had been carried safely into the flower-house . . . and when the gale continued to roar hour after hour reminding me every minute that a harvest had been saved. This is what was to happen that Wednesday.

I was followed down to the California meadow by Jeannie and then, a few minutes afterwards, by a dozy Jane. I had ruthlessly asked Jeannie to wake her up.

'Sorry about this, Jane,' I shouted into the wind. I was only politely sorry. I was, of course, thankful to see her once again in a Minack meadow.

And when within an hour the meadow was cleared and the daffodils were safe in the flower-house, I said to the two of them that we could now spend the rest of the day in peace. I had not guessed that we were about to experience the most ferocious gale in the Penzance area within living memory.

As soon as breakfast was over, Jeannie and I started to bunch the daffodils we would be sending by the afternoon flower train; while Jane began to sort out her various exhibits. There was a great deal of work for her to do. She was thus content to leave the Carbineer in the greenhouse, for she believed that another hour or two in the warmth would form the blooms to perfection. She needed twenty-four bunches, twelve blooms in each, to be packed in two boxes, as her entry for the Prince of Wales Cup. Also two perfect bunches to be placed in vases above the boxes.

'I think I'm right, don't you?'

'It can't do any harm, Jane.'

That was at nine o'clock.

At ten I said to Jeannie: 'Am I imagining it or is it in fact blowing twice as hard as when we were picking the California?'

'Frankly,' she said, and she was smiling at me, 'I'm terrified.'

'What about you, Jane?'

'It does sound a bit rough. I think I'll get the Carbineer.'

They were in the big greenhouse in front of the cottage and so, when Jane collected them she had only to dash from the flower-house perhaps twenty yards there and back.

I opened the flower-house door for her. It swung viciously on its hinges so that a gust whipped inside.

'Look out,' called Jeannie, 'those daffs are knocked over!'

The gust had indeed knocked over two jars of daffodils Jeannie was keeping for the Show. But, instead of sympathising with her, I was transfixed by a sight which I had never seen before and hope will never see again.

'Jeannie!' I called out, 'the greenhouse is going!'

The greenhouse was swaying like a tree. A hundred feet long and twenty feet wide, it was lurching first to one side, then to the other; and I suddenly saw a terrible suction effect which made the glass roof appear to leap upwards. A pause; and then the whole massive structure began swaying again. And all the while there was the roar of the gale, so deafening, that although I was standing just outside the flower-house Jeannie could not hear my shouts. I went back inside.

'Jane,' I said, 'I'm sorry. The greenhouse will crash any second. You can't possibly fetch your flowers.'

'It'll only take a minute!'

'Jane,' I repeated firmly, 'you can't do it. If you open the greenhouse door that will be the end.'

There was plenty of work inside the flower-house to keep us busy. Jane had her other exhibits to attend to, while Jeannie and I had to bunch the daffodils that filled the galvanised pails lining the shelves. Bunching can be a peaceful task that allows your thoughts to roam. You bunch automatically. You instinctively select the blooms, three to each row, then two rubber bands to hold the stems, and another bunch is done. A therapeutic task if you are not expecting to hear, at any second, the crash of breaking glass.

'I'm going out to have a look at the mobiles.'

I could not pretend to be calm like Jeannie and Jane appeared to be. My nerves were too raw to cope with routine. I could not confine myself to the flower-house. I felt impelled to watch the destruction which seemed inevitable. I went outside and struggled up the lane to the mobiles; and for ten minutes watched uselessly and with fascination. Then I came back and stared at the big greenhouse. Through the glass I could see Jane's Carbineer in their pails. Never, I thought, had daffodils that were scheduled for the Prince of Wales Cup been in such danger.

At lunch-time Jane said she thought the gale was easing.

'You're an optimist.'

'I think it's easing too,' said Jeannie.

'You're both optimists.'

As the time passed there was in fact no pause in its violence. It thundered on and on. The noise was so terrible that sometimes I thought it was the collapse of the greenhouse that I had heard. Then I would look, and miraculously it was still intact.

At three o'clock I loaded the flower boxes destined for Covent Garden into the back of the Land Rover. I was thankful that action was required of me. I would now be doing something that demanded all my concentration and for an hour I would be relieved from watching the heaving, swaying greenhouses. I could balance my own fears by seeing what had happened to others.

I reached Newlyn Bridge and a policeman turned me left into the Coombe. The coast road was impassable. Great gaps had been ground from the sea wall. I joined the line of traffic that travelled up Alverton, through the town and to the station. On the platform the indefatigable George and Barry who handled the flower cargoes greeted me with the news that I was just in time. The evening tide, they reckoned, would flood Penzance station and cut the railway line which ran to Marazion parallel to the shore. It did.

When I got back to Minack an hour and a half later, I drove down the lane murmuring to myself that all I could expect to see was debris; and I found myself wondering what one did with heap upon heap of broken glass. But first I saw the Robinson mobiles were still there. Then the big greenhouse. I marvelled at our good fortune and my reaction as soon as I pulled up at the cottage was to find Jeannie so that I could share my pleasure.

The storm by now was reaching its peak. Seldom does a gale maintain its momentum for hour after hour, viciously hitting the innocent, as if it were a cruel boxer who was meeting no opposition. But as Wednesday afternoon turned into evening, and growers all over the area were desperately arranging their long-planned entries for the Show, the storm increased. By eight o'clock that evening it was diabolical.

I had got back and found Jane bunching her Carbineer.

'Heavens, Jane, how did you get them?'

I knew it was an unnecessary question. Jane and Jeannie were in league together and as soon as I was out of the way they had proceeded to carry out what they had already planned. They watched the canvas hood of the Land Rover disappear. Then they acted. Within a few minutes, Jane had hopped into the greenhouse and brought out her flowers.

Of course, I was delighted she had done it. I had been spared any sense of responsibility, Jeannie's support has been justified, and now we could all hope that Jane would win.

At nine o'clock the Land Rover was ready to go into Penzance again. There were seven entries from Jane and six entries from Jeannie, and they were placed in the well of the Land Rover as if they were jewels. Along with them went enthusiasm, tenacity and courage.

14

Jane won the Prince of Wales Cup, the youngest competitor ever to do so.

She also won four other prizes including three more cups. And when we came back to Minack after she had been presented with her trophies, we were given a welcome which belonged to the life Jane had lived with us.

Knocker, the gull, was on the roof; Lama was rolling on the path looking inviting; and Boris waddled towards us and followed us up to the door. The gale was over. They were all at ease again.

As for ourselves, we were bewildered by the strain and the success. We were all very quiet. I remember coming into the cottage and saying to Jane what a wonderful experience it had been for Jeannie and me that the schoolgirl who had once called on us for a job had won such a victory. The sound of the storm was still in my ears. I was still dazed.

Then suddenly I heard Jane's soft voice; and what

she said brought to the surface why, in fact, we were so quiet.

'How Shelagh would have loved these past two days!'

Jane was sitting on the same chair where she sat the day she first came to Minack, Jeannie was sitting opposite her on the sofa. I picked up a pipe from my desk and began to fill it.

'A year ago she was celebrating her prize for bunched violets. She was so pleased with that win,' I said.

The gull was crying up on the roof.

'What happened to Bingo?' Jane asked.

'The RSPCA found a good home for him . . . Spotty and Sooty were put to sleep when she left the caravan. They were ill.'

There was silence for a moment. Then I said: 'She didn't suffer. She was unconscious even when she fell off her bicycle. When she was a child she had been in hospital with heart trouble.'

'She never showed any signs that anything was wrong while I was with her.'

'None of us had any warning.'

Jeannie was stroking Lama who had jumped on her lap.

'You were great friends, Jane,' she said, 'I will always remember you together.'

'Oh yes. She was coming to stay with us on Tresco last Easter, the week she died.'

Jeannie turned to her; and at this instant I found myself seeing again Shelagh's delicious smile when she was very happy.

'Just think, Jane,' Jeannie said, 'how glad she would be for you today.'

A Donkey in the Meadow

1

'When do we go?'

It was a sunny April morning, and we were sitting on the white seat beside the bare verbena bush eating our breakfast; a liner aslant from the Lizard on the horizon, Lama, the little black cat at our feet, and Boris, the muscovy drake, staring at us a few yards up the path.

'Have you really made up your mind?'

I knew what Jeannie was thinking. We had discussed holidays before. We had perused the map, had our passports renewed, thought about Brittany, decided on Paris, then changed our minds to London, and in the end had gone nowhere.

'Yes,' I said, 'you have persuaded me.'

A holiday sometimes begins as a course of duty. There are people, for instance, who have to be exploded out of their homes in order to escape to the enjoyment of a holiday. I am one of them.

'The point is,' Jeannie had said to me earlier, 'you haven't been away from Minack for eight years.'

'I haven't wanted to.'

'You've worked very hard all these years on the flower farm.'

'You too.'

'You've also written two books that in successive years were high up in the *Sunday Times* best seller list.'

'Flattery!'

'You've also sold one for a Walt Disney film.'

'What's all this leading up to?'

'It's time you saw one of your books in a London bookshop.'

'You're appealing to my vanity.'

'Seriously . . . I'm suggesting you see in their own surroundings the people you work with.'

'A business holiday.'

'If you like to put it that way. You would be able to wake up in the morning without having to worry about gales or what's made the tractor break down or what disease has hit the freesias . . . and concentrate on your other career.'

'And find out which is the more satisfying?'

'You can't deny,' said Jeannie, flinging a bacon rind at Boris, 'that things have been changing. I mean pressures have been put on us that remind us of the reasons why we left London to come to Minack.'

'The grit in the oyster.'

'And because of these pressures you haven't been able to put your mind to the flower farm as you used to do.'

'The old story of being unable to serve two masters.'

'Sooner or later we'll have to reconcile the two, and by going to London it might help. Afterwards we might see things in better perspective.'

'I doubt it,' I said, 'we'll have a gay time in London, a time of forgetting, that's all. When we get back we'll have to face facts. We'll have to make a choice. We'll have to decide whether to keep on the flower farm. And the only way to solve that problem is here at Minack.'

'You don't have to explain,' Jeannie said, and Lama was gently rubbing against her leg. 'I know you're right. We can't go on as we are. But in the meantime it would do you good to have a holiday.'

'You too. Especially now after the flower season.'

'Well?'

'I agree then,' I said, 'when do we go?'

Minack is a lonely spot with the nearest farm a half mile inland. The cottage sits snug by a wood, an old granite cottage with a massive chimney which in olden days was a beacon to sailing ships making their way across Mounts Bay to Newlyn. It has one large room, a small bedroom, and a spare room and bathroom. The site is carved out of a hillside and it faces, after a few hundred yards of moorland, the expanse of the bay. There is no other building except our old barn in sight, no road, no pylons, nothing to offend the view. The eyes peel across the gorse and the bracken, old hedges and boulders, to the sea and the distant shapes of houses far away on the Lizard peninsula.

Our fields slope down to the cliff, a hundred feet above the sea, then are replaced by a series of small meadows tumbling in odd shapes down to the rocks. Here grew our earliest daffodils, blooming so early in the year that they rivalled the pampered, heated daffodils that come from the vast glasshouses of Spalding. We had several tons of daffodils in our fourteen acres. We also had four large mobile greenhouses covering two sites, a small and a large static greenhouse in front of the cottage, and all of them were heated by oil burning heaters each with an electric fan. The fans drove the hot air through polythene ducting.

Had we foreseen, when we first came to Minack, such equipment and opportunity we would have been goggle eyed with excitement. We possessed then only our hands, enthusiasm and ignorance to drive us forward in the pursuit of making a living. We had no capital. There was no route for a car to reach the cottage. There was no water except the rain from the roof, and thus no bath. Our light came from paraffin lamps and candles and, as now, we had no telephone. But we had in our hearts the exquisitely sweet relief of being freed from twentieth-century entanglements. The deceptive gloss, the gritty worship of false values, the dependence on the decisions of tin gods, all these we had escaped from; and we had the years ahead of us in which to dwell with the primitive and to discover whether within ourselves we could earn contentment.

One discovers in these circumstances that one's own shadow remains the enemy. During the honeymoon of the first years a magical impulse drives you forward, seducing you into believing that each set-back is a jest and each complication a momentary bad dream which has no reality in the life you are leading. It is easy to believe, at this time, that you have devised for yourself a way of life that for ever will be protected from the tendrils of computer civilisation. You delude yourself into believing that you have the same freedom as an aborigine of the South American jungle. Cut off from the do-gooders and the progress makers you feel able to find your own level of happiness. Unharnessed by man-created shibboleths and conventions you feel you at last have the opportunity to release the forces of your secret self.

The balloon of these inspirations remains inflated until the setbacks and the complications begin monotonously to repeat themselves; and then it gradually dawns on you that the period of illusion is over, that it ended as abruptly as a school holiday without the merit of your knowing it, and that considerable determination will have to be exercised to stop yourself drifting.

Of course, it is pleasant to drift, as it is to lie in bed in the morning half awake. I was once a beachcomber on the island of Toopua two hundred miles south of Tahiti where my only neighbours were a Tahitian family; and

I was contentedly able to develop a beachcomber mind because I knew my indulgence could not possibly last for long. I had a boat to catch and I had to come home.

There was, however, no timetable to govern our lives at Minack. Time was our own. We could lie in bed all morning if we wished, or treat hot summer days like holiday makers, or start a job of work, get bored and give up. We had a roof over our heads in a setting we loved, and so long as we had enough to pay for our food we could wander along in indefinite idleness. A perpetual holiday, in fact, leading nowhere. The convential conception of the escapist.

We were able easily to reject such an attitude, but in doing so we made a miscalculation. We still imagined we could remain in isolation spiritually, if not materially, from the force of twentieth-century progress, and from the consortium of greed, envy and guile which sponsors the rat race.

Such a foolish error was due to the rawness of the life we led. Our pleasures were not designed for us at great expense by others. We had only to go and look out of the door, and whether the sun shimmered the Lizard in haze, or a raging storm thrust the foam and the waves into a darkening, winter sky, or the moon silvered the grey rocks that heaped around the cottage into the illusion of fairyland, we had only to see these things to shout to the heavens that we were alive. The sea breathed into our souls, the wind talked. We were part of the ageless striving of the human being. There around us, reflecting from the rough granite grey stones fingering up the walls of the cottage, were the calls of haymakers and the echo of carthorses, fishermen bringing their catch to the door, centuries of truthful endeavour, blazing summers, gales sweeping in from the south, justice in uncomplicated judgement, babies born and wagons carrying the old. All this we were aware of. All this elated every moment of our life at Minack. All this was our stronghold.

We had yet to learn that no one can escape from his shadow, and in order to survive in our new kind of life we had to compromise. We had to pay court to those who project the success of others. We had to flirt with the sponsors of the rat race. And by embracing the slippery, transient applause we faced losing what we had set out at Minack to achieve.

2

April is the between-time of a Cornish flower farm. Where once bloomed violets, anemones and daffodils, there are wastes of green. Soon the anemone plants are ploughed into the ground, and those of the violets split up into runners and planted again to flower the following winter. Only the daffodil beds remain and the foliage, as the summer advances, withers to yellow pointing to the moment when the bulbs, if need be, are dug, separated, sterilised and planted again.

It is a time of planning. Shall we have the violets again this year? They take much time to pick and to bunch. If the weather is kind they flower profusely and a glut is inevitable. If it is bad, prices may be high but there are few blooms. And anemones? They too are at the mercy of the weather, so could not the time involved in looking after them be better employed in other ways?

We had decided this April to streamline our programme. We would concentrate on crops in the greenhouses, except for the outdoor daffodils. Thus tomatoes were already planted in neat rows in the greenhouses, two thousand five hundred of them; and by the beginning of May we would have planted the freesia seeds. Some would go in a couple of thousand whalehide pots, and the rest would be planted in the open sites of two mobiles; and they would all be covered by glass as soon as the tomatoes were finished.

'Obviously,' I said firmly, 'this is the time to go for the holiday. Now. Immediately.'

'Hey!' said Jeannie. 'You take eight years to decide on going away, and now everything has to be arranged overnight.'

'I've got myself excited about it,' I said, 'I want to get away before any doubts set in.'

'Why should there be any doubts?'

'Doubts always set in if you stop to think.'

'Don't think then.'

'I'm not going to, but I have to plan. I have to plan the work for the student and arrange how he and his wife are going to look after Lama, Boris and the others.'

The student came from an agricultural college and was working for us while he looked for a place of his own to go to. He was the only help we had.

'What are you going to do about Lama, for instance?' I asked. 'She's never been left on her own before, and without us she might go wild again.'

'I think the best thing is to give her plenty of her favourite foods,' said Jeannie, 'and then we can hope that she will sleep most of the day.'

Lama came into our lives three years before. A mysterious arrival. The vet who then examined her said she was three months old, an exquisite little black kitten with one white whisker. It should have been easy to trace where she had come from because farms and cottages in our district are so few and far between. We visited each one for miles around. Nobody owned up to her. So where had she spent her first three months?

My first sight of her was at the beginning of that daffodil season, a black spot in the distance; but a couple of weeks later I was passing by a meadow of marigolds when I suddenly became aware of her scrutiny. She was three-quarters hidden within a mass of orange flowers, a small black velvet cushion with a pair of yellow eyes which followed me as I went by. I was acutely conscious of her steady stare; and I felt I was being assessed by a possible employer as to my qualifications in regard to a job.

My first touch of her was nearly disastrous. I found her one morning in the chicken run, and foolishly believing we could be friends I advanced to pick her up. Instead she hurtled herself against the wire netting, crazily tried to thrust her head through the small holes, then escaped from my fumbling hands by shooting up a tree and leaping like a monkey from one branch to another until she jumped clear, and disappeared into the wood.

Jeannie's approach was more subtle. She wooed her by placing saucers of milk at strategic places distant from the cottage, then reporting excitedly when the saucers were found to be empty. This courtship, this fencing between Lama and ourselves, continued until Easter Sunday afternoon when a tremendous storm blew in from the sea.

We were sitting in the cottage, the roar of the gale battering the walls and the roof, and Jeannie was reading her diary of almost exactly the year before. Monty, our old cat, was then dying and she read from her diary the account of the efforts she had made to save him. She also recalled what I had said to her at the time. I had said that as far as I was concerned, and she agreed, we would never have a cat again because we would never be able to repeat the love we had for Monty. Then I added, and this she also recalled, I would be ready to make one possible exception to this decision. That was if a cat, uninvited and untraceable, came crying to the door in a storm; but it had to be *black*.

Here we were then, on that Easter Sunday, sitting in

the cottage when above the noise of the gale, I heard a miaow, and another, and another. I leapt from my chair, opened the cottage door; and into our lives came Lama.

Lama, therefore, while we were away, had to be suitably cared for, and so Jeannie decided she would have her favourites. Cod and whiting would be in the deep freeze, an emergency packet of Felix would be in the pantry; and to launch our departure there would be a special supply of pig's liver. Fed at steady intervals by the student and his wife, Lama would sleep and forget us. That, at any rate, was the aim.

There remained Boris, Knocker, Squeaker and Peter. Boris, the Muscovy drake, had measured habits which had to be adhered to. He was a strong character who lived alone in the large one-time chicken-house deep in the wood to which he retired without persuasion every evening as dusk was falling. He would waddle there, taking his time, then fly ponderously up on to his perch; and later we would come along to lock up his door and safeguard him from any prowling dangers of the night.

In the morning he could be difficult. He would explode in wrath if we were late in letting him out, hissing his fury and flapping his wings, charging after us as we returned to the cottage so that sometimes I have found myself murmuring: 'I'm sorry, Boris.'

He had arrived at Minack three years before in the arms of Jane, the young girl who then worked for us. A young farmer had attempted to woo her by bringing Boris in a sack to her cottage, and offering him for her dinner.

Her response was to burst out in anger, remove Boris quickly from the sack, and take him up to her bedroom where he remained for two days. Then her mother thought it was time for him to move, and Jane brought him to Minack.

His sense of independence, however, would make it

easy to leave him. He enjoyed being undisturbed. He pottered about in the grass, dipped his yellow beak frequently in the pail of water kept full for the purpose, and two or three times a day plodded up the steep path to the door of the cottage for any titbits that might be available. He would, of course, miss these rewards, and Jeannie decided to compensate him by preparing a plentiful supply of his favourite home-made bread.

Knocker, Squeaker and Peter were the gulls. The first two were the owners of the roof, the latter a friendly, intelligent gull who arrived when the others were absent. Knocker and Squeaker fiercely defended their territory, and Peter would wait far off in a field until he saw the roof was clear; then sweep majestically towards us. I had a special fondness for Peter and he would sometimes go for walks with me. He would fly and swoop over my head, alight on a boulder a few yards ahead of me, then surge into the sky again when I reached him. Knocker and Squeaker were more opportunist. They would parade the apex of the roof day after day, and in the winter would squat side by side on the chimney, content with its warmth. When they were hungry, if we had failed to attend to their needs, Squeaker would squeak and Knocker would bang on the roof with his beak. Many a time he has deceived us into thinking there was someone at the door, so insistent, so loud has been his knock. These three also had to be looked after. They were not, however, going to be pampered. They did not like shop bread but they would have to put up with it.

All the instructions for the student and his wife were neatly typed. We had bought our tickets to Paddington. We had decided to stay at the Savoy, the first time together there since Jeannie had written *Meet me at the Savoy*. We both had a pleasant sense of anticipation of the gay time ahead. It was Friday and we were going to leave by the Sunday night train. Everything, in fact, about the holiday was organised, when the Lamorna postmaster strode down the lane with a telegram. The message said simply:

'Got donkey.
                    Teague.'

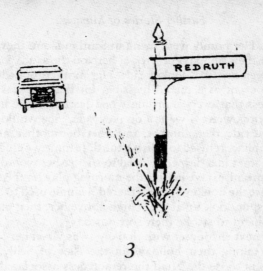

3

I looked at the telegram in dismay.

'Heavens, Jeannie,' I said, 'now what do we do?'

Mr Teague, a Dickensian, toby jug of a man, kept the Plume of Feathers at Scorrier near Redruth. He was also a cattle dealer, a horse dealer, a dealer in any kind of animal. We had had a drink with him a couple of weeks previously.

'I never said *definitely* I wanted one,' she murmured. 'I only *talked* to him about it. I never thought he had taken me seriously.'

I glanced at her suspiciously.

'You promise you didn't make some secret plan with him? . . . arrange for him to produce a donkey just as you arranged with your mother to give us Monty? . . . presenting me with a *fait accompli?*'

'Don't be silly.'

'You've always been so dotty about donkeys that I could believe anything.'

Her addiction to donkeys began when she first learnt to

toddle. Her family were living in Scotland, and they used
to take their holidays at Troon; here on the sands Jeannie
was given her first donkey ride. Her mother looked back
on the event as a mixed blessing; for the ride was such
a success that every morning when Jeannie woke up her
first words were: 'I want a donkey ride.' She would have
first one ride, then another, and when her mother, aiming
at discipline, refused to allow a third, Jeannie would howl.
Her mother in a desperate need to silence her would offer
a compromise, a visit after the morning play on the sands
to where the donkeys were tethered. Jeannie used to arrive
at the spot, look up at them high above her, then put out
a tiny hand to stroke their soft noses.

Her next encounter with donkeys was when her family
began taking their holidays in the Isles of Scilly. The
islands in those days had the remoteness associated with
islands. There was no mass invasion of holiday makers.
There were no telephone kiosks or cars, and electricity
was limited to those who made their own. It was a magical
place to visit, sailing, fishing, lying in the sun on deserted
beaches, somewhere in which time seemed to be poised in
space. The war was close, but Jeannie and her friends used
to play there, deaf to the noise of the dictators, gloriously
believing there was no end to any day, bronzed youth
swimming in still blue water, shouting to the heavens
their relish of living.

She used to stay in those days in the Atlantic Hotel on St
Mary's overlooking the harbour. And when she was there
in the spring she used to lean out of her bedroom window
in the early morning and watch entranced the sight of the
donkeys and their little green carts bringing the daffodil
boxes to the quay. Then she dressed and went down to the
breakfast tables and took lumps of sugar from the bowls.
Many a donkey was pleased to see her as it waited for its
cart to be unloaded.

And later in the day she used to make a regular sortie
to a field where a favourite donkey was put out to graze.

First there was one donkey, then another and another. She had the childish delight in fancying that the donkeys had gossiped as they stood by the quay, spreading the news that a girl visited a certain field with a pocketful of sugar. Then one day there were more than twenty donkeys in the field, and it was not fun any more. They barged their noses into her pockets, pushed and shoved her, until she became frightened and began to run away from them. Her father who was watching her said it was a very funny sight . . . the Florence Nightingale of the donkeys racing across the grass and twenty sugar-mad donkeys close behind her.

I also had been chased by a donkey.

My earliest memory, so distant that I sometimes wonder whether it may be my imagination at work, is lying in a steep grass field staring up at the grey underbelly of a donkey. The field itself, and this I remember clearly, fell from the road to the seashore at the river end of Porth beach near my childhood home at Newquay. I was very small, and in my haste and terror as I ran from the donkey I had tripped, tumbling over into the grass, desperately aware that my future lay at the mercy of the beast which was soon upon me.

I am able to believe in the reality of my story so far, but there is also an event in my memory so horrifying that it is strange that no one in my family can vouch for it. My mother when she was alive, and when I asked her about it, laughed at my foolishness, and surely she would have remembered so violent an incident to her youngest son.

The donkey, so my memory tells me, kicked me in the teeth as I lay helpless beneath him.

This memory, or childish nightmare as it must have been, was vividly present during my conversation with Jeannie. Donkeys, as cats had once been, were to me unfriendly creatures; but whereas my original distaste for cats was merely because I thought them vulgar, detached and selfish, I was, as far as donkeys were concerned, a little scared.

They were bony and heavy, and dull witted. I did not see how one could trust a donkey. A cat at least was not dangerous. It might scratch when frightened, or might even lacerate you if enraged, and you happened to be in the way. That was all. A donkey, on the other hand, was an unruly creature. It might kick without reason. Or bite. It was uncouth. I could not foresee how a donkey could ever enter the stream of our life except to excite our pity. There it would stand forlornly in a meadow, nothing to do, reproachfully demanding our attention which it would be too stupid to appreciate.

Jeannie, of course, had long ago forgiven her sugar-mad donkeys, and I guessed she only needed a little encouragement from me for her to answer the telegram by setting out forthwith to have a look at the donkey. I, on the other hand, remained on guard.

'The first thing I'm going to do,' I told her, 'is to have a word with Jack Baker.'

Jack Baker was a landscape gardener, and at this time was designing a new part of our garden. He was a practical man, an expert horticulturalist, a mechanic, a tree feller and, what interested me particularly, he had had experience with donkeys.

'Tell me, Jack,' I said when I found him, 'what do you think about keeping a donkey as a pet?'

Jack had a merry eye but a lugubrious nature. He wanted to enjoy life but the fates had checked him so many times that he was inclined always to outline the tedious side of a problem at the expense of the happier side. He was in his fifties, tall and broad-shouldered, an individualist who, during the war, preferred to remain a sergeant in the Guards rather than accept the commission he was offered. He was one of those rare people one would instinctively want to be with in a jam. He would, I felt sure, be calm while the threat – whatever it was – received his attention. I anxiously awaited his donkey views.

He took the pipe from his mouth, knocked the ash from the bowl on a rock, then pronounced:

'You'll have a packet of trouble.'

I was, of course, prepared for a douche of cold water. He was only being true to my knowledge of him, a harbinger of bad news before good; and yet his attitude, because it coincided with my own, was pleasing to listen to.

'How do you mean?' I asked.

'Well, the first thing you'll find out, for instance,' he said solemnly, 'is that it will eat up the garden.'

Even to my ears this remark sounded biased. What about a horse or a cow? Wouldn't they eat up the garden if they were given a chance?

Jack was leaning on his shovel, amused, delighting in his mission to discomfort me.

'Ah,' he said knowingly. 'A horse or a cow can be kept in a field, and it's only bad luck if it gets out. But a donkey! You can't keep a donkey loose in a field. It'll get out. It'll jump a fence or a wall, and go roaming all over the district. And it'll be eating up other people's gardens besides yours.'

'What do people do about donkeys then?'

He grinned at me.

'Best thing to do is to tether it. You get a swivel anchor from the blacksmith, fix it firmly in the ground, and the donkey goes round and round eating the grass. Then twice a day you move it.'

'Twice a day?'

'Oh yes, otherwise as soon as it has eaten the grass it will start braying.'

'It's a bit of a job digging up the anchor and then fixing it again, isn't it?'

'Certainly. But that's what people do.'

I could not see myself doing it.

'There's another point,' Jack went on, and he was now talking as if he believed he had got me on the run, 'and that's water. A donkey drinks a lot, and you'll have to keep a bucket always full beside it. If a donkey is thirsty even for a minute the braying will start up.'

'How loud is the braying?'

'They'll hear it in the next parish.'

'But surely,' I said, 'you're exaggerating. You're making out that a donkey is only fit for a zoo. After all, lots of people *do* keep donkeys.'

'Not for long. They're excited when they get them at first but soon tire of them when they find out the trouble they cause.'

I found at this moment, contrary to reason, that Jack's attitude was engaging my sympathy for donkeys. His arguments against them seemed, even to me, to be over-loaded.

'Now tell me honestly,' I said, 'how *friendly* can a donkey be?'

He sat down on a rock, put his palms on his knees, laughingly looked at me with his head on one side, and replied:

'How friendly? You ask me how friendly? . . . all I can say I would never dare keep a donkey myself!'

This should have been enough to make up my mind. Armed with Jack's arguments I could have gone to Jeannie and explained to her that a donkey at Minack was quite impracticable. He had confirmed my suspicions. A donkey would only be a nuisance.

But there were other factors involved which I felt would be fair to consider. Jack himself, for instance. He knew us both well enough to realise that in any case Jeannie would have her donkey if she really wished, and, therefore, he could without qualms take humorous pleasure in trying to scare me. He had had his joke but, contrarily, he had awakened my interest. My talk with him had the effect of an appetiser; and I was beginning to be intrigued as to where the ownership of a donkey might lead me.

I had also to admit that Minack would provide a wonderful setting for a donkey. It could roam along the grey boulders of the moorland, wander down the steep slopes of the cliff to the sea's edge, and for most of the year when the daffodils were not growing, it could be loose in the bulb fields. There was land enough, therefore, for it not to have any reason to escape; and I also saw a practical advantage. A donkey would help to keep the grass down.

Nor could I forget that in the past I had always objected to the arrival of a new pet, and then soon agreed that my objections had been wrong. I had not wanted Monty or Lama or the drake or the fox cub which Jeannie looked after when it was brought to her with an injured foot. I suffered the contradictory emotions of enjoying responsibility once it had been imposed upon me, but of fearing any addition to those I already held. An animal was a responsibility. I had been brought up to believe that once an animal is accepted into a household it must be treated as a member of it, and not as a piece of furniture. And I remember my father telling me, when he gave me my first puppy, that it was my job to make the puppy happy, and not the other way round.

I was, therefore, in two minds what to do; and in the end I decided to surprise Jeannie. I would act in a holiday spirit. When she set out to persuade me to go and have a look at the donkey, I would immediately agree. What harm could there be in just having a look?

So an hour later we were in the Land Rover, and I was innocently driving towards Mr Teague. We were about to arrive when Jeannie suddenly said, 'If we like it, we will have the donkey, won't we?'

'No,' I said firmly, 'certainly not.'

And I knew I was lying.

4

We reached the Plume of Feathers soon after opening time, and Mr Teague greeted us with a glint in his eye. He saw a sale in the offing.

'Come in,' he said jovially from behind the bar, 'have a drink. What'll you have, Mrs Tangye?'

Mr Teague, or Roy as he now insisted on us calling him, was in the fortunate position of being able to do his bargaining on his own licensed premises. Sales could be conducted in convivial circumstances, and though a purchaser might succeed in reducing a price or a seller in increasing it, the cost of the evening had to be considered. I was aware of this. I had therefore decided, in the event of us wishing to buy the donkey, to complete the deal with the minimum of argument. I might lose a pound or two on the price, but this was a sensible sacrifice if it meant we could speedily return to Minack.

'We've just looked in to see the donkey,' I said casually, 'it was very nice of you to send the telegram.'

'Not at all,' he said, 'I've got a nice little donkey and thought I'd let you have the first chance.'

He had got us our drinks and was now leaning with elbows on the bar, hands interlocked. I could see he was about to turn his charm on Jeannie. She was a vulnerable target.

'Lovely tempered little donkey,' he said, smiling at her, 'good as gold. Comes from Ireland, from Connemara or somewhere like that. They ship them over by the dozen these days.'

'What for?'

'They go for pet food mostly.'

'How cruel,' said Jeannie.

He was now fiddling with an empty ashtray on the counter.

'The only trouble is she is not in very good condition. Nothing serious. Nothing that Dr Green can't soon put right.'

'Dr Green?' I asked, puzzled.

'Grass.'

'Oh, of course.'

He turned again to Jeannie. His eyes were twinkling.

'And there's another thing. Something, I bet, you never bargained for when you came along here. She's in foal. Two donkeys for one. What about that?'

I took a gulp at my drink.

'Good heavens!' I said.

'Now, now, now,' he answered, looking at me and sensing a momentary set-back, 'as soon as she's had the foal I'll buy it off you. Nothing could be fairer than that, could it?'

He turned again to Jeannie.

'Have you ever seen a little donkey foal? Lovely little things they are. Just like a toy. You can pick it up in your arms. I've seen a child do that, honestly I have.'

I watched Jeannie melting. The practical side, the prospect of *two* donkeys charging about Minack did not concern her at all. All that she could imagine was the picture card idyll of a donkey and its foal. The deal was advancing in his favour. Somewhere in a field behind the pub was a donkey which was on the brink of being ours.

And then Mr Teague played his ace.

'Sad thing about this donkey,' he said, fumbling again with the ashtray, 'very sad thing . . . by the way, Penny's her name. Pretty name Penny, isn't it?'

'You were saying.'

'Yes, I was going to tell you that if you don't like the look of her, I've got a buyer. Made a good offer he has too, but it's a sad story.'

'Why so sad?'

'Well, I wouldn't like to see it happen. You see the idea of this buyer is to wait for the foal to be born, then put it in a circus. A donkey foal in a circus would be a big draw, especially on the holiday circuit. Can't you see the children flocking round it?'

I could see he was genuinely concerned.

'What happens to the mother?'

He glanced at me, appreciating that I was on the wavelength.

'That's the point. That's what I'm worried about. That's why I want to find her a good home, and thought of you two.'

'How do you mean?'

'The idea of this buyer friend of mine is to send Penny to the knacker's yard as soon as the youngster can get along without her.'

'But that's awful.' I could not help myself from saying what I knew was in Jeannie's mind.

'And what's more,' went on Roy Teague, 'when the season is over and they've got their money's worth out of the youngster, it'll be too big to keep.' He paused. 'They'll send it to the knacker's yard as well.'

The emotion he expected erupted.

'I must go and see her at once.' Jeannie was picking up the gloves she had dropped on a stool. She looked pained. She was at that moment the ideal example of a salesman's victim. She was hooked, and so was I. However bad was the donkey's condition, we must buy her. It was our duty. We had been given the chance of saving her, and of giving a home for her foal. Here was an opportunity which reached far beyond our original inclinations. We would not only be giving a donkey a home, but also acquiring a donkey which would otherwise be doomed ... first by sadness because of being parted too soon from her foal, then by the journey which ended in the knacker's yard. I was a donkey buyer with a mission. I had better begin negotiations.

'You go ahead,' I said to Jeannie, 'have a look at her and see what you think. I'll have another drink.'

My purpose in not accompanying her was to appear nonchalant in front of Mr Teague. I intended to go through the form of bargaining, the pause between sentences, the changes of subject, the sudden return to a point that appeared to be forgotten, the mock laughter over a price which in reality I didn't think too high, the pretence that I had, in fact, no intention of wanting the donkey at all; all those machinations which one feels one ought to pursue despite the fact that an immediate deal would produce a shout of joy.

'I suppose you're getting ready for the season,' I said, after Jeannie had disappeared to the paddock behind the pub where the donkey was temporarily grazing, 'all ready for the rush.'

'That's right. Winter in a hammock, then a sprint.'

'I don't know how you stand it night after night.'

'It's a job. Like any job you have to stick to it.'

'Not for me. I wouldn't stand it for any money.'

He took my glass, and swung round to the optics.

'Mrs Tangye is dead keen on that donkey, isn't she?' He had his back to me, a finger on the lever of the optic of the whisky bottle. 'Dead keen, I should say.'

He was forcing the pace.

'She's always liked donkeys ever since she was a child,' I said, as if I were talking about the weather, 'of course she's got a kind heart, and that story you told her upset her a bit.'

'It's true.'

'Now, Roy,' I felt that I could sound intimate, 'I believe you are a fair man. What price have you in mind for the donkey?'

He looked at me shrewdly, bright eyes from a red, jovial face. He had no intention of exploiting me, that I was sure; but naturally he would like to make a maximum profit. He pushed my glass across the counter.

'Have it for twenty-seven pounds.'

I fumbled for a packet of cigarettes, found it, pulled out one, lit it. I apparently succeeded by this delay in conveying to him that the figure had shocked me.

'I'll tell you what I'll do,' he said, speaking quickly, 'I'll throw in a shay with the price. A donkey and a shay go together, everyone used them in the old days. It's good fun. If the car breaks down I can see Penny taking you and Mrs Tangye into Penzance!'

I couldn't, but I joined in his laughter.

'It's worth five pounds,' he said.

At this moment, before I could answer, the door at the corner of the lounge was flung open, and in rushed Jeannie. One glance at her and I knew the donkey was ours, whatever the price, whatever its condition. Roy looked at her happily.

'She came to me as soon as I called her!' she said excitedly, 'came right across the field as if she knew me, as if . . .'

'I know, I know,' I said, 'as if she knew you were the one person in the world who could give her a happy home.'

She ignored me.

'. . . as if she were hungry.'

'Not much grass in that paddock, true enough,' said Roy, 'but you'll soon put her to rights. Eat anything, donkeys will.'

'Now look,' I said, trying to sound sensible, 'there are one or two things we ought to clear up. How old is she, for instance?'

'She's four. Can't be more than four.'

'And what about the foal. When is the foal expected?'

'A month perhaps. Five weeks. Difficult to say.'

Then he added quickly.

'I'll buy the foal back, mind. Give you ten quid, I promise.'

A promise I knew would never be put to the test.

'And what,' I went on, 'does one do about the confinement?'

'Leave her out,' he said briskly, 'leave her out and she'll look after herself. No trouble at all.'

I envied his casual efficiency. All his life he had been accustomed to the arrival and the departure of animals; and he was naturally impatient with my doubts as to how to treat properly a donkey and its foal. They were a production unit as far as he was concerned. Something which could make a sale and a profit and, without being heartless, something he considered as inanimate as tins in a grocery shop. He would never carry on his business as a dealer had he thought otherwise. And yet I felt he was sentimental enough to be glad that Penny was about to leave for a good home.

'Well,' I said, 'about the price. We don't want the shay, you can keep that. I'll give you a cheque for twenty-five pounds.'

'That'll do me.'

'What about the delivery charge. Who's going to pay that? I mean we'll have to hire a horse box.'

He grinned at me, giving the empty ash tray another twirl with his finger.

'Don't need a horse box. Got a Land Rover outside

haven't you? Put her in that. My daughter fetched a donkey in one from Exeter the other day. No trouble at all.'

This was a situation I had not foreseen. Indeed had I had an inkling when I set out for the Plume of Feathers that I would leave it with a donkey in the back, I would have stayed at home.

'But surely she might be dangerous,' I remonstrated weakly, conscious I risked being labelled a coward, 'she might get in a panic as I was driving along, lash out and all that. She might bite.'

I hoped that Jeannie would agree.

'Come and see her,' she said soothingly, as if I were making a fool of myself, 'she's as quiet as an old sheep dog. I certainly don't mind myself if she comes with us.'

And she did.

Half an hour later we were racing along the Redruth by-pass with me at the wheel, Jeannie beside me, and between the two of us, shoulder level, the solemn, patient face of Penny the donkey.

5

'You know, Jeannie,' I said, as we turned off the by-pass and drove up the hill into Camborne, 'we've got ourselves in a fix. We can't possibly leave a donkey which is going to have a foal.'

'I realise that too.'

'So that's the end of our holiday before it's begun.'

'Are you very disappointed?'

'It seems to me to be sheer lunacy to give up a long-overdue holiday just because we take pity on a wretched donkey.'

We were passing the Holman engineering works on our left, and the road to Illogan where my grandfather was born on our right.

'Turn round and take her back then.'

'I'm thinking,' I went on ignoring Jeannie, 'of all the trouble involved in putting everything off. What do I say? And how is your mother going to react when you tell her you can't go to London because we've bought a donkey in the family way?'

'She'll laugh.'

A huge lorry ahead slowed us down to a crawl.

'I had got myself attuned to the idea of seeing the bright lights again. I was looking forward to a frivolous time.'

'You can go on your own.'

'Don't be silly.'

'There's such a change in you. First I have to knock you on the head to make you go, and now you're moaning away because you can't.'

'My contrary self.'

I changed gear, accelerated and passed the lorry blowing the horn. I found comfort in doing so.

'It means,' I said, 'we won't have the chance of going away again for a year. You know that. We won't have a chance what with the tomatoes, the freesias, the daffodils all following on each other. We're committed to fight it out this year.'

'You can write a book about the year in between.'

'Between what?'

'The year in which you decide whether to work with your mind or work with your hands. The year in which we decide whether to continue with the flower farm.'

'It is a question of labour. There is so much manual work to be done. That's all the trouble.'

'Cheer up. You're forgetting you're going to have another interest.'

'What?'

'A year with two donkeys!'

At this moment Penny, who was standing in the well of the Land Rover and small enough to be clear of the canvas hood, pushed her head forward and, to my concern, rested it on my shoulder. Thus, as I stared at the road ahead of me lined at first by squat houses and shops, then by the open fields leading to Connor Downs and Hayle, I could see out of the corner of my eye a large white nose; and I felt a weight on my shoulder like the hand of someone wanting to reassure me.

'She seems to like you.'

'I think I'm dotty.'

'But don't you feel happier?'

'I suppose so.'

'You're a misery!'

The time was seven o'clock and we had a little over an hour before dusk. Clouds were looming up over the distant Zennor hills, hiding the sun. Penny's head remained resting on my shoulder, and I took one hand off the wheel and stroked her nose. Even so early in her life with us, she was placid. It was if she had had many journeys such as this one, shifted from one place to another, railway trucks, the boat from Ireland, cattle lorries, herded with other donkeys at auction sales; and these experiences had made her resigned. Here she was travelling to another paddock, another brief period of affection or work, then on to somewhere else as soon as the originality of her presence had worn thin, or her usefulness had expired.

We were nearing Connor Downs.

'Let's stop for a drink at the Turnpike,' I said. I said it doubtfully. I was prepared for Jeannie to say that one didn't leave a donkey in charge of a car while one went inside a pub.

'All right, but I'll stay with her. We have to get her out of the Land Rover before it is dark. We can't be long.'

I had good reason to stop at the Turnpike. Jack Edwards, the landlord, had been a gamekeeper for most of his life, and whenever Jeannie and I wanted experienced advice on a section of country life he could be relied upon to supply it. A few weeks before, for instance, we had called in to see him about a dying fox we had found in the lane a few hundred yards from the cottage.

Foxes and badgers are numerous around Minack, and often in the early morning we can lie in bed watching a fox through the window nosing about the field opposite. We pretend to ourselves, and we may be right, that we can identify each one. This particular spring there had been two dog foxes we had watched, one whose territory seemed to be the field opposite, the other who spent his time in a neighbouring one. I would watch them through field-glasses stalking a mouse in the grass, alert and ears cocked, a pause before the pounce, then the attack and the spreadeagling of legs like a cat. We were amused when the attempt misfired. There was the same posture of disappointment, then the same nonchalant pretence that failure did not matter which we had seen so often displayed by Monty and Lama.

One of these two, the one in the neighbouring field, appeared to be younger than the other. He seemed to be bigger, a better sheen on his coat, and his brush was huge. He was also more adventurous and we would often watch him slink over the hedge before darkness fell, then up and over and along the track that led away from the cliff country into the hinterland. And then in the morning we would watch him return, tongue hanging out, a tired fox, and we would wonder how many miles he had travelled; and of the angry conversation someone at that very moment might be having about a fox that had raided the poultry during the night.

One evening soon after dusk we were still bunching daffodils in the packing shed when we heard a scream up the lane as wild as that of a hyena. Then another and another, such a cacophony that it was as if there had been a collision of screams. After ten minutes, during which time there were momentary silences and a gradual lessening of the noise as it moved away up the lane, I said to Jeannie that we had better go and find out what had happened. We did not really expect to find anything. We were just being curious.

We had gone half-way towards the farm at the top without seeing anything and were about to turn back when my torch shone on what looked like a dog curled up in the middle of the lane. As we walked closer it began to move, dragging its body towards the ditch; and we saw it was a fox. There was nothing we could do except to leave it without it being frightened by the sight of us. We saw that its front paws were terribly mangled and it could not possibly go far whatever its other injuries. We left it lying in the ditch and half an hour later when I returned it was dead.

The following morning through our bedroom window we saw the field opposite was empty, but the neighbouring one had its usual occupant, the splendid-looking young dog fox. As we watched, he jumped over the hedge into the field which hitherto had been forbidden to him, and began wandering around as if he owned it. The same thing happened morning after morning, and so we concluded that he had fought and killed his rival, and he was the new king of the territory.

In due course I had described the episode to Jack Edwards. I also told him that a trapper I knew had said that our conclusion was wrong. The trapper maintained that a young badger had been the killer. Who was right?

'When the fighting was going on,' asked Jack Edwards, 'did you hear any grunting noises?'

'None at all.'

'Badgers grunt when they fight.'

'There was only an endless screaming.'

'That confirms your conclusion was correct and the trapper was wrong.'

'What happened then?'

'Foxes fight on their hind legs like horses. They box each other. I reckon the young fox was quick enough to seize the old one's paws as they fought, and that's why they were mangled. That's what happened.'

I now turned the Land Rover off the main road and drew up in the Turnpike car-park.

There was no one else in the bar.

'Jack,' I said, coming straight to the point which was still bothering me, 'are donkeys difficult to keep?'

'How do you mean?'

'Are they the asses they're supposed to be?'

He lit a cigarette and smiled.

'I've known some intelligent donkeys in the past. Like everyone else some are clever, some are not.'

'Can they be a nuisance?'

'They're certainly very affectionate.'

'Which means?'

'They need a lot of attention . . . but what's all this about?'

At this moment there was a wail outside like that of a banshee. A gargling noise on a high note.

'Heavens,' I said, 'she's calling me!'

'Who?'

'The donkey.'

'God bless my soul!'

'We've just bought one from Roy Teague.'

'What about Mrs Tangye . . . where's she?'

'She's out there too.'

'Mrs Tangye guarding the donkey? . . . Look, I'm taking her a drink straight away.'

We went outside and up to the Land Rover; and as Jack walked forward, glass in hand, a face was thrust through the driver's window. It had a large white nose.

'I sign the pledge!' cried Jack.

Penny pushed her head forward as if she were making to bite the glass. She looked quite fierce. I did not realise until later that she was only thirsty.

But at the same time an unpleasant thought crossed my mind. She was showing restlessness. She might, for all I knew, be vicious. Dusk would be falling when we reached Minack, and Penny in a strange place without an expert to handle her might not be so placid at her journey's end as she had been at the beginning.

How were we to remove her from the Land Rover on our own?

6

Rain began to spatter the windscreen as we turned from the main road into the bumpy lane which led a mile away to Minack. Clouds, low and lugubrious, swirling in from the sea and the south, were hastening the dusk to fall before its time.

'I feel very pleased with myself,' said Jeannie suddenly.

'Why's that?'

'Well,' she said, 'before we left and when you were out of sight, I got hold of Jack Baker and asked him a favour.'

'And what was this favour?'

'It was his idea really.'

'Come on, tell me what it was.'

I felt irked that I had not been previously informed.

'You know that big iron bar which is used for levering rocks?'

'Of course I do.'

'Jack Baker suggested it would make an ideal tethering post for a donkey.'

'Reasonable enough.'

'And so before we set off just in case we *did* buy a donkey, I asked him to fix it.'

'You seemed very certain in that case that we *would* buy a donkey.'

'The only trouble is,' she said, ignoring me, 'that he couldn't put it upright as the soil was too shallow. He therefore planned to anchor it into the ground horizontally, helped by a couple of big rocks at either end of the bar.'

A journey into detail was unlike her. She was hiding something.

'The bar,' she went on, 'is all in the ground except where the rope is tied. The other end of the rope we join to the halter we've brought with us. It means that Penny can't run away.'

We passed the jumble of farm buildings which stood at the top of the valley, then began to descend the last stretch to the cottage. And all the time Penny's head rested firmly on my shoulder.

'Whereabouts,' I asked, 'am I going to find this contraption?'

'On the lawn.'

I calmed myself. I kept my hands on the wheel. I said nothing.

'I know what you're thinking,' she went on, 'I can guess. But . . . honestly, it isn't much of a lawn. Now is it?'

'I should certainly think not after you and Jack Baker and the donkey have carved it up.'

'Don't be silly.'

'What do you expect me to say? You've seen me enough times cursing and sweating, keeping the grass cut with the motor scythe, the most exhausting machine ever devised.'

'It still isn't really a lawn.'

'It was improving.'

'Where else can we put her? The stable is full up with

junk and we couldn't possibly clear it out tonight. And if we put her in a field she might jump over the hedge and be lost.'

'I suppose it never occurred to you that you could have put the contraption in a field?'

'Oh yes,' said Jeannie softly, 'I thought of that, but you see, she would be lonely. By having her on the lawn I can keep a watch on her through the bedroom window.'

'All night?'

'Every now and then I could look out and see she's all right.'

'Are you sure you wouldn't like me to carry out an armchair? You could sit beside her under an umbrella.'

'What a good idea!' she said laughing.

There was a jerk as the Land Rover went through the stream that crosses the entrance to Minack, the stream we call Monty's Leap. It was here, when at last we had arrived at Minack, that on a magical moonlight night Monty had nosed his way puzzlingly down the lane; and on reaching the stream had ignored my readiness to lift him over and, instead, had leapt majestically across. It was here, too, beside this stream that he was buried.

'Hell,' I said, 'it's started to pour.'

I drew up outside the cottage and as I did so I saw the rain dancing on the bonnet; and when I switched off the engine I could hear the wind sweeping through the elm trees.

'It's going to be a dirty old night.'

'What a beginning for her.'

'She's got to get used to it sometime. And, anyhow, didn't she come from Ireland?'

'That doesn't mean she *enjoys* rough weather.'

'Nor do we. And we are about to be soaked trying to lure a donkey from the back of a Land Rover towards a contraption outside our bedroom window, and keeping it from running away.'

'I'm ready.'

The lawn has a steep slope, the size of half a tennis court, and a section of the bottom end merged with the parking space for cars. I proceeded to back the Land Rover to this spot so that when the rear was unlatched the well of the Land Rover was level, within a yard or two, of the lawn. Hence Penny had only to jump this short distance to be on firm ground. Unfortunately her bottom faced the wrong way.

'Come on, Penny,' I said, gently pulling the rope of the halter, 'turn round.'

She stayed staring across the front seats at the windscreen.

'Do *please* turn round.'

I pulled again, firmly this time. It was like pulling a tree trunk.

'For heaven's sake, Penny, TURN ROUND.'

No response.

'I'll get a carrot,' said Jeannie, running indoors and returning with a handful.

'Look Penny,' I said, tugging at her again and holding a carrot like a flag, 'look what I've got.'

There was an imperceptible movement of her head, an intimation that she was giving me a sideways glance, no immediate surrender to greed but one sensed a thought was passing through her mind; when did I last have one of these delectable things?

I pushed the carrot up to her face, then cunningly traced it along the side of the canvas hood so that she had to turn her head to watch it. I knew victory was near. The ancient carrot trick was about to work. I stood at the open end of the Land Rover and waited.

She did a neat turn. The well of the Land Rover is only four feet by three, a small space for a donkey in foal, but she manoeuvred herself with the ease of a large dog. Her bottom to the driving seat, her face thrust forward, peering into the rain and growing darkness, she now expected her reward.

'I'll let her have a nibble,' I said, 'just to whet her appetite. Then I'll do the trick again to get her out.'

Her idea of a nibble was to grab the carrot from my hand. A huge mouth, then crunch, crunch, crunch. It was a succulent sound, the forerunner of many, many such crunches. Here was enjoyment of high degree, the luscious favourite dish of a gourmet, the wild abandon of someone who had forgotten good manners in the pursuit of exquisite flavours. I felt, as I listened, my own mouth watering, and I thought of my supper, and I cursed the rain. Penny might be enjoying herself but it was time we reached the comfort of the cottage.

'Here you are,' I said, dangling another carrot invitingly, as I stood on the lawn three yards from the crunch. 'Here you are,' I said again.

I have learnt now that you do not eat a carrot in the way you eat a handful of hay or a slice of bread. These are ordinary things. A carrot requires respect, and after the crunch there follows the lick. The purpose of the lick is to recapture the original delight, an attempt to linger the pleasure, mirrored by an indulgent look in the eyes of the licker. The licker prefers to lick a hand, or a stone if it is handy, but it can be perfectly satisfied by its own solid looking mouth. In any case, the observer, the provider of the carrot, must be patient.

'Look, look,' I said, backing away up the slope, 'another carrot!'

I felt the rain filtering between my neck and the collar of my shirt, while Jeannie, scarf over her head, was clutching the rest of the carrots, allowing me to conduct the campaign on my own. Both of us were growing impatient.

Lick, lick; like a cat after a capture.

'Come on, Penny,' I said, 'jump out into your new home.'

She did not jump, she scrambled; and in one awful moment three of her legs were on the ground while the other was left sprawling in the Land Rover.

'Look out, she'll break her leg,' cried Jeannie.

'I'm doing my best!'

I was holding the halter, unsure whether to let it lie loose so that she could make her own recovery, or to pull it tight and so attempt to pull her with it. And I was angry with myself. I was angry that we should have been so foolish as to bring her home in such conditions of rain and darkness and ignorance. We should have gone back for her in the morning, or at any rate stopped at the farm at the top and asked Jack Cochram, the farmer, to come down and help us. It had been laziness on my part, or a vain wish to prove my independence, and Penny was paying for it.

But, as it happened, in this instant of my panic I had over-dramatised the situation. My habit of seeing disaster before it has occurred danced me to a conclusion which was quite invalid. Penny, realising her predicament, paused a few seconds to gain balance on the three legs already on the ground, then leapt forward bringing the fourth one clear.

'Our first lesson,' I said, mockingly serious, 'let her look after herself.'

For Jeannie, however, this was not a lesson that was easy to accept as I learnt during the course of the night. A donkey in the darkness of a strange place, standing in driving rain and a gale, was certain to excite her pity.

We tied Penny to the contraption on the lawn, fed her with a pound of carrots, three apples and half a loaf of home-made bread, and put a pail of water beside her. The adventure, as far as I was concerned, was over for the time being. I wanted my own supper, and a good night's sleep.

But Jeannie had no such intention. Twice during supper she dashed outside with a torch; and when we went to bed, no sooner had I turned out the light than she was at the window gleaming the torch through the rain at the bedraggled donkey ten yards away on the lawn.

'Poor thing,' she murmured.

'Hell to it,' I replied, 'I want to go to sleep.'

I awoke soon after dawn and I lay there listening to the dawn chorus, sleepily attempting to identify the many songs. The storm had passed and it was still again; and through the window I could see the crescent of the sun climbing behind the Lizard. It was a heavenly morning, and for a brief moment I believed I possessed no cares. Then suddenly I realised why I had woken so early.

There, just outside the bedroom window, was a donkey. A responsibility. I had waited for years for a holiday and I had sacrificed it to a four-legged creature which would be useless for any practical purpose. There would be nothing for it to do except mooch about demanding attention. And soon there would be the foal. Two donkeys mooching about.

They would live for years and years; and every day I would be waking up, half worrying what to do with them. Should they be in this meadow or that? Have they got enough water? We had burdened ourselves with two large permanent pets, remote in manner but utterly dependent upon us. I had been rushed into making a purchase that any cool period of thinking would have made me check, see reason, and halt from making. On this lovely, fresh early morning I was angry with myself.

And then I found myself wondering why I was vexed. True I had made an unreasonable, over-excited gesture, but it was a gesture which tied me even more closely to Minack; and Minack was a home neither of us would ever want to leave. So why was there a demon inside me who resented another anchor?

I lay thinking and was unable to answer. There was just this vague, tenuous sense of distress that I had committed myself. Perhaps I had discovered for myself the reason why so many are scared of the affection of animals. They do not want to be tied. They do not want anchors. Their lives are complicated enough without having to worry about a creature on four legs.

I was fully awake by now. I also found that a curiosity was already replacing my negative thoughts. How was she? What was she doing?

I got out of bed and looked out of the window.

Penny was happily eating the lawn I hadn't cut for a month.

7

Penny was black, and this had disappointed me from the first moment I saw her. Only the bottom half of her nose, the rims round her eyes, and a rotund girth were white or a light grey. I felt as I did when, years ago, I went to Tahiti and found the sands which edged the lagoons were black. In both cases my preconceived ideas had been affronted; sands of the South Seas should be white, coat of a donkey should be grey.

We were later to be told by a horsey gentleman who came to inspect her that he considered her to be of Arabian donkey stock.

'Look at the way she holds her head,' he said, 'she has the nobility of a thoroughbred.' Then he added, 'I've got a fancy she was bred for racing.'

We were impressed.

Neither Jeannie nor I understand the language of horsey people. We listen but cannot match it. Jeannie, when she was at the Savoy, listened a great deal to English, French and Irish talk about horses; jockeys, trainers and owners gave her advice, and once she won £50 on the Derby. Usually it was talk that was painfully forgotten.

Even to our eyes, however, Penny was a beautiful animal. Her head, when she was alerted by some noise or by some sight she did not understand, was elegantly intelligent with eyes sharp on the look-out and her large ears pointing inquisitively towards the mystery. After Penny came into our life we were never able to look at a horse without thinking how funny its ears looked.

On this particular morning, her first morning at Minack, Penny could not possibly have earned flattery from anyone.

We had moved her after breakfast from the lawn she had close cropped during the night to the stable meadow, so called because an ancient cowhouse and stable border one end of it. Here in early Spring, stretching towards the sea and in close view of the cottage, a variety of daffodil called Oliver Cromwell flowers profusely, defying the experts by doing so year after year without at any time receiving special attention. The bulbs have been in the ground for so long that I cannot find a person in the parish who can remember when they were planted.

A gentle slope falls to the end opposite the stables, then a stone hedge, and on the other side of it the big field which was our special pride when we first came to Minack. It was wasteland, covered in gorse and brambles, and gradually we brought it into cultivation until one year we grew four tons of potatoes. The field is called the cemetery field because in olden days dead cattle were buried at the bottom of it; and here at this point the field is poised above the cliff, the cliff which is cut into small meadows that fall steeply to the rocks and the sea of Mount's Bay.

On one side of the stable meadow is a finger of land which is the watercourse of the stream; lush in spring and summer with wild parsley, mint and watercress, it is in winter a haven for snipe. We do not allow anyone to shoot them.

On the other side is the path which leads down from the cottage to the cemetery field and the cliff. A low stone hedge divides it from the stable meadow, and it is a path which was in due course to give endless excitement to the donkeys.

Whenever they were in the stable meadow, and this was often, they would keep a watch as to who was passing by; and as soon as they caught sight of one of us they would race across the grass, then prance parallel to the hedge as we walked down the path until they reached the gap at the end where we had put a wooden fence.

Then, if we continued to walk on towards the cliff, there would be snorts and bellows, such a hullabaloo that we would be forced to turn back to talk to them. Often, in fact, we found it simpler to avoid the path and go across a field out of sight when we wanted to go down to the sea.

Here was Penny seeing the meadow for the first time and when I unfastened the halter, letting her be free, she looked around her for a moment, placidly without fear; and then began ravenously to eat the grass at her feet.

'That is the Dr Green Roy Teague talked about,' I murmured.

'We must get the vet as well,' said Jeannie.

There were bare patches on Penny, like moth-eaten patches on a discarded fur, and her coat was dull, like old silver waiting to be polished.

'No wonder she might have gone to the knacker's yard after the foal is born,' I said, 'she's scraggy, despite the foal.'

'I'll go and phone the vet straightaway.'

We had no telephone at the cottage, sure that by being without one we were spared complications that we could gladly do without. Thus, when we wanted to telephone, we either went to a call box two miles away or, when it was particularly urgent, asked permission to use the phone of our neighbour, Jack Cochram.

The vet was a Scotsman whom we had known for many years. A shy, polite man, he had the combined gifts of compassion and zeal which knighted his technical experience with a special quality. He was ready to make his skill available at any hour, there was never any suggestion that one might be wasting his time; and this attitude, together with that of his staff, induced many people to wish they were an animal instead of a human being.

The treatment he prescribed was simple if unpleasant. We had to rub her coat every other day for a fortnight with a delousing powder.

'Do this,' he grinned, 'and let her eat as much grass as she wants. Then you'll find she'll be as right as rain when His Nibs arrives.'

He was always to call the foal 'His Nibs'.

'And when can we expect him?'

'In about three weeks. You'll go out into the field one day and find him beside her.'

'It seems very casual.'

'She'll prefer it that way.'

During the following fortnight we conscientiously carried out our instructions, helped by Penny who displayed no objection to the smelly powder with which we dusted her; and at the fortnight's end a stubble of hair had begun to cover the bare patches. But her coat was still dull, and her feet were awful. We were, in fact, filled with embarrassment when anyone asked to see her.

Her feet, particularly the two front ones, had the shape of Dutch clogs; and they were so long that she gave the impression that she walked on her heels. The cause of this was that the hooves of a donkey grow fast if they are not subjected to the wear of a hard surface; and so a donkey which does nothing else but graze all day requires a regular pedicure, performed by a blacksmith with a large file, a pair of clippers, and a strong arm with which to check any protest that the donkey concerned might try to make. It was the fear of this protest, and the fierce struggle that might ensue, which decided us to postpone Penny's pedicure until after the foal was born.

Penny, meanwhile, was oblivious there was anything in her appearance of which to be ashamed. It was clear by her gentle manner that she was exceedingly content. Here was grass galore, titbits which included carrots, apples, currant cakes and home-made bread, and a pair of humans who fussed over her as if she were a Queen. There was also a cat.

Lama's attitude was one of benign approval from her first sight of Penny. One might have expected upright fur and an arched back, a mood of anger or terror, when Penny like a moving mountain advanced towards her, a black cat so small that some people still mistook her for a kitten. Not a bit of it. There was not a quiver of a whisker nor a twitch of the tail. She was serenely confident that Penny threatened no harm.

This belief of Lama that nothing, not even a motor car, possessed any evil intentions towards her, frequently caused us alarm. How was it possible that the character of a cat could so change? Only three years before she was wild, and now nothing scared her. If a car came down the lane she lay in the middle until the car had to stop. If a dog lunged from a lead and barked insults, she complacently stared back, a Gandhi policy of non-violence. If a cat hater tried to avoid her, she pursued him with purrs. Once I saw a fox cub taking a look at her from a few yards off as she lay, a miniature Trafalgar lion, in the grass. When she became aware of his attention she got up, stretched and walked peacefully towards him. What does one do with a cat so trusting?

Soothing as it is to watch a creature so happy in its surroundings, there are some moments when the onlooker is scared stiff by its amiable antics. Penny was one day in the middle of the stable meadow munching away at the grass when I saw from the window the silky black figure of

Lama advancing towards her. It was a deliberate, thoughtful advance because the grass was cat high, not high enough to advance in secret, not short enough to walk briskly through; indeed the grass was at that particular stage of growth when an intuitive, experienced cat leaps at one moment, then crawls at another. These alternate gestures brought her in due course to Penny's hind legs. They were powerful legs. They looked so powerful to me that, despite the nonchalant contentment Penny so apparently displayed, I quickly skirted them whenever I was having the fun of making a fuss of her. I respected the potential kick. I was not going to risk a sudden outburst of unreasonable, donkey temper. But Lama!

I watched her reach Penny, then frantically I called out to Jeannie. Lama, at that particular moment, was reaching a peak of her amiable confidence. And when Jeannie joined me I pointed to what was happening.

Lama was gently rubbing her head against one of Penny's hind legs; the loving, the embracing, the idiotic gesture of an idealist who had never been shocked into realism.

We held our breath as Penny continued to munch. Rub, rub, rub. First the head and the ears, then the cheek and the chin, even from a distance we could sense the ecstasy that Lama was enjoying.

'Shall I shout a warning?'

'Better not,' said Jeannie, 'or Penny might be startled into realising what is happening.'

But Penny knew all the time who was there, and she didn't care. We saw her glance round, observe Lama for a second, then back again to her munching. And Lama continued her display of affection until suddenly she heard a rustle in the grass a little way off. Penny's hind leg was forgotten. A mouse was on the move. A more important task lay ahead than displaying her trust in a donkey.

We never tethered Penny again after her first night at Minack. We also learnt that it was even safe to take her for

walks without a halter; and she would solemnly walk up
the lane with us when we fetched the milk from the farm,
requiring watchfulness on our part only when she passed
a flower bed. Flowers, especially roses, had an irresistible
attraction for her.

The third week went by without any hint of the foal
and, as the news had now circulated that we possessed
a donkey which was expecting, we were subjected to
an endless number of solicitous inquiries: 'Any news
yet?'

In the middle of the fourth week we had taken Penny
for a stroll before breakfast along one of the paths, and
on returning to the cottage had put her in a small meadow
near by. We then went in for our breakfast.

An hour or so later Jeannie went outside while I was
at my desk writing a letter. Suddenly I heard her excited
voice calling me. I dashed out of the door murmuring to
myself: 'It's arrived!'

I nearly trod on Lama on the way, came face to face
with a hissing Boris waddling up the path, and then in
amazement saw why it was that Jeannie was calling
for me.

A huge horse was standing in the small meadow with
the donkey beside it.

'Good God,' I said, 'where has it come from?'

'Not the faintest idea.'

Our reaction was a mixture of merriment, irritation
and concern. It was absurdly incongruous standing there,
a giant of a horse, a chestnut, and it glared at us; while
we in the meantime were smiling to ourselves at its funny
little ears.

'What is it?' I asked cautiously. 'Male or female?'

'A mare.'

'I'll dash up to the farm. Jack will know where she
comes from.'

In due course the owner arrived, a very old man with
watery eyes and a squeaky voice and no hat covering his

bald head. I recognised him as a new arrival to the district, and owner of the cottages in one of which Jane Wyllie the young girl who used to work for us, once lived with her mother.

The mare took no notice of him except to edge away when he approached.

'Judy, Judy,' he coaxed on a high pitched note.

The mare replied by dashing through a gap in the hedge which surrounded the meadow. She was out on her own now and into another. The old man was already out of breath but he bravely followed her.

'Judy, Judy.'

When the mare ignored him again, he turned to me.

'Bring the donkey out. It will quieten her down if she has the donkey with her.'

'Hell, I won't,' I said, 'that donkey is going to foal any time, any *moment*. I'm not going to bring her out within kicking distance of *your* monster.'

It was perhaps the harshness of this sentence that inspired the mare to take the violent action which now took place. She ignored the old man, thundered past him, then over a hedge and into the stable meadow. Over another hedge which I had thought unjumpable and then a dash down the lane. To my horror Jeannie was in her way. As soon as she had sensed there was going to be more trouble than we had expected, she had hastened to look for Lama. There she was, without having found Lama, bang in the way of the mare.

As if it were a circus trick, the mare jumped over her. And a few minutes later we watched the back of the old man panting up the lane, a galloping mare far far ahead and out of sight.

He caught her, we heard later, three miles away.

On the following Monday Jeannie and I and her mother, who was staying with us, went out for the day. When we returned to Minack, we met Jack Cochram who had been digging potatoes in his cliff which lies beyond the cottage. He had to pass the field in which we had left Penny.

He grinned when he saw us, a gay, amused grin.

'It's arrived!' he said happily. 'It's waiting for you!'

I have never gone down the lane so fast.

8

They were standing in the big field below the stable meadow, and beyond them the sun glinted on a still sea, disturbed only by the Stevenson fishing fleet out of Newlyn, their engines thumping, sailing like an Armada to distant fishing grounds.

Penny paused in her munching, strands of grass hanging out of her mouth, a proud mother no doubt, but still looking careworn, bare patches still on her back and her coat dull in the sunlight. The toy donkey huddled close to her, looking up at us inquisitively but without fear.

'It's so pretty I can't believe it's true!' laughed Jeannie. 'To think it might have gone to a circus!'

'Oh, Penny, you're a clever girl!'

We heard later from Jack Cochram that he had passed through the field at half-past eleven with his little girl, Janet, and Penny was on her own. There was a cloudburst shortly afterwards which continued for half an hour; and he came back across the field with a load of potatoes at half-past twelve. He looked towards Penny, and there was the foal.

'Look out,' I said, 'it's wobbling.'

It wobbled, lost its balance and collapsed on the grass. A ridiculous sight. All legs and fluffy brown coat, huge ears like old-fashioned motoring gloves, a tail like a fly whisk. I saw a comic eye, staring at me in surprise, and I had a feeling which made me smile, that it was furious. The indignity and the stupidity, just as it was introducing itself! It struggled, tiny hooves trying to get a grip on the grass, then a lurch, and it was upright again.

'What do you think it is?' I asked. 'Boy or girl?'

'Shall we find out?'

'Well,' I said cautiously, 'it's a bit of a risk, isn't it? We haven't had any experience of this kind of thing.'

The little toy donkey now moved unsteadily under Penny who lifted her head from the grass and waited patiently while it had a drink of milk. The legs were like four matchsticks propping a matchbox.

'I think it would be wiser,' I went on, 'if we asked Jack Cochram to investigate. Foals and calves are his business after all.'

'Seems a funny thing to have to ask him to do.'

'Might be funnier if we tried to find out ourselves.'

'I think you're a coward!'

'You said the other day if it were a girl you'd like to call her Marigold. You never mentioned what you'd call it if it were a boy.'

'Yes, I did,' said Jeannie, 'I thought we might call him Fred.'

Marigold or Fred. I looked at the unchristened creature who was now gazing thoughtfully back at me. Its nose was white like its mother's, and I noticed for the first time it had eye-lashes which were absurdly long. As I watched it took a few uncertain steps towards me, pushed its head forward, and gently nuzzled its nose in my hand. A sweet moment of trust.

'I think we had better get them up to the stables,' I said, 'the hay is spread on the floor.'

'Shall I carry the foal or will you?'

Jeannie was always so firm and yet so gentle when handling birds or animals. When she was a child she had wanted to be a vet, she had the patience and the quiet courage and the intuition to have made a successful one.

'You, of course,' I said, 'if it's not too heavy.'

Too heavy! She picked up Marigold or Fred as easily as if it had been an Alsatian puppy, holding it in her arms with its head drooping over her shoulder, and off we went across the field, then up the path to the stables. It was a gay procession. Jeannie leading the way murmuring sweet nothings to the foal, Penny in the middle snatching at succulent grasses as she passed them, exuding pride in her achievement, supremely confident that Jeannie ahead of her was taking her foal to safety. Here was her home. Nothing to fear now. Here at last was the foal she had carried with her on her journeys from Ireland, there in front of her, on the way to a warm stable, and time lay ahead together.

As for myself, as I walked up the path behind them, I was pondering on the value of the moment. Had we ignored the call of the telegram, had we taken the night train to London, we would have returned to Minack with memories of many faces, lunches in hot restaurants, late nights and thirsty mornings, packed tubes and rushing taxis, a vast spending of money, much noise, and yet a feeling of satisfaction that we had at last pushed ourselves again into the circle of sophisticated pleasure; and it was over. Instead we possessed two donkeys; and the magic of this moment.

It is a sickness of this mid-twentieth century that the basic virtues are publicised as dull. The arbiters of this age, finding it profitable to destroy, decree from the heights that love and trust and loyalty are suspect qualities; and to sneer and be vicious, to attack anyone or any cause which possesses roots, to laugh at those who cannot defend themselves, are the aims to pursue. Their ideas permeate those who only look but do not think. Jokes and debating points, however unfair, are hailed as fine entertainment. Truth, by this means, becomes unfashionable, and its value is measured only by the extent it can be twisted. And yet nothing has changed since the beginning. Truth is the only weapon that can give the soul its freedom.

As we reached the stables I had a sudden sense of great happiness, foolish, childish, spontaneous like the way I felt when my parents visited me at school. Free from dissection. Unexplainable by logic. Here were these two animals which were useless from a material point of view, destined to add chains to our life, and yet reflecting the truth that at this instant sent my heart soaring.

'Do you realise, Jeannie,' I said, after we had put them safely in the stable and were leaning over the stable door watching them, 'that people would laugh at us for being sentimental idiots?'

'Of course I do. Some would also be angry.'

'Why?'

'They are afraid.'

'Of what?'

'Of facing up to the fact they are incapable of loving anything or anyone except themselves.'

Guerrilla warfare continues ceaselessly between those who love animals and those who believe the loving is grossly overdone. Animals, in the view of some people, can contribute nothing to the brittle future of our computer civilisation, and therefore to love them or to care for them is a decadent act. Other people consider that in a world in which individualism is a declining status, an animal reflects their own wish to be free. These people also love an animal for its loyalty. They sometimes feel that their fellow human beings are so absorbed by their self survival that loyalty is considered a liability in the pursuit of material ambition. Animals, on the other hand, can bestow dependable affection and loyalty on all those who wish to receive it.

'It's odd in any case,' I said, 'that whenever one uses the word sentimental it sounds like an insult. Sentimental, before it became a coin of the sophisticated, described a virtue.'

'In what way?'

'It described kindness.'

'Surely in excess?'

'Only later, in the Victorian age. In those days people were nauseating in the way they fussed over animals, and this was reflected in those awful pictures we all know. Such an over-flow of sickly superficiality became a middle-class curse to avoid. Animal haters like to keep alive the idea that Victorian sentiment is synonymous with animal loving. It eases their consciences.'

'Anyhow, I'm sentimental,' said Jeannie, 'and I see no reason why I should be ashamed of it. I only wish human beings were as giving as animals.'

'Don't be so cynical!'

'Well you know what I mean. Human beings can be so petty and mean and envious. You can't say they are progressing in themselves as fast as the new machines they're producing.'

'That's true.'

'One can rely on animals to give kindness when one needs it most.'

'One has naturalness from animals and one is inclined to expect the same from human beings.'

'And by that you mean we expect too much?'

'Yes. Animals do not have income tax, status symbols, bosses breathing down their necks.'

Penny came and pushed her nose at us over the door and below her, so that we had to lean over and stretch out an arm to touch it, was the absurd little foal.

'Anyhow,' I said, 'I'm now very glad we've given a home to these two. They will amuse us, annoy us in a

humorous way, trust us, and give others a great deal of
pleasure.'

'Silly things,' said Jeannie, smiling.

'And so let's be practical. Let's find Jack, and ask him
to discover whether we have Marigold or Fred.'

Jack Cochram, dark with wiry good looks, looked like a
Cornishman but was born a Londoner. He was evacuated
to Cornwall during the war, and has remained here ever
since. His farm has fields spread round Minack, and he
and his partner Walter Grose were neighbours who were
always ready to help. Walter lived at St Buryan and came
to the farm every day. Jack and his wife lived with their
children Susan and Janet in the farmhouse at the top of
Minack lane, an old stone-built farmhouse with windows
facing across the fields towards Mount's Bay.

After a while in the stable Penny had made it quite
plain that she wanted to move, and so we had taken her,
Jeannie carrying the foal again, to the little three-cornered
meadow where she had had her encounter with the mare.
It was close to the cottage and we could keep an eye on
them both.

An hour later Jack Cochram arrived, and unfortunately
I had been called away. Jeannie therefore led Jack to
the meadow and showed him the foal on the other side
of the barrier I had erected at the entrance. Jeannie
said afterwards that as they stood there, Penny stared
suspiciously at them. This was the first time a stranger
had seen her foal, and she was on guard. It would have
been wiser, therefore, had they waited, allowing Penny
to become accustomed to Jack; or if Jeannie had fetched
her a handful of carrots to bribe her into being quiet. But
Jeannie had been lulled by Penny's previous serenity, her
placid nature, and she failed to understand that Penny
might believe her foal was about to be stolen. Jack, in
his kindness, jumped over the barrier, picked up the foal,
and immediately faced pandemonium.

Jeannie was terrified. She saw Penny rear up, bare her

teeth, then advance on her hind legs towards Jack while pawing the air like an enraged boxer with her front legs. Jack quickly put the foal to the ground, but by this time Penny was in such a temper that she failed to see it, and she knocked it flat as she went for Jack. When she reached him she was screaming like a hyena, and he was standing with his back to a broken-down wall in a corner of the meadow. He put up an arm above his head as she attacked him, trying to punch his way clear; and then, seizing a split second, and also swearing I am sure never to investigate the sex of a donkey again, he jumped over the barrier to safety.

Jeannie, meanwhile, was in the meadow herself, kneeling beside the foal which was lying on its side, eyes shut, tongue out and breathing in gasps. She knelt there stroking its head, Penny somewhere behind her calm again, and thought it was dying. Then she heard Jack cheerfully call to her, unperturbed by his experience: 'It's a girl!'

She told me later that Marigold, at this exact moment, opened an eye and flickered an eyelash. Jeannie said it looked so bewitching that she bent down and kissed it at which Marigold gave a deep sigh. Then a few minutes later she struggled to her feet and sturdily went over to Penny who licked her face, then waited as she had a drink of milk. When Jeannie left them they were standing together; and they may well have been laughing together. They had reason to do so.

When our friend, the vet, arrived early in the afternoon, and after we had toasted the health and happiness of Marigold, we learnt that Jack had made a mistake.

Marigold was Fred.

9

Jeannie's mother was staying with us when Fred was born, and she was a participant in his first escapade. She it was who had connived with Jeannie to defeat my then anti-cat attitude by introducing Monty into our London household when he was a kitten; and now the happiness that Monty gave us, first in London and then at Minack, was to be repaid in part in the few months to come by Fred. Fred captured her heart from the first moment she saw him; and when she left Minack to return to her home, she waited expectantly for our regular reports on his activities.

He was inquisitive, cheeky, endearing, from the beginning; and we soon discovered he had a sense of humour which he displayed outrageously whenever his antics had embroiled him in trouble. A disarming sense of humour; a device to secure quick forgiveness, a comic turn of tossing his head and putting back his floppy ears, then grinning at us, prancing meanwhile, giving us the message: 'I know I've been naughty, but isn't it FUN?'

He was a week old when he had this first escapade, a diversion, a mischievous exploration into tasting foal-like independence. Perhaps his idea was to prove to us that he could now walk without wobbling, that he was a sturdy baby donkey who could dispense with the indignity of being carried from one place to another. If this was so it was a gesture that was over-ambitious; and though the result caused us much laughter, Penny on the other hand was distraught with alarm at her son's idiotic bravado.

I had guarded the open side of the little yard in front of the stables, the side which joined the space in front of the cottage, with a miscellaneous collection of wooden boxes, a couple of old planks, and a half-dozen trestles which during the daffodil season supported the bunching tables. It may have been a ramshackle barrier but I certainly thought it good enough to prevent any excursions by the donkeys, and in particular by Fred. I had omitted, however, to take into account that there was a gap between the legs of one of the trestles suitably large enough for an intelligent foal to skip through. Suitably large enough? It was the size of half the windscreen of a small car, and only after the escape had been made could I condemn myself for making a mistake.

The first to be startled by what had happened was Jeannie's mother who was sitting on the white seat beside the verbena bush reading a newspaper. She was absorbed by some story, when suddenly the paper was bashed in her face.

'Good heavens,' she said, 'Fred! You cheeky thing!'

She explained afterwards that Fred appeared as surprised as herself by what he had done, though he quickly recovered himself, danced a little fandango, then set off like a miniature Derby runner down the lane in the direction of Monty's Leap. Meanwhile there had developed such a commotion in the yard behind the barrier, where Penny was snorting, whinnying and driving herself like a bulldozer at the trestles, that Jeannie and

I, who were in the cottage, rushed out to see what was happening.

We were in time to see Fred waver on his course, appear to stumble, then fall headlong into a flower bed.

'My geraniums!' cried Jeannie. The reflex cry of the gardener. Only flowers are hurt.

'Idiot!' I said.

Penny by now was frantic and as I dashed down the path I saw that the battering ram of her shoulders was just about to break a way clear for her. I left Jeannie to join her mother who had already reached Fred, and set about calming a rampaging donkey which looked prepared to eat me if I gave her a chance. A minute later Fred appeared in Jeannie's arms.

'Not a scratch as far as we can see, and thoroughly ashamed. Aren't you, Fred?'

He had grown so fast in a week that Jeannie could no longer carry him, as she did at the beginning, like a puppy. It was an effort to hold him, and his legs dangled close to the ground.

But he did not look ashamed to me. For here was the common denominator of all things young, the foolishness of enterprise before it is ready, the gusto of such foolishness, the bruised vanity after being found out, the genius of making the error appear inconsequential.

I moved a trestle, shielding it against Penny so that Jeannie could drop Fred in the gap without fear of attack from his hysterical mother. She *was* hysterical. She was like a wild beast in her distress.

'There you are, Penny,' said Jeannie, putting Fred to the ground and pushing him through the gap, 'nothing to worry about.'

I fancy that Fred expected a joyous reunion, a pat on the back for being so original as to attack a newspaper, to startle an elderly lady, to cause consternation within a week of his arrival. He was mistaken. Penny was as angry as she was relieved at being united with Fred; and she chased him. She chased him with her nose, chastising his buttocks with her soft white nose as if for the moment she considered it a whip. She chased him round the yard and into the stable, and out again. She was so furious that she wanted to teach him a lesson he would never forget. Not on our behalf, but on hers.

Fred's reaction seemed to be a relish that he was loved on both sides of the barrier, a wonderful hint that if the imponderables went well, he would for ever and for ever have the most wonderful life imaginable. And so when Penny's fury had subsided, when Fred found himself once again a young donkey freed from his mother's strictures, he smiled, putting his ears back and shaking his head. I am certain he was saying that he enjoyed every minute of his escape, the fall didn't matter, life was fun and mistakes didn't count so long as there were years ahead in which to correct them. I feel sure that when he came rushing up to my hand which I held out to him, nuzzling it with his nose, he was telling me what a hilarious time lay ahead of us.

'I have a feeling,' said Jeannie's mother later, 'that this donkey is going to be a nuisance!'

She did not mean, of course, this to be a reproach. Nor for that matter a warning. It was a gentle joke, said in a soft voice with just the trace of a Scottish accent. I realise in retrospect that her affection for Fred stemmed from something deeper than a superficial enchantment for a Disney-like creature. He was to her, in the last few months of her life, a link with the future. Her intuition made her aware that time was against her, and so she was glad to find in this absurd little donkey a bridge. Jeannie's uncle told Jeannie how a few weeks later he was with her mother waiting for a bus to take them from Gloucester Road to Hyde Park corner. They waited twenty minutes at the bus stop, not because there were no buses. Three went by; but Jeannie's mother went on talking, and the subject was Fred. The poor man cursed the donkey as he stood there, listening patiently. He did not know the secret.

Fred, at that very instant, running free on the Cornish cliffs, the skies and wild winds, sunny days and torrential rain, the sea lurching then calm, scents of the salt, wild grasses, pinks, meadow sweet, puzzling cries of gulls, woodpeckers laughing, badgers solidly plodding ageless paths, foxes alert, exultant chorus of the early morning, marsh warblers, summer larks, blackbirds trumpeting, wrens erupting; for all these Fred was the spokesman. These pleasures, enriched by the eyes and ears of centuries, projecting the kindness of permanence and security, dwelt there hopefully in her mind.

And there were the incidents of which she had been a witness at Minack. Visits at daffodil time and potato time, Jeannie coming into the packing shed with baskets of flowers in either hand, Jeannie in shorts under a blazing sun grubbing through the soil quicker than anyone as she picked up the potatoes. Glorious moments of anticipation when arriving for Christmas, carefully thought-out presents in gaily coloured paper awaiting disclosure, champagne on the day – shall we have the turkey for lunch or for dinner? Times of disaster when gales and salt spray cut the potato tops like a scimitar, leaving a barren harvest in their wake; and a terrible spring when a disease attacked the daffodils, spotting the petals with a brown mould, making them useless for market so that the compost heap grew higher and higher with thrown-away stems. She had been at Minack when Lama was first seen, a black spot in a meadow, and when Monty died. She had known Jane and Shelagh of *A Drake at the Door* when each had first arrived, Jane with the corn-coloured hair touching her shoulders, Shelagh with the shy smile, both with the gift of making us feel happy that they were with us. Funny times . . . she was in the cottage on Jeannie's birthday when, after a night of raging wind, I went out to find the cloches scattered across their field. I was fighting in the gale to save those which were left when suddenly I saw Jeannie, struggling towards me.

'A cup of tea with Glucose,' she shouted above the noise. I was grateful she had taken pity on me, and I seized the cup and took a gulp. It tasted like acid. 'Hell,' I shouted, 'have you poisoned me?' When I got back to the cottage her mother was waiting at the doorway. 'Look dear,' she said gently, 'you opened the tin of Epsom salts.' Quiet times, when there was the idleness of a deck chair in the wood, or a stroll to the cliff to watch the little fishing boats feathering for mackerel and the big ones on their way to and from Newlyn. Or just sitting on the white seat where Fred bashed the newspaper.

A month after she had returned to London, and Jeannie was with her, I took a pair of scissors and cut a small piece of Fred's mane and sent it to her tied with a pale blue ribbon. It was still in her handbag eight months later when she died.

'Whatever else he does in his life,' said Jeannie thoughtfully, 'Fred has justified his existence.'

10

Fred now faced a glorious summer of adulation. Nobody could resist him. Children and grown ups both uttered cries of delight as soon as they saw his gambolling fluffy figure, cameras were poised, small hands held out to stroke him, picnic baskets searched for sugar; and his response was to pander to his admirers in various fetching ways. Sometimes he would stand beside them soulfully staring into the distance as they stroked him, sometimes he would surprise a new admirer by a comical, harmless dance, sometimes he would show off his speed by sprinting across the meadow, sometimes he would hug close to Penny, but always sooner or later he would allow every admirer to fondle him.

Jeannie and I soon found that his presence was exceedingly helpful. When one writes about the place where one lives, it is to be expected that strangers will call. Seldom a day passed in the summer without someone arriving at Minack; and as we were so far off the beaten track it was a feat of exploration to have found us.

Visitors were of all ages and came from all parts of the country. The snag of these visits was that we were always caught by surprise. We would have to emerge from a greenhouse in which we had been tending tomatoes, and appear in the role of host and hostess with our hands and faces green with the juice of the leaves. Or we would be disturbed at some peak time when we were wanting to rush something into Penzance. One daffodil time a couple arrived as we were packing our flower boxes as fast as we could into the Land Rover so that we could catch the flower train to London. We also knew that we were far behind in our picking, and there was a whole meadow awaiting our urgent attention. I suggested to the couple that they might like to see such a beautiful sight, and off they went. When they returned, the woman in a lofty voice said: 'I would have thought you would have found time to pick those daffodils!' Jeannie had to stop me from braining her.

Once we had a visitor who looked up at the gull on the roof and asked: 'Is it plastic?' There was a man who arrived on a bicycle and, pointing to the pedometer on the front wheel, said: 'I've ridden three hundred and seventy miles to prove to my wife that you are not fictitious!' Another time we had a car load of people whose car got stuck at Monty's Leap, the low slung chassis was jammed on the bed of the stream; they were there for four hours. We have had strangers who have brought us presents. We frequently met people with whom afterwards we kept in touch; and at all times Jeannie and I found it a wonderfully rewarding experience that any of these people had taken the trouble to find their way to Minack.

Such visits, however, inevitably took time because we could not just say hello and goodbye. Tasks we were performing had to be suspended and, if they were tedious tasks like hand weeding the freesia beds, we often found it difficult to return to them. The nature of the visit was likely to have disturbed our sense of routine, and we were inclined to relax and await the possible arrival of another visitor.

Our usual procedure was first to show these visitors the gull on the roof, provided one of the gulls was there; but it was maddening how often Knocker, Squeaker or Peter would let us down, and would only sail into view after the visitors had disappeared up the lane. Boris, the drake, however, could always be relied upon. He enjoyed attention as long as no one tried to touch him. He squatted imperiously in the shade of the flower house or in the grass by the elms, eyeing the strangers, stretching his neck forward towards them, hissing gently at them if they seemed to be coming too close, hissing loudly if they did and at the same time raising the feathers on the top of his head as a cat will lift its fur in anger. Then he would rise majestically to his large yellow webbed feet and waddle away, waggling his olive green tail feathers in protest.

Lama's behaviour, as one might expect, was unpredictable. Sometimes she was in a sociable mood and she would appear jauntily with a hop, skip and miaow. At other times she would remain obstinately in her hiding places while we rushed round the usual sites bleating for her. At last the visitor would say: 'Don't bother to look any more. It doesn't matter. We didn't come specially to see her.' Then, of course, Lama in a trice would be with us.

There were many occasions, however, when people did come specially to see her. Her particular attraction was that she had been a wild cat; a cat who had spent extreme youth in the cold but now was conquered by comfort, an irresistible situation for cat admirers, a cat who had been tamed, a human victory over the feline species. Jeannie and I, on these occasions, would anxiously watch how she would behave because there was one thing she loathed and that was sugary flattery. Any visitor who tried to win her that way was beneath her contempt. Hence if someone began cooing at her in the manner so often adopted towards cats, Lama would stiffen in disgust. I have often seen her in the arms of a visitor who was cooing like mad, have seen the danger signal, then leapt forward and snatched her away a split second before harm was done.

The presence of the donkeys now produced a major diversion. Sometimes I had found a conversation difficult to sustain and I would stare out to sea, the visitor beside me, murmuring foolishly over and over again: 'Isn't it a glorious view?' There was now no fear of a faltering conversation, no cause for me to fill a silence with an inane remark. The shyest visitor was filled with rapturous excitement as soon as I said: 'Have you ever seen a baby donkey?'

I thereupon led the way to the meadow, and it was usually the stable meadow, where Penny and Fred were perusing the green grass around them.

'Penny! Fred!' I would call out authoritatively, as if it were the most natural thing in the world for them immediately to obey me.

'Penny! Fred!'

They would stare from afar and make no move.

'Come on, Penny!' I would shout again, wanting to prove to my visitors that I was in command. 'COME ON!'

I soon noticed, before he was even a month old, that Fred was usually the first to react. He could be in deep slumber, lying flat on the ground with Penny standing on guard beside him; but when I called he would wake up, raise his head in query, scramble to his feet, pause while looking in my direction, then advance towards me. First a walk, then a scamper.

'He's a very intelligent donkey,' I would then say proudly. A sop to the fact that Penny had ignored me.

But Penny at this time was still a sorry sight, the sores had gone but her coat was still thin. We had to excuse her appearance by repeating the story of how we had found her. We explained her elongated feet by telling how we had waited for Fred to be born before dealing with them, and that now we were waiting for the blacksmith. We chattered on with our excuses and then realised no one was listening. All anyone wanted to do was to fuss over Fred.

'Aren't his ears huge?'

'I love his nose.'

'Look at his feet! Like a ballet dancer's!'

'What eyelashes!'

'Does he hee-haw?'

I remember both his first hee-haw and his first buttercup. He was a week old when he decided to copy his grazing mother, putting his nose to the grass without quite knowing what was expected of him. He roamed beside her sniffing importantly this grass and that; and then suddenly he saw the buttercup. A moment later he came scampering towards me with the buttercup sticking out of the corner of his mouth like a cigarette, and written all over his ridiculous face was: 'Look what I've found!'

The first hee-haw was to occur one afternoon in the autumn when Jeannie and I were weeding the garden. There was no apparent reason to prompt it. They were not far away from us in the meadow, and every now and then we had turned to watch them contentedly mooching around. And then came the sound.

It was at first like someone's maiden attempt to extract a note from a saxophone. It was a gasping moan. It then wavered a little, began to gain strength and confidence, started to rise in the scale, and then suddenly blossomed into a frenzied hiccuping tenor-like crescendo.

'Heavens,' I said, 'what an excruciating noise!'

'Fred!' called out Jeannie, laughing. 'What on earth's the matter?'

At this moment we saw Penny lifting up her head to the sky. And out of her mouth came the unladylike noise which we had already learnt to expect. No bold brassy hee-haw from her. It was a wheezy groan which at intervals went into a falsetto. Here was a donkey, it seemed, who longed to hee-haw but couldn't. All she could do was to struggle out inhuman noises as her contribution to the duet. It was painful not only to listen to, but also to watch. This was donkey frustration. The terrible trumpet of her son had reawakened ambitions. She wanted to compete with him, but she hadn't a ghost of a chance.

Meanwhile, as the summer advanced, Penny had developed a role of her own towards the visitors. She was clearly, for instance, used to children and although it was Fred who received the initial caressing attention it was Penny, because she was full grown, who only could give them a ride. Ignored during the first ten minutes, she then became a Queen in importance, and she would patiently allow a child to be hoisted on her back, and a ride would begin.

But Jeannie and I soon found that her job was far easier, far less exhausting than ours. One of us had to lead Penny by a halter, and as she would not move without Fred, Fred had to be led along as well. I had bought him a smart halter of white webbing within a few days of his being born, and he never resented wearing it. He wore it as if it were a decoration, a criss-cross of white against his fluffy brown coat giving him an air of importance. One visitor said he reminded her of a small boy who was allowed to wear trousers when all his friends were still wearing shorts.

Up and down the meadow we walked and all the while we had to be on guard against accidents. We had a nightmarish fear that a child might fall off and so while one of us led the donkeys, the other walked alongside holding the rider. We spent hours that summer in this fashion.

There was no doubt, therefore, that the presence of the donkeys was a huge success. People who had come to see Jeannie and me went away happy because they had met Penny and Fred.

'The donkeys have *made* our day,' said two strangers who had driven specially from a distance to call on us.

And there were other occasions when I sauntered out of the cottage on seeing strangers draw up in a car, a bright smile on my face.

'May we,' an eager voice would ask from the car window, 'see the donkeys?'

11

An eloquent feature of the donkeys was their stare; and
we never succeeded in growing accustomed to it. It was
a weapon they used in morose moments of displeasure.
There they would stand side by side in a meadow stead-
fastly watching us, exuding disapproval, condemning us
for going about our business and not theirs.

The stare increased in its frequency after the summer
and the visitors had disappeared; for Fred, by this time,
expected attention like a precocious child film star who
believes that adulation goes on for ever. He missed the
applause, lumps of sugar, and posing for his picture. He
was a Prince without courtiers. He was at a loss as to how
to fill his day. So he would stare, and hope that we would
fill the gap.

'Why can't we go to another meadow?'

'I'd like a walk.'

'Oh dear, what *is* there to do?'

And when finally we relented, yielding to the influence
of the stare, and dropped whatever we were doing, and

decided to entertain him, Fred would look knowingly at Penny.

'Here they come, Mum. We've done it.'

Penny's stare was prompted by a more practical reason. True she enjoyed diversions but they were not an innocent necessity as they were for Fred. She was old enough in experience to be phlegmatic, her role as a donkey was understood; she had to be patient, enduring the contrariness of human beings, surprised by the affection she was now suddenly receiving, and yet prepared it might end with equal suddenness. She didn't have to be amused. All she had to remember was to have enough milk for Fred, and that the grass was losing its bite. Her stare was to induce us to change to another meadow or to take her for a walk, not for the exercise, but for the grasses and weeds of the hedgerows. A walk to her was like a stroll through a cafeteria.

It did not take much to amuse Fred. He liked, for instance, the simple game of being chased, although he and I developed together certain nuances that the ordinary beholder might not have noticed. There was the straightforward chase in which I ran round a meadow panting at his heels, Penny watching us with an air of condescension, and Fred cantering with the class of a potential racehorse; there was a variation in which I chased them both, aiming to separate them by corralling one or other in a corner. This caused huge excitement when my mission had succeeded with Penny in a corner and Fred the odd man out. He would nuzzle his nose into my back, then try to break through my outstretched arms, snorting, putting his head down with his ears flat, and giving the clear impression he was laughing uproariously.

He loved to be stalked. In a meadow where the grass was high I would go down on my hands and knees and move my way secretly towards him. Of course he knew I was coming. He would be standing a few yards off, ears pricked, his alert intelligent face watching the waving grass until, at the mutually agreed moment, I would make a mock dash at him; and he would make an equally mock galloping escape. This was repeated again and again until I, with my knees bruised and out of breath, called it a day.

I think, though, that our most hilarious game was that of the running flag. I would get over the hedge to the meadow or field he was in, then run along the other side holding a stick with a cloth attached high enough for him to see it. It baffled him. It maddened him. He would race along parallel to unseen me whinnying in excitement; and when, to titillate his puzzlement, I would stop, bring the stick down, so suddenly he saw nothing, nine times out of ten he would rend the air with hee-haws. Of course he knew all the while that it was a pretence; and when I jumped back over the hedge to join him he greeted me with the cavorting of an obviously happy donkey.

These were deliberate games. There were others which came by chance. Electricity had at last come to the cottage and on one occasion I saw a Board Inspector running across the field with a joyous Fred close behind him. The Inspector, I am sure, was glad when he reached the pole he had come to inspect, and could speedily climb out of reach.

It was a fact that Fred enjoyed the chase as much as being chased. He was fascinated, for instance, by Lama and Boris. As soon as he saw the little black cat he would put his head down, move towards her, struggling to free himself from the halter with which I was holding him. Or if Lama had entered the meadow in which he was roaming, his boredom would immediately vanish. Why is she here? How fast can she run? Let me see if I can catch her.

And yet I never saw any evidence that there was viciousness in his interest. Lama, because of her trust in all men and things, gave him plenty of opportunities to show the truth of his intent; and his intent seemed only to chase to play. It was the same with Boris. On one occasion Fred escaped from his halter, saw Boris a few yards from him and, head down close to white feathered tail, proceeded to chase Boris round the large static greenhouse in front of the cottage. The waddle and the hiss of Boris was distressing to behold and to hear, but I found myself watching without fear that Fred might do any harm. It was clear that Fred was only nudging him. Here is my nose, there your tail. Go a little faster, old drake.

The donkeys now spent much of their time in the field adjoining the cottage, and it was here that Fred had his first major fright. The field was so placed that the stare could be imposed upon us in a particularly effective fashion. It was a large field sloping downwards to the wood with a corner which was poised shoulder high above the tiny garden. Hence when the donkeys came to this corner, which was often, they looked down at us. They could even see into the cottage.

'The donkeys are wanting attention,' Jeannie would say as she sat in a chair by the fire, 'shall I deal with them or will you?'

There were other occasions when they chose to stand in the corner purely, I am sure, to emphasise the toughness of their lot. When there was a storm with rain beating down on the roof and the wind rattling the windows they would stand in view of our comfort. Two miserable donkeys who could easily have found shelter under a hedge. Two waifs. Fred with his fluffy coat bedraggled and flattened against his body like a small boy's hair after a bathe. Penny, years of storm suffering behind her, her now shiny black coat unaffected, passing on her experience to Fred.

'Put your head down, son. The rain will run off your nose.'

But the day that Fred had his fright was sunny and still, an October day of Indian summer and burnished colours, the scent of the sea touching the falling leaves, no sadness in the day. Fred, now a colt not a foal, was enjoying himself grazing beside Penny, nibbling the grass like a grown up, when under the barbed wire that closed the gap at the top of the field rushed a boxer.

Had Boris and Lama witnessed what followed no doubt they would have laughed to themselves . . . a taste of his own medicine . . . that is how *we* feel when he comes thundering after us. The difference, however, was that the boxer was savage. It chased Fred as if it were intent on the kill. It had the wild hysteria of a mad wolf. It ignored the galloping hooves. It tried to jump on Fred's back, teeth bared, its ugly face ablaze with primitive fury. And all the while Fred raced round and round the field bellowing his terror like a baby elephant pursued by a tiger.

I had arrived on the scene at the double to find Jeannie already there running after the dog with Penny trumpeting beside her; and a man walking unconcernedly across the field towards the cottage. The contrast between calm and chaos was startling.

'I have lost my way,' said the man when he saw me, 'can you direct me to Lamorna?'

His nonchalance astounded me. My temper was alight.

'Is that your dog?' I shouted back.

'Yes,' he smiled, 'he's having a good time.'

'GOOD TIME? What the hell are you saying? Look at that baby donkey, look at your dog!' I was incoherent with rage. I raised my arm and wanted to hit him. 'How dare you come through private property without a dog like that on a lead!'

'He doesn't like a lead.'

It was fortunate that at this precise moment I saw that the boxer had broken away from the chase, that Jeannie, after a moment's soothing of Fred, was hastening to my support. The sight restrained me.

'Get that dog, then get off my land!'

Even this was not the end of it. Indifferent to my anger, oblivious that Jeannie had now joined in the attack, he took the dog by the scruff of the neck and began to climb down into the garden from the point where the donkeys liked to stand.

'Not that way!'

I had visions of the dog breaking free, and indulging his stupidity by wringing the necks of Lama and Boris.

'But I want to get to Lamorna,' said the man plaintively, 'and surely I can go up that lane?'

'You can't, and that's that. You can go back to wherever you came from, and go quick!'

It always surprises me why so many dog owners are dull minded. They thrust the bad manners of their dogs upon the rest of us. They ignore the possibility of damage that dogs can inflict. They are deaf. I have known a dog which would bark for two hours on end, its owner close by insensitive to the people miles around who were cursing. I like dogs. I only blame their owners. I might even have liked the boxer.

The attachment between Penny and Fred was intense. If a gate was shut and Penny was one side of it, Fred the other, both would show signs of great distress. There was never any question of taking them out each on their own. In the meadows they were always within a few yards of each other; and when Fred lay down for a sleep, Penny would stand guard beside him.

Fred was always particularly perturbed by Penny's six-weekly pedicure. Along would come the blacksmith armed with a massive pair of cutters and a large file, and Penny would be ushered into the stables while Fred remained outside. He was certain something awful was happening to his mother, and this was not helped by the tantrums Penny sometimes displayed. On one side of the stable door the blacksmith was holding the leg of a plunging Penny; on the other, Fred was behaving as if he were never going to see her again.

These should have been signs enough to put Jeannie and me on our guard. The uncontrollable affection was a potential explosion. We only had to provide the opportunity, by testing it to breaking point, for a situation to arise in which someone was hurt. And this is exactly what happened.

We decided one evening to take the donkeys for a walk up the lane, and into a field which led through the top end of our wood. Jeannie, because she has always maintained a wondrous, innocent, totally trusting attitude towards the behaviour of all animals, was not only riding Penny but carrying Lama as well. She had done it a number of times before. She held the rope of the halter as a single-sided rein while a comfortable Lama sat snugly with her two front paws around Penny's mane. Lama enjoyed it, Penny displayed no objection while I, though appreciating the pleasant sight of cat, donkey and my pretty wife, also viewed the whole affair with a tolerant suspicion. It seemed to be asking for trouble. My weakness, however, was that I did not feel strongly enough about this to complain.

We were in the field and were on the way back, a pastoral scene. Jeannie in pink pants astride Penny, Lama beatific and merging into Penny's glossy coat. Fred and I a few yards ahead. Nothing untoward seemed about to happen. We were all enjoying ourselves. Jeannie was telling me that Lama was purring, Penny was pausing at intervals to snatch a mouthful of grass, Fred wearing his bright, white halter was taking a great interest in all around. Why this? What's that? In every glance one sensed the gay inquisitiveness of the very young.

Fred and I reached the open gateway of the field, then turned right down the sloping lane leading for the cottage. It was, on my part, a thoughtless mistake. I was so amused by the way Fred was enjoying himself, leading me by his halter instead of me leading him, that I never thought of waiting for Jeannie. The setting was too normal and peaceful for me to imagine that Penny might panic when Fred disappeared out of her sight.

Suddenly I heard Jeannie shout. Then I saw Penny come out of the field at the gallop, jump a ditch, and in an instant she was dashing towards me. Her head was down, she looked wild, and had she been by herself I would have jumped aside and let her race on. But to my horror Jeannie was still astride her, vainly trying to grip with her legs . . . for in her hands she held Lama.

She said afterwards that her only concern was to save Lama. Lama, she visioned, would be trampled on. Lama was the only one in danger, not herself. But for me who was standing there in her path, a flash of my life which seemed an eternity, her fall at speed to the granite based, jagged stone surface of the lane was inevitable. Lama, as far as I was concerned, could look after herself.

Jeannie was slipping to the side on my right. She was silent, no calling out for help.

'I'm going to the right,' I shouted.

My instinct was to try to catch her, cowboy fashion, taking her as she fell, leaving Penny to gallop on. I let Fred go and held out my arms.

I do not now think I had a chance to succeed. Penny was moving too fast, too heavy for me to check her, and indeed the very fact that I was standing there made her swerve as she reached me; and that was the moment when Jeannie fell.

My right hand seemed to clasp her for a brief instant, and then I was buffeted as Penny raced past me. The sound of the hooves disappeared. Incongruously I was aware of a lark singing. A rattle of a tractor came from a distance. All was normal again, quiet and peaceful and pastoral, as it had been five minutes before.

I knelt down beside Jeannie, quite still and eyes shut, and cupped her head in my hands.

12

Jeannie was unconscious for three or four minutes, and I was at a loss to know whether to stay with her or leave her and hurry for help. I took off my jersey and made it a pillow under her head. And I had just decided to rush up to the farm, when she opened her eyes.

'Where's Lama?' she murmured.

Hell, I said to myself, here I am frantic with worry and all she thinks of is Lama.

'Lama's all right,' I said soothingly, 'what about you?'

As it happened I hadn't a notion what had happened to Lama. I remembered that as Jeannie fell she flung Lama forward so that Lama flew past me like a small black football. Then she disappeared into the pandemonium of Penny's gallop.

The fact, however, that Jeannie had spoken sent bells ringing through me. The question of Lama could wait, so also the whereabouts of the donkeys.

'I had better get you to hospital.'

'No fear.'

'Come on, no argument, please.'

I was delighted, of course, that she did choose to argue. Here was the good sign. The bossy, if faint, contradiction. Her injury could not be serious.

I helped her to her feet and I walked with her leaning on me, slowly back to the cottage.

'Please don't take me to hospital.'

Her chin was cut and bleeding.

'All right,' I said, thankful for the alertness she was showing, 'we'll compromise. We'll see if we can find an off-duty doctor.'

We had reached Monty's Leap. A few yards further on there was a grass verge, just big enough for us to park the Land Rover sometimes during the daffodil season. It was opposite that section of the stables we used as a packing shed.

'Now look . . .' And I couldn't help smiling.

'Donkeys!' said Jeannie. And she too smiled.

Two shamefaced donkeys. Halters still harnessing their heads, the ropes dragging the ground. They stood there waiting patiently for us to come to them, Fred so close to Penny that they were touching.

'Wasn't really our fault, was it Mum?'

'Quiet, son.'

We saw no sign of Lama, and as it was growing late I decided I had to wait until we got back before I searched for her, and search I did when an hour and a half later we returned from the doctor. It was dark. Jeannie, with a bandaged chin and mild concussion, had gone to bed. And for the life of me I could not find Lama.

'Lama! Lama!'

Lama was usually an obedient cat, if it is possible to call any cat obedient. She obeyed because I would choose a moment to call her when I guessed she was in the mood to respond. If my guess was wrong, if my echoing voice reached her while she was on sentry duty beside a tuft of grass or a hole in the hedge, she of course ignored me.

Thus her reputation of being obedient depended on me; and a reliable occasion when our minds coincided was at night. She always came home to the comfort of the cottage, to a saucer of milk, to a Jeannie prepared plate of some delicacy, to a deep slumber on our bed. What, then, had happened to her?

I searched the customary hunting grounds, went into the wood flashing my torch, walked round the greenhouses, came back by a bank where for two or three days she had been picking off a family of mice one by one. Then down the track towards the sea, back again to the cottage and up the path to the well. No sign whatsoever, and I began to worry whether Penny in her mad gallop had kicked her; and Lama was lying injured and unable to move. If that were the case she would probably have dragged herself into the undergrowth near by where the accident occurred.

I had now been searching for over an hour, and I wasn't surprised when Jeannie opened a window and called out for news. Nor was I surprised that such was her anxiety she dressed and joined me. Nothing would stop her staying up all night whatever the doctor's orders unless Lama was found.

We had had, of course, these alarms before, and each one had a freshness, an original urgency, a sense that this particular one was at last going to justify our most terrible fears. From a gentle call to a cross one, from a cross call to an anxious one, from an anxious call to loud bleats at the top of our voices: 'Lama! Lama!' And when there was no response, no welcoming small shadow to light up the darkness, we wondered secretly in ourselves in what way the fox had caught her. Had the end been quick or had he carried her away to his earth?

Such foolish fancies vanished like childish nightmares as soon as Lama, having heard us all the time, displaying no remorse, confident of her charms to secure instant forgiveness, suddenly appeared at our feet.

'I've got her!' the favoured one would shout.

The pattern was the same on this occasion. The difference was in the location. The incident of the lane, her flight through the air as Jeannie was falling, her crash among Penny's galloping hooves, had deposited her into a new hunting ground. Never a wanderer far from home, circumstances had forced upon her the opportunity to explore a forbidden land; and when we found her, when my torch shone on her crouching figure, she was awaiting adventure on the edge of a track which Jeannie and I had known since we first came to Minack as a highroad for foxes.

The accident, understandably, had a salutary effect upon us. When next day we held an inquest we admitted we had been growing over-confident, and that the donkeys in future had to be treated with greater respect. We had been behaving towards Penny as if she were an amiable lady without any emotion, and towards Fred as if he were the equivalent of a cuddly puppy. An amateur's attitude. It was high time we imposed discipline upon ourselves in the way we dealt with them.

The first step I took was to ban them from the greenhouse field; and I do not now understand how I had allowed them there in the first place. Four large mobile greenhouses looking like aeroplane hangars were at the mercy of their kicks; and it was a miracle that the only near-damage they ever did was the result of a comical sortie by Fred. One of the mobiles was covering a crop of Christmas lettuce. One day we noticed a series of indentations in the soil and we quickly came to the conclusion that mice had been at work. No plants had been damaged. There were only these holes between the rows.

But Fred was the culprit. He had managed to squeeze through the partly open glass door, and later that day I discovered him making a tour of inspection within. Heaven knows why he did not step on the plants themselves.

The student had left us by the time of this incident and in his place we had a manager; and the object of such a high sounding title was to employ an expert who could steer us away from the confusion in which we were becoming increasingly enmeshed. We had been continuing to lose grip of the flower farm. In the old days when Jane and Shelagh had worked for us, and reliable Geoffrey who had left to go into the building trade, there were no outside commitments to disturb us. We all joined together in the volume of work to do, the slow, meticulous work of a flower farm which has to be done by hand because it cannot be mechanised; and we were, in a sense, all partners. We now looked back with nostalgia to their loyalty and enthusiasm as we struggled to find a way out of our problem. The slow, meticulous work still remained but there was little time to spend on it; and when such work is not regularly and carefully performed, the seasons begin to catch up on each other, crops are planted too late and weeds flourish. I had been seduced from the steady tempo of the past. I was now divided between a life controlled from the city and the life of the peasant which had made Jeannie and me so happy; and what I gained from the one, I lost in the sacrifice of the other. I sat at my desk when my hands should have been in the soil.

We had therefore decided that if we could find a manager, someone so experienced in horticulture that he would demand a high salary, he would take control of the flower farm while I continued with my other work. I would be spared the day-to-day problems and activities but at the same time have the satisfaction of knowing that the flower farm was going to flourish; and of course Jeannie would continue to help with the flowers while I would be there whenever I was needed. In the peak months of the daffodil season, for instance, we would both be happily rushing the flowers away to market as quickly as possible.

I had realised that the type of person we required would be difficult to find. I was warned in fact that the person did not exist; and so I was greatly impressed by the gesture of an applicant who made a special visit from the Channel Islands to see me. He was the only applicant I saw. Because he was so keen to start working at once I engaged him immediately. True enough I was, in any case, in a hurry. The programme of the flower farm had to be kept in motion and there was no time to lose; but I made the error of willing myself to believe he was the man who would suit us, instead of giving time for my head to decide.

He was charming, and had a special wish to live in Cornwall. He won my sympathy because he had been a prisoner of the Japanese. He showed me photographs of his three pretty children. A reference from the market garden where he had been employed for some years was excellent. He liked the cottage I was to rent specially for him. He said he would bring his car over from the Channel Islands and so I took it for granted that he could drive; and of course a driving licence was essential if Jeannie and I were to be spared the time consuming task of driving the Land Rover whenever a routine journey was necessary. But the day after I had given him his written contract, and I had suggested he collected some things in Penzance, he looked at me with a smile. 'Oh, I don't drive myself,' he said disarmingly, 'my wife does all the driving in our family.'

It was an ominous beginning to our plans for rescuing the flower farm.

13

When the foghorns of passing boats hooted in Mount's
Bay, the donkeys answered them. They were half believing, I suppose, that somewhere out in the fog were
other donkeys. Penny would thrust her head forward
and upward and emit the excruciating warble which was
her speciality, a wailing saw, a falsetto groan. Fred, still so
small that the top of his fluffy back was only just above the
level of Penny's rotund belly, followed in a more dignified
manner; a real genuine hee-haw, in fact a whole series
of hee-haws rising to a crescendo then descending again
until it ended quietly in a grunt.

'I laughed out loud alone in my boat,' a fisherman
said to me one day, 'listening to your donkeys in the fog
yesterday.'

They had, of course, other more subtle forms of communication than their bellows. The snort was a joyous
affair much used when they were released in a meadow
they hadn't been in for a while; a scamper, a kicking
of heels, a friendly dash at each other, heads down and

snorts. It was a rich sound. A quick roll of bass drums. A proclamation that they were happy. At other times, I fear, the snort was only a tickle in the nose, grass seeds in a nostril; and then they would stand looking at us by a gate, or peering down at us from the field above the cottage, shaking their heads and snorting, as if they were blaming us for their temporary vexation.

A persuasive, eloquent sound was their whimper. There was nothing obsequious about it. It was a means of making known the fact they had observed us pass by and would appreciate attention or a titbit. They would stand side by side, Penny's white nose topping Fred's white nose, trilling away like birds in a bush; and when we responded, when we advanced towards them speaking words of affection, they changed their whimper into a series of rapid sigh-like sounds. A rush of breath through their nostrils. A curious, puffing method, it seemed, of saying thank you.

They had wonderful eyesight. Sometimes Jeannie and I would go out on a walk to the Carn that we can see from the cottage, a jagged pile of rocks like an ancient castle falling down to the sea. It was a walk on which they generally accompanied us, but as there were succulent grasses all the way on either side of the narrow path, such a walk took a long time. So sometimes we liked to go on our own. Their revenge was to stand in a meadow and watch us, so that when we looked back we could plainly see two reproachful donkeys, ears pricked, staring in our direction.

'They make me feel awful,' Jeannie would say inevitably, yielding them their victory.

Their eyesight and their acute sense of hearing made them wonderful sentries. Time and again they would warn us by their alertness that a car was coming down the lane long before we heard the tyres on the gravel or that there were voices in the distance. They would point like a game-dog.

'On guard, Jeannie! Look at the donkeys!'

And thereby we had a few minutes grace before the visitor arrived.

One October night, a still, unusually warm night of dense fog, the watchfulness of the donkeys was challenged by an event of great drama. We had left them down in the cliff meadows and this in itself was an adventure for them. They loved these meadows. Not only was there a profusion of their favourite grasses in various stages of growth, but there were also the evergreen privet and escallonia. I had taken them there many times during the daytime but this was the first occasion they had been allowed to stay for the night; and I had done so because when at nightfall I had called them from the gate to come up, they had not taken the slightest notice. They were steep, pocket-sized meadows intertwining one into the other, cascading like stepping stones downwards to the rocks and the sea. Once I used many of them for early potatoes, heaving the sacks up the cliff path; but now they were our daffodil meadows, and in January and February they danced with yellow, the splash of waves on rocks their orchestra. As yet, in October, not even the spikes of green had appeared; and we even, flatteringly, praised the donkeys for being useful. They at least were helping towards keeping the grass trimmed.

I will always wonder whether they were frightened by what happened. Did Fred, more highly strung than Penny, begin immediately to hee-haw? And was he heard by any of the men hanging to the driftwood? It seems certain that he was. And did Penny join in, so that the two of them tolled for the doomed? I can see them in my mind, ears upright like Churchill's victory sign, keen eyes blind in the darkness, noses quivering, listening to the mysterious noises, useless sentinels of disaster.

Jeannie and I were sound asleep with Lama curled at the bottom of the bed. The window was open and as usual, before I went to bed, I had fixed the contraption which we had used ever since, years ago, Monty was nearly caught by a fox as he jumped out of the window on a nightly jaunt. It consisted of wire meshing fitted to a wooden frame the exact size of the window; and so although we could see out and also have the fresh air, Lama was contained in the cottage. It was unsightly but useful; and as soon as we got up it was whisked away.

Anyhow there we were when suddenly I began climbing out of a deep dream, fighting my way reluctantly, until I reached the nightmarish reality of the sound of a car outside the cottage. It was pitch dark, and the car arrived at such speed that when it drew up it woke me by the screech of its brakes. Never before, not even in daylight, had a car arrived so fast. It shot me out of bed. It shot Lama off.

'What's happened?' asked Jeannie dreamily, and in such a tone that I half expected her to tick me off for leaping out of bed and waking her.

'A wreck!' I knew this immediately.

I heard the voices of the men in the first car disappear down the path towards the sea, high chatter folding into silence. Then, as I was struggling into my trousers, another car arrived, then another and another. There were shouts, and orders and counter orders; and when I got outside headlights lit up the grey rocks and the old barn, and pushed their beams at the cottage.

'Here they come,' someone shouted.

There in front of me lurching through the dip of Monty's Leap there came an old jalopy of a van, no, not a van for it had no sides and no ends. Was it a converted hearse? It had a top supported by metal posts at each corner of its chassis, and it carried huge boxes like coffins, and clinging to the sides and heaped on the boxes there seemed to be a legion of swarthy men in woollen skull caps. Heavens, I said to myself, if this weren't the twentieth century these would be pirates. The old jalopy roared up from the Leap, rattling like a hundred clanking tins, a Genevieve of a vehicle, and pulled up inches from a flower bed. The Life Saving team had arrived.

At this moment I smelled the oil.

I wondered why I had not noticed it before as soon as I had woken up. It was not just a whiff of diesel oil. It was as heavy and persistent as night scented stock on a hot summer's night. It filled the air like wood smoke. A ghostly smell, a smell of death, the marker buoy of a wreck. And the reason why I hadn't noticed it before was because, as I learnt later, for over three hours I had been breathing it as I slept, I had become used to it.

It was now half-past six and the fog had gone. A glimmer of light wavered behind the Lizard peninsula and as I looked at it, knowing that within half an hour it would be light and rescue made more simple, a plane roared overhead.

'Where is the wreck?' I asked a man in coastguard's uniform; and as I spoke I thought how absurdly remote I sounded. Here was Minack the hub of the rescue, and I did not belong. I was an onlooker, and I was asking the onlooker's feeble questions.

'We think on the Bucks.'

There was an Inner Buck and an Outer Buck, and in days of sail the scene of many wrecks. They were half a mile off shore from our cliff, small hillocks at low tide, obscured at high tide.

'What kind of boat?'

'Don't know. We've been looking for her since three this morning.'

At a quarter to three Land's End radio had picked up a Mayday signal. It was very feeble and did not last for long. The operator heard enough to learn it was a Spanish ship called the *Juan Ferrer*, but the sender of the signal did not know where he was. He thought, he said, he was near Land's End and he added that the ship was breaking up on the rocks and the captain had ordered her to be abandoned.

Those in charge of the rescue operations were in a quandary. How do we find her? They decided to order the launching of the Sennen lifeboat with instructions she should search the coast between Cape Cornwall and Gwennap Head, the head which is, in fact, the southerly corner of Cornwall, about five miles up the coast from Minack. They also sent out scouts to scour the cliffs, alerted the Mousehole based Penlee lifeboat but did not order her to be launched, and instructed the Life Saving team with their heavy equipment to concentrate in the Land's End car-park where the headquarters of the rescue operations were set up. For over three hours, therefore, the main rescue services waited patiently in the fog in the car-park, no news from the Sennen lifeboat, no news from the scouts, until at last a report came in that the *Juan Ferrer* was disintegrating on the Bucks.

But the report was wrong. The Life Saving team had already unloaded their equipment from the jalopy and were heaving it down the path, through our big field to the top of the cliff meadows, when one of their number who had gone ahead shouted back that there was no sign whatsoever of a wreck on the Bucks.

The sun behind the Lizard was now brimming over into a canopy of sky, familiar places were becoming recognizable again. I could see the long stretch of sand at Loo Bar, the crinkly cliffs round Mullion, the hills behind Prah Sands pushing like a clenched fist into a low cloud. Closer, I could see again the Carn and the outline of its rocks cascading down to the sea, and the elderberry tree which marked the biggest badger sett in the district. Car lights were switched off. Figures became faces. Torches were put into pockets. Cold realism began taking over from the intangible fantasies of darkness.

A police radio car was now parked opposite the flower house and I could hear distorted voices coming from its loudspeaker. Senior police officers in peaked caps, coast-guard officers with weatherbeaten faces, the Life Saving team in their skull caps, all stood around, disconsolate, puzzled, asking themselves over and over again: 'Where's the wreck?'

A field opposite, the one with the gate where the lane turns right for the last hundred yards to Minack, had been turned into a car-park. First one car, then ten, then thirty, their wheels slithering as they turned on the unfamiliar grass. Press photographers and reporters, overdressed for the occasion in neat suits and shiny black shoes, hastened to the cottage. Can we borrow your phone? Sorry, we haven't got one.

And now helicopters from the naval station across the bay at Culdrose began to roar and to hover, up and down the coast. We stood and stared. There in the sky the mid-twentieth-century rescue service, here in the shadow of the ancient cottage standing around me the rescue tradition of centuries. 'I dearly love a wreck,' I heard a man say.

At half-past seven someone pointed to a helicopter that was hovering low down off the entrance to Lamorna Cove, a mile or two away, and on the other side of the Carn. 'She's gone in there,' a man said brightly, 'that's what it is. She's gone in the other side of the Carn.'

I felt the sense of relief around me that something positive had been suggested. The men in skull caps lifted their weighty boxes once again and staggered off. A constable went ahead. Pressmen conscientiously set out to wade through the undergrowth. The sun was out, the sea was lazy, shimmering no hint of danger, a robin sang in the wood and a woodpecker laughed, and over everything lingered the smell of oil.

Jeannie suddenly appeared beside me. 'Have you seen the donkeys?' she asked, 'I've been down the cliff and there isn't a sign of them.'

'Oh dear,' I said, 'I'd forgotten about them.'

A policeman on a motor-cycle rode up at that moment, stopped and with measured dignity got off. 'Did you see any donkeys up the lane?' I asked. He looked surprised. 'No sir. I didn't.'

I realised now that they would have been scared out of their wits when the advance party of the Life Saving team dashed down through the meadows, leaving the gate open no doubt for they would hardly have expected to meet donkeys.

'They're probably miles away by now,' I said to Jeannie, and as I spoke I saw in my imagination a bewildered Fred and a distraught Penny plodding along some distant road. 'On the other hand,' I added soothingly, 'they may have only escaped to Pentewan.' These were the neighbouring cliff meadows which we used to rent but gave up after a sequence of gale-ridden crop disasters. 'I'll go and have a look.'

It was past eight o'clock and at the busy centre of Minack there was still no report of the whereabouts of the wreck. Aircraft were zooming overhead and as I made my way over to Pentewan I saw strung along a mile or more offshore a company of ships . . . the Trinity House vessel, the *Stella*, a Dutch tug which was spending the winter in Mount's Bay at a second's readiness to speed for salvage, a Fishery Protection boat and, close to the cliffs as if they were searching the inlets, were the two lifeboats. The *Sennen* which had been out since the beginning, the *Penlee* which had been out since half-past six.

I looked over towards the Carn. The group which had set out from Minack were straddled around it. I saw no urgency in their movements. There did not appear to be any reason to believe that they had found the wreck. The only thing which did seem clear to me was that a large number of people other than all of us at Minack must by now know its exact location. The sea was calm, the visibility was excellent, both ships and aircraft must have inspected the length of the coast.

I reached the Pentewan meadows and was passing through what we used to call the thirty lace meadow when I observed piles of driftwood, gulls sweeping and calling above it, drifting eastwards in an endless line towards Lamorna Cove. I had been joined in my walk by a stranger with an important air.

'That settles it,' I said, 'the wreck is the other side of Pentewan cliffs, just beyond the top of that lane we can see. The wreckage is drifting with the tide.'

'The tide has changed,' the man said loftily.

'You mean the wreckage having drifted one way is now drifting the other?'

'I do.'

I could not contest the views of such a seafaring looking character. It was not my business to inform him that the tide did not change till ten o'clock. But I made up my own mind that the *Juan Ferrer* was on the rocks just over the point ahead.

So it was.

She had rammed the rocks at Boscawen Point within two miles of Minack, a five-hundred-ton cargo boat on passage from Bordeaux to Cardiff with a mixed cargo of onions, plywood made of cedar and thousands of chestnut stakes destined for Welsh farms.

She had gone ashore within four sea miles of the Penlee Lifeboat station; and so if her Mayday signal had been louder, if her position had been able to be plotted, rescuers would have reached her within an hour.

Three survivors jumped ashore. Two men drifted with the tide and the wreckage, and were picked up by the helicopter we saw hovering off Lamorna Cove. Eleven were drowned, their bodies having also drifted with the tide.

And the donkeys? Did they hear the last cries of those men as they drifted past our meadows? And those two who were saved?

It was a special pleasure when all the excitement was over to find they never did run far. While it was still dark and I was dressing, they must have rushed away from the cliff, through the open gate which normally stopped them from cavorting in the garden, into the wood past Boris's house, then on to the farther part of the wood.

When it was all over, when the long adventure ended at nine and we had begun our breakfast, a banshee wail and a tenor-like trumpeting joined in a duet in the corner of the field overlooking the cottage.

Everyone had gone. Minack belonged to its occupants again.

14

The *Juan Ferrer* shuddered on the rocks at Boscawen Point for a couple of days, half submerged, disgorging its cargo: and all along the coast men were busy salvaging the stakes and the squares of cedar plywood as they drifted forlornly ashore.

And there were the sightseers. A wreck, like all disasters, has a morbid fascination for those who live safe lives. They heaped themselves on the cliffside, little groups staring in silence, breaking it occasionally to ask the lone policeman, incongruous in helmet, some question he had already answered many times before. Below them, like a whale in its death throes, the object of their entertainment floundered in the waves, sea spouted from the broken windows of the wheelhouse, a rope flopped about the deck, a bell clanged uselessly; and all the while the hulk was heaving this way and that, scraping and banging the rocks, an echoing orchestra of doom, giving a sad, despairing value to the gaping crowd before its inevitable end.

Many of the sightseers came charging along the cliff

through Minack meadows to reach their destination. A fanatical lot, a glint in their eyes, walking faster than usual, driving themselves through the undergrowth as if the hounds of hell were after them. 'Where's the wreck?' they panted.

Fred viewed this invasion first with suspicion and then, as the scope of its possibilities dawned upon him, with relish. Here were people galore to show off to. He could divert them from their object, lure from them the praises which would relieve an otherwise dull day. Flattery would be assured. His charm would be irresistible. I am a baby donkey, have you ever seen one before? Look how I can kick my heels and don't you think my fluffy coat adorable? My nose is very soft if you would like to fondle it. Who is the other one? She's my mother. Rather staid. What have you got in that bag?

I might have moved them from the pathway of such attention into the isolation of some other field, but I was in fact delighted there was something to occupy their minds. They were doing no harm, and Fred had a whole series of toys apparently to play with. Each person who passed through was there for his entertainment, and I felt sure he would give value in return.

I was happily believing that this was so when, as I sat at my desk, I saw through the window a hatless elderly man come puffing up the path from the direction of the field, followed a moment later by a formidable looking lady. I dashed out of the cottage to meet them, sensing immediately that something had gone awry.

'Can I help you?' I said, using my usual method of introduction, smiling politely, and at the same time wondering what on earth had happened to cause such obvious excitement.

'Are those your damned donkeys in the field we've just come through?' barked the man. He was out of breath as if he had been running and as he spoke he mopped his bald head with a handkerchief.

'Yes,' I replied doubtfully, 'anything wrong?'

'Very much so,' interrupted the lady grimly looking at me from under an old felt hat, 'the young one snatched my husband's cap and is running round the field with it.'

How had Fred managed it? Had he sneaked up behind the couple as they hurried along, annoyed they had taken no notice of him, and then performed a ballet dancer's leap to take the cap from the gentleman's head?

'Good gracious,' I said, 'I do apologise for this. I'll go ahead straight away and catch him.'

I ran away from them laughing, down the path to the field, asking myself what I would have to do if Fred had gobbled it up. But as I did so I suddenly saw a galloping Fred coming towards me, tweed cap in mouth, and just behind him a thundering, rollicking Penny; and the two of them gave such an impression of joyous, hilarious elation that I only wished that Jeannie had been with me to see them.

The cap was intact, a little wet, but no sign of a tear; and when I thankfully returned it to its owner I asked what had happened. It was simple. It was almost as I imagined it. The couple had sat down on the grass for a rest; and then up behind them came Fred. And away went the cap.

This episode, I am afraid, set the tone of Fred's behaviour towards other sightseers. The trouble, I reckon, was that they were too intent to reach the wreck for them to dally in the way Fred would have liked them to dally. They had no time to play with a donkey. The magnet of disaster destroyed any wish to pause on the way. Morbid curiosity displaced idle pleasure.

Thus, when Fred discovered he was being ignored, he set out to tease. He would watch a group coming along the path from the Carn in the distance, then canter straight at them scattering them in all directions. I found, for instance, three small boys way off the path and waist high in undergrowth, and when I asked how they were there, one of them mournfully replied: 'The donkey chased us, and we're trying to get round.' Of course I then escorted them through the zone of danger and Fred, satisfied with his moral victory, followed meekly behind us until we reached the end of Minack's boundary. Then he scampered back with me, nuzzling me, no longer meek, impatient to play the game again.

He later inveigled me to act as an ally. I began to dislike the ghoulish groups as they strode through Minack private land, not caring about its beauty or that they were there by courtesy, and so I devised a game to play with Fred. He and I would stand in a corner of the field, waiting and watching for a group who looked as if they deserved a surprise. Then, when the chosen victims had reached half-way up the field I would give my order: 'See 'em off, boy!' Away Fred careered, not in an unimaginative dash straight at them, but in a circular movement like a dog rounding up sheep. And after a pause I would hasten after him to reassure our victims that there was nothing really to be scared of in the cavalry charge of a baby donkey.

While the *Juan Ferrer* settled on the bottom of the sea, emotionalism went into action. I have often marvelled how emotionalism, skilfully conducted, can achieve results which the basic facts do not warrant, while other campaigns more worthy but less imaginative in appeal stutter into failure. It is, I suppose, mainly a question of timing. If the perimeter influences are favourable, if the event concerned is sufficiently vivid to act as a flag on a masthead, if worthy people are interested who want an outlet for their energy, if there is a chance for a few to achieve a personal advantage, if all these factors combine to push a cause which appears superficially justified, then the chances are that emotionalism will succeed at the expense of realism.

The object of this particular campaign was to persuade the authorities to build an ocean-type lighthouse a short distance away from Minack in the area Jeannie and I called the Pentewan cliffs. These cliffs and meadows belonged to one of the few remaining unspoilt stretches of the Cornish coast. You could see it from the Carn with the rocks like an ancient castle, and people would stand there and marvel that they could look upon a scene that had been the same since the beginning of time. No man-made ugliness, no breeze block buildings to offend them.

'Every day of our lives,' I wrote in *A Drake at the Door*, 'was spent in unison with this coast, the rage of the gales, salt smearing our faces as we walked, east winds, south winds, calm summer early mornings, the first cubs, a badger in the moonlight, wild violets, the glory of the first daffodil, the blustering madness of making a living on land that faced the roar of the ages.

'The cliffs fall to rocks black and grey where the sea ceaselessly churns, splashing its foam, clutching a rock then releasing it, smothering it suddenly in bad temper, caressing it, slapping it as if in play, sometimes kind with the sun shining on the white ribbon of a wave, a laughing sea throwing spray like confetti, sometimes grey and sullen, then suddenly a sea of ungovernable fury lashing the cliffs; enraged that for ever and for ever the cliffs look down.

'And among the rocks are the pools; some that tempt yet are vicious, beckoning innocently then in a flash a cauldron of currents, pools that are shallow so that the minnow fish ripple the surface as they dash from view, pools so deep that the seaweed looks like a forest far below, inaccessible pools, pools which hide from everyone except those who belong to them.

'High above, the little meadows dodge the boulders, and where the land is too rough for cultivation the bracken, the hawthorn, the brambles, the gorse which sparks its yellow the year round, reign supreme. This is no place for interlopers. The walkers tamed by pavements, faced by the struggling undergrowth, turn back or become angry, their standardised minds piqued that they have to trace a way through; and it is left to the few, the odd man or woman, to marvel that there is a corner of England still free from the dead hand of the busybody.

'Here, on our stretch of the coast, man has not yet brought his conceit.'

For some years there had been murmurs about erecting a small, harbour-type light and fog signal near Lamorna Cove to act like a street lamp for the benefit of local fishermen on their way to and fro from Mousehole or Newlyn; and this indeed was a reasonable proposition. But the wreck of the *Juan Ferrer* gave a new twist to this idea, and the cry went up for an ocean-type lighthouse, as powerful as that on the Wolf Rock and the Lizard; and the cries became louder after a television film was compiled called Cornish Wrecks. It was a stirring production and somehow succeeded in giving the impression that there had been twenty-three wrecks in twelve years on this southern coast of the Land's End peninsula which the new lighthouse would serve. Almost two wrecks a year within a distance of ten miles! The film caused a furore.

This was wonderful material for the campaigners and I watched with fascination how they reacted. Women's organisations were roped in. A petition was organised and signatures were collected by door-to-door canvassers. A letter was sent to Sir Winston Churchill. A question was asked in the House of Commons. A special programme of the T.V. film was shown to Mr Marples as the man finally responsible for instructing Trinity House to build the lighthouse. Veiled accusations were made that Trinity House should have acted before. The Minister must act! Gradually, with the persistence of a steamroller, the illusion was fostered and believed that a new lighthouse would banish wrecks from the Cornish coast for ever.

The snag of the illusion lay in the facts which the campaigners seemed to avoid. There had not been twenty-three wrecks in twelve years; there had been four wrecks in over fifteen years. And there were other facts which the campaigners ignored with aplomb as they hurried on their emotional way. Another four wrecks, in as many years, had occured within a few hundred yards of lighthouses; two off the Longships near Land's End, two at Pendeen near Cape Cornwall. Seventeen had died in one of them the year before.

The claim, therefore, that lighthouses provided immunity to those who sailed in their neighbourhood was unfortunately untrue; twentieth-century methods of safeguarding shipping were required, not those of the seventeenth. Moreover, in the case of the new lighthouse, it was to be situated at a position which many experienced sailors found incomprehensible. Tater-du, as the position is called, is five miles from the headland called Gwennap Head marking the southernmost point of the Land's End peninsula; five miles, in fact, inside Mounts Bay. 'If they want one at all,' said an old fisherman to me who had sailed this coast all his life, 'put it on Gwennap Head or close to it. There it might help shipping coming up the Channel or across from the Lizard. But it's crazy to put it so far inside the Bay as Tater-du for a score of reasons.'

The campaigners swept forward, irresistible, vociferous, unreal in their arguments, thriving on the unproven slogan they were saving lives; and there is today a lighthouse at Tater-du. In this age of electronics, of radio direction finding and radar, a lighthouse of hideous utility design with huge electricity pylons marching across the skyline towards it, the first to be built in this country since the last century, costing many thousands of pounds, now climbs into the sky, a phalanx of concrete blocks, on this lovely once lonely coast.

A monument to what happens when emotionalism goes into action.

15

Fred met his first winter and viewed it with apprehension. No one to visit him. No flavour in the grass. Hedgerows bare. Long nights with nothing to do. Driving rain to flatten his fluffy coat. And gales.

How he hated gales. Rain, however heavy, was only an inconvenience in comparison. He would stand in the rain hour after hour, spurning the welcoming open door of the stables, looking miserable nevertheless, taking apparently some kind of masochistic pleasure out of his discomfort. I was sorry for him in the rain but I did not feel I was under any obligation to take steps to protect him from it. A really persistent long day's rain would put him in a stupor, and if I called him he would pause a moment or two before lifting his head dazedly to look at me. He seldom showed any wish to come to me; he and Penny, heads down, the rain dripping off their noses, bottoms towards the weather, would stand stoically content in what I would have thought were intolerable conditions.

But in gales he needed protection. He became restless

as soon as the first breeze, the scout of the gale, began hurrying across the field; and he would begin to hee-haw, lifting his head to the scurrying clouds so that a mournful bellow joined the swish of the wind in the trees. He would not stand still, racing round in small circles, then dashing off to another part of the field; and instead of following Penny dutifully about as was his usual custom, Penny would be hastening after him. He was the leader. It was as if he believed that something tangible was chasing him, not a gale but an enemy with plans to capture him. A foolish fantasy of the very young, faced by the unknown.

Penny herself, with private memories of the Connemara mountains, was unperturbed. She felt, no doubt, that Fred's fears were part of his education, and that repetition would dull them. She plodded after him as he ran hither and thither like an old nanny after a child, and when he grew tired she nudged him along to the shelter of a hedge. Penny was very weather-wise. She had mapped each meadow with a number of tactical positions to suit every variation of the wind; a series of well worn patches on the ground disclosed them. Thus, if a westerly moved a few points to the east resulting in her current position being exposed, she cunningly led the way to the next patch.

But there were times when the gales roared like a squadron of supersonic hedgehopping aircraft, deafening us in the cottage so that when the news came on I had to switch the radio at full strength if we were to hear the announcer. Lama would be curled up comfortably in a chair, Boris in his house in the wood would be sitting on his perch; the gulls, Knocker and Squeaker or the lonely, friendly Peter, would be safe beneath some leeward cliff until many hours later the gale died down and they set off to fly to the roof again.

It was at a time like this that I indulged in protecting Fred. At first I used to lead the two of them to the shelter of the wood, and they would stand around the outside of Boris's house among the ivy covered trunks of the elms, the wind slapping the tops, swaying, branches cracking and falling, an invisible angry hate hissing its fury, mad with rage that its omnipotent, conquering, horizon-leaping triumph over the sea was being checked by hands held high; trees and hills and houses and sudden valleys, old buildings and church spires, hedges acting as ramparts. Penny and Fred would stand there with the roar of the gale above them and the roar of the sea behind them. They did not like it.

And so in due course, whenever a gale blew, I took them to the stable meadow where the security of the stable awaited them. In a severe gale you would find both of them within. In any kind of wind you would always find Fred.

The stable was dilapidated but solid. It was an ancient building with arm-length thick walls made of stone in all shapes and sizes and bound together by clay. The clay in many places outside had cracked and fallen away over the years, and sparrows and blue tits made use of the holes in the spring; one wall was so popular with the sparrows that their nests resembled a series of flats, each one above the other. Huge beams stretched across the battered ceiling inside, rusty hooks where once hung harness stared from the walls, cobble stones like knuckles of a hand lined the floor, and in the corner there was the broken frame of a manger.

On Christmas Eve we took mince pies to the donkeys in the stable. A lighthearted gesture, a game for ourselves, an original diet for them.

'Donkeys! Donkeys!' Jeannie called into the darkness of the meadow. 'Come into the stables. We've got something for you.' And after a minute or two, their shadows loomed, heralded by inquiring whimpers.

'Fred,' I said, 'you're about to have your first mince pie.'

Inside we lit a candle in an old-fashioned candlestick and put it on the window sill. The light flickered softly. It flickered on their white noses, their eager faces, their giant rabbit-like ears. They pushed their heads forward, nuzzling us in expectation.

'Patience, patience!' said Jeannie, holding the mince pies high in her hand. 'Don't be in such a hurry!' And then with a quick movement she gave one to each of them.

As I stood there watching I began to feel the magic of the occasion. Our intention had been to have a joke, to enjoy the merry spirit of Christmas and now, unexpectedly, something else was taking place.

'Look at their crosses,' I said to Jeannie. The cross of Penny was black merging into black, but that of Fred was easy to see; the dark line tracing up the backbone beneath his fluffy brown coat until it reached his shoulders, then stopping abruptly when it met the two lines tracing down each foreleg. 'Here we are,' I went on, 'with two biblical creatures eating mince pies.'

'In a stable.'

'On Christmas Eve.'

There was the gentle sound as they shifted their feet on the cobblestones, and I was aware too of the musty scent of their coats. Ageless simplicity, laughed at, beaten, obstinately maintaining an individuality; here indeed was a moment when there was a communication with the past. Struggle, self sacrifice, integrity, loyalty; how was it that the basic virtues, the proven talisman of man's true happiness, was being lost in the rush of material progress? Why was it that civilisation was allowing its soul to be destroyed by brain power and the vacuous desire it breeds? Why deify the automaton when selflessness has to be won? For a shimmering moment we felt the race halted. No contrived, second-hand emotion. We were not watching, we were part. As it always had been, so it was now.

We had changed since we had first known each other,

Jeannie and I. Once we had both fought hard to savour flattery and power, to be part of a glad world of revelry, to be in the fashion, and to rush every day at such speed that we disallowed ourselves any opportunity to ponder where we were going; and now we were in the stable at a customary moment of merriment, perfectly happy, alone with two donkeys. It is easy to remain in a groove, a groove which becomes worn without you realising it, only recognisable by friends who have not seen you for a long time, and it is usually luck which enables you to escape. Jeannie and I had the luck to feel the same at the same time, and so we had been united in forcing ourselves to flee our conventional background. There had never been any argument between us about the pros and cons, gradually the standards we once believed so important appeared sadly ineffectual, only vital until they had been experienced. Moreover the merciless zest required to achieve them became an exhausting effort as soon as the standards, reached at last, had to be maintained; for it became obvious to us that in most cases the banners of success were made of paper, waved by *entrepreneurs* who were temporarily leeching on the creative efforts of others.

Thus Jeannie and I belonged to the lucky ones who, having seen their personal horizon, had also reached it; and yet in doing so there was no possible reason for self satisfaction. It was true that contentment was always near us, but there was an edge to our life which stopped us from ever taking it for granted. What had become our strength was the base to which we could retreat. We had a home we loved. Around us was the ambience of permanency. We had roots. And so, when we became involved in sophisticated stresses which touched us with memories of other days, there was a moat behind which we could recharge. We then could observe quietly the enemy; envy, for instance, the most corroding of sins, the game of intrigue which fills so many people's lives, the use of the lie which in business is considered a justifiable weapon, the hurt that comes from insecurity, the greed which feeds on itself, the worship of headline power without quality to achieve it. We watched, and sometimes we were vexed, sometimes we were frightened. Across the moat we could see the reflection of the past.

On occasions we were interviewed for magazines, radio and television, and Jeannie usually had to take the brunt of the questions. And how weary she grew of that inevitable question: 'Don't you miss all the gay times you had at the Savoy?' She would smile brightly and say no, and there would follow the second stock question. 'Don't you ever say to yourself that you would like to go back?' These leading questions demanded an affirmative answer, or at least a hesitation on Jeannie's part. Instead the second no was as firm as the first. Jeannie always failed to gratify any outsider's hope that she might be dissatisfied in a life so different from that she described in *Meet me at the Savoy*.

One day a distinguished interviewer arrived with a caravanserai of cameramen and others at half-past eight in the morning at Minack. Dapper and trim in a city suit and shiny black shoes, looking like a stockbroker on the way to the office, he stepped up the path and into the cottage. He left over twelve hours later. An illuminating day.

The tone was set by a tough, preliminary cross-examination, as if Jeannie and I were suspected partners in crime; and in the best tradition of detection, we were questioned separately. First myself, then Jeannie; and when we compared notes afterwards we found we had each endured a similar, attacking interrogation the aim of which was to discover the weakness in our happiness. '*What* do you quarrel about?' was the first question he put to Jeannie.

But as the day wore on, we became aware once again of the loneliness which besets an idol whom everyone admires but few have time to know. He did not wish to hurt us. His screen self was confused with his true self. He had to maintain his image and so he was trying to knock us down. Perhaps he saw in us what he wanted for himself, a happy marriage and the time to enjoy it; and thus he hoped to explode our way of life in order to reassure himself that conventional happiness was impossible. He wanted reality but was trapped by outward success; he had to live with the bathroom door open or the public would rage. I found it strange to watch him straddled in an armchair at the end of the day, staring gloomily into the fire, whisky glass in hand, and to know that he represented in the eyes of millions their imaginary ideal of twentieth-century contentment, a conqueror of the small screen. All I saw myself was a man who spent his life shuffling from one arc lamp to another, secretly cherishing a hope that a home one day awaited him.

Jeannie and I had the home but we were, on the other hand, disorganised. I sometimes felt I behaved like a rabbit caught in the glare of headlights dashing this way and that without purpose until it zigzags its way to the safety of a burrow. I seemed incapable of solving the problems around me. I would have one idea, then another, then another, and none of them would ever quite come off. I was safe at Minack but I was not progressing. My imagination became congealed, for instance, by the tedious detail of spending three days, Jeannie beside me, on my hands and knees weeding freesias; and we would both become doped by the simplicity of the task. We would cheer when we had finished. We would gaze in admiration at the neat beds and convince ourselves that something worthwhile had been achieved. So it had been. Unhappily it was at the price of thinking. There is a soothing, narcotic daziness in weeding which pleasingly seduces you from concentrating on plans for the future. A day of weeding might satisfy our consciences but it did not advance us. It only helped to obscure the trouble we were in.

The manager remained charming and anxious to please. He laughed often and apologised handsomely whenever it was necessary, but as we shivered slowly towards the daffodil season, it was clear he was not the man we had been looking for. Able in many horticultural departments, always pleasant and amiably tempered, it was no fault of his good nature that he did not unfortunately fit into our type of flower farm. Thus Jeannie and I were now in a web of our own making, and our position was far more difficult than before he arrived.

We were, for instance, embroiled in the man's life. We were not a large soulless organisation which could upturn the life of an individual 'for the good of the Company'. His three children were now at local schools. There were no other jobs in the district which would suit his managerial manner. Thus if he left us the children's schooling would be disrupted when they were just growing accustomed to their new surroundings. The family had no permanent home. The cottage we rented for them was their home until they could find somewhere else to go.

'We'll have to compromise,' I said at last.

'How?'

'The best thing we can do is to concentrate on the next three months, keep him for that time, and let the summer look after itself.'

It was the only thing we could do. The daffodil season was advancing upon us with the massive inevitability of a steam roller. There would be three hundred thousand individual blooms to pick, bunch, pack and send away to Covent Garden. Every day would be a race against time, against the lowering of prices, against the gales which always threatened; the blooms were never secure from being destroyed in the meadows until they rimmed the pails in the packing shed. And I was still writing *A Drake at the Door*. I could not break away and put my full mind to the flower farm. All I could do was to shut my eyes to the future, and aim to salvage what we could from the huge harvest of daffodils. I had no time in which to attempt a reorganisation. I had to muddle through; and when it was all over, and we were in a vacuum, we would then pause and ponder which way we had better go.

We would then decide whether to continue with the flower farm or to give it up.

16

When the snow came after Christmas we shut the donkeys in the stable at night. We did it for our own peace of mind. We could not bear to lie in bed and think of them out there in the dark becoming snow donkeys; and yet, as experience proved, they did not seem to object. One evening when we returned home late and snow was falling, we found the two foolish things out in the meadow despite the fact the comfort of the stable awaited them.

Fred was like a small boy in the snow. The first morning he was introduced to it, he came rushing out of the stable, stopped in his tracks when he saw it, began pawing with his front feet, put his head down and pushed his nose into it, then in wild excitement started a fandango of flying kicks which made me speedily run away from him. Then he raced into the middle of the meadow and without more ado sank to his knees which was, of course, the preliminary to a roll.

The roll, in normal circumstances, was a solemn ritual. The ceremony was performed on a small circular patch in a carefully chosen position and, as it was well worn, the ground was either dusty or muddy according to the weather. This, however, had no bearing on the success of the ceremony, for the roll was a donkey bath; and whether Fred rose from his roll in a cloud of dust or caked in mud, he was satisfied. As far as he was concerned he was clean. He had had his wash.

Penny, like a fat lady on the seashore, had to watch her dignity when she followed suit. She would collapse to her knees, fall over to one side, then begin to wriggle this way and that in an endeavour to complete a roll. It was an embarrassing sight. She would get on her back, a huge grey barrel facing up to the heavens, then miserably fail to force herself over. Nor would her attempts be silent. She, like Fred, accompanied her efforts with repetitive, body-shaking grunts. A desperate sound, like a wrestler in combat; and when, if we were watching, she at last succeeded in making it by a final glorious lurch, Jeannie and I would send up a cheer. She would then get up, turn her back on us, stare at an imaginary interest in the distance, and pretend that nothing whatsoever untoward had happened.

Fred's roll in the snow, however, was purely a gesture of joy. He was captivated by the feeling of the powdery stuff, and he rolled this way and that snorting with pleasure, kicking his heels in the air, and when he had had enough and stood up again, he looked as if he were a donkey wrapped in cotton wool. He then hoped for a game. Ears pinned back, head on one side, one could sense he was laughing at the huge joke of it all; and when I began gently throwing snowballs at him, I was surprised he did not pick one up himself and chuck it back. He wanted to, I'm sure.

We had no fear that the bitter weather might affect our daffodils. It delayed them, of course, and for weeks they stayed constant a few inches above the ground, too cold to move; and instead of starting to harvest them in the middle of January, we had to wait until the middle of February. Our main concern centred round the freesias, for their peak flowering time coincided with the day and night frost. It was awful. We had a splendid crop but our heaters did not have the power to lift the temperature sufficiently, and although they kept the frost out they did not make the air warm enough to bring the buds into bloom. The heaters, using huge amounts of oil, curled the equivalent of pound notes into the chill air, but the plants did not move, and because of this the roots began to develop a disease. Then, when one week we picked enough to send a consignment to Covent Garden, they froze on the way. The van was unheated, and the consignment was unsaleable.

The donkeys, meanwhile, were becoming restless. There was nothing for them to nibble, and we fed them on pellets, hay and anything they might fancy. It was one long round of eating, and as the ground was too hard for any serious exercise, they began to store up energy; and the energy unleashed itself as soon as the soft winds began to blow again and the frost disappeared. And then twice they disappeared.

At other times of the year we would have been annoyed, but not worried. But on these occasions their disappearance coincided not only with the time the daffodils were coming into bloom; it was also potato planting time. Neither among the daffodils nor on the newly-turned soil could donkey feet be anything else but a trouble maker.

I had already suspected that some of our neighbours might have considered the donkeys as parasites. After all we had been asked any number of times during the summer by visitors, 'Don't they *do* anything?' And if the visitors asked such questions it was understandable that farmers might be asking them too. They could see them meandering aimlessly around the meadows, creatures that wouldn't draw carts, couldn't be milked, and incapable of performing any farming activity. Nor were they proving the success at keeping the grass down that I had hoped. They were choosey. They would eat certain grasses and certain weeds, but I was astonished how much was always left behind; and a meadow had still to be cut down after their presence had been intended to clear it. We felt they *ought* to do something, and so when the daffodil season began we got hold of two Spanish onion baskets. We tied them together and put the rope across Penny's back so the baskets rested against either flank, then we led her to a daffodil meadow and filled the baskets with the stems we picked. It was a total failure. For one thing it was obviously much simpler and quicker to fill an ordinary hand basket, then put it in the back of the Land Rover; for another, Fred, who was too young to be asked to share in the task, treated the whole effort as a game. He butted the baskets with his head. He whinnied. He was, in fact, a nuisance.

I could not, therefore, tell anyone that they performed any useful function, but it was easy to answer the other regular question: 'What do you have them for?' I explained they gave pleasure both to ourselves and to strangers, and that they were plainly happy in themselves. Every day they were becoming more affectionate and more trusting; and the responsibility of looking after them, which once I had feared, had turned instead into a reward. They enriched the tapestry of our life at Minack; and by touching us with their mystical quality of antiquity provided a reminder that in an age when the machine is king, all life is still sacred whether it has wings, or two legs, or four. There was another, more personal feature about them which perhaps only Jeannie and I could understand. They had become to us a symbol. They were the tangible reflection of the simple life which we were struggling to maintain in the face of the outside stresses which were trying to envelop us.

Such thoughts, however, would not excuse damage to

the crops of my neighbours, and the first time they disappeared I got into a panic when a passing hiker told me he had seen two galloping donkeys half a mile away over the opposite hill. There was, I knew, a field of broccoli in that direction, and another field of freshly planted potatoes; and I saw in my mind an enraged farmer striding towards me. And so Jeannie and I set off at the double, halters in our hands, praying silently that no neighbour would see us and that the capture would be quickly achieved and that no damage had been done in the meantime. Ten minutes later we arrived panting at the open gate of a grass field, and in the far corner stood the donkeys. Even from that distance they gave the impression of solemnity. They were in a fix, they were far from home, and they were wishing they had never started on their escapade; and so when Jeannie called out, 'Donkeys! Donkeys!' they turned their heads in our direction, then meekly, thankfully trotted towards us.

They disappeared for a second time three days later and the panic was repeated because the direction we guessed they had taken was towards Jack Cochram's cliff potato meadows. He and Walter Grose had just completed the laborious task of planting them by shovel, the centuries-old method which could not be improved upon because no machine would work the small meadows which fell like stepping stones to the sea. And I knew that if the donkeys began prancing over the newly-turned earth, real damage would be done. Their hooves would crush the seed potatoes which were only a few inches beneath the surface.

So once again Jeannie and I rushed off with the halters, this time with a certain impatience. We had thought the previous excursion had taught them a lesson, that they were ashamed of themselves, and that they would cling to Minack land in the future; and we were in part correct in our assumption. We did not find them among Jack and Walter's cliff meadows. We found them among ours. I had left the gate open at the top of our cliff and I found them at the bottom, roaming contentedly in a splendid meadow of Magnificence daffodils which were waiting to be picked.

They did not escape again. Instead, as the daffodil season increased its speed, leaving us no time to dally with them, they would stand and reproachfully stare at us. They could not understand why we were rushing about so fast. Neither did the gulls who cried from the roof for their bread, nor Boris who flapped his big wings in impatience as he waited at the door for his scraps. This was the time when every minute means money, and we could not break away from our routine to pander to them. Only Lama remained serene. She pottered about catching mice in the grass and the hedges, resting herself in the lane after a capture, silky black against grey chippings, paying us a call in the packing shed, jumping up on a bench, purring for a while among the daffodil pails, then off again on her business. She was as tired as we were when the day was ended.

We began the season by bunching the daffodils in bud, the new method of bunching which means the daffodils last far longer after they have been bought in the shop. Formerly the markets insisted on the blooms being full out when they arrived in their boxes, and inevitably this usually meant that they were a few days old when they reached the customer. The new method is also far more convenient for the daffodil grower because he can pick the buds, put the stems in water for a couple of hours, then pack them and send them away the same day. Previously the daffodils had to linger in pails perhaps for two or three days before they were ready for market; and this resulted in valuable space being taken up in the packing shed. Buds, therefore, are an excellent idea both for grower and customer despite the fact they may not appear so attractive to buy. Unfortunately on this particular occasion in this particular season, Jeannie and I were faced with a snag. We could not pick the daffodils fast enough to stop them coming full out naturally in the meadows.

It was a sweet spring. No gales seemed to threaten us, and following the bitter winter the various varieties leapt forward together as soon as the earth was warmed. It was a bumper crop, every bulb burst into bloom instead of the customary misses, and Minack meadows were covered with potential income. And when these meadows are yellow against the backdrop of a deep blue sea even the cynic will marvel, even the man whose salary is derived from destroying by words or by vision, even the devil would not deny it is one of the most beautiful sights in the world.

My first job in the morning was to drain the pails of water so that the daffodils we had bunched the previous day had time to dry before Jeannie began packing them. She was a deft packer. I would help her by getting the boxes ready, cardboard type boxes which arrived from the suppliers in large flat bundles, and I had to fold each one into shape; and into the boxes Jeannie would pack sometimes twelve bunches, sometimes fifteen, sometimes eighteen, depending upon the variety. Then I would tie the boxes in couples, label them, stack them in the Land Rover, and rush off to Penzance station to catch the flower train.

All day we would bunch. It is one of the most soothing tasks you could wish for, and as each bunch is completed and you hold it up and look at it to make quite sure that each bloom is perfect, you experience the naïve pleasure that within forty-eight hours it will be lighting up a room; and you feel you are lucky indeed to be performing a task which earns such a reward.

And while we bunched, the manager was conscientiously picking in the meadows. He would fill the baskets, carry them to the Land Rover which I would leave in some convenient place, then report to me that all the baskets were full; and then, because he could not drive,

I left my bunching and drove the Land Rover back to the packing shed.

After he had gone home for the day, Jeannie and I would go out together to pick and as, bent double, we went up and down between the beds we would call out to each other inconsequential remarks.

'Strange how the Mags never flower as well as California.'

'Do you remember Jane in this meadow shaking a shovel above her head at an aeroplane because she'd read in the paper it was testing West Cornwall for uranium?'

'And it was over there behind those elders that Shelagh hid to watch the cubs play.'

'This basket is too heavy for me. Could you get me another one?'

'Here comes the *Scillonian*. She's done an extra trip today so that means the market will be flooded tomorrow.'

'Damn, I've pricked my finger on a bracken stump.'

'Look at this lovely rogue! What daffodil can it be?'

'Silly name, rogue. Who gave it I wonder? And yet it's graphic. A daffodil which doesn't belong to the variety which one is picking.'

'I wish Geoffrey was with us. We would have finished picking this meadow ages ago. The fastest picker I've ever known. I bet he'd prefer doing this to driving a lorry for a builder.'

'I wonder if he would.'

The shadows fall early on our cliff. The setting sun is still comparatively high behind the hill when the rocks begin to point their fingers towards the sea. It becomes cool when on the top of the hill it is still warm. You soon have a sense of impending sleep, a settling for the night as the confetti of gulls drift against the dying sky, floating to smooth rocks, calling from time to time. I would then carry the baskets we had filled up the steep path to the field, load them into the Land Rover, and the two of us would drive up the field and along the track to Minack.

The same track, the same view awaiting us, as when years before, at a moment of despair, we looked ahead of us, and Jeannie called out as if our problems had been solved: 'Look! There's a gull on the roof!'

17

The daffodil season was over, and we were once again sitting on the white seat beside the bare verbena bush having our breakfast. Like the wink of an eyelid the year had gone.

The familiar beds of green foliage, spattered by occasional left-over blooms, stretched side by side in the meandows of the cliff. Wasted flowers straddled the compost heap outside the packing shed. And in the shed itself there was the usual collection of cardboard flower boxes, half-torn pieces of packing paper, a ball of string with a pair of scissors across the top of it, three bunching cradles, galvanised pails on the shelves, the odd crushed stem on the floor, invoice books and contents labels lying on the table, all waiting for the spring clean we would be giving the packing shed as soon as we had had a pause.

'Well, the season's over,' I said, watching Boris waddling towards us, 'and I'm sorry.'

'Me too.'

'Now we have to face facts.'

Lama was stalking past Boris. His friendliness towards her was often tinged with jealousy. He was now hissing away at her like an old steam engine, stretching out his neck and beak as if he would dearly like to take a bite out of her tail. She was, as usual, beatific in her indifference. She was immune from danger. She had a great love for everyone and everything around Minack, so why should she worry? She was not jealous of Boris. Her life was too idyllic for mean thoughts.

'I told the man,' I went on, breakfast over and fumbling for my pipe, 'that his family can stay on in the cottage until the school term ends in July.'

'I can't see what else we could have done,' said Jeannie, making a grab for Lama as she passed by but missing her, 'but without a cottage we haven't got a hope of replacing him.'

At this moment a tremulous hoot, rapidly changing into a hiccuping, roaring bray echoed from the field above the cottage. A calculated thought behind the noise. A cunning knowledge of the power of such blackmail. A certainty that the summons would be answered.

'Fred,' I said solemnly, 'is requiring attention.' And we got up from the seat to go and talk to him.

Our problem had the same common denominator of all people who work on their own. When everything goes smoothly one can rejoice that one is not answerable to any boss. One is independent in a regimented world, and one is inclined to believe that one is also independent of trouble. Unfortunately trouble when it comes is magnified; and a problem is more difficult to solve because there are no reserves to draw upon.

In our case there was the inescapable fact that without reliable help I could not work the flower farm and at the same time cope with the sophisticated, other side of our life. There was so much heavy work to be done, tractor driving and ploughing, keeping the meadows in trim, all the slogging work of a skilled labourer. I had done all this in other years, and would have done it again if there had been time, but now there was no time. I had legions of letters to answer, people endlessly calling to see us, and there were too the painful, slow hours of writing. I had gained so much, but I had lost much too. And amidst all the kindness that Jeannie and I were receiving, there were signs of the same jarring influences which we had disliked so much before we came to Minack. The standards of the competitors in the rat race seemed more offensive than ever.

Fred was in a thoughtful mood when we reached him. He stood on the edge of the field staring down into the small garden, a gentle, harmless little donkey who could not possibly have been responsible for the appalling noise of a few minutes before. Penny was a few yards away up the slope of the field, silhouetted against the sky and looking alertly in our direction, her coat now glistening black, her splendid head etched like a thoroughbred. Then, not wishing to miss any gifts which might be available, she trundled towards us. They stood together, nose beside nose.

'Here you are both of you,' said Jeannie, and she gave them each a jam tart, 'you can't have any more because these are the last in the tin.'

They ate the tarts, waited hopefully for more, then ambled away together into the field. We paused for a moment watching them, the blue sky as a backdrop, first nuzzling each other, then breaking away and racing each other at the gallop to the far end where the wood joins the field. Jeannie suddenly said: 'I've got a wonderful idea. The donkeys have given me it!'

'Well?'

'A year ago we were about to have a holiday when Penny's arrival stopped it.'

'Needless to say I haven't forgotten.'

'We can't possibly think of going away in the foreseeable future because there is no one to look after the animals.'

'Agreed.'

'So why don't we behave like the donkeys . . . and be idle?'

I put my arm round her shoulders. I was laughing. 'Such a suggestion,' I said, 'is amoral.'

'We would be holiday makers,' she said, ignoring me, 'like all those people who come to see us.'

'And close our eyes to crops, weeds and the existence of greenhouses?'

'Yes . . . and stop worrying about labour problems!'

'You're persuading me, Jeannie.'

'We would have the time to watch the summer peacefully instead of fighting against it.'

'Just laze on the rocks.'

'And fish. I've always wanted a fishing rod.'

'I can't see you taking the fish off the hook once you've caught it.'

'I'd have the leisure to work on the garden and experiment with all sorts of recipes.'

'You're making my mouth water.'

'Don't laugh at me.'

'I'm not. I am thinking how strange it is that you should lead me astray.'

'That's not true. A time comes for everyone when they need a pause. And that's what I'm suggesting.'

'Isn't this a surrender?'

'Of course not, you idiot. I'm only saying that instead of struggling with the impossible we should have an interval.'

'And be Micawbers during the course of it.'

'Yes.'

'All right,' I said, 'you've convinced me. When shall we start this idleness?'

'Why not this morning?'

I was laughing again. 'If that's the case the donkeys deserve a reward. I'll fetch them an apple each.'

For a month we were as gay as could be. Jeannie had her

fishing rod, dangled a line for hours into our teaspoon of a bay, and caught nothing. I pottered about, leant against rocks staring vacantly out to sea, pretending there never would be worries again. People called and instead of being as polite as was necessary before brushing them away, we indulged in their company. There was no cause for impatience. There was no tedious task niggling our minds, no weeding, no sense of duty to make us feel we were wasting time by talk. We were relaxed. We behaved as I would have expected two people to behave who had rented Minack for a holiday.

But when the month had gone, there slowly began to build up an unexpected dimension in our lives. Our consciences started to prick. We found, for instance, that a greenhouse which is left empty when by natural right it should be occupied develops an air of resentment; and we had six greenhouses. They stared at us day after day, huge canopies of glass, and although we tried to keep our eyes averted as we passed them, they forced us to look; and we shuddered increasingly at the sight of the weeds growing with lush abandon. At the end of the month the contents resembled a section of the South American jungle.

A further discomfiture was not only did we feel guilty, but we were publicly proved guilty. When callers arrived we of course could not prevent them from observing what was happening, or coming to their own conclusions; and so we imagined their eyes became shifty, as if they believed they had discovered the skeleton in our cupboard; and that we were now playing at flower farming because we had been seduced by the shadowy rewards from the city. We became increasingly uncomfortable. We shuddered in guilty anticipation as soon as we saw a car coming down the lane. And every day the weeds prospered abundantly.

Callers reserved their comments until they had left us. Friends didn't. Sage advice has often been heaped upon us by friends enjoying a Cornish holiday. Normally the safety of an office protects one from the amateur, but in our case the office was there for all to see. Everyone could participate. And often we have been maddeningly irritated when friends, having absorbed our time, have innocently commented on some feature of the flower farm with which, in any case, we ourselves were dissatisfied. A question of rubbing salt in a wound.

This time, however, our friends were blunt. And in the wake of their remarks, however unreasonable they may have been, we found ourselves wallowing in wordy explanations.

'It is beyond me why you've left these greenhouses empty. They look a mess.'

'What is in that meadow over there, the one with all the nettles in it?'

'Surely you could find time to grow cucumbers. My aunt grows them and finds them very easy.'

'I hope you realise that these greenhouses are depreciating all the time, and you're not getting a penny interest on your capital.'

In other years we would have loftily dismissed these strictures as an unasked-for interference, grumbled together privately, then forgotten them. This summer, however, with our consciences pricking, we were peculiarly sensitive to criticism and so sometimes we accompanied our wordy explanations with a dash of bad temper. The truth is that the honeymoon of doing nothing about the flower farm was soon over. Worry took its place again.

I am among those who can be down in the depths one moment and up in the heights the next. I also wilt, my imagination becomes stifled, when faced by people who show no likelihood of ever sharing my wavelength; and the fact they so obviously believe in their superiority over me only increases my frustrated fury. But I take wings when I meet someone who possesses the gift of enthusiasm and who distributes it among those with whom he has dealings. My mind awakes. I am willing to climb Everest.

One hot afternoon we had a caller who was the salesman for our flowers in Covent Garden. Of all the business people I have ever met, flower salesmen are the most genial, despite the early morning hours they have to keep, and the dark, cold conditions of the market in which they work; and for the 10 per cent they receive from sales, they also give the grower much enthusiasm and very helpful advice. This, at any rate, is what Jeannie and I have found over the years in sending all our flowers to the same firm in Covent Garden. Moreover, they took such a personal interest in the flowers they received that once a year, during the daffodil season, the head of the firm paid Cornwall a visit; and later on, between seasons, his representative. And it was his representative who arrived on that hot afternoon when Jeannie and I were despondent.

He was in a hurry. He had another appointment for which he was already late, and he said he knew we would understand. A brush off possibly, almost inevitably, if spoken by another kind of person. He knew we would understand, he said, because never from the beginning of the season to the end were there ever any complaints about our flowers. They ask for them specially, he said, and it is always a pleasure to open your boxes and show them.

'You give something to the flower trade, you two.'

I believe when he said this that both of us felt so emotional that we wanted forcibly to restrain him from leaving us. He had given us the key. He had made no deliberate effort to do so but his antennae, without which a talented person will be ordinary, had sensed we needed a lift. And we were able excitedly and so happily to respond. Here was an instant of good luck without which no endeavour can succeed; and the only issue at stake was taking advantage of it. The hot afternoon, after he had left, had to be made to work.

As soon as his car disappeared up the lane, we realised

too where lay our friends; and although our connection
with them might be by the tenuous communication of
newly turned soil, daffodil bulbs, flowers, picking and
bunching them, rushing them to the station, and awaiting
the post for the envelope containing the prices, the world
they lived in was indeed a real world.

We knew also that we must not betray all the struggle,
sacrifice, and enthusiasm which led the way to us receiving such a compliment. We must attack. This collision
between despondency and the praise we had received was
a reflection of all the years we had been at Minack. The
earth and the rain and the wind may have hurt us but
they had never, I felt, dimmed the truth of our optimism.
We struggled where we loved. Failure was in the hands
of the gods, not in the hands of human beings. When
we fought for our survival, we did not have to weary
ourselves waiting upon the whims of other people. We
were alone. We were together.

'Jeannie,' I said, such relief in my mind and the enthusiasm simmering again which had been curbed in the tight
circle of wavering defeatism, 'let's give ourselves one more
chance!'

'Oh yes, I agree.'

'I want to see Minack a show place of daffodils. I
want to fight all those things which have been dulling
our happiness.'

Jeannie was smiling at me.

'Don't get too fierce!'

'Oh I know I sound melodramatic, but that's how
I feel. For better or for worse I want to slam them
all!'

'You will.'

'And so I'm going to play a hunch. The only person
I know who can help us to achieve what we want is
Geoffrey. I saw his father the other day and it is just
possible Geoffrey wants to return to Minack.'

'He loved the cliffs.'

'I'll write to him and ask him whether he will come and see us on Wednesday evening.'

Wednesday was the day after the morrow. It was also Fred's birthday.

18

I was up early in the morning, a glorious, hazy, warm May morning, and went down to the rocks for a bathe. Fishing boats, a half mile offshore, were hurrying to Newlyn market and gulls swirled in their wake. Two cormorants on the other side of the little bay, black sentinels in the sunlight, were standing on a rock regally surveying the scene; and on my left, up in the woods of the cliff, wood pigeons cooed. The scent of the sea filled the air, crystals sparkled the water, and the sound of the lazy, lapping waves was like a chorus of ghosts telling the world to hush. No angry engines in the sky disturbed the peace of it. No roar of traffic dulled the senses. Here was the original freedom. Here was poised a fragment of time when the world was young.

When I returned to the cottage, Fred and Penny were standing in the field looking down into the garden, and Jeannie was at the door.

'We've been waiting for you,' she said, laughing, 'Fred's been getting impatient.'

He began to whimper, nostrils quivering, the prelude

to a bellow. 'Hold it, Fred, hold it,' I called, 'we've got a present for you!' Then Jeannie went inside and brought back a huge bunch of carrots. 'Happy birthday!' we said, holding the bunch in front of him.

Fred, and Penny for that matter, was clearly surprised at such an array of carrots so early in the morning. They were even more surprised when ten minutes later two children's voices came singing round the corner; 'Happy birthday to you!' Susan and Janet from the farm at the top had arrived, like Cornish pixies, with their presents. More carrots! And it was not yet eight o'clock.

Fred, in a way, had become a mascot to the children of St Buryan parish in which we lived. They had been told of the days when donkeys clip-clopped the lanes of the district; and how the fishermen of Sennen Cove had the finest collection of donkeys in Cornwall, racing each other through St Buryan village on the way to Newlyn with their catches; but these seemed like fairy stories to those who had never seen a donkey. An old doctor on his rounds, before the First World War, was the last to be remembered using a donkey cart in St Buryan parish; but no one could remember when a donkey was last born. Fred, therefore, was a character of the imagination which had become real. His birthday, his first birthday, was an occasion. And the children were going to celebrate it.

Fred now had time to digest his early morning presents. There was a pause in his festivities and he roamed around the field flicking his tail and nibbling the grass, then suddenly appeared again to look down into the garden.

'Fred seems to be hinting at something,' said Jeannie.

I looked up at him. Fluffy brown coat, a brown pillow of a fringe between his two big ears and the white of his nose, a sturdy, slightly arched little back, the black cross easy to see, and a pair of intelligent eyes which were saying: 'She's right. I am!'

'Nothing doing, Fred,' I said, 'you must wait for the party this afternoon.'

At that moment I heard the postman singing his way down the lane on his bicycle. Part-time postman, cobbler, hairdresser, fish and chip merchant, he had a key part to play in the coming events. He also sold ice-creams. And he also always arrived at Minack happily smiling, whatever the gales, the rain or the snow.

'Lovely morning, Mr Gilbert,' I said.

'And a lovely morning for a donkey's birthday,' he replied. He began to search through his satchel. 'I've got something here I've never carried before. A telegram for a donkey! And there's a big envelope for Fred too. Birthday cards from the school.' He paused, still searching. 'Ah, here they are . . .' Then he added when he had handed them to me: 'I've seen the schoolmaster. Thirty-two will be coming from the school, and so what with the grown-ups I reckon forty cornets will see it through.'

'Leave it to you,' I said.

'I'll be down soon after half-past three.'

A telegram and, within the envelope, thirty-two birthday cards! We were under an obligation to play the game with respect. Much earnest thought and trouble had gone into the making of it. A ritual had to be observed. Whether Fred was personally interested or not, each greeting had to be read to him; and in any case Jeannie and I were exceedingly touched that the children should have remembered him.

'Many happy returns to Freddie. Love Sally and Linda,' said the telegram. How had they remembered the date? Two schoolgirls from London who had come to Minack as strangers to see if they could meet the gull on the roof; and then had spent the afternoon playing with Penny and Fred. I held the telegram up to him and he pushed his nose into it. 'Do you remember how Sally spent an hour grooming you and you loved it?'

There were carrots galore on the birthday cards. Each card had been individually drawn in coloured crayon, imaginative, primitive drawings, the figure one prominent in all of them, some with poems attached, cut-outs of other donkeys painstakingly pasted on thick paper, messages of good wishes in carefully written script, joke drawings like donkeys fishing ('I hope you catch your carrot.'), romantic drawings of a donkey ruminating in a pasture, another with ships as a background; all kindly and thoughtful and original. Something so much more important was there than the cards themselves, and we now awaited the arrival of those who sent them. And so did Fred.

When they came he could have been excused if he had been startled by their number. He had never seen so many children before, so many gay, shouting children who tumbled out of cars, running up the path to the field, calling: 'Happy birthday, Freddie!' This was a carnival of a party, a boy was dressed as the Mad Hatter, battered top hat and tails too big for him, another wore a huge mask of the March Hare, girls in party frocks with ribbons in their hair, boys chasing each other, all converging on Fred who stood his ground half-way up the slope of the field with ears pricked; and I would have forgiven him if he had turned and fled. Thirty-two children swarming towards him, screams of laughter, yells of glee, this cacophony of happiness made noise enough to scare him into leaping into the next field. He did not budge. He awaited the onslaught of arms being flung around him, ears pulled, mane ruffled, nose kissed and kissed again, pats on the back, tail tugged, as if it were an experience to which he had long been accustomed. All through the afternoon he allowed himself to be treated as a toy, and not once did he show impatience. Dear one-year-old Fred. This was indeed his hour of glory.

There were rewards, of course. His guests, for instance, vied with each other in their generosity, eating part of their ice-cream cornets then pushing them towards a large, welcoming mouth. He had always loved ice-cream. And there were the sticky lollipops, the shape and colour of carrots which Jeannie had bought; and these too were dangled before him in such a way that when accepted, kudos was obtained.

Penny, meanwhile, was having her own passage of fame. Fred, being too young to carry anyone, Penny had to play the role of the patient beach donkey. Can I have a ride? Can I? Can I? Up and down the field she went, solemnly and safely. Sometimes two astride her back, sometimes even three. She plodded on in the manner of a donkey who knew how to earn its living. She waited quietly as someone was heaved upon her back, she moved on at the right moment, she halted as soon as a fair ride had been completed. Can I have a ride? Can I? Can I?

There they were, two donkeys with ice-cream smeared about their faces, sucking lollipops; Fred a toy donkey, Penny a working one, when the time came for The Cake. Jeannie had made it, a table on the field was ready for it, and there was a single candle.

The air was still, and with ceremony the candle was lit. The table was at the bottom of the field above the wood and so its shelter helped the flame to burn steadily and with no fear of it flickering out. All around were Fred's guests. There was chattering and laughter, and from somewhere in the background a small voice began the customary birthday song.

'Too soon!' someone else shouted.

Fred, at that moment, had not arrived. He was a few yards away in a cluster of admirers, a girl with golden hair holding the halter, and all of them edging Fred towards the climax of his party. He did not want to be rushed. He was going to arrive in his own good time. And suddenly the shouts went up: 'Here's Freddie! Happy birthday, Freddie! Good old Freddie!' Treble voices sailing into the sky. A moment in time that many years away, most would remember. Nothing complicated. The same pleasure that centuries have enjoyed.

Fred reached the table. The candle on the cake, a strong,

confident flame, awaited him. But I do not think anyone who was present believed he would so successfully fulfil their secret hopes.

As the children sang his birthday song, Fred pushed his head forward inquiringly towards the candle, snorted; and blew it out.

The children had gone, Minack was quiet again, and we now awaited Geoffrey; and we soon saw him coming down the lane. There was a sense of continuity about the sight of him, as if it were one of those days years ago, when he worked at Minack; and it would have been easy had I shut my eyes, to believe that Shelagh was riding down the lane behind him on her bicycle, and that Jane too had arrived across the fields from her cottage above the cliffs she loved. These three who in a period of struggle for survival, had given us their loyalty and enthusiasm; and now that I saw him again, his presence drove a sharp awareness into my private world of doubts and frustrated plans that once again we could set about building upon the base of Minack.

In this impermanent world in which restlessness is a deception for contentment, in which the individual can only salvage what he can from the twilight pressures of the mass, in which to be sensitive is no longer a grace, in which haste without purpose, second-hand pleasures, package thinking and noise for the sake of it are the gods of millions; in which truth is an expendable virtue in the pursuit of power, and in which youth is compelled from the beginning to worship materialism, Jeannie and I could touch the old stones of Minack, brace ourselves before the gales, listen to the sea talking and to the gulls crying, be at one with the animals, have time to search our inward selves and fight the shadow which is the enemy; and to marvel at the magic which had led us to a life we loved so much.

'Do you realise,' said Jeannie, after Geoffrey, as enthusiastic as we had hoped him to be, had gone back up the lane and the date of his return had been agreed, 'that we now can go away as we planned a year ago?'

'I do.'

'And neither of us now want to?'

'Neither of us.'

'It seems to prove something.'

'What?'

Jeannie paused for a moment, leaning against a rock and staring out into the wide sweep of Mount's Bay.

'I suppose I mean,' she said, 'that if individuals are to be truly happy they should have a purpose in life which does not trample on others.'

'Only a few can have such an opportunity. The rest have to fight for a living in jobs they do not enjoy.'

'That's what I mean. We are one of the few . . . and we have realised it.'

'We have solved what we set out to solve a year ago.'

'Yes.'

The dying sun was beginning to touch the fields across the valley. The shadows of boulders were sharp. The pilchard fleet of Newlyn was busily setting out towards the Wolf Rock. A happy day. A soft breeze off the sea, curlews flying high and calling, a woodpecker laughing.

'Let's go and see the donkeys,' I said.

We reached the field and saw no sign of them.

'That's funny, I hope I didn't leave the gate open.'

'Look there they are!' said Jeannie.

At the far end of the field beneath the distant hedge I saw Penny standing dozily upright. On the grass beside her lying outstretched was Fred sound asleep. A donkey who had had a party, enjoyed every minute of it, and was now exhausted.

We did not disturb them.

Sun on the Lintel

1

New Year's Day and a black easterly was blowing in from the sea and The Lizard.

'I want you to listen to me.'

'I'm listening.'

From where I was standing with my back to the fireplace, my head level with the great granite lintel which had been heaved into place when the cottage was built five hundred years before, I could see Jeannie in our galley of a kitchen, concentrating on a recipe book open before her.

'You're not listening,' I said, 'or if you're listening, you're not hearing.'

'I won't be a second.'

A problem of two people being happy together is that they talk too much to each other. A thought comes into the head, and it has to be shared. They are inclined to prattle, gushing their thoughts into words, hoping for instant reaction from the other.

'It's not important,' I said, 'it can wait.'

The kitchen is very small, eight feet long and five across; and yet it has numerous small cupboards with natural wood doors that go from floor to ceiling, an electric stove, a sink, a dishwasher, a refrigerator, a Kenwood Chef, and of course a space where the food is prepared. Jeannie drew the design for the kitchen, though it was I who, from time to time, had insisted on buying the electrical extras.

But at first I was against the installation of electricity. For ten years Jeannie and I had lived with paraffin and calor gas and an old petrol pump which had brought the water up from our well; and we were content. There were no groans from Jeannie when she cooked breakfast on the paraffin stove, no groans from me when I dipped the lighter into the methylated spirit bottle, then fixed it to the paraffin lamp, lit it, waited for its warmth to light the mantle of the lamp, then pumped it into brightness. There was pleasure in these basic acts. A sense of freedom in being so dependent on primitive necessities.

It was during this period that we learnt to distrust a world in which the people threw up their hands in horror if there were a bread delivery strike, an electricity strike, a milkman's strike, or any strike which interrupted the conveyor belt method of their living. It seemed to us that the people had created a spiritual vacuum, so that they possessed no peace of mind once a cog in their material existence jammed.

We had our problems, many of them, but we appreciated that the base of happiness did not depend upon man-made technical tricks. We could survive happily without electricity, or main water, or a telephone. These, we learnt, were not the essentials for a happy life. We were spared, also, from any 'keep up with the Joneses' attitude because we had no Joneses to keep up with. We never had to suffer from that material hunger which has no end to its appetite. True, occasionally we would have happy times with witty friends, lots of laughter, jokes at other people's expense, a wish superficially to please . . . but we were aware, as we poured out the drinks and laughed and listened and enjoyed such moments of gaiety, that we were living again our London selves which we had run away from. For I had learnt that gregariousness hides you from yourself, and that if you want to know the real truth of living it is found in solitude. Then, if you are patient, a window opens upon a multitude of subtleties to which you were blind and deaf before. You even become aware of man's trivial living time, and marvel at the conceit with which he fills it.

Then one day the electricity planners came to Minack, part of a scheme to steer this part of the Land's End peninsula into the modern era; and I proceeded to object to the wooden poles which were to come through our wood, refused to have one planted adjacent to the cottage, later insisted that one pole should have a couple of feet cut off because it appeared above the tops of the trees. I was like a tribesman in the jungle, whose instinct was against the benefit of change.

I did not, however, obstinately maintain this attitude once the electricity was installed. True, I continued to resent the fact that, instead of sitting in a cottage which was totally independent of the outside world, I was now tied by a cable to a generating station . . . but, at the same time, I began to learn to accept the advantages. I learnt, for instance, that the simple life can be enhanced by modern gadgets; and once converted to this point of view, I behaved as a convert is inclined to do. My enthusiasm for the cause became greater than that of those who were born to it.

Jeannie, for instance, was suspicious of dishwashers until I arrived home with one in the back of the car after I had been to St Ives to pay a visit to the dentist. A shop next door had a dishwasher displayed in the window, and when I came out of the dentist's, bemused perhaps by what had been done to me, I went into the shop and bought it. It was a whim, a sudden act which had to be done before I thought twice about it, even before I knew how it could be squeezed into the kitchen; and to make sure there would not be a moment's delay before its installation, I called on a plumber friend, and he came out to Minack that same day. It is so important never to delay turning a whim into reality.

There was also sense in my extravagance. Electricity now provided the opportunity of saving Jeannie tedious work, and so gave her the opportunity to make use of her talents. Jeannie finds, like many of us, that manual labour is easier than mental labour. Hence, instead of writing or painting, she will gladly undertake any task such as ironing, making an unnecessary cake, weeding the garden, rather than concentrate her mind on the tasks her talents deserve of her. It was because of this attitude of hers that I once regularly kept her locked in the wood cabin where we bunched violets in our early days at Minack, a cabin which has since been joined to the cottage and become a spare bedroom, in order to make certain that she completed her book *Meet me at the Savoy*; and I repeated the exercise when she wrote her novel *Hotel Regina*, and again when she wrote *Home is the Hotel*. I too, however, am a dallyer, and so I do not complain if she, in turn, locks my door when I am working.

'I'm ready,' said Jeannie, closing the recipe book, 'what is it you want to say?'

'I want to list my New Year resolutions.'

She laughed. 'How very funny.'

'I'm serious.'

'Oh really . . .'

New Year resolutions are, of course, a perennial joke. They are made to be broken. As a twelve-year-old I resolved to read a page of a French book every day of the holidays . . . this resolution lasted two days.

'There are certain things I want to do,' I said, 'and I am always putting off doing them. Sensible things. And perhaps if I parcel them together in a package

of New Year resolutions I might make myself carry
them out.'

'Perhaps . . .'

Jeannie, however, is less of a dallyer than I am. I am
naturally lazy. I gaze into space, I meander on a walk,
I roam around mental corners before making a decision
. . . unless an incident suddenly inspires my imagination.
Then I act quickly.

Jeannie is inclined always to act quickly. She is like
a rider who fearlessly jumps fences, not worrying what
may happen on the other side. When we were making up
our minds whether to leave London and make a new life
at Minack, it was Jeannie who led me to the decision. I
wavered. I foresaw the problems. But Jeannie, once her
mind was made up, had no doubts; and when she closed
the door of suite 205, her office at the Savoy Hotel, for
the last time, she had no fear of the future. She, who was
the personal friend of the great names of an era, showed
no hesitation in exchanging her luxury life for a Cornish
cottage which had no running water, or bathroom, or
electricity. She had decided where the true values lay, and
in the years we have been at Minack I have never known
her question the correctness of her judgement. Not even
in some emotional moment has she declared her wish
to return. Not even when she has received handsome
offers to do so, like the time she was asked to handle
the publicity for Charlie Chaplin's last movie. Minack
was her harbour, and that was all there was to it.

'All right,' she said, curling herself on the sofa, 'tell me
about your resolutions.'

Jeannie is slim and dark, and a mixture of Scots, Irish
and English. Sometimes I have clear evidence of the Scot
in her, sometimes of the Irish, sometimes of the English.
This means that my life with her has never been dull.

'Well,' I said, pausing for a moment while I prised out
with a matchstick the ash remnants of my pipe into the
ashtray on my desk, 'I want to start my New Year

resolutions with what I am doing now ... instead of spilling the ash carelessly on the desk, which it is my habit to do, I'm going to knock the ash cleanly into the ashtray like so ...'

The ash, with the aid of the matchstick and a knock, fell neatly into the tray.

'That's a good start,' said Jeannie laughing, 'what next?'

The surge of enthusiasm one has about New Year resolutions is intoxicating. A glorious self-confidence overwhelms one.

'I'm not going to be bossed by Oliver and Ambrose,' I said, 'nor by Penny and Fred.'

'I think you're rather hard on them!'

'Not at all,' I said firmly, 'I think there's something weak about my character the way I pander to them. I'm going to correct this.'

'How so?'

I realised there was a hint of defiance in my voice, a tone of aggressiveness which one adopts when intending to change course from the accepted routine.

'For instance,' I said, 'Oliver and Ambrose are infiltrating more and more into our lives. Before long you'll find they'll stop sleeping in the porch and be on our bed instead.'

'What would be wrong in that?'

'What would be wrong? My dear girl, I have spent most of my married life with a cat on the bed, first Monty then Lama, and the prospect of having two on the bed is impossible to contemplate.'

'We'll see.'

'You won't get round me this time. None of you will.'

Of course, she knew that my attitude was a vulnerable one. When I first met Monty, the beautiful ginger cat who came with us to Minack when we left London, he was playing with a string on the green carpet of Jeannie's office at the Savoy. He was a tiny kitten, obtained by

Jeannie's mother from a hairdresser's in St Albans, and I, a cat hater, was expected to be thrilled by the sight of him. 'I'll throw him over Hammersmith Bridge on the way home,' I murmured threateningly. But Monty passed safely over the bridge, and on into Barnes and to Mortlake, where he lived for the next seven years in our cottage on the river overlooking the finishing post of the Boat Race, then to another seven happy years at Minack. He conquered me, enslaved me, and when he died I swore I would never have another cat.

I did, however, in this moment of sad emotion, add a curious condition. Curious, because at the time I was not hoping that it would come true. I said to Jeannie that the only way in which I would ever have another cat was if it were all black, came to us in a storm and there was no trace whence it came. Lama fulfilled these conditions. Lama, who sat on my lap for hour after hour while I wrote my books about Minack, was all black, came to us in a storm, and came from no human home we could trace. Like Monty, she became the repository of my secret thoughts. As with Monty, I began to be afraid when she grew old.

Three years before she died, however, another black cat started to appear regularly in the vicinity of Minack, and we had reason to believe that it was the same black kitten we once discovered in a small cave down the cliff. The mother of the kitten was a little wild grey cat, whom we always considered to be Lama's mother, and in that case the kitten and Lama were relations. The kitten had certainly looked exactly like Lama when she was young . . . and the black cat which now had appeared had the same uncanny resemblance. The same shaped head, the same compact body, and only the tail was different. Lama had a plushy tail, that of the new arrival was thin like a twig.

I told what happened during these three years in *A Cat Affair*. Oliver, as we called the black cat, persistently stayed in the neighbourhood, though at first he was far too nervous for us ever to approach him. It seemed that, though he wanted to be near us, he did not yet expect to be part of us; and this, of course, was fortunate because our love centred around Lama, and on no account did we want her peaceful routine disturbed. But, as time went by, Oliver slowly became more confident. We had now to be on guard that there was no confrontation; and, although he still remained remote, still did not demand of us any special attention, it was clear that he was ready and waiting to be a Minack cat. Lama knew he was there, and did not like it.

Then, two years after we had first seen him, Oliver played an ace card. One Sunday morning I was taking a meandering stroll and had reached Monty's Leap, the little stream which guards the entrance to Minack, when I found that Oliver had come up close beside me. He began to miaow. A second later, to my astonishment, I heard another miaow, a squeak of a miaow, in the brush a few yards away on the other side of the white gate. To my further astonishment, a tiny ginger kitten suddenly appeared, and Oliver rushed up the lane to join it. And what was so extraordinary was that the markings of the kitten were exactly the same as those of Monty when he was a kitten. Thus, out of the nowhere land of the Cornish cliffs, had come first the double of Lama and then the double of Monty. I was bemused. I, the one-time cat hater, was being chased by cats.

Jeannie gave the name of Ambrose to Monty's double but, although he had the markings of Monty, he was very shy. Monty lured me to love him. Ambrose showed no desire to do so. It was, however, clear that he was as devoted to Oliver as Oliver was devoted to him. Oliver watched him, took him for walks, educated him by slapping him with a paw if he were too familiar, taught him to wash . . . but both of them remained the outsiders. They slept in an outhouse. A plate of food was given them on the mud floor of the shelter. They were not going to receive any special favours. They could hang around Minack, but they were not going to be allowed to belong. Lama was the Queen . . . and she was not going to yield an inch of her territory.

When Lama died, however, Oliver soon began to infiltrate. Ambrose, on the other hand, remained elusive, superior in his attitude to human beings. He would never come near enough to be touched. If either of us stooped to stroke him as he drank his milk, he would dash away. He had no wish to be seduced by human condescension. He intended to keep his independence. He didn't want to fall a victim to flattery.

And then he began to falter. Though still elusive, he began to show an interest in comfort. The successful rebel, who reluctantly becomes aware of some of the advantages of the establishment. I saw the danger signals. I realised he could be skilful enough to worm his way into the establishment and, in a little while, boss it.

'I absolutely refuse,' I therefore repeated to Jeannie, 'ever to have those two cats sleeping on our bed. One resolution I certainly mean to keep.'

'Bravo,' Jeannie replied in an off-hand way, stroking Oliver who, a second before, had jumped on her lap.

The donkeys, Penny and her son Fred, had a less obvious way of interfering with the pattern of my life. They interfered by staring at me. They stared whenever they wanted to be moved from one meadow to another, or when they decided they would like a walk along the cliff path towards Lamorna, or when they were bored and wanted to be amused. I would come out of the cottage in the morning, intent on pursuing some personal task, then observe that the donkeys were staring at me and, if I took no notice of them, hooting at me. They had a subtle form of blackmail . . . if you love us, as you say you do, prove it.

Of course, it was always pleasant to prove it. I had been

proving it constantly from the first time I saw Penny, an emaciated black donkey standing in a field outside the Plume of Feathers at Scorrier, a field which has now become the concrete beginning of the Redruth by-pass . . . from the moment I first saw Fred, born to Penny a month later. I was always yielding to them both, especially in the mornings when I had letters to write, bills to pay, accounts to unravel, for then they gave me a chance to change my plans. 'Oh well,' I would say to Jeannie, 'it's a lovely day, let's take them for a walk.' I would thereupon revel in the hour and a half that followed, though when I returned, when I arrived back at the cottage to pursue the tedious duties I had set myself, I would find that my good intentions had disappeared. The letters, the bills, the accounts, would remain untouched.

I can, perhaps, plead justification for this dilatory behaviour because of the kind of life we led at Minack. We felt detached from the outside world. The outside world, it seemed, was imposed upon by publicity-minded men and women who, in order to maintain the momentum of their ambitions, thrust their views upon the public, irrespective of whether these views mirrored sincerity. Thus, ugly moods and situations which might have faded into oblivion, were magnified into major issues; and grievances, real or imaginary, were manoeuvred on to national platforms; and, at all times, envy was worshipped. Yet the pressure of modern life is such that the people accept the brainwashers. They have no time or energy to challenge them. Materialism is all that matters; and survival.

We, too, have our materialistic problems. We, too, are influenced by the brainwashers. We, too, have tensions. But we are among the lucky ones because our environment gives us the chance to see our lives in perspective; and if we do not take this chance to do so it is our fault alone. We are not rushed. We wake up to the sound of gulls crying, instead of traffic. We have no office to hasten to, no clocking in at a factory, no days ahead full of strain-filled appointments. Thus time is inclined to stand still, and we dream, and we stare out across the moorland to the blue expanse of Mount's Bay, and engross ourselves in small, unimportant pleasures; and then feel guilty over such periods of pleasant idleness. The donkeys made me feel guilty.

'Nor am I going to be bossed by the donkeys,' I said to Jeannie. 'No more walks in the morning when I have other things to do. No more being hypnotised by their stare.'

'He's tough,' said Jeannie, stroking Oliver between his ears. 'You and the donkeys will have to look out this year.'

'It's for my own protection.'

'Why?'

'I want to be organised. I want to be like one of those people who have their desks neat, their lives orderly, who are able to do all sorts of things which I never have the time for.'

'And you blame Oliver, Ambrose, Penny and Fred for your present failure?'

She was teasing me.

'Yes,' I said, playing up to her.

I walked over to the wicker basket beside the fire, picked up a log, and placed it in the grate.

'What else,' she went on with mock solemnity, 'have you in mind for your list of resolutions?'

'I'm going to grow our own plants for the garden,' I said, 'and I'll write out a list of the seeds we want during the course of this week. I'm not going to bother Percy this year.'

Percy Potter was in charge of the Sutton Seed Trial Grounds at Gulval outside Penzance, a master gardener, who provides a superb display of summer colour in the gardens overlooking Mount's Bay, and who, in other years, had often provided us with plants.

'That's a good idea. More?'

'Make up our minds whether we can continue with the flower farm, wages and costs being what they are.'

'That's a serious resolution. I don't want to hear about that.'

'It will have to be faced.'

'Perhaps . . . but I only want to hear about the fun resolutions.'

'Well,' I said, 'I intend to become a cook.'

'Wonderful!'

'Don't forget I used to cook. I gave you your first lesson.'

'Hardly.'

'Well, that first meal you cooked for me . . . the bubble and squeak, I mean. You didn't even know you had to put fat in the frying pan first.'

'I have progressed since then!'

'You certainly have . . . and now I would like to compete with you.'

'It will be a relief for me if you do. What sort of cooking have you in mind?'

'Do you remember that Prunier dish I did one day in Mortlake just before we came to Minack'

'Years ago, and I will never forget it.'

'Prawns and lemon sole and rice, and the hours I took over the sauce?'

'Sheer artistry.'

'That's the kind of cooking I would like to do again.'

'A great occasion it will be, if it comes off.'

Oliver, at that moment purring on her lap, pressed his claws into her leg. Ecstacy on his part, pain on hers.

'Oliver . . . don't!'

And Oliver jumped to the floor.

'Any more resolutions?'

'Oh yes,' I said, 'plenty . . . but I think I'll keep them to myself. It will be safer.'

'I won't broadcast them.'

'One of them I'll tell you about,' I said, 'is my intention to read *Remembrance of Things Past* again.'

'I never reached further than *Swann's Way*.'

'Well, I never read all of it. I skipped a lot. But that doesn't alter the fact that Proust had a huge influence on me when I was young. At the time I believed my personal thoughts, my personal fears and contradictions were exclusively my own. Proust showed me they were not.'

'He helped to guide your growing up.'

'Yes. I would like to find out what effect he would have on me now.'

A gull was crying on the roof. Probably Philip. He was an old gull and he made a habit of coming when the other two regulars, Flotsam and Jetsam, were absent. He had special treatment when he was on his own, a slice of meat or of cake.

'I also,' I said, 'intend to go through the papers stacked in Labour Warms.'

Jeannie was laughing.

'There are oceans of letters and notes and papers!'

'That's what I mean. It's time we sorted them out.'

Labour Warms was an institution in my life. A massive teak cupboard that was in my nursery at 48 Bramham Gardens, Kensington, then in my nursery at Glendorgal, our one-time family home near Newquay in Cornwall. Then it was installed in my bachelor flat in Elm Park Garden Mews near the Kings Road, and later followed me to Cholmondley House on the river at Richmond, and after that to Thames Bank Cottage at Mortlake. It was a family heirloom, a reminder of Victorian solidity, of the British Empire at its peak ... and across the top of the cupboard, painted in blue against the brown of the teak, was the warning:

LABOUR WARMS. SLOTH HARMS.

An appropriate motto, it seemed, for the coming year.

2

I have seldom been the person I wished to be, because the person I wished to be changed so quickly that I was unable to catch him. My Walter Mittys have been numerous.

Sometimes I have wished to be a steady, conventional type, playing safe. Sometimes I have wished to live a Bohemian life as varied as that of Augustus John. Sometimes I have wished to be a pianist, sometimes an England cricketer, sometimes an art collector. Sometimes I have wished to enjoy the deceptive applause of transient success, sometimes to run away from it and hide. Sometimes I have wished to be an intellectual, praised by the few, though unintelligible to the many. Sometimes I have wished to be gregarious among the sophisticated, sometimes to live the life of a hermit. Walter Mittys have filtered through my life, changing their roles with bewildering rapidity, providing me in their aftermath with many conclusions. Among them is a distaste for those who relish exercising power over their fellow human beings; another is that a fundamental contemporary need is to delve into one's own secret thoughts before becoming anaesthetised by the opinions of a crowd . . . and another is my everlasting gratitude to the Walter Mitty who led me to Minack.

On New Year's Day, however, it was a Walter Mitty of good intentions who had embraced me . . . but who, within twenty-four hours, had deserted me.

I had sat down in the corner of the sofa for a moment, when Oliver jumped on my lap . . . just after breakfast, and I was about to go to my desk and answer letters.

'Oliver,' I said, 'get off. I don't want anything to do with you!'

Purr, purr.

'Oliver,' I repeated, though I cursed the half-hearted tone which had crept into my voice, 'get off. I have other things to do.'

Purr, purr.

It was as if I had Lama on my lap again. The same silky black fur, the same neat head, the same unwillingness on my part to move.

'Jeannie,' I called out, 'please help me!'

The same cry as many times before. The same wish for a diversion. A saucer of milk or of fish. Anything to lure away the purr on my lap.

'You're too indecisive,' she said, coming in from the porch and proceeding to fulfil the task expected of her. 'All you have to do is to push him off.'

Quite so. All I had to do was to push him off, and yet a part of me refused to act. Why?

I had a special reason. I remembered the three years before Lama died when I had treated Oliver as a pariah, shouting him away from the cottage, frightening him by savagely scraping my feet on the gravel if he advanced too close. I had aimed to make him feel unwanted, hoping to force him back to the place whence he came, and so leave Lama in peace. I didn't care how unhappy I made him provided Lama continued her reign undisturbed. Lama belonged to Minack. Oliver was an interloper.

Propinquity, however, is a danger. A relationship between two people can blossom when their work brings them together, or they share a regular journey, or other circumstances beyond their control make them see each other often. Against their will they begin to love. Against my will, Oliver began to creep into my affection.

It was his persistence that caused this. He was so determined to become a part of Minack that he was prepared to accept any insults and much discomfort. When he first began to hover around the neighbourhood, and for many months afterwards, he used to sleep at night on a bank of grass and bracken beside the lane on the far side of Monty's Leap. He huddled himself into a little cavity, seemingly unperturbed by the rain and the gales; and in the daytime he would sit for hours by the white gate staring up towards the cottage, fleeing away into the undergrowth whenever we walked towards him. Minack was a magnet, but it gave him no confidence.

Jeannie, in her role as a lifetime lover of all cats, was the first to show pity; and she found a wooden box which she placed in the undergrowth near the white gate, lining it with straw. Oliver liked it immediately; and later I improved this dwelling by covering it with polythene and hiding it with bracken, and making a tunnel of an entrance, and a back exit out of which he could escape if frightened by an inquisitive fox. Our mistake, however, was the choice of site. It was close to a gully, and when the gully was flooded by the winter rains so too was Oliver's dwelling. The morning following the first flood, I found him perched on the branch of an old gorse bush, miaowing. I thereupon rebuilt his dwelling elsewhere.

Some time after this episode, I saw him hobbling up the lane towards the cottage on three legs. Lama was out of the cottage at the time and, at first, I thought it was she who had been injured. From a distance they looked so exactly alike that it was easy to make such an error, and I called out to Jeannie: 'Lama's coming up the lane and there's something wrong with one of her legs!' Jeannie, who was in the tiny front garden, called back that I had made the usual mistake: 'It's Oliver, not Lama . . . Lama is with me!'

I watched Oliver hobble up the lane, then turn right into the stone building which serves as the garage and disappear under the Volvo. I had never seen him behave in such a determined fashion, nor had I ever seen him go into the garage before. His back legs were sound, so also the right front one, but I clearly saw the left one was dangling.

'Oliver needs your help, Jeannie . . . you'll have to examine him.'

'But he would never let me!'

'You'll have to try.'

To her surprise, Oliver this time showed no fear of her. He remained quite still as she examined him and found that his paw had a deep cut.

'Looks as if he's been caught in a snare.'

'Damn them,' I said.

Each day he let her bathe it with the liquid of Exultation of Flowers that comes from Nairn in Scotland, and a bottle of which Jeannie always keeps handy . . . and, after a week, the wound was healed. But, by that time, our relationship with Oliver had changed. He had won a victory, and he knew it. From now on Jeannie and I were on the retreat, facing the fact that he was here to stay. The prospect did not please us. For Lama's sake, we now had to be prepared to chase away a cat who had won our affection.

There are, of course, many who would call our attitude a sentimental absurdity. Why bother about the feelings of a cat? Why waste time on animal love when the human race can obliterate itself at the touch of a button; when twisted minds leave random bombs in crowded places;

when schoolchildren threaten their teachers with flick knives; when there is a perpetual economic crisis? Animal love, in such circumstances, does seem absurd. It is an irrelevancy compared with the problems of the day. No wonder that pragmatic people condemn animal lovers. Life is too serious for such indulgence.

Unashamedly, however, Jeannie and I allow ourselves such indulgence. Animals offer stability in this unstable world. They do not deceive. They soothe jittery moods. They offer solace in times of trouble by the way they listen to you. They may not understand a word you say, but that doesn't matter, because it is a dumb sympathy that you ask of them and they give it; an extra-sensory understanding, which is the more comforting since it is secret. You have no regrets afterwards for having disclosed too much.

I am not, on the other hand, an indiscriminate animal lover. Indiscriminate animal lovers can be so lavish in their love that they seem to suffer from a form of disease. Their emotions are highly pitched, and they agonise over the welfare of animals to such an extent that their home lives become warped . . . horses, ponies, donkeys, lost dogs, cats and kittens, and any other unhappy animal they may find, take over. I admire the selflessness of such people, but I have to admit my love for animals does not embrace such selflessness. My love for an animal is based on a friendship, and I cannot offer this to animals in quantity. I want it to be concentrated on the few. If I once allowed myself to succumb to the lost look of the animal kingdom, I too would catch the disease. I would lose my sense of proportion.

Sometimes, however, I have been close to catching the disease. I am, for instance, irrational as far as snares and the trapping of animals are concerned. When we first came to Minack, gin traps were still legal, and we used to listen to the trapper hammering into the ground the stake to which the trap was attached, knowing that in the evening the cries of the trapped rabbits would begin. First a number of cries after the rabbits had come out from their burrows, then more spasmodically during the course of the night. It was a brutal experience and, when the day came when Monty was caught in one of the traps, our emotions exploded. Jeannie picked up the trap after we had released him and flung it away into the undergrowth . . . only to receive a visit from an angry farmer, who accused both ourselves and Monty of trespassing. He was justified in doing so, and I had no right to argue. We were newly arrived city folk, who did not understand the standards of those who had long experience of the land. Rabbits to us were pretty things, but to the farmer they were vermin . . . like mice in the kitchen.

When the gin trap became illegal, the rabbits had already been obliterated by myxomatosis and, for some years, there was peace at night in the countryside. Then the rabbits gradually returned and large scale snaring began, and the snares are more diabolical in many ways than gin traps. A snare, for instance, can catch an animal around its body and squeeze it; and, apart from rabbits, I have known many a cat caught in this manner. I haven't, however, seen a rabbit snare in this area for a long time because myxomatosis came back yet again and so there was no need for snares. Snares and gin traps, therefore, had become a part of unpleasant history, or so I thought. I had no idea that another kind of snare existed.

For a number of years, a group of influential Cornish farmers had been conducting a campaign alleging that badgers, the most hygienic in their habits of all British wild animals, were carriers of tuberculosis, and that they were the cause of tuberculosis in cattle. Cattle T.B. is obviously a serious matter and the Ministry of Agriculture takes every possible step to control it. The herd of each farm is regularly tested, and whenever an animal is found to be infected it is slaughtered. If a herd, therefore, is badly infected the financial loss to the farmer is severe.

The veterinary advisers of the Minsitry of Agriculture

have constantly been trying to discover the cause of the disease. One theory is that farmers overstock their land with cattle, producing conditions similar to those that account for T.B. in humans who live in overcrowded and underfed areas. Another theory is that the modern intensive method of farming and the use of chemical fertilisers are the cause. Theories have abounded, but without any fundamental evidence to support any one of them.

Thus some farmers became angry, mystified and frustrated, and began a witch-hunt against the badger; and they pressed the Ministry of Agriculture so successfully that the Ministry agreed to examine the health of badgers in the West Cornwall area. Badger dropping samples were to be sent for laboratory tests and bodies of dead badgers were to be examined. All this was a conscientious attempt to solve the T.B. problem and it had the advantage that, if the laboratory tests were to prove negative, badgers would be cleared conclusively as the cause of the trouble. The Ministry, however, did not disclose how the dead badgers were to be obtained. Jeannie and I were to find out.

Meanwhile, we have had our own badger problems. A badger, for instance, will sometimes take a fancy to a meadow of bulbs and proceed to dig up a patch, or he will roll on the daffodil foliage, or play a game in a meadow where the daffodils are soon to be picked. He will also keep obstinately to the track which his forbears have used for hundreds of years, and so, if the track runs across a daffodil meadow, nothing we can do will ever make him abandon it. These antics do not disturb us. No major harm occurs. We accept the badger presence.

I was not, however, so tolerant of the badger who developed a passion for carrots last summer. The carrots were sown in long double rows at monthly intervals in an area of ground beyond the greenhouses where we had our tomatoes. Nearby were rows of peas, runner beans, raspberry canes, lettuce, strawberries, turnips, beetroot and other produce of a kitchen garden for our own use . . . but the carrots, though we needed some for ourselves, were chiefly grown for the benefit of Penny and Fred. This was their winter fodder, succulent carrots which we would dry and store and produce by the handful for donkey delight when the grass in the fields had lost its nourishment. The first sowing was patiently weeded and thinned and, at last, had reached the stage ready for pulling, when overnight they disappeared. Fragments of carrot foliage lay scattered on the ground, but not a carrot was to be seen. It was as if foraging pigs had been let loose on the patch.

'Disaster!' I said to Geoffrey, our help, standing beside me. 'What are we going to do?'

'Can't do anything,' he replied, cheerfully. 'They've gone.'

'Of course they've gone,' I said, impatiently. Geoffrey is inclined to show a macabre jollity when things go wrong. 'But what are we going to do about it?'

'Dunno.'

I had heard in the past of badgers eating carrots, but they had never before come to Minack. We have had carrot-eating mice, and carrot-eating rabbits, but they had been leisurely eaters. They enjoyed their nibbles, then returned to their quarters. They never gorged a double row of carrots, each row seventy feet long, all in a night.

'Well,' I said, 'we have to save the next batch, and I've got an idea how to do it . . . we'll lay a roll of wire netting all along the two rows, flat on the foliage. A badger would never dare to go under that. He'll think it's a trap.'

'If he has a mind to do it, it won't work.'

'We'll try.'

The roll of wire netting was laid down, the slim young carrots began to bulge, and not one of them was disturbed.

'The trick is successful,' I said.

'Too soon to say that,' replied Geoffrey. 'The carrots aren't ready for pulling yet.'

And he was right. The day that the carrots were ready

for pulling, the day that we were prepared to do so, a sequence of visitors arrived and the time was spent talking instead of pulling.

Next morning the carrot ground resembled the aftermath of a battlefield.

We still had a third batch of sowings and, this time, I said to Geoffrey it was up to him to devise their protection.

'I reckon,' he said, 'that he comes up from the cliff. I'll put wire netting along the cliff side and that will stop him.'

'What about the wood? He might come from there.'

'I don't reckon he will.'

So the cliff side of the greenhouse field was closed by wire netting, and the carrots were considered to be safe. As August arrived, they bulged in weight, and on a Friday night when I paid Geoffrey we agreed to pull them on Monday after he had picked the tomatoes.

On Sunday night, a moonlight night, I slept uneasily for reasons quite unconnected with carrots . . . and when, in the early hours of Monday morning, I was lying awake, my mind buzzing around without purpose, I thought to myself that I would be better off if I took a stroll. I might even have a look at the carrots.

I strolled down the lane, across Monty's Leap, and turned left through the gap. I walked quietly towards the wire gate Geoffrey had made, and into the kitchen garden . . . and within sight of the carrots. The moon was full, glinting on the glass of the greenhouses, shining on two annihilated rows of plump carrots . . . and on a badger. He was young, I could see that, and he was moving slowly and swaying. A badger bursting with carrots, and the pleasure of a wild night out. A badger without a care in the world; a glorious, self-indulgent sleep ahead of him, his mind awhirl, his belly full. He did not even notice me as I stepped up close to him. He had created, by his discovery of the donkey carrots, his perfect world. He was carrot-drunk.

How had he penetrated Geoffrey's wire netting? Simple. He had dug under it.

The incident caused me to contemplate how I would have felt if I had been a farmer with a field of carrots which had been destroyed by an army of badgers. My loss was comparatively small, although Penny and Fred would not consider it small. They had lost their winter fodder, but at least I could find something to replace it. A farmer, on the other hand, who has lost a crop also loses his income. It explains, perhaps, why some farmers are so ruthless in their attitude towards animal life. Survival is at stake, and a wild animal which threatens their livelihood is an enemy. Badgers, for instance, were enemies in the minds of those who believed they were the carriers of T.B. Any step to kill them was a good step.

One evening I saw two dogs hunting together on the other side of the valley towards Lamorna. They were tearing up and down a field, and dashing into the moorland and back again as if they were following a trail. I did not take much interest in them, except to be irritated by their barking, and I didn't notice their breed or recognise them as belonging to anyone I knew. They were obviously enjoying themselves and they could continue to do so as far as I was concerned. I reckoned they would not stay long in the neighbourhood, and the barking would cease and it would be quiet again.

An hour later, however, there was still the sound of barking; a muffled sound of barking, and I remarked to Jeannie that one of the dogs was likely to be at the entrance of a badger sett. This had happened before in the area concerned. A terrier of a Lamorna friend of mine used to scare his owner by going down into a badger sett, going so far that the barks became hardly audible. On this occasion, therefore, I continued to take little notice, and we had our supper of poached lemon sole, which came from the fish market at Newlyn, and listened afterwards to a Fauré concert from the Royal Festival Hall, and then went to bed early.

Our bedroom window faces across the shallow valley

to the other side where I first saw the two dogs chasing the trail. We were lying there, hoping to sleep, and being checked from doing so by: 'Bark, bark!' It was a resigned bark. No urgency in it.

'The dog's getting tired,' I murmured to Jeannie. 'Will stop soon.'

'You don't think it's in trouble?'

'Of course not. It is an obstinate dog, which is frustrated. It's reached the end of the trail it followed, and now is baulked from fulfilment. It will tire before long, and go home.'

'Sure?'

'Yes . . . now go to sleep.'

I have always been vexed by three o'clock in the morning. Why is it that you can go relaxed to bed at ten, then wake up at three in a state of apprehension? All the mixed-up stresses are present. A challenge is too big to cope with. Your money affairs are insoluble. Your job in danger. You lie awake with your mind tight, ideas racing each other, and wonder how it is possible to survive. On this occasion, however, it was not personal apprehension that woke me up at three o'clock in the morning. The apprehension concerned the dog. I lay there in bed hearing it bark for half a minute, then silence for three, then another bark. Jeannie, too, had woken up.

'It *is* in trouble,' she said.

'Can't think how.'

A bark, silence, a bark.

'We had better get up and have a look.'

'Not yet,' I said. I was comfortable. I selfishly had no wish to leave the warmth of my bed to go searching for a dog in the dark. Anyhow, I said to myself, it couldn't be in serious trouble. There was nothing to cause a dog trouble. It wasn't as if the gin traps were still around. It was probably just waiting for a badger to come out of its sett, or a fox from its earth.

A long silence.

'There you are,' I said, sleepily. 'It's given up and gone home.'

Bark.

'You're wrong . . . come on, get up.'

I obeyed. I dressed, found the torch, a beam torch which shines like a searchlight, and we were about to set off when Jeannie said: 'You had better bring the secateurs.' I picked up a pair which were on the shelf in the porch and put them in my pocket. 'It may be lying hurt in a thicket,' she added, 'and we might have to cut our way through.'

We walked down the lane towards Monty's Leap, past the stables on our right, past two large shadows that loomed beside the hedge of the stable meadow. A soft whinnying noise sounded from one of the shadows.

'Quiet, Fred,' I said. 'We don't want any ballyhoo from you.'

Fred, if he saw us out at unusual hours, was inclined to announce the matter to the neighbourhood. I have known him shatter a soft summer night, soundless except for the sea lapping rocks, with a crescendo of blaring hee-haws.

'Quiet, Fred,' I repeated. And he was quiet.

We passed, and went on up the lane. It was a dark, moonless night and, therefore, we relied on the dog continuing to bark to give us our bearings. We trudged up a grass-covered path into the moorland, and then along a track bordered by blackberry brambles, and all the while the dog was silent. I was sure we were going in the right direction, but I knew that, unless the dog barked, we would never be able to find him. We had begun to walk downhill towards the sea when, suddenly, to my left I heard a kind of strangled cry of a dog, a sad cry, no bark this time. It was as if he had heard us and feared we would go by, and all his previous barking would be wasted. Yachtsmen in need of rescue must feel like that, when they watch a ship pass by without observing them.

'In there,' I said to Jeannie. 'Through that bracken, by

that elder tree beside the hedge.' I was beaming the torch in that direction. 'That's where it is.'

We plunged into the high bracken, and I promptly fell over because I went too fast and a foot stepped into a hole. Then Jeannie did the same, and there we were, the two of us, on a dark night on a Cornish cliff, just out of a comfortable bed, floundering in the undergrowth. The dog cried again, and it sounded as if it were at my elbow, and when I got to my feet the torch shone on the dog five yards away beneath a small elder tree. A front leg was strung up high above its head. I could see a thick wire circling the trunk of the tree four feet from the ground, and from this wire sprouted the snare, and the dog had run into it, and it had pulled pincer-tight just above its right paw.

'Hell,' I shouted. 'A badger snare. I didn't know they existed!'

The dog was a beagle hound, and I had never seen it before. It stared at us quite quietly and never for a moment did I think that, out of panic, it might attack me as I tried to release it. Other dogs might have done, but not this one. I sensed it was gentle, and that I could set out safely to do the job.

'Thank goodness, Jeannie,' I said, handing her the torch, 'that you had the idea of bringing the secateurs.'

They were not sharp. They were not wire cutters, and the wire of the snare was a quarter of an inch thick and made up of strands of wire. It was five minutes before I was able to cut through it, and then I had only been able to cut the wire attached to the tree. A length was still attached to the beagle, and there was a horrible lock on it which I found impossible to prise open.

'The only thing to do,' I said, 'is to carry it home and I'll have another try there.'

So we stumbled back the way we came, through the moorland to the lane, up towards the cottage and across Monty's Leap, the beagle becoming heavier and heavier in my arms. The donkeys were where we had passed them before, and the light shone on Fred's quizzy face, and he began again to make a snuffling noise.

'Quiet, Fred,' I repeated.

One glance at the wire in full light was enough to show that I would not be able to release it. An expert was required, and quickly. The dog had been trapped for eight hours or more. We couldn't wait for the morning.

'We'll go straight into Penzance,' I said, 'and I'll ring the vet on the way.'

Thus, at four in the morning, I was standing in a telephone kiosk close to the promenade talking to a sleepy vet, who told me to take the dog to the surgery and a colleague would come round and see to the matter. No grumbles on his part. No doubts that I might be wasting his time. And when the colleague arrived, a young Australian from Queensland, he looked at the snare and said it was diabolical. It took half an hour before the beagle was finally freed.

We took it back to Minack after that, and gave it a meal and a bowl of water, and made a bed for it in the greenhouse. Later in the day, a harassed gentleman arrived, saying he had lost a beagle and had we seen one? 'Oh yes,' I said, and took him to the dog and watched the reunion.

But what would have happened to Nonny, as we learnt was her name, if we hadn't heard her barking? True, she ought not to have been on the land in the first place, but there had been no public notice that badger snares were in the neighbourhood. And supposing it had been a badger instead of a beagle? How long would it have suffered?

I rang the Ministry of Agriculture at Truro and they admitted that snares (and there were others besides the beagle's one) had been set under their auspices. The 1973 Badger Act, aimed at preventing badger persecution, I was told, did not apply to the Ministry . . .

First Oliver in a rabbit snare, then the beagle in a badger snare. I was glad we were able to help both of them.

3

I had, of course, made resolutions on other New Year Days. All of them had soon fled away out of sight; all of them, that is to say, except the one which concerned Martha.

Martha is the help in the cottage. Martha is responsible for the cleaning, dusting and hoovering. Martha is furious if anyone forgets to wipe the mud off their shoes before coming into the cottage, or if anything is spilt on the carpet. Martha shakes the cushions on the sofa, removes untidy newspapers, sees that the scuttle is full, carries away the ash from the fire, removes any cobweb in a ceiling corner, dusts the frames of pictures. Martha, if in a good mood, is an admirable servant. Martha was born of a New Year resolution. Martha is me.

Martha was first created by A. P. Herbert on one of the occasions he was staying with us. He had sympathy for the biblical Martha with all her comings and goings; and he had an admiration for Jeannie's conscientious activities of cooking, looking after the cottage, and earthy work in the fields. Thus Jeannie became the first Martha at Minack, and A. P. H. gently praised her with a song called 'When I'm Washing Up', set to music by Vivian Ellis in *The Water Gipsies*, that A. P. H. wrote at Minack. Later, outsiders helped in the cottage and, although each one at the time eased the tediousness of Jeannie's routine, there were also disadvantages. We were not independent. We had to organise the day to suit the help; and when at last Jeannie and I decided to care for the cottage on our own, I celebrated by buying from an antique shop a small Bristol glass hand-bell. We call it the Freedom Bell, and periodically I ring it just to remind us how pleasant it is not to be under an obligation to anyone.

After my New Year resolution to take my share of the housework, after I had proved to be serious about doing so, Jeannie began to call *me* Martha. A silly game, though a game that turned tiresome chores into those of amusement. Like Jeannie saying: 'Martha, you haven't hoovered the carpet today.'

I do not mind her catching me out. Only when I was young did I believe there was a virtue in having someone looking after the place where I lived. I once thought of myself becoming a kind of Bertie Wooster, with an amiable servant to tolerate my eccentricities; a rich young man who was cosseted by his servant. But I was never rich, and never had such a servant, though when I had my first flat in London in Elm Park Garden Mews close to the King's Road in Chelsea, there was the wonderful Mrs Moon who cleaned the flat. She doted on me, was tolerant of my misbehaviours, was ecstatic at seeing my name in large letters on the sides of London buses at the time when I was writing a column in the *Daily Mirror*; and, after her first visit to the countryside, she swore she would never go again because the silence frightened her. The *Luftwaffe* over London, on the other hand, did not frighten her to the same extent. 'Old 'itler won't get me down,' was a remark she made.

Mrs Moon was an historical Londoner. London was her being.

There were others who tended me. Mrs Youdall was married to a chauffeur who drove gilded young ladies to their débutante dances. Mrs Chevins came for one day and never returned. Mrs Benson was housekeeper when I lived in Richmond, and her chief merit was the marrows she cooked, stuffed with minced meat and herbs. I was fond of Mrs Benson, but she left a curious memento after packing her bags and marching out one day. I found a dead bat hanging in her cupboard. There was Mrs Clarke, who was with me when I married Jeannie, and who tormented us after the marriage ceremony by insisting on walking close beside us as we walked down the path from the church door to the car. 'Go away, Mrs Clarke!' I was spitting, while the photographers clicked their cameras. 'Go away!'

Then there was the elderly lady who was a thief, though I never caught her in the act. Small articles disappeared, small change. At last came the moment of embarrassing circumstantial proof. I had a number of guests for a cold Sunday lunch, Poles, Yugoslavs, American journalists and a prominent Communist and his wife. Before lunch, we adjourned to a neighbouring pub, leaving the house empty save for the elderly lady concerned. When we returned, the pretty wife of the Communist looked for the handbag she had left behind in the drawing room. She found the handbag, but the contents were missing. Eight pounds.

At Minack, however, we do not have parties. Indeed, we are antisocial in the sense that we have little wish to be guests in other people's houses and we seldom invite people in advance to Minack. Advance invitations demand of you so much in self-conscious preparation; and so, by the time the guests are due to arrive, I find myself at the window, alternately looking up the lane or looking at my watch, wondering how late they are going to be, and in a mood that inclines me to regret that our invitation has ever been made.

We prefer the unexpected visitors, those on our wavelength who have suddenly decided to take the trouble to see us and arrive, not knowing whether we are here. It happens quite often. It has a pattern. They may arrive around mid-day and we offer them a glass of wine, and by one o'clock they are murmuring about leaving so that 'you two can get on with your work'. We offer them another glass, and with a show of reluctance they accept ('half a glass, please') . . . and an hour later they are delving into the pâté, cheese or whatever else that is available. The advantage of such an occasion, or of any occasion which has not been pre-fixed, is that no shadow has been thrown over the previous hours. Martha has had no domestic work to do in preparation. Jeannie hasn't had to worry what clothes she ought to wear, or what lunch she should give. The guests are treated as birds of passage. The occasion is uncomplicated. It is fun.

Sometimes, of course, the unexpected guest can cause a problem.

We had a gentleman with a high-pitched voice, who would take the bus out from Penzance, walk down the mile-long lane and present himself at our door just as I was about to settle down to cheese, biscuits and William Hardcastle's *World at One*.

We welcomed him the first time. We yielded to him the second time. The third time, a week later, we were lucky enough to spy his dapper figure crossing Monty's Leap, and we escaped through the back door into the wood, where we hid, listening to the high-pitched voice enquiring of Geoffrey where we were. We thought we were safe, and it would have been so if it had not been for Fred. At that very moment, in Houdini fashion, he succeeded in unlatching the gate of the stable meadow. Geoffrey saw him do it, and we heard him shout . . . 'The donkeys are out!'

A minute later, our unwanted guest saw us dash out of our hiding place and run up the lane and beyond. He had caught us. We had still to catch Fred.

We do not often have people to stay, and when we do, if it is a couple, we move out of the cottage and sleep in the one-time stable which is now my office, and the couple have our bedroom. We moved out for George and Sophie Brown when they came to stay with us not long after he had resigned from being Foreign Secretary. We had become friends when he stayed at Lamorna before the 1964 election, and we used to meet again periodically in the ensuing years when we went to London. He had now invited himself for five days, and the prospect alarmed us. Five days with a turbulent George Brown in a small cottage, a mile off the road, and without a telephone could be explosive. Nor did the day of his expected arrival augur well.

At mid-day we received a telegram: 'Very sorry. Must cancel visit.'

This was a let-down. Preparations galore, and now a void. We felt sorry for ourselves until tea-time. Then another telegram arrived: 'On our way. Arriving midnight. Much looking forward to holiday.'

'What's the reason, I wonder, for all these changes of mind?' I said.

'Sophie,' Jeannie said. 'I expect Sophie has persuaded him after all.'

Sophie Brown is a gentle person, tolerant, kind and easy to be with. Jeannie says she is the kind of woman that other women always like to have as a friend.

'How are we going to stay awake?' I asked. We always go early to bed. It is the Cornish air. It is sleep-making.

'Matchsticks,' said Jeannie, laughing.

This was the joke which was produced whenever there was a need for us to stay up late. It began when I was writing a book about the British Empire and I had to work into the early hours of the morning. I used to say that I kept awake by keeping my eyes open with matchsticks.

At midnight – it was the end of July – we positioned ourselves at a spot above the cottage beside the well and stared northwards to where we would first be able to see the lights of a car coming along the lane from the main road.

An hour went by, and the lane remained in darkness; and then at last we saw a smear of light, and we watched it coming nearer and nearer, the smear growing larger until it reached the farm buildings at the top of the lane, when the smear turned into headlights before it began to descend our lane, and then the headlights turned into a smear again because of the high hedges.

'He's travelling very fast,' I said, nervously.

'He's remembered the way,' said Jeannie, 'and I expect he's thankful the journey's over.'

The car had now reached the turn at the far side of Monty's Leap so that the headlights shone directly towards the cottage. There was no slackening in its speed.

'I'm a bit scared,' I said, joining Jeannie in hastening down the path to the space beside the barn covered with stone chippings where all cars had to stop.

The car had now leapt Monty's Leap. It was heading straight for Jeannie.

'*Stop*, George,' I heard her call out.

And the car stopped.

It was a police car.

George Brown had had a collision at an Exeter round-about ('*not* my fault' he explained later) and he had asked the police to let us know that the car had to be repaired, and he was staying the night in Exeter, and would not be arriving at Minack until late in the afternoon.

'Thank you very much for your trouble,' I said to the two police officers.

'Great chap, George Brown,' said one.

'He's honest,' said the other one. 'That's what one likes about him.'

Arriving late in the afternoon . . . the snag was that we were opening the Lamorna Fête that afternoon with Penny and Fred. This alone was trouble enough for one afternoon. We had to walk Penny and Fred to the field beside the Lamorna road; we had to persuade them to enter the field, and we had the responsibility of giving rides to dozens of children. It was a worrying prospect, and now there was the additional worry that the Browns, in a battered car, might arrive in our absence. Jeannie, therefore, left the Fête early, leaving me to take the donkeys home on my own.

We were half-way up Boleigh Hill, the donkeys and I, when there was a toot on a horn, and a Jaguar with a battered front drew up beside us.

'George!' I called out, with pleasure, and Fred immediately shied to my right . . . 'Welcome!'

It was a solemn George, a solemn Sophie. Hardly a smile. Hardly a greeting.

'Jeannie's waiting for you,' I said, cheerfully. 'You remember the way? Turn left by the milkstand, then up the lane with the barn on your left!'

They moved off, and I watched them disappear up the hill.

'Come on, you two,' I said to the donkeys, pulling at their halters. 'Hurry up . . . we have got a lugubrious ex-Foreign Secretary on our hands, and you'll have to help in dealing with him.'

I have sometimes felt envious of men of power because life must be simpler if you know exactly where you want to go, what you want to achieve. Men of power are not fogged by contradictions within themselves. Their ambition is as clear as the moon on a summer's night. They want to control their fellows. They want the obedience of the mass. They want applause.

But did George Brown ever possess the real, biting

ambition for power? I do not believe so. Events pushed him; he did not push himself. His heart was too big to allow him to be cunning, and men of power have to be cunning if they are to survive. He was aware of this weakness, if it were a weakness, within himself, and it was the cause of his celebrated outbursts. He was shouting in the dark. He was raging against the fates which offered him prizes which other men longed for, but which he, basically, did not feel able to accept. The public sensed this and loved him for it; still do for that matter. A man with a heart is always likely to be more loved than an intellectual.

'Oh, George is tired,' said Sophie that evening. 'Oh, he's tired. This is his first holdiay for four years.'

The evening was easier than I expected. Easier, I believe, than George expected. He thawed with the help of a glass or two of La Guita sherry, a good dinner from Jeannie, and a bottle of wine; and we finished the evening with Jeannie and Sophie talking at one end of the room, while George and I sat at the other end, listening to records of Callas and Stephano in *La Bohème*, George extravagantly performing the motions of a conductor.

The following morning the cottage curtains were still drawn at ten o'clock. I had already been to Newlyn to buy mackerel and the newspapers. While I was there, I met a die-hard Conservative.

'I hear you've George Brown staying with you,' he said.

'News certainly travels fast.'

'I hope you shoot him.'

Nobody emerged from the cottage until eleven o'clock. It was then that I was startled by a curious noise coming from the donkey field just above the cottage garden. I hurried up the path to have a look and, as I drew near, the noise rose to a crescendo . . . and when I turned the corner I saw the cause of it. George, in open-neck sports shirt on this sweet summer morning, was still in a Puccini mood, and he was singing into the skies *Your Tiny Hand Is Frozen*. That was not all. Fred, close to him but above in the field, was also singing. Fred always appreciates a chance to hee-haw and the louder George sang, the louder was his hee-haw. Up and down the scale, head pointing to the heavens, clear notes, tremolo notes, hysterical notes. . . . Fred was countering George's baritone with a tenor-like bellow.

George saw me.

'Ah,' he said. 'I've made a friend!'

'How did you sleep?'

'First time I've had a full night's sleep in years.'

'Glad of that,' I said, relieved.

Shortly afterwards I handed him the newspapers I had brought back from Newlyn. He glanced at the front page of one of them.

'Damn lie. I never said that. Pure invention . . .'

He was still at the time Deputy Leader of the Labour Party and there were those who were pushing him to resign. He was intending to resign, it seemed to me, but he wasn't going to be manoeuvred into resigning by intriguers. No bile, however, on his part. I heard him speak criticism of some of his colleagues, but there was never a word of viciousness.

The weather was fine all through the five days. He sat often the bridge, as we call it, facing the sea and the wide sweep of Mount's Bay. Directly in front of him was a small bed of mignonette, where bees hummed and settled on the serrated little flowers.

'Look,' he said. 'The bees have red socks' (the bees having touched the pollen). 'Good socialists obviously.'

We were in tomato time. Geoffrey picked the tomatoes three times a week, carrying them into the packing shed, grading them, and then driving the chip baskets to the wholesaler in Penzance.

'You're packing them wrong, Geoffrey,' said George one morning. Geoffrey now had the advice of the man who once had the responsibility for the economic affairs of the United Kingdom, the man whose Declaration of Intent foreshadowed the Social Contract.

'How?' said Geoffrey. Geoffrey was often blunt.

'Back the car,' said George, 'so that the rear is at the packing shed door. You're wasting minutes of your time loading the car with the bonnet facing the shed.'

Geoffrey obliged.

I asked him later what he thought of George.

'Seems a nice enough chap,' he replied.

We never left the environment of Minack during their stay, except once when I took George down to the Wink at Lamorna. It was not a success. George was in one of his silent moods, monosyllabic answers, pursed lips, a bit scaring. There was no one to spark him in the pub.

He preferred to stay at Minack. Late waking up, a mackerel breakfast, a stroll, a talk with Penny and Fred, lager at mid-day, teasing of Jeannie.

'Are we having runner beans tonight? Let me help you pick them. Let me shred them.'

He had a passion for fresh runner beans.

Jeannie said to him one afternoon:

'Why don't politicians guide people into realising that the true values of life are free like the sun, kindness, seeing the best in other people's natures . . . instead of always insisting that materialism is the key to happiness?'

He waggled a finger at her.

'My dear, politicians cannot promise the public other than money because they would receive no votes. If politicians advocated the kind of pleasures you find pleasure in, simple pleasures, the public would say it was a dodge to cheat them out of the next wage rise.'

Another time; another question.

'What is this perfect life,' I asked, 'that politicians are always promising us? A sort of mass playground?'

I knew too well that one had to be on guard when

asking him a question. Ask it in the wrong tone and he could explode.

But he answered gently:

'In time, the new society will learn to enjoy the subtle pleasures of life. It will take time. One has to be patient.'

'And, meanwhile,' I said, somewhat boldly I realise in retrospect, 'the more people are promised, the greedier they become, and the more violent they are ready to be to satisfy their greed.'

I waited for his reply, but he said nothing. He was staring moodily in front of him. Then suddenly:

'What you need in West Cornwall is a balanced new town. You don't want all these retired people cluttering up the place. You need a reason to keep the young here. What are the youth migrant figures in Cornwall? If I were in office I would send for them.'

'But, George,' I said. 'What's wrong with retirement? Why do planners always make retirement sound as if it were a dirty word? These people have worked hard all their lives to be happy for the last years of their lives . . . and they spend their pensions and savings in the area. They are as useful as any imported industry and without doing any harm to the environment . . . and much more useful than the multiple stores who take their money out of the county.'

Again he did not reply.

His mind had wandered. He was no longer listening to me. He would have replied to me with invective had he been in the mood.

Another time:

'I'm so relaxed,' he said, 'that here I am looking out to sea, listening to sounds, watching small things.'

'Like the bees with red socks,' I said, 'who are socialists.'

Strange, I thought, that when he first came to Minack the great Offices of State lay ahead of him, and there had been in him a great, driving hope for the future. He had been turbulent then, determined to act, an evangelist with clear-cut solutions. Notable occasions were awaiting him. Meetings with de Gaulle, Willy Brandt, Lyndon Johnson, Kosygin, Nasser, Mrs Golda Meir, all the great figures of that era. The destiny of the British people could be influenced by him. He could win the applause of the United Nations. He could lead us into the Common Market . . . and now, as he looked at the bees, what had been achieved?

The Common Market, yes. That was his greatest achievement.

'One day you'll be back,' I said.

'Resigning politicians never come back,' he replied.

'Churchill did.'

'Ah, he needed a war.'

'You both have a common denominator. You both had violent opposition within your own parties . . . and you both had a charisma with the public.'

He looked glum, pursed lips again. No wise man asks George further questions when he is in that mood.

Minack had soothed him, I think that. When he left, I heard by chance a remark he made. I wasn't meant to hear it. I was about to carry his suitcase out to his car, now repaired, when I saw him turn suddenly back. He was making a sentimental gesture.

'Goodbye, little bedroom,' he was saying, 'goodbye.'

A man with a heart, I said, is more likely to be loved than an intellectual. The trouble about intellectuals is that they live in a rarefied atmosphere. Watch them discoursing on television and you find their attitude to humanity is that of a theorist, something to argue about, but never to analyse if it conflicts with a pre-conceived opinion. Intellectuals are seldom generous-minded. They like to find faults in other people's efforts, real or imaginary, and to debase the achievements of their fellows. They are very glib. They do not seek what is best in people or in their work. They do not accept simplicity as a virtue. Truth is something to be knocked, they will steer away from it, clouding it with complications. For the most part they are *poseurs*, pretending to live a life of wit, charm and knowledge, when all that is happening is that they haven't the courage to face their true selves. The most terrible experience of an intellectual, for instance, is to meet someone who is happy.

One such person, a distinguished, world-weary intellectual, came to Minack not long after George Brown's stay. I listened to his comments on world politics, his sweeping generalisations as to why America was doing this and Russia doing that, what was wrong with this politician and that author, what the government should do, and so on. Then, in a gap of his conversation, I began to talk about ourselves. He listened patiently for a while as I explained the kind of life we led. Then suddenly he exploded, and he turned to his wife:

'Good God,' he said, in a tone that suggested I had insulted him. 'These two are *happy*!'

Occasionally, very occasionally, we have that formal lunch party we prefer to avoid. One day, we received a letter from the editor of *Gourmet* magazine in New York, the sophisticated American food and travel magazine, saying that she was coming to Cornwall and would like me to write an article about Minack. Lunch was arranged. Jeannie developed a build-up of apprehension (what do you give the editor of such a magazine to eat?), while Martha worked overtime making the cottage a joy to behold.

I met the editor at the Queens Hotel in Penzance to avoid the likelihood of her losing her way in trying to find Minack; and when I arrived I found, instead of the formidable business lady I expected, a soft, soignée, very attractive New Yorker called Jane Montant; and she had accompanying her a photographer, Ronny Jaques, who travelled the world for *Gourmet*, a marvellously evocative photographer as I now know, and who reminds Jeannie and me of Bob Capa, the *Time* and *Life* magazine photographer, legendary pursuer of wars, who was killed in Vietnam. Bob Capa was with us the night our home in Mortlake was bombed. I can see him now at the half-opened front door, a cigarette languidly dangling in a corner of his mouth, counting the stick of bombs as they fell towards us: 'One, two, three . . . *now!*' I could also see Ronny Jaques behaving as nonchalantly in the same circumstances.

I brought these two back to Minack, and Jeannie gave them her carefully thought out lunch . . . fresh crab and her own special mayonnaise, followed by thunder and lightning (treacle tart and Cornish cream), or alternatively hazelnut flan with raspberries, and there was cheese, of course, and wine.

We finished the lunch and they showed no signs of wishing to leave. Nor did we ourselves want them to do so. It is one of the advantages of living in an isolated cottage where there is no telephone, no sudden ring of a bell to interrupt a flow of conversation, that time passes by without being aware of it. Conversation roams on, arguments and views are expressed, and wrong impressions corrected at leisure. Such occasions create friendships in a few hours which otherwise might take years.

A copy of *Gourmet* is now sent to us every month and, since that lunch, we have often been with Jane Montant and Ronny Jaques; and we have written other articles for *Gourmet*, including, by Jeannie, articles on the Savoy, the new Berkeley Hotel and Claridge's. And it was a recipe from *Gourmet* that sent me off to fulfil my New Year resolution to become a cook.

I had been sitting in the cottage looking through the most recent issue when Jeannie arrived back from a visit to Penzance.

'A wonderful *Gourmet* issue this month,' I said.

Jeannie paused.

'Containing more recipes for me to follow, I suppose.'

'Not only you.'

'Don't tell me you're going to fulfil your cooking resolution.'

'I am.'

'Heavens . . . what's it to be?'

'Onion soup,' I said.

'I don't believe you.'

'Why?'

'Onion soup, well . . . it's so ordinary!'

'Not the way I'll prepare it. My onion soup, you'll find, is a great delicacy.'

Jeannie looked at me, doubtfully.

'We'll see,' she said.

4

'I'll need your help.'

'But it's *your* onion soup.'

'Well, there are just one or two items . . .'

'Such as?'

'I must have two pints of stock.'

'Surely you know how to make that?'

'Not absolutely certain.'

'I've both beef and chicken stock cubes. Which is it to be?'

'Chicken,' I said, decisively. I hoped I was correct. The *Gourmet* recipe made no mention of chicken or beef stock. It just said stock. Two pints for four portions.

'I also need,' I continued, 'one and a half ounces of butter, a tablespoon of flour, salt and pepper, and a bayleaf.'

'Now, Derek,' Jeannie said, patiently, 'the idea was for you to make this onion soup, and yet you are expecting me to do all the preparing.'

'Certainly not. All I'm asking is for you to give me the

ingredients, and then I'll do the rest. I've already got the onions.'

We grow onions. We used to buy them from a Breton onion seller who called twice a year, and who came from Camaret on the Brittany coast where live a number of people with the name of Tanguy. The Tangye family originally came from Brittany and my father wrote a booklet in which he tried to trace its background. He based his research around the Tannegui du Chatel family, whose ruined château still exists at Kersaint in Finistère. One of these, Guillaume, was killed in a naval battle with the English and, to avenge his death, his brother Tannequi, Chamberlain to Charles VI, Provost of Paris, and who fought at Agincourt, came to the west of England in 1404 'with 400 men at arms and wrought much damage on the English in the course of two months' stay, after which he returned to Brittany laden with heavy booty'. My father gently suggested that he met a Cornish lady during his stay and that she was the mother of John Tayngy, the first recorded name similar to Tangye. My father also traced a Saint Tanguy, although he was unable to record the gentleman's saintly virtues.

'So if you'll give me these ingredients,' I went on, 'I'll take them down to the field kitchen and get on with the job of chopping the onions. And, oh yes, I want a large saucepan and another for the stock.'

'You're sure you wouldn't like to go for a walk, and let me make the soup instead?'

'Don't be unfair.'

The field kitchen is in the small greenhouse close to the cottage, in a meadow circled by elm trees with a view of the sea in the distance. It is here that we bunch daffodils in the spring and grade tomatoes in the summer. It serves other purposes as well, such as being a dumping place for a variety of things which I cannot make up my mind whether to keep or not, and for old newspapers galore containing articles I intend to cut out, but never do . . . and as a field kitchen.

This field kitchen was my idea, inspired by Oliver and Ambrose or, more accurately, by the smell of their fish in the cottage when it boiled on the electric stove. Why, I thought, do we not install camping equipment in the greenhouse so that we could be spared the stink? I thereupon acquired a calor gas cylinder and a double burner and, from that moment, the greenhouse endured the stink instead; and it also became the scene of other cooking, messy cooking for the most part, like the making of tomato purée . . . and now of onion soup.

Oliver and Ambrose, however, believed that whatever the culinary activity in the greenhouse, the result was always to be meant for them. Hence, after the burner was lit and the contents of the saucepan began to simmer, they would mysteriously respond to the delicious aromas by suddenly appearing, and behaving in that special cajoling fashion which is the habit of cats when anticipating a feast . . . walking round in circles, arching of the back, a quite unnecessary rub of the head against the leg of a chair. This ritual was understandable when fish was in the saucepan. It made them look foolish when the saucepan was filled with stewing tomatoes . . . or onions.

Ambrose was about to look foolish.

I had been standing for a few minutes at the bench chopping the onions, the stock saucepan on the burner beside me beginning to warm, when Ambrose appeared in the doorway. He paused for a moment, gave a squeak, then hurried past me with tail in the air, and jumped on the bench a few yards away. Again a squeak.

'Idiot,' I said, puffing at my pipe. 'What an idiot you are to think you would like onion soup.'

I was contemplating, as I spoke, how effective a shield the pipe smoke was against the tear-jerking effect of onions. Perhaps I had made an important culinary discovery. No tears in my eyes as I chopped. No tears in any housewife's eyes if she puffed at a pipe. A tip, I lightheartedly said to myself, that I must pass on to Jeannie.

Squeak . . . squeeeek . . . a prolonged squeak.

'Idiot,' I said again.

I continued to chop the onions while he stared at me. Dark ginger stripes between his ears, dark ginger shapes on his body resembling miniature shapes of clouds in the sky, a small, white shirtfront, white whiskers and a pink nose, a plush tail with ginger circles, pale ginger paws. His similarity to Monty and Jeannie's paintings of Monty which hang in the cottage was becoming more remarkable every day as he grew larger.

Squeak.

This squeak was Ambrose's signature tune. He squeaked instead of miaowing, an absurd noise like a mouse in trouble. He might be sitting on the green carpet of the cottage, keeping his distance, when Jeannie emerged from the kitchen with his supper . . . squeak! Or, I might meet him outside and have a passing word with him, and again he would reply with a squeak. It was a juvenile sound. I had compared it to that of a boy's treble, and thought he would grow out of it. He had not done so.

Squeak.

Neither of us had yet come to terms with Ambrose, nor he with us. If, for instance, I had moved from my onion chopping towards him, he would have scampered away. He would never allow himself to be picked up, nor to be stroked, and it would certainly never enter his head to jump on a lap. At this period of his life, he treated affection as a nuisance. Only sustenance was required of us.

Squeak . . . squeeeek.

I had by now placed the butter in the second saucepan, and it was beginning to sizzle and to froth, and so I gathered up the chopped onions in my hands and dropped them in. On the one burner the cooking onions, on the other stock coming to the boil. And in came Oliver.

He arrived in the manner of someone late for a party. He hurried in through the greenhouse doorway, paused at my feet, making the sound of his own particular signature tune which is a strangled cry reminding me of the yap of a small dog, and then proceeded to circle round and round one of the legs supporting the bench, rubbing his head against the wood. He too anticipated a feast.

'I thought you were an intelligent cat, Oliver,' I said.

There are some, of course, who decry the habit of those who talk to animals. Silly, sentimental nonsense, they claim it to be. They may even suggest it is a weakness of the brain on the part of the person who does so. Reason may support them because it does seem eccentric to talk to something which cannot answer back. Yet, is the vapid chatter between two people any more sensible?

'Oliver,' I went on, 'you and your son are potty.'

He had now jumped on the bench and, after a head rubbing head welcome with Ambrose, he approached the saucepans. Sniff, sniff, sniff . . .

'Stupid boy,' I said, quoting Captain Mainwaring's frequent remonstration to Pike, then adding a remark of my own. 'Is it really true, Oliver, that you cannot tell a fish from an onion?'

His reply, if it were meant for a reply, was to retreat to the lemon tree, branches of which now covered the far end of the bench, and where Ambrose was already crouched, staring at me; and there the two of them remained, huddled side by side, green leaves around the two cats waiting for a feast they were doomed never to receive.

The lemon tree had been grown from a pip by Jeannie's mother in her Kensington flat, and Jeannie had brought the seedling to Minack after her mother had died several years ago, and had planted it direct into the soil in the corner of the greenhouse. It thrived, and there came a memorable summer when there were flowers on the branches, and in the autumn they began to change into fruit, and by January they were bright yellow lemons; and

I was able to say to Beverley Nichols, who was paying us a visit:

'Would you like a lemon with your gin and tonic?'

'Yes,' he replied.

'Come and choose your own lemon,' I was then able to say. We had more than a dozen bright yellow lemons that year . . . but since then not a flower, not a lemon. Only a profusion of lemon-scented green leaves on spiky branches which reach to the greenhouse roof.

We have, however, set out to find what is at fault, and whenever a gardening expert visits us we ask for advice. We learnt, for instance, that we had made a fundamental mistake. We had pulled the lemons off the tree instead of cutting them . . . for it is essential to leave the 'button' intact at the apex. It became clear also that we had failed to prune sufficiently because all weak shoots, all old and bare wood, all long branches, should be cut from the tree. Then there was the condition of the soil, and although it was rich and we kept it well watered, we were told one day it lacked one essential ingredient: wood ash.

Our informant was the noted garden expert Shewell Cooper, who breezed into Minack during a tour of the West Country. An extrovert, large and boisterous, he succeeds by his enthusiasm in making the solution of all gardening problems appear to be as simple as adding two and two together. He is an apostle of organic growing, and he is responsible for the Good Gardeners Association, whose headquarters at Arkley Manor, near Barnet, provide a practical demonstration of what organic growing can achieve. He is against all forms of chemical fertilisers, believes compost can provide most of the manure a garden requires, and that in a well-balanced soil the worm population is sufficiently active to take the place of hand digging and cultivating. His rhetoric is persuasive on these matters. He once lectured at a meeting in Bradford and, a year later, he received a solicitor's letter from that city. 'If you are the person,' the letter read, 'who lectured on compost a year ago, I have good news for you. A lady who was present has left £1,000 to you in her will.'

He looked, therefore, at our sterile lemon tree and declared: 'Wood ash round the roots, that's what's needed. Wood ash will work wonders . . . also some pruning.' He proceeded to do the pruning himself. 'That advice is worth five pounds,' he said, laughing, his shoulders heaving.

As soon as he had left – it was evening time in late summer – I observed Jeannie set off into our copse-size wood with a basket; and in due course she returned with it full of small broken branches. Then she went off again, then again, until there was a pile of broken branches available for a fire. Our Courtier stove in the sitting-room had been unused since the spring. It was now to become active for the sake of a lemon tree.

Unfortunately, Jeannie had made a miscalculation. I, too, for that matter. I had watched her stuff the stove with wood, watched her light it, and had been totally blind to what could be the result.

It was a delightful soft summer evening, and I went up to the bridge for a drink. The bridge which isn't a bridge, but provides the effect of a ship's bridge as one stands there, gazing out across Mount's Bay to the Lizard . . . I was standing there, facing the moorland and the sea, when I observed thick smoke emerging from the chimney. It is a small granite chimney, square, and on cold winter days Philip the gull, or Flotsam and Jetsam, the other two gulls who regularly visit us, like to sit there warming themselves. The chimney has also played its part in the sea annals of Mount's Bay because fishing boats, as they came into the Bay heading for Mousehole, Newlyn or Penzance, used to line up the chimney with the great rock that balances on another at Carn Barges which we see from our windows; and when the Carn and the chimney were in unison, they knew they could turn to their harbours. The chimney stands there, prodding into the sky, a small monument to centuries of history.

After a few minutes the smoke began to thicken into a menacing plume and, because it was a still evening with no breeze to disperse it, the smoke began to drape itself over the roof so that Philip the gull, who had been waiting for a nightcap of a piece of cake, became so uncomfortable that he shuffled his wings and flew off.

I ran down the few paces to the cottage, calling Jeannie, and into the cottage, and there she was in front of the stove, a pile of broken branches beside her, stuffing them into the now blazing grate.

'Stop it!'

'Why? What's wrong?'

'The chimney's on fire!'

'Rubbish.'

'It is, I tell you!'

Jeannie is single-minded when she gives herself a job, and it is better not to try and interrupt her. But the trouble about this particular job was the possibility that the cottage might catch fire.

'You *must*,' I said, 'stop feeding the fire with those branches.'

'They burn quickly.'

'Too quickly,' I said.

'Shewell Cooper said that the lemon tree needed wood ash, and that's what I'm getting. In a few minutes, I'll have a whole heap of pure wood ash . . . and I'll spread it around the lemon tree.'

'Sure, sure,' I said. 'But in a few minutes we may have no home. Don't you understand the chimney is on fire? If we were in a town the alarm bells would be ringing; neighbours would be rushing to help us . . .'

'Serious as all that?'

'Yes . . . so *please* stop feeding the fire and come outside and see for yourself what is happening.'

The whole environment around us was now covered in smoke, and our old granite chimney was belching out the stuff as if it belonged to an old-fashioned factory complex.

'You're making too much fuss,' said Jeannie, looking up at the smoke.

'Golly,' I replied, 'what more do you want to happen to realise the seriousness of the situation?'

I could scarcely see the greenhouse, or the barn, or the sea which is normally only obscured by thick fog.

'Calm down,' she said. 'You're over-excited. It is only the chimney on fire.'

'Only . . .'

I have always been fascinated by fires. One of my earliest assignments as a junior reporter on the *Daily Express* in Manchester was to cover a mill factory fire in the Ancoats area. I was so entranced by the blazing flames that the *Daily Express* had to send out another reporter to discover what had happened to me. I was standing, mouth open, gaping at a wall of fire which was about to lurch a wall of the building to the ground, when there was a tap on my shoulder: 'The editor wants to know whether you're feeling all right.'

This, however, was a personal emergency. I could not feel detached. I could not allow myself to be hypnotised. I had to act.

'I'm going to call the fire brigade.'

The fire brigade was in Penzance and, at best, it couldn't be with us for half an hour. First I had to go up the hill to the Trevorrow farm and use their telephone, then the journey of the fire engine along the winding road would take at least another twenty minutes.

Sparks had now joined the smoke from the chimney.

'Damn the lemon tree,' I said.

'*Don't* get so excited!'

I would have preferred not to be so excited. I hated the prospect of calling the fire brigade. I was subconsciously concerned that the fire engine might charge down Minack lane on an unnecessary errand, that Jeannie's calmness might be justified and that, by then, the fire would be out. True, I was over-excited but, at the same time, I was only too ready to do nothing. I was in favour of Jeannie's calmness. I had no wish to make a fool of myself, or to cause trouble. If *only* the smoke showed signs of diminishing.

'Well?'

'Well what?'

'I thought I was about to see you disappear up the lane.'

'I'll wait another five minutes . . . if there is no improvement, I'll go.'

Jeannie's calmness was deceptive. It was not born of assurance, rather it was born of a sense of guilt. She was responsible for the situation. She lit the fire, built it up . . . and she could best counter this innocent foolishness by appearing to believe that all would be well.

'Look,' she said a moment later, 'not so much smoke is coming out now. And anyhow, *why* are you afraid that a chimney fire might spread to the cottage?'

That was a good point. She was attacking me, not defending herself; and why, in fact, was I so worried? The actual fire was caused by the soot inside the asbestos flue which ran up the length of the massive old chimney. The asbestos would withstand the heat caused by the fire, and so there was nothing in near contact which would cause it to spread. The smoke might look fearsome, but that was all.

'One has to be prepared,' I said, lamely.

'Agree, agree, but you can overdo it.'

I now knew that I was overdoing it. The chimney was still belching, but it was a harmless belch. There was no threat to the cottage. Jeannie was right. I had over-reacted. She may have been at fault in setting the scene, but she had now recovered her position. She had proved that I, too, had been foolish. We were equal.

The pity is that the lemon tree did not benefit. The tree had its wood ash, but we never had our lemons.

*   *   *

After half an hour of gently stewing in the butter, the onions had become soft and golden brown, so I emptied the tablespoon of flour into the saucepan and stirred it until it had been absorbed in the juices; and then I picked up the saucepan from the other burner and poured in the stock. At that moment, I saw Oliver and Ambrose advancing towards me across the bench; a pair of greedy cats, who thought it was time to participate. I waved the empty saucepan at them.

'Do try and be sensible,' I said, and they retreated back to the lemon tree.

I am now an experienced maker of onion soup. I have onion soup days during which I make a quantity of onion soup, storing it in containers in the freezer, so that there is always some available when I am in an onion soup mood. But, on this first occasion, when I had no knowledge of what the result of my efforts might be, I had a delightful sense of excitement. I saw a hint of the horizon which chefs seek. I was about to create a subtle delight and I was able to sniff the approaching results of my handiwork. I watched the soup simmer, bubbles fluttering in the centre, and as I waited for the simmering period to be completed, I frivolously remembered the pleasure of other onion soups. Two Parisian onion soups in particular.

I was for a while a ghost writer for Schiaparelli, the legendary dress designer, and I used to go to Paris once a month to collect material from her for the article she was under contract to sign in the Sunday newspaper I worked for. She was a thin, gaunt figure, very elegant, with a severe manner, and I found her a little unnerving. The first time I met her was on one of her visits to London, and I was sent to interview her; and when the results of the interview appeared in the paper, she informed the editor that she was so pleased with it that she would like to write a series of articles, so long as I was the one who ghosted them. I was very young, and I was delighted. I foresaw this lady of fashion introducing me into the mysterious, chic Parisian society about which I was currently reading. Schiaparelli, I half hoped, might do for me what Madame de Guermantes did for Proust.

However, this was not to be. The first time I went to Paris to see her set the tone for my other visits, so each visit was to prove as unsatisfactory as the first. I arrived one morning at the appointed time in her salon in the Place Vendôme and sat waiting, observing elegant clients come and go, for an hour before Madame was ready to see me. Then I was ushered into her office with a huge desk between me and her, and listened to half an hour of staccato advice as to how young women should dress.

It was good advice. It was advice which still holds good. Her main point was that elegant fashion of whatever period is always basically simple. A flurry of fussy clothes might excite spasmodically from time to time, but such a mood was too brash ever to last very long. Thus I remember her saying that women should base their wardrobes on simplicity, but bring change to such simplicity by having a large variety of accessories ... handbags, fashion jewellery, belts, shoes, silk scarves, and so on. She was particularly keen on scarves because, she said, they *disguised* often worn suits and dresses.

Our discussion lasted for an hour and when it came to an end I had hoped, or expected, she would ask me what I was going to do in the evening, and that when I replied that I had nothing planned she would say she was having a small party at her home and that she would be delighted if I would attend. I even began imagining, during the course of our discussion, that she might be thinking of me as a Chéri and herself as a Colette; and that, therefore, I was about to enter an exciting, dangerous relationship which also might be instructive. After all, I was very young, and she had specially asked me to come to Paris.

My expectations did not materialise. Instead, as she said goodbye, she briskly informed me that her public relations director would take me out to dinner: an elderly, motherly

American who, in due course, I found sitting opposite me at Fouquet's, a solemn restaurant in those days, while I wondered, despairingly, how long my evening with her would have to continue. At last it came to an end and I set off to walk the streets of Paris in a determined mood for adventure, and somewhere in the area of Montmartre I found a girl in a bar and I drank Pernod and then she suggested a tour of the seamier side of Paris, and long after dawn had broken I was sitting with her in a scruffy café in Les Halles . . . drinking onion soup. All around me others were drinking onion soup. I was having my first experience of the national soup of France.

My other Parisian onion soup memory took place years later when Jeannie and I spent a month in Paris together. We began our stay in a penthouse suite at the *Georges V* thanks to Jeannie's Savoy Hotel influence, and that first evening as we sat in the balcony garden looking out over the rooftops of Paris, drinking champagne, we experienced elation . . . a month in Paris and this the first evening! We dined on the Ile St Louis, then on to a nightclub in Montparnasse, and a wandering journey back towards the *Georges V* on foot and, on the way, we found a café with an array of lighted candles in the window. We went inside and there at a table was a quartet of people drinking onion soup. That early morning Jeannie, too, had her baptism of the national soup of France.

My own version was now ready. I switched off the calor gas, took hold of the saucepan in both hands, and set off out of the greenhouse and up the path to the cottage. This was a notable occasion. I had started to fulfil a New Year resolution for one thing and I had, judging from the aroma, a delicious Parisian memory to enjoy for another.

I was half-way to the cottage when I glanced behind me. Two cats, tails up, one nudging the other as they walked, benign expressions of expectation on their faces, were a yard or two behind me.

5

'Delicious,' said Jeannie, after savouring the soup.

'Thank you.'

'You have a natural cooking talent.'

'You think so?'

'I'm sure of it. A soup can be very ordinary. This is exceptional.'

'I'm overwhelmed by your compliments.'

'The flavour is so subtle . . . just think how enthusiastic we would have been had it been served in a restaurant.'

'Oh well,' I said, modestly.

'And now that you have made such a good start,' Jeannie went on, 'I urge you to develop your talents.'

'Always pleasant to be encouraged.'

'You've made a good beginning towards fulfilling your New Year resolutions.'

I looked at her. I sensed there was a snag in this flattery.

'What are you hinting at?' I asked.

'Simply that one soup doesn't make a feast.'

'Of course it doesn't.'

'Well then, what are you going to do about it?'

'Ah,' I said, 'you mustn't push me. I must have time to plan.'

She laughed.

'I know what that means,' she said. 'You'll go on thinking about that onion soup and live on its memory.'

'You're unfair.'

'We'll see.'

'Anyhow,' I said, 'I won't have time now. Geoffrey thinks the daffodils will be in with a flood by the middle of the week if this weather lasts.'

'You're stalling. The trouble with you is that you have no follow-through. You start something and then lose interest.'

'I haven't lost interest. I just like to take things slowly. You wait until the daffodil season is over.'

'I'll be waiting,' she said, laughing.

Jeannie, however, was right. I can be conscientious and persistent if the task involved is one of necessity, but I am inclined to drift, to behave like a schoolboy uninterested in his subject, if there is no crystal-clear reason why I should perform it. I realise also that I could be more positive in other matters. I sometimes say to myself, for instance, that I should participate in public causes, serve on the committee of this or that worthy organisation, or make the effort to push myself into spheres which might bring me useful advantages. My reluctance to do so, I believe, centres around my suspicion of the motives of some of those who act in this way. Many, of course, are selfless and dedicated, but there are those who treat their involvement in public activities as a method of boosting their own egos. They fussily attend their meetings in an aura of such self-importance that their friends and acquaintances, even their families, are duped into believing they are doing something worth while when, in fact, they are only motivated by self-aggrandisement.

Such people behave as if the outer façade is a substitute for reality.

Then there is the example of politicians, union leaders, and other public figures of our society, who have a similar façade. They become so confused by the volume of their work, by the endless contradictory reports on this or that, by pressure groups, by cunningly led minorities, by political manoeuvring, that they give up the attempt to keep in touch with truth. They have no time to do so and, as a consequence, they adopt attitudes, holding on to them whatever the evidence may be that such attitudes are false.

I, therefore, do not cherish the idea of moving out from my miniature world. I prefer to heed the dictum of A. P. Herbert that writers should be read and not heard. I prefer to drift. I prefer to stay as I am . . . except I am aware that, from time to time, I will behave out of character.

Each year when the daffodil season begins we are in the mood of pool investors waiting for the Saturday results. We are always hopeful. We always begin by believing that the combination of circumstances required for a successful harvest will materialise and that, during the few weeks of the season, we will earn the money which we have been hoping for all through the year.

First, however, there are the preparations. We have, for instance, to decide where we are going to market the flowers and, this year, we were changing our tactics. Hitherto we had acted on our own, but now we had joined the local Society of Growers, which had wholesaler connections in all parts of the country.

The Society was not a co-operative in the sense that all the produce it handled was sent to the markets under a single brand name. Each grower continued to send his consignments under his own name, thus conserving his individuality, but he enjoyed the use of the Society's marketing organisation which had its headquarters at Long Rock just outside Penzance. This served as an intelligence centre, and here a grower could find out what price his produce had fetched a short time after it had been sold; and he could compare the prices in the various markets and receive advice as to where best he should allocate his sendings of the day.

Thus I might be advised not to send more than thirty boxes to Covent Garden, or ten to Derby, or twenty to Southampton, though it was up to me to make the final decision. Then, all I had to do was to staple a card on the lid of each box containing the name of the chosen wholesaler and the destination, and take them to Penzance station. The Society also had the advantage of a contract with British Rail whereby there was a fixed transport charge of 18p per box regardless of where the box was being sent, or the number of boxes in the consignment. An individual sender, on the other hand, was charged different prices for different places and the fewer boxes he sent to each place the higher the charges were per box. Hence an individual sender was always tempted to send a large consignment to a single destination rather than spread it around a number of them.

The theory boys suggest that the principle behind this kind of co-operative is the answer to all grower problems. Thus a number of growers should be joined together in one unit, and then proceed to benefit by the advantages of bulk buying (of containers or fertilisers, for instance), the sharing of equipment, and the sharing of labour. Such an ideal has a delightful appeal to those in Whitehall offices and University colleges. It looks neat on paper. It can be eloquently championed on television. It fits the image of brilliant men, operating behind the scenes, who are able to solve the country's economic problems. The truth is, of course, that the theory boys often do not have practical experience in the things they advise about and confuse dreams with reality. They are academics.

Hence their theories of co-operation, of brotherly love, of the practical advantages of sharing, do not materialise in practice; and a main reason for this is the weather. However skilful the grower, however scientific the methods he uses, God remains always in charge. A long period of rain bogs the ground; warm weather in winter brings on a crop too fast; gales may blacken another; a sudden hard frost in spring may destroy another or, ironically, a spell of perfect growing conditions will probably cause a glut. A consequence of this lottery life is the belief amongst growers that independence is a necessity. If, for instance, a group of growers shared the use of an expensive tractor and there came a gap of fine weather after a period of wet, who would be given the chance to use it when each member of the group required it as urgently as the others? Or, when a crop is to be harvested, how is the available labour to be shared when everyone wants it at the same time? Perhaps in some areas of growing, the organisation of such sharing may be possible, but it will be at the sacrifice of that sense of liberty which the majority of growers and small farmers still cherish. They would have to come under a central authority. They would have to be ordered what crops to grow . . . and in the end they would still be at the mercy of the weather.

The sense of liberty, however, is a deceptive emotion. No one is free today. We are watched by computers, blackmailed by minorities and ruled by envy. We have no spur, as our fathers had, to heighten standards, to explore the subtleties of life, to escape from coarseness. We are enclosed in a society which worships the supermarket, and noise, and treats the charm of solitude as a vice. The odd man out is a nuisance and must be stamped upon. We must all be lemmings. We must hide ourselves in groups, hide our individualities, hide our quest for self-fulfilment. We must learn to accept the notion that it is naughty to desire privacy. We must make ourselves believe that it is antisocial to have saved for years so that we can be ill in a private bed without strangers prying upon us, that such saving is a sin compared with spending the money at bingo. We must adjust ourselves to these attitudes, and be careful not to challenge them. If we challenge them, we will be given a label and our views will be ridiculed. Yet all we are doing is speaking for liberty and for those who have died, sacrificing their lives for liberty:

> 'Went the day well? We died and never knew
> But well or ill, freedom, we died for you.'

The killed did not just die for the lemmings. They died also for those of us who wish to live as individuals; and liberty is the power of the individual to follow his own way of life within a framework of commonsense laws and conventions. Now, however, the laws have become so extensive and complicated that only the few can understand them and so liberty, as our fathers knew it, is fading away. We can no longer follow our dreams. We need no longer reach for the stars because there will be no reward in reaching them. We must conform. We must pretend that we are all equal in brain power, talent, and the capacity for hard work. Like the fast ship in a wartime convoy, we must proceed at the pace of the slowest.

It is a situation, ironically, which suits my idle nature. I do not have to feel guilty when I do not stretch myself. I can drift without conscience. I can confine any hard work to doing just enough to preserve our happiness. I need no longer aim to earn a bonanza because the bonanza will not be allowed to stay with me. Ambition, as far as money is concerned, has been quelled. It is a soothing emotion.

There is, however, a snag to this comfortable attitude. I still have to earn a living, and so it is easier for me to talk about my *laisser-faire* behaviour than it is to put it into practice. I do, in fact, perpetually worry about my financial affairs and it has been a chronic habit for me to do so all my life. I cannot keep money, I cannot save; and when on occasions I have collected a large sum I spend it, then worry and wonder why it is still not in the bank. Thus, when the daffodil season comes around, we are on tenterhooks. During the two months it lasts we hope to earn between fifteen hundred and two thousand pounds.

I arrived one morning at the Long Rock headquarters of the Society of Growers.

'Hello, my old cock.'

A Mousehole expression.

'Fine, Ben.'

Ben Green was the impassive, genial, humorous manager of the Society of Growers from Mousehole. I had known him since the early years at Minack when we used to grow potatoes, and I would carry the day's digging in the back of the Land Rover to the Nissen hut in the Marazion railway yard, where the company he then worked for had its headquarters. I would pester him and Ken Lakeman, his colleague, for the price the load might fetch in the market, or I would rage because of the low price of the previous day's load. They were very patient. They understood the frustration of growers, and they would try to calm me by explaining that Pembroke had started digging, or that Jersey was at its peak, or, most dangerous of all, Lincolnshire had begun. Or they might have cheerful news . . . gales had blasted the Pembroke crop, or frost had cut the Lincolns, and the price was picking up. Just the information I wanted to hear, not caring for anyone else's misfortune, and I would hurry back to Jeannie with pleased excitement.

'And what can I do for you?' asked Ben.

Outside in the Long Rock yard and in the shelter of the vast hangar, mammoth lorries with bearded long-distance drivers stood loaded with crate upon crate of broccoli. Soon they would be setting off on their journeys through the night to cities all over Britain, and I always marvel at the organisation that lies behind those journeys. Broccoli cut in the field, carried to a collection point, transported to Long Rock, and then Ben Green and his small staff deciding upon which lorry and to which city they should go.

'The daffs have started,' I said.

'Good, good.'

'Only two boxes,' I said, meekly, thinking of the broccoli and the lorries outside.

'Splendid, Derek,' he said, in a tone which suggested I had brought in myself a vast load of broccoli. 'Talk to Russ about it. He's the flower man.'

Russ I had also known since our potato days. He was an office boy then, and later a van driver. He was now, as I was to learn during the next few weeks, someone who is unable to terminate a telephone conversation. Thus I would make a visit to Long Rock for the purpose of finding out the prices, and then wait, and wait, and wait, while Russ conducted a conversation with some farmer or far distant wholesaler. On, on, on, would the conversation go with Russ at this end replying in monosyllables while the wholesaler or farmer at the other end poured out his troubles.

Russ was free of the telephone on this occasion.

'Yes, my old cock?'

'Just sent two boxes of Mags to Covent Garden on the train. What's trade like?'

Mags, or Magnificence as they are properly called, are daffodils with a golden yellow trumpet and a soft scent, and they grow in meadows down our cliff, our earliest daffodils.

'A bit dodgy, Derek.'

'But the season hasn't yet begun!'

'A lot of Spalding stuff coming in. Glasshouse stuff.'

Stuff is the word. Once upon a time the first bunch of daffodils in a city florist was the true herald of spring. You bought them out of emotion, conjuring up sunny days in the Scilly Isles and the far west of Cornwall, out of expectation of the coming spring, out of the thrill of having a bunch of natural flowers in your dreary city surroundings. Then along came the business men, who saw the prospect of producing daffodils as if on an assembly line in a factory, and they erected vast areas of glasshouses and filled them with bulbs, forcing them to grow quickly in heat. Spring, in the shape of these *ersatz* daffodils, now begins before Christmas, and the wonderment of the true spring flowers is lost; and after Christmas into January and February they fill the florists and supermarkets, anaemic blooms and spindly stalks for the most part, a short life, and a mockery of the true daffodils which last twice as long.

I was to see them, later in this particular season, in Covent Garden. I was astonished to find that they were picked and packed even before the calyx surrounding the bud had broken so that they had the appearance of grass. We ourselves never pick a daffodil until the bud has begun to bulge because, if one picks it before, the bloom will never grow to its normal size; and this, of course, means going over a meadow several times. The glasshouse growers, it seems, do not bother to do this as it would increase their labour costs so they take everything in one picking session. Hence the grasslike daffodils they send to market.

On my return from London, I sallied forth to Long Rock, found Ben and Russ and another man in the office, and proceeded to give vent to my indignation about such Spalding rubbish. I had spoken for a couple of minutes when I sensed a strain in the atmosphere. Ben was shuffling his papers, Russ was looking out of the window, and the man was glaring at me. He came from Spalding.

We had Carol helping us this spring. We usually have someone from a distance who comes for three weeks or so. We had Fran one year, an Australian girl who was on a world tour, then a New Zealand girl, and now Carol. She was tall and slim with long dark hair and wide eyes, and the glasses she wore suited her. She was a secretary when she first paid a visit to Minack, coming to Penzance for a week's holiday, then walking all the way out to the cottage. She was talented in homely matters like knitting, and making original toys, which parents would pounce upon if they saw them, and sewing, and the pressing of flowers, and making people feel at ease. She was quiet and quick in perception, and she provided the steady background Jeannie and I needed during the stress of the flower season. She had now given up being a secretary and, in a wild wish for independence, she had opened a shop in her village of Awsworth near Nottingham where she sold, helped by her mother, her toy ideas and the results of the sewing and the knitting; and this gave her the independence to come to Minack during the daffodil season.

'How are you doing, Carol?'

'I've done twelve dozen bunches in an hour.'

'Geoffrey says you ought to do seventeen dozen.'

'Ah well, you know what Geoffrey's like.'

Geoffrey, in a cheerful mood, enjoyed being a slave-driver; and in any case he was a fast buncher himself.

The small greenhouse where we bunch has the work-bench looking out to the sea in the far distance, through the circle of elms, and across the moorland. We can stand at the workbench and stare far away as we automatically bunch, finding our minds roaming as we do so. It is a mood that dissolves all daffodil seasons into one. Long silences; and then a sudden remark.

'You don't eat enough, Carol,' I said.

She was a vegetarian.

'Enough.'

'If you ate more you would bunch faster.'

'You're as bad as Geoffrey.'

'You'd have more stamina.'

'Rubbish.'

'I don't understand you vegetarians. You make eating a science. You make such a fuss about your proteins, too many or too few of them, that you miss all the enjoyment of good food.'

'We manage.'

'It's so clinical, like sick people who are forced to keep to a diet.'

'He's provoking me, isn't he, Jeannie?'

'Don't take any notice of him.'

Silence again. The bunches pile up on the bench beside each of us and, when there are enough, we gather them up and put twenty into a tin. A round number like that made it quicker for Jeannie when she came to pack. Most varieties have forty in a box.

'I see Broadbent over there,' I said. 'Over by that branch above the woodpecker's hole.'

Broadbent was a jackdaw which I nearly buried a couple of years before because I had thought he was dead. Birds do, unhappily, fly into the panes of the greenhouses from time to time and, on this particular occasion, I found this jackdaw lying on the grass just as we were about to begin a day's bunching. There was blood on his head and his eyes were closed and his body was so limp that there didn't seem any point even to try to revive him. I thereupon found a trowel and a little cardboard box and was about to dig a hole in the ground when, still with no sign of life from the jackdaw, I changed my mind. Instead I took him to a nearby wall and placed him in a crevice between two stones; and then returned to the greenhouse to begin the day's bunching.

At lunch-time, I walked over to the wall, glanced at the crevice and found no jackdaw. My surprise was mixed with the pleasure of having been wrong . . . or had the body been taken away by a magpie, even by Oliver, or Ambrose, or Lama who was still with us at the time? I looked around the immediate vicinity and found no sign of it and then, just as I was going away, I saw movement among the lush green leaves of a campion at the base of one of the elms. It was the jackdaw, trying to hide among them. It was a curious experience, seeing something alive which I had been sure was dead.

In due course, we had him in a box with a wire netting as its front, a box which acted as a sickbay whenever we had a hurt bird, but there was the problem of where to put the box. We would normally have put it in the small greenhouse but, as we were using it for the daffodils, we would obviously scare the jackdaw if we put it there. He would be scared in Geoffrey's hut too if we put it there; and so we decided to leave the box in the open, fixed in the wedge of two trunks of a tree where the jackdaw could rest in natural conditions, and yet be safe from marauders.

Very slowly he recovered. We nursed the wound in his head with the ointment of Exultation of Flowers and, in the early stages, we also dosed him with its liquid. From then on it was a question of feeding him with meal in order to build up his strength. One afternoon he was fluttering in the box so strongly that I realised the time had come to free him, and I did so. The jackdaw, which I had been about to bury with a trowel, flew away into the sky, over the cottage chimney, over the meadows and fields towards Pentewan Cliffs. I always knew he came from there. An age-old colony of jackdaws have their home on that grey, granite jagged cliff. A living echo of centuries of times past.

I never expected the jackdaw to come back. I thought he would be absorbed again in his colony. The Pentewan jackdaws were never the social kind of jackdaw you hear about. They always kept aloof. But Broadbent did, in due course, return to Minack, and he has been here ever since. He squats at one end of the roof while the gulls are at the other, and he competes with them for the bread and other scraps we throw up. He is a shy, lonely bird. I have never seen him with a companion, and he has made no response to my attempts to be friendly with him. He has adopted us, but only in a remote fashion. He is, however, resourceful. The other day, I decided we had kept a carton of pâté too long, and so I took off the wrapper and placed it on the bird table for the birds to peck at. Shortly after I saw Broadbent swoop down, seize the side of the carton in his beak, and fly the whole thing away.

Why did we name him Broadbent? I used to have a close friend, a renowned newspaperman, called Jack Broadbent. Both of us still often think and talk about him . . . but more of that later.

'A bit dodgy,' Russ had said of the daffodil trade when we sent our first two boxes, and 'a bit dodgy' it remained for the whole season. It was too warm for one thing; and, while people were going around saying what a beautiful February the country was having, Jeannie and I and all daffodil growers were cursing the sunny days. We should be used to these warm Februarys by now, we have had four of them in a row, followed by sharp frosts as soon as the early tomato plants, requiring oil heating, have been planted in the greenhouses. Every daffodil grower, therefore, was financially suffering from a surfeit of daffodils when another hazard, a man-made one, made our situation even more difficult. A railway strike prevented the growers from sending their flowers to market at the most crucial period of the season.

Strikes, sudden unofficial strikes, or union top-brass-blessed strikes, are so common that we are brainwashed into accepting them as an everyday feature of life. Everyone is treating everyone else unfairly, and we are so momentarily impressed by the arguments posed by the glib spokesman of the illtreated that we sigh and endure. When, however, a strike hits one's pocket, the mood changes. One is no longer an observer, detached, switching off the television because the strike does not concern one, or skipping the paragraphs about it in the daily paper. You are involved because your livelihood is at stake. Your views sharpen, so does your temper.

On this occasion, there were two simultaneous strikes, an unofficial one of porters at Paddington, who refused to shift the flower boxes, and an official one of engine drivers. I never have any sympathy for the former because with almost annual regularity they stage such a strike at some time of the daffodil season. The engine driver strike, on the other hand, although it stung me into such a fury that I sent a telegram of protest to the secretary of their union, would, in calmer times, have extracted from me some sympathy . . . anyone, it would seem, who has the skill and courage to drive a train at a hundred miles an hour deserves the salary of an airline pilot.

However, if these strikes enraged me and my fellow daffodil growers, we were also full of admiration for those who tried to solve our problems. There was, for instance, the sympathy from the staff of the Penzance station. They have always been sympathetic. I have never been to Penzance station without feeling I am in a pleasant club. Perhaps it is because it is at the end of the line, with a sense of finality where dreams end and reality begins, that it invokes such a mood of comradeship. Perhaps it is because the sea is beside it. Perhaps it is because we all feel involved with each other, whatever our tasks, and feel superior to those who live their lives in envy.

And so, when I arrived at the station and asked if there were a chance of a train getting away, I knew I was among friends. Big Donald, normally jovial, but now very concerned; Sailor, incongruously wearing a scarf and no cap, philosophised on the breakdown of standards; and George Mills, who has known us since the beginning when we used to arrive with a load in our Land Rover OPA 40 with seconds to spare and George calling out: 'Make way everyone, make way . . . here comes the Home Farm!' . . . George would now look sorrowful, aware that the livelihood of Cornish growers was being lost, and murmur: 'It's bad luck, it's just bad luck.' Even Sam (short for Samantha), the station's tabby, was sympathetic. Sam owns Penzance station, owns the trains as well for that matter, and periodically she takes a trip on one and ends up at Crewe or Paddington or Bristol; and a message comes over the railway 'phone that Sam is being looked after until the next train home. Even Sam showed her understanding one day when I was standing on a platform, wondering what to do with the flowers. She, who seldom approaches a stranger, actually rubbed against my leg.

Over at Long Rock they were practical in their help.

'We've got a lorry going to Derby,' Ben Green would say. 'Do you mind Derby?'

'Don't mind anywhere,' I would reply.

Lorries, scheduled for broccoli, now had to take daffodil boxes as well. Not good companions. The cardboard boxes were at the mercy of the wooden crates.

'Trouble is, Derek,' said Ben, 'we have to use what lorries are available, and so the markets we send them to will get more flowers than they need.'

Scores of daffodil boxes were heaped around the hangar.

'Hell to the strike,' I said, and marvelled at the calm way with which Ben was dealing with the chaos.

'The lorries leave here around four,' he said, 'so try and bring your loads by lunch-time to give plenty of time for them to be loaded.'

The days went by with this haphazard way of marketing, and the prices got lower, and tempers shorter. Then, at last, the strike was settled and we rejoiced and, although it was now too late to recover our losses, too late ever to expect anything near the turnover we had hoped for, we could now resume the normal method of distributing our daffodils.

That night, the night of the day when the strike had been settled, a ferocious gale blew up from the south. I lay in bed listening, though not worrying about it because we have long become accustomed to ferocious gales. It spat and roared and groaned around the cottage, and I lay marvelling at our good fortune that nature, not humans, was in a rage around us, that the wind thundered, not guns. At such moments one luxuriates in awareness of the real freedom. Nature is the king, not man. Nothing organised is attacking. No computer is smugly playing a trick. The gale blows, and is master.

We were up early next morning, eager to bunch a record number of daffodils so that we could make best use of the ending of the strike. I can take forty-two boxes in the Volvo and, as we would have as many as eighty boxes, two journeys to the station would be necessary.

I set off with the first load, and twenty minutes later I was there in the yard and saw George Mills standing at the entrance.

'Thank God the strike's over,' I said, cheerfully.

'Yes,' he replied, gloomily, 'but it's going to take some time to get the railway stock back where it should be.'

'Is there trouble then? I mean, aren't the trains running as normal despite the strike being over?'

'Worse than that.'

'Why?'

'The station is out of action. It's the gale . . . the sea has flooded the line between here and Marazion. No train can get there, no train can come here.'

Strangely, I did not mind. I had no feeling of anger or frustration. Nature as an adversary, however cruel its effect, can have a calming quality.

I had a sense of relief that there was nobody to whom I could send a telegram of protest.

6

Oliver and Ambrose did not enjoy the daffodil season. The bustle, after a period of winter serenity, upset them. They were vexed, for instance, by the field kitchen reverting to its proper use. Daffodil tins were no substitute for a fish saucepan, and they found it infuriating that chatter, activity and an unreadiness to pander to them now dominated the days.

For Ambrose, this was confirmation that the human race was unreliable. Oliver, on the other hand, was puzzled. What had he done wrong to be so ignored? Why should I hurry past him when he curled upside down on the path in front of me? Why should I not pause and listen to his purrs? What made me shout at him in such an excited way when he was sauntering down the lane just as I was about to rush to Penzance with a cargo of flowers? The shouts, the tone of my shouts, were like those that frightened him when first he appeared at Minack, when Lama was Queen. Daffodil days were not pleasant days for Oliver, and he was glad when they were over. So was I.

It had been a poor season. We had taken only £900 compared with the £1,500 or more we had hoped for when the season had begun. The warm weather and the railway strike had been the cause of this, but I feared there was another underlying reason. Too many daffodils were chasing too few customers, and the big growers, with their streamlined costs of production, were ousting the small growers. The same story, in fact, as the supermarket taking away the business of the corner shop.

However, the season was now behind us and we could take up our slow lives again; and Ambrose could be courted; and Oliver receive the attention he longed for. He had a vulnerable nature, a shy mood about him as if he were still not sure that he had settled in the home of his dreams. Lama, when I look back on her life, was a composed cat compared to Oliver. Lama had come to our doorstep when she was less than twelve months old and so she was very young when she realised she had a home for ever. Oliver was seven and a half, for it was seven and a half years since we had found the little black kitten down the cliff, before he could call Minack his home. There was reason for him, therefore, to feel insecure. Years of wandering, of looking for permanence, prevented him from being able to take Minack for granted. He might be thrown out at any time.

His efforts to please me were touching and, if I went for a stroll, I would find him trotting behind me, a black shadow; and although such a gesture did, in fact, please me it also made me nostalgic. Lama used to walk with me in such a manner. Every path, every meadow had seen her with me in all my moods and, at the time, she had seemed to me to be immortal, as all those we love seem to be. Of course, in this functional age, I should have forgotten her by now. Sentiment, for some reason, is a sin, while the sneer is a virtue. I have never been able to understand why.

Thus, when Oliver came on walks with me, he came as

half Lama, half himself, and I found myself being sorry for him that my nature was such that I could not treat him as a personality on his own. I was unable, as many people are able to do, to substitute one animal for another, as if one were substituting one piece of furniture for another piece. The changeover had to take time. It could not be hurried.

I was, however, at ease with Oliver. He did not make me self-conscious by his presence in the way I was self-conscious in Ambrose's presence. Ambrose had to be flattered, and yet still remained maddeningly remote. Oliver only wanted to be loved. Ambrose was like a teenager experimenting with life. Oliver had suffered and now only wanted peace. Ambrose, at this stage, was a taker; Oliver was a giver. The same labels that can be given to human beings. The givers and the takers.

'I'm going for a walk.'

After breakfast one April morning.

'I wish I could come with you.'

Jeannie was packing the dishwasher.

'Why can't you?'

'I'm waiting for the dough to rise.'

Jeannie's home-made bread was so delicious that Flotsam and Jetsam, and Philip, turned up their beaks when offered the steam-blown bread of a baker's shop.

'I won't be long,' I said.

'You go ahead. I might follow you . . . but, if I've time, I want to write to Tannie. I owe her a letter.'

Tannie was my eighty-nine-year-old aunt who lived happily alone in a flat in Chelsea, absorbed in Walpole, Trollope, the Brontës, and any other cultivated writer of the past; and absorbed also in the present activities of a legion of young people, who were fascinated by the way she listened to them. Later in the year, there was to be a special party to celebrate her ninetieth birthday.

'Don't forget to tell her about Mary Stewart.'

A strange incident had taken place ten days before. I

had been rummaging one afternoon through a drawer full of photographs when I came across one of Mary holding in her arms her beloved cat, Troy. Troy had been with her in her Edinburgh home during the years of her rise to fame and she and her husband Fred, now knighted for his public services, were selfless in their love for this beautiful black and white cat. Indeed, Mary, during a nationwide tour of bookshops to boost her lovely book *The Hollow Hills*, insisted on returning home to Edinburgh just for the one day to see Troy because he was ill, and then back she came to London and continued her tour.

Troy was nearly eighteen years old and, therefore, there was good cause for her to make that journey. I, however, had no cause to act so strangely when I picked up the photograph of Mary holding him in her arms. I had never met Troy. I had not seen Mary for three years. Yet, when I picked up the photograph, I had a feeling of great sadness; and I said to Jeannie that I was sure Troy had died. Three days later came a letter from Mary. I had been right. Troy had died in the morning of the day I had picked up the photograph.

I set off on my walk with the intention of taking the coastal path to Carn Barges, and then going inland to the top of the valley in which Lamorna lies. It is a pleasant, up and down walk through gorse-covered land with the gorse in places so high that, even in high summer, you are walking in the shade; and you pass through a copse where, in this particular year, I had heard the first chiffchaff in the second week of March, and you cross a little stream which tumbles speedily towards the sea, then onwards through bracken country and past bramble tendrils which try to sneak across the path so that I always take secateurs with me to cut them back. It is a walk that the donkeys love to take and, when I go on my own, I always feel a little guilty that I have left them behind.

I had, however, only just passed through the white gate which leads to the big field, or Fred's field as we call it, because he was born there one May morning beside a flat rock in the centre, when Oliver rushed past me, then came to a full stop and stared back at me.

'I'm going too far,' I said. 'You won't want to come where I am going.'

I went on down the path to the boundary wall and clambered over it and, as I did so, Oliver rushed past me again, then came to a stop in a damp patch of the path, around which wild mint grows.

'You won't like it,' I said. 'You'll start miaowing soon.'

I felt a mild irritation that I was about to be cheated of my peaceful walk. A sunny morning, no troubles on my mind, the air full of April scents and gulls' cries, and I was to be baulked by a cat.

Miaow.

'There you are, Oliver. I knew it.'

Miaow, miaow.

I had left him behind beside the wild mint.

Miaow!

It was a foghorn of a miaow. A miaow so demanding in its tone that I knew now that my happy walk was ruined. I had to surrender to him. I had to turn back. I had to walk where *he* wanted to walk.

'You're scared, Oliver,' I said, 'because you're outside your territory.'

I turned back, over the boundary wall again, Oliver now silent behind me, and then towards the gate of the Minack cliff, brushing as I went the foliage of the scattered Golden Harvest bulbs. Years before, I had invested in Golden Harvest bulbs, a foolish investment as it turned out because the soil on this bottom part of Fred's field where we had planted them did not suit them. It was too warm in summer, causing the bulbs to rot and die, so that now we only had a few scattered ones left.

I reached the gate, unlatched it, and walked down the rough steps which led to the first meadow. I had lost my mild irritation. I was even grateful to Oliver for steering me back to our own land on this lovely April morning; and I paused for a moment thinking back . . . Lama was a part of this cliff all her life; Monty for seven years. Two cats who had witnessed our endeavours and struggles for survival. And now there was Oliver beside me, the twig of a tail gently switching across his front paws, an air of assurance about him because we had returned to his territory. He was home, like Lama and Monty before him . . . and a few yards below us was the little gap in the rock where Jeannie first saw him, the little black kitten on dry leaves, curled asleep in a ball.

A wren rattled its warning note. Why are wrens so foolish? They are small enough to hide in the undergrowth from any prying eyes, human or animal, and yet they are so easily alarmed that they rattle their warning notes, and so bring unnecessary attention to themselves. Oliver, however, showed no interest. He had been a part of the wild, and he was tolerant of wren eccentricity, and so he continued lazily to flick his silly tail, content enough that he had proved his influence over me.

'Oliver,' I said, 'I'll stop contemplating, and we'll go on down.'

The trouble is that it was so easy to contemplate, to let my mind wander. A soft haze waiting for the sun to break through, no human being in sight, no garish building, no man-made noise, only soothing things to watch and hear. A cormorant was drying its wings on the rock called Gazelle and, a few yards away in the sea, a couple of seagulls swayed in the swell. A chiffchaff sounded from the blackthorn to my right, and somewhere behind me a robin sang and was answered by another.

I moved from the first meadow to the second, and paused again. I thought back to the time when we planted this meadow with the bulbs of the Magnificence daffodil and how, three years ago, we conscientiously dug them up and transplanted them elsewhere. It was ironic, I now thought as I stood there, that the bulbs we had transplanted failed in their new meadow, while the rogue bulbs we left behind had multiplied so that there were now as many as when we first planted the meadow.

I went through the California meadow below, treading carefully because the foliage of the daffodils was beginning to flatten, spreading over the narrow path, making it slippery; and I fleetingly remembered how Jeannie's sister, Barbara, staying with us once at this time of the year, slipped on such foliage and fell and broke her arm. An admirable guest. She never complained.

Oliver was close behind me and, as I passed near the little cave, or gap in the rock, where Jeannie first saw the little black kitten curled asleep on the dry leaves, I wondered whether he would take a look at the spot. He didn't this time, though three months later, one morning when he and Ambrose had accompanied Jeannie and me down the cliff, he dashed to it as if he instinctively remembered it as a place of safety.

He and Ambrose had been playing together, chasing each other in and out of the meadows when suddenly the game became too rough for Oliver, and I saw him dash for the little cave, just as a hunted fox might dash to his earth; and when he reached the cave, and Ambrose still rushed towards him, Oliver stood and spat at him. It was enough to stop Ambrose. The game was over, and Ambrose immediately left the vicinity, making a passing sniff at a pink campion as he went, then finding a sudden interest in an untidy clump of couch grass . . . an imaginary mouse, no doubt.

I went down the cliff path, Oliver still at my heels, until I stopped where the palm tree grows. The first palm tree was planted by me when my mother died, and it grew tall enough for passengers on the *Scillonian,* as she passed to and from the Islands, to notice it; and then, a couple of years ago, the fronds began to brown and I, thinking I was helping the tree, used to pull them off. I realise now that I was not helping it, that I was in fact helping it to lose its strength, though I am still not sure whether this was the cause of its dying. Beetles were eating into the bark, thousands of them, and I reckon they must have been the cause, a kind of Dutch Elm beetle. Anyhow, when it was obvious it was not going to recover, I bought a seedling palm; and now, as I stood beside it with Oliver, it was growing healthily upwards only a few feet away from where the first one grew.

I have a letter from my mother which I have never opened. She wrote it to me from London when I was living on an island two hundred miles away from Tahiti in the Pacific; and it never reached me because I had left the island when it arrived. It was forwarded on to me from one address I had just left to another, and another, until finally it reached me months later after I had returned to England. I remember holding it in my hand for several minutes wondering whether to open it and, in the end, I decided not to do so. My reason, I remember, was because the war had begun and the envelope was a gossamer connection with the halcyon days I had lived on the island . . . the envelope had actually *been* to the island. I, therefore, put it in a drawer and as, during the coming years, I moved from one home to another, I continued to keep it in a drawer. It is here now at Minack. Will I ever open it?

My mother was in the tradition of selfless mothers. She hadn't a care in the world provided her three sons were happy. She helped Jeannie and me in many practical ways when we came to Minack, and I do not believe we could have survived had it not been for her enthusiasm and confidence that we had made the right decision to leave London. We were always short of money, critically short, and my mother, unknown to us, would pay periodic visits to her bank manager to whom she would vividly describe the great job we were doing in producing food for the country, potatoes in fact. She was so persuasive that he would agree to advance money through her account on our behalf; and she would send us the money, hiding the fact that she had borrowed it. My mother loved Jeannie, and never lost faith in us.

Around the palm tree and along the banks surrounding the meadows were clumps of primroses, wild violets and celandines and peering from the green of young stinging nettles was the occasional bluebell. The elders were breaking their foliage, and the harsh branches of the blackthorn were a blur of white. Jeannie has a nineteenth-century book on wild flowers, which tells what wild flowers meant to people of those days.

I did not know, for instance, that in Arabia they used to make sherbet by pounding the flowers of violets and boiling them in sugar, or that they used to cultivate great quantities at Stratford-upon-Avon for medicinal purposes, or that there are six different kinds, including the Dog Violet, the largest (though scentless) of the six. We used to grow commercial violets at Minack, but I never thought of extracting a medicine from them, or of pounding them into sherbet. We grew Governor Herrick and Bournemouth Gem, a variety with a long stalk and fragrant scent, though the variety I have always liked most is the traditional Cornish violet called Ascania. We still have it growing in patches around Minack, but the flowers are too small for a commercial market.

The petals of the primrose and the celandine once upon a time were turned into ointment and used to ease sores. The sticky juice of the bluebell, or wild hyacinth, was put to even more practical effect. In days when very stiff ruffs were worn, the juice was made into starch and used to stiffen linen; and it was also used by bookbinders as a glue to fasten the covers of books.

I knew about the elder; that to have an elder growing near your home keeps the evil spirits away and ensures happiness. Unfortunately, elders are tricky things to keep growing. They have a comparatively short life, twenty years or so, before their sap stops running and the trunk and branches dry up; and then, it is said, you must refrain from the temptation of using the dead branches as firewood because to do so is unlucky. No one, however, preaches doom in regard to the picking of the flowers or the berries for the making of wine, and we make the wine every year.

I prefer the white elderflower wine to the red made from the berries and, with its gentle sparkle, it makes a fine summer wine. Picking the flowers is a ceremony, an exciting ceremony because we take the donkeys along to help us, choosing a sunny June morning after the dew has dried from the flowers, and we come down the cliff to the meadows surrounded by elders, and while we pick, using scissors to cut the stems, the donkeys play games. Fred will rush from meadow to meadow, followed by Penny kicking her heels in pleasure, a hilarious demonstration of happiness that they are free to have such a pleasant change from solemnly cropping grass in a field. Then, as we continue to pick, they will suddenly change their tactics and come rushing up to us and nudge us, or Fred will push his woolly face into the basket of flowers. Part of the pleasure when drinking the wine is to remember how the harvest was gathered.

The sun had now broken through the haze and it dazzled a path on the sea, silhouetting the rocks below me, hiding in darkness the gulls that were perched there, so that I heard them squawking without seeing them. Aeons of time and here was the same scene, the same etched lines of the rocks, the same language of the gulls, the same celandines, rose-pink campions, bluebells, wild violets around me, the same greening of the elder trees, the same white of the blackthorn, the same young ferns, the same bridal sprays of the sweet-scented sea-sandwort on grassy banks. A morning to be aware of one's luck. A morning to shout one's gratitude to the heavens. A morning to sympathise with those on trains and buses crowding into cities, or those passing through the factory gates to join the din of machinery. Here was peace. Here was the ultimate which man seeks. Nothing in a supermarket, nothing which could come from the success of a wage claim, nothing that a millionaire could buy, nothing that greed or envy could win, equals the reward of a spring morning on a lonely Cornish cliff, so quiet that you are truly at one with nature, listening to the sea touching the rocks, sinking one's mind into unplanned beauty.

A miaow. A sharp miaow, almost a yap. Oliver, a couple of yards away from me, turned on his back amid a cluster of celandines, and looked at me from his upside down position.

'Why,' I asked, 'do you think, do many cats think that it is so attractive to be upside down?'

A quiver of the paws.

'All right, I'll tickle you.'

It wasn't, of course, strictly a tickle that was being demanded of me. It was attention. Cats may meander on their individual ways, may haughtily pass by a human who is frantically trying to woo them, may refuse a purr when there seems to be no reason not to purr, yet . . . there are moments when an uncontrollable desire comes over them to be loved. Thereupon they produce one of their endearing tricks, or what their past experience has proved to be endearing . . . they will jump on a lap just when a meal is beginning, or when the owner of the lap has just decided to rise from his seat, or jump on a bed and snuggle up to the occupant at the moment when the occupant is about to get up. The upside down trick is particularly successful out of doors. It is never performed too close to the person for whom it is being played, because the purpose of the trick is to watch its effect. Thus, when cats perform this trick, they do so at a distance of three or four yards from the victim. Upside down they go, wiggle a little, and watch. Oliver watched, and won.

It is, however, unwise to offer a cat too much evidence of his victory because, if you do, he will have a second one. Suddenly, as you are murmuring suitable remarks to him, bent double as you stroke him, he will do a twist and turn and be on his feet and away. One moment seductively appealing, the next, elusive and remote, making you feel a fool. I had no intention of letting Oliver make me feel a fool and so, while he was still blissfully happy on his back, I seized him in my hands and marched him off through a gap between two rows of blackthorn, down a step to the bottom meadow of the cliff and over to a grassy bank of primroses and the scented white flowers of the sea-sandwort. I was proving to him that I was in charge. My one-time anti-cat feelings were always waiting to reassert themselves.

Oliver did not, however, show any signs of resenting my outburst of discipline. Indeed, he was a cat who so rejoiced in the life he had found for himself that he was tolerant of any demands I made on him. Only Ambrose annoyed him sometimes; and then, in an eruption of bad temper, he would have a bash at him with his paw. It was as if, on such occasions, he was thinking: '*You* have no idea of what the struggle of life is about. You have never suffered like me. You have everything given to you without struggling at all.'

7

Thus Oliver and I sat there in the meadow close to the sea for an hour or more. Oliver, from time to time, would wander off for a while, then come hastening back as if in fear that I might have gone away and left him; and he would greet me with a noisy miaow followed by a purr as he settled himself on my lap. He would purr for several minutes, and then it was time for him to be off again among the primroses, bluebells, the dying daffodil foliage, and time for him to investigate again the mysteries which lay in the undergrowth of the blackthorn. I would watch him go, musing, thinking of the New Year resolution I had begun to fulfil a couple of weeks before, that of reading Marcel Proust again, his *Remembrance of Things Past*.

Proust was not fashionable, as he is today, when I first began to read him; and I would not have known of his existence had it not been for an erudite Egyptian, Georges Cattaui, a Secretary in the Egyptian Embassy who, in eccentric fashion, used to skate round Grosvenor House ice rink reading passages from Proust aloud. Grosvenor House ice rink, during this period, was the gathering place on Sunday afternoons of the prettiest girls in London, young actresses, models, débutantes, and I, along with other young men, used regularly to attend these occasions in hopeful expectation. Thus I would spy a pretty girl gliding round the arena in a skater's mini-skirt, aware that I did not have to devise a formal introduction because all I had to do was to skate in her vicinity, then cunningly, as if by mistake due to the mêlée of the other skaters, bump into her. I had many successful bumps and several friendships as a result.

I was not, however, as confident within myself as my actions would appear. Thus I would make a bump, mutter my apologies, perhaps gain a response from the girl, even find her accepting my invitation to tea on the balcony overlooking the rink, but then, alone with her, I would have nothing to say. My mind would be blank. There I was with the gorgeous result of my bump beside me, and I was tongue-tied.

I was also, at this stage, suffering from the mistaken belief that my whims, my doubts, my desires, my sense of inadequacy, my foolish ambitions, were exclusive to myself, and that no one else suffered in the same way. Then, one Sunday afternoon as I skated round the rink with Georges Cattaui, small and dapper, with an expressive use of his hands, a neat black moustache, a black suit, bursting into French as often as he spoke in English, he pronounced to me that if I were to understand the language of love, or of culture, or of grace and manners in aristocratic places, I must follow his example and become a student of Proust. I do not know if he himself ever learnt much about love, though he was certainly well acquainted with aristocratic places. Like Proust, he was an appalling snob.

It was the wisdom of Proust, however, in which I was interested, just as I was at the time in the wisdom of

Somerset Maugham. Maugham was more practical, easier to understand; his stories were related to the present, and they possessed tension. Proust, as I was to learn, had little tension in his chronicles and, unlike Maugham, he demanded of the reader much patience and concentration. Both, on the other hand, shared one quality in common, and that was the gift they gave to a young person, a young person of any period for that matter, of reflecting the emotions of those they wrote about as if in a mirror. A reader looked into the mirror and saw himself.

I have the same volumes of Proust on my shelves as those I bought after Georges Cattaui became my temporary Svengali; and when, the other day, I began reading them again, I was fascinated by the pale pencil marks I had drawn against those passages which had then interested me. They interested me again. The first moment of enlightenment is seldom forgotten.

Here are a few of the passages:

How often is the prospect of future happiness sacrificed to one's impatient insistence upon an immediate gratification.

In this strange phase of love the personality of the woman becomes so enlarged, so deepened that the curiosity which he could now feel aroused in himself, to know the least details in her daily occupation, was the same thirst for knowledge as when he once studied history.

He would at once detect in the story one of those fragments of literal truth which liars, when taken by surprise, console themselves by introducing into the composition of the falsehood which they have to invent, thinking that it will be safely incorporated and will lend the whole story an air of verisimilitude.

She failed to see the meaning of his tirade, but she

grasped that it was to be included among the scenes of reproach or supplication, scenes which her familiarity with men enabled her to conclude that men would not make unless they were in love: that from the moment they were in love, it was superfluous to obey them, since they would only be more in love later on.

We must confine ourselves to what is possible: no use wasting time in proposing things that cannot be accepted and are declined in advance.

In strange places where our sensations have not been numbed by habit, a girl is remembered and we refresh, we revive an old pain.

Our desires cut across one another's paths, and in this confused existence it is but rarely that a piece of good fortune coincides with the desire that clamoured for it.

A prolonged separation, in soothing rancour, sometimes revives friendship.

With women who do not love us, as with the 'missing', the knowledge that there is no hope left does not prevent our continuing to wait for news.

We tremble when we are in love: but when she has ceased to control our happiness how peaceful, how easy, how bold do we become in her presence.

There can be no peace of mind in love, since the advantage one has secured is never anything but a fresh starting point for further desires.

There are many such passages with the pale pencil marks alongside, and I smile when I look back and remember how important these sagacious remarks were to me at the time. They interpreted the behaviour of a girl towards me, or my behaviour towards her. It was wonderful to have such a secret guide to the peculiar emotions of love. I was now free from the hitherto black and white moods which my solid upbringing had taught me to expect in my relationships with girls. You love her, or you don't love her. You want to sleep with her, or you don't. I was no longer to be held by invisible reins of reason. I now knew that others felt with the same complexity as I sometimes felt. My doubts, conflicts within myself, confidence at one moment, fear of what the girl may be thinking of me making me dumb at the next, were not, as I now learnt, the unique feelings of myself. Proust, at that stage of my life, provided me with the education I required.

I found, however, on re-reading him that he was as heavy going as ever. Page after page of long, rambling sentences seem to be leading nowhere, and then suddenly you find a flash of enlightenment and your patience is rewarded. He has now, of course, become a fashionable writer among intellectuals and so his work, and himself, are subject to a plethora of treatises, theories, sneers, interpretations, and all the other kinds of self-conscious attention which the famous receive when they are in vogue.

On the other hand, although he may be in vogue, he will never be popular. His world of Dukes, Duchesses, Barons and Parisian Society hostesses is archaic now that 'working class' has become the snob phrase of the age. He is also too introspective for the majority. Union leaders, the prophets of today, are unlikely to urge their members to look inside themselves, instead of inside their pay packets; and the rest of us in our hurrying lives, absorbed by financial self-survival, shy from the discipline which is necessary, preferring to find relaxation by letting our minds go blank and staring vacuously at the television screen, meekly surrendering the opportunities of getting to know ourselves. Instead, we drift with the herd, making ourselves believe that the hysteria of mass decisions, mass emotions, mass pleasures, provide the answer to our lives. Yet it does not require much effort of thought to realise that this is a false belief. Each of us was born with an ego, a soul, or whatever you like to call the sense of Being; each of us is unique, and each of us is a puzzle which we should try to unravel. Otherwise, we are like a man with the key to his own house, who refuses to unlock the door.

It was around the time of my introduction to Proust that I discovered Rabindranath Tagore and his *Sadhana*, the Realisation of Life, and also the Edwin Arnold translations of other Indian philosophers. I still have my original copy of *Sadhana* and it, too, has many passages with pale pencil marks alongside. This careful documentation of my reading suggests I was an earnest young man. Not so. I was a deb's delight at the time and seldom went to bed before dawn. Then, bleary-eyed, I would arrive four or five hours later at Unilever House, Blackfriars, to pursue my job as a clerk filling in ledgers. My fellow clerks were delightful, my work horribly dull. Thus, with debs by night and ledgers by day, I am surprised I found the time to explore strange horizons.

The *Sadhana* passages I marked, as with Proust, are the same as I would mark today if I were reading them for the first time. They had a contemporary importance then, as they have now. Here are a few of them:

Man's cry is to reach his fullest expression. It is this desire that leads him to wealth and power. But he has to discover that accumulation is not realisation. It is the inner light that reveals him, not outer things.

Only those of tranquil minds, and none else, can attain abiding joy, by realising within their souls the Being who manifests one essence in a multiplicity of forms.

We are frantically busy making use of the forces of the universe to gain more and more power; we feed and clothe ourselves from its stores, we scramble for its riches, and it becomes for us a field of fierce competition. But were we born for this, to extend our proprietary rights over this world and make of it a marketable commodity? When our whole mind is bent only upon making use of this world it loses its true value. We make it cheap by our sordid desires; and thus to the end of our days we only try to feed upon it and miss its truth, just like the greedy child who tears leaves from a precious book and tries to swallow them.

The West seems to take a pride in thinking that it is subduing nature; as if we are living in a hostile world where we have to wrest everything we want from an unwilling and alien arrangement of things. This sentiment is the product of the city-wall habit and training of mind. For in the city life man naturally directs the concentrated light of his mental vision upon his own life and works, and this creates an artificial dissociation between himself and the Universal Nature within whose bosom he lies.

Man must realise the wholeness of his existence, his place in the infinite; he must know that hard as he may strive he can never create his honey within the cells of his hive, for the perennial supply of his life food is outside their walls. He must know that when man shuts himself out from the vitalising and purifying touch of the infinite, and falls back upon himself for his sustenance and his healing, then he goads himself into madness, tears himself into shreds, and eats his own substance. Deprived of the background of the whole, his poverty loses its one great quality which is simplicity, and becomes squalid and shamefaced. His wealth is no longer magnanimous; it grows merely extravagant. His appetites do not minister to his life, keeping to the limits of its purpose; they become an end in themselves and set fire to his life and play the fiddle in the lurid light of the conflagration. Then it is that in our self-expression we try to startle and not to attract; in art we strive for originality and lose sight of truth which is old and yet ever new; in literature we miss the complete view of man which is simple and yet great, but he appears as psychological problem or the embodiment of a passion that is intense because abnormal and because exhibited in the glare of a fiercely emphatic light which is artificial. When man's consciousness is restricted only to the immediate vicinity of his human self, the deeper roots of his nature do not find permanent soil, his spirit is ever on the brink of starvation, and in the place of healthful strength he substitutes stimulation.

A long passage, but read it; and again.

I was endeavouring at this stage of my reading to form a philosophy in which I could believe out of personal conviction, and not because it was imposed upon me. I could not accept, for instance, the value of the notion that all men are equal in the sight of God, when it was so perfectly obvious they varied drastically in their physical and mental attributes. It seemed absurd to me that someone who was born to permanent ill-health should be considered to have the same chance for a happy life as the man who was capable of breaking the four-minute mile; and equally absurd to accept the cry of 'fair shares for all' when some are born with much talent, and others with none; when there are some who become great musicians, others who remain tone deaf; some who become skilled in their professions, others who are fit only for manual work; some who are scholars, others who are dunces; some who have the flair to organise, others who can only follow; some who have criminal minds, others with integrity; some who are mean, others who are generous . . . I could not accept that the multitude of permutations involving the personality of human beings warranted the belief we were all equal; and that we each had one life, and were then wafted to heaven or hell. The prospect did not satisfy me.

It was unfair; and it was ludicrous to expect the unfairness could be corrected by laws, regulations, and political dreams. The unfairness was fundamental, not man-made. Nor had it anything to do with the environment in which one was born, for history had shown the rich could be dunces; the poor could provide a genius.

I also could not accept the way religions competed for converts, as if they were postage stamps for a collection. I was influenced against these methods when I lived in the South Seas and saw, even on small islands, missionaries of various faiths, Protestant, Roman Catholic, Jehovah Witnesses, selling their faiths to the confused and hitherto happy inhabitants as if they were representatives of competing industrial companies. People, I feel, should find their faith without being threatened by a form of spiritual blackmail.

My own faith, and I have no strident zeal about it, no wish to convert anyone, inclines to the doctrine of the transmigration of souls. The doctrine was established and accepted by the Hindus of Buddha's time, the period when Jerusalem was being taken by Nebuchadnezzar, when Nineveh was falling to the Medes, and Marseilles was founded by the Phoenicians. This Indian doctrine long ago helped to persuade me that a human being, in whatever circumstances he has been born and whatever his talents, or lack of them, is judged by the way he conducts himself during his life. If he strives to improve his mind and his talents, he will be promoted, mentally and factually, when he returns to this earth; if he squanders his talents, he will sink lower. Of course, you may scoff at this theory but, to me, this is a religious thought that offers a practical aim for mankind; and it is an explanation of why there are those who are far superior in intellect, or physical achievement to the rest of us. Thus the sick, the unlucky, those who strive without success, those who are selfless in helping others, those who are very poor, those who are stupid, all have a target to aim for. By their conduct in life, in their different lives for that matter, they can still reach perfection. They can become a *rishi*. Who are the *rishis*? Here is Tagore again:

> They who having attained the supreme soul in knowledge were filled with wisdom, and having found him in union with the soul were in perfect harmony with the inner self; they having realised him in the heart were free from all selfish desires, and having experienced him in all the activities of the world, had attained calmness. The *rishis* were they who having reached the supreme God from all sides had found abiding peace, had become united with all, had entered into the life of the Universe.

The sweetness of this attainment is that it does not depend upon the conditions in which you live. It is the peace which you can find in your soul which counts; and the soul is your personal possession throughout your journey towards perfection.

Thus I am happier in prayer alone on a Cornish cliff than I am being part of a crowd in a church. For I am unmoved by the mumbo-jumbo of the normal religious services, because they seem to me to reflect an automaton form of worship. The details of the service and the manner of those conducting it seem so contrived that the service makes an artificial impression upon me. It has no meaning. My heart is not touched, nor is my mind. I am watching a charade.

Religion for me, therefore, is not a question of dutifully

attending religious services of one denomination or another. Religion for me is a secret affair, very personal, and requiring no conventional religious umbrella to shelter under. I do not believe I would be a better person if I read from the Koran every day, or conscientiously attended Communion, or fasted, or lit candles and confessed away my conscience. I could still be a heathen in my behaviour to others. I could still have only a façade of goodness. I could still be a bigot. I could still be a man of violence. The evidence of this surrounds us today. Religious fervour does not bring peace of mind; and peace of mind is what man searches for.

There are those who help you forward on your search by their example, and priests of all denominations are naturally among them. They do not require the trappings of a stylised service or a formal habit in order to gain respect, because their influence among people arises from their integrity and selflessness and compassion for humanity. Jeannie has an uncle who is such a person: Canon Martin Andrews, one-time Rector of Stoke Climsland in Cornwall and a Chaplain to the Royal Family. He is not strictly an uncle; he is a cousin but, because he is many years older, she has always called him uncle.

When he retired from Stoke Climsland – the living and the district belong to the Duchy of Cornwall – he went to live at Downderry in a house with a garden edging the cliff, the outline of Looe Island in the distance, and the light of the Eddystone winking at night. He is ninety years old. After the First World War he became a personal friend of the then Prince of Wales and with his encouragement he set up a market garden based on the Rectory in order to help the unemployed and, at one time, employed a hundred men. During the last war he kept open house at the Rectory for Australian airmen. One of these, Peter Stafford, manager of the Mandarin Hotel in Hong Kong, has never forgotten the peace he

found there on his leaves and regularly, once a year, flies
back to England to see him. Martin Andrews is that kind
of man. Friendship with him is for ever.

Jeannie and I have a hilarious time when we visit him.
He has such gusto and perception and dry humour.
Jeannie brings an offering of a bone for Honey, his golden
labrador, before we have an opulent lunch prepared by
Vincent Curtis who has been with Martin since a boy.
Vincent used to manage the market garden. Vincent
is also known as one of the most imaginative flower
arrangers of today. He is a man of many other gifts
and he might have made use of them in other spheres,
but he is devoted to Martin and, therefore, inevitably he
is happy at Downderry.

Recently Martin wrote his autobiography, *Canon's
Folly*. A. L. Rowse wrote the Foreword and part of
this is worth quoting because it explains why Martin
Andrews is one of those who, by their example, help
people forward in their search for peace of mind:

> Martin Andrews [writes A. L. Rowse] will disap-
> prove of what I am going to say . . . humble man of
> heart that he is; but I don't care: I have got to say why
> it is that we all love him, not only here in Cornwall,
> where he has spent so much of his working life, but
> everybody who has come in contact or worked with
> him . . .
>
> What a happy life it has been, brimming with good-
> will, crowded with fascinating incidents and people
> from the top to the bottom of society, from the Royal
> Family who have found a friend in him from one
> generation to another, down to the poor fellows out
> of work in the 1930s and the soldier to be shot at
> dawn for desertion at the Front in the horrors of the
> 1914–1918 war.
>
> The sheer goodness of the man and what he has done
> for others, in a life lived for others. The humanity of it

all, the compassion for men's suffering, the immediate readiness to do something about it, the understanding patience, and good humour . . .

As A. L. Rowse expected, Martin did disapprove. 'Far too kind, dearie,' he said. 'Not me at all.' He addresses everyone as 'dearie'.

He loves donkeys, and he always wishes to know about Penny and Fred. He once had a donkey called Alphonse at a time when he was a parson in Khartoum; and he used to ride Alphonse around his parish. It was suitable, he said, that a parson should ride such a holy animal; and when one day he was invited to return to England, the only doubt in his mind about accepting was whether he could leave Alphonse. He respected donkeys.

'After all, dearie . . . few animals are mentioned in the Bible more often than the donkey. The infant Christ was saved from Herod by the donkey who carried him safely into Egypt . . . and it was the donkey who carried Christ in triumph to Jerusalem on that first Palm Sunday. No wonder, dearie, that all donkeys have the Cross on their backs.'

It so happened that, shortly after this particular visit to Martin, we were informed that the new Bishop of Truro, the Rt Reverend John Leonard, intended to pay us a 'visitation'. The prospect of such a 'visitation' mildly alarmed us, as we had no experience of Bishops except at long ago Confirmation time when, I remember, I was petrified. I was the last in a long line of boys in Harrow School Chapel who had to advance up the aisle to the then Bishop of London. No reason at all for such nerves, except shyness.

The Bishop, we were warned, would be on a rush tour of the district and would be with us at half past two and stay for a quarter of an hour. I ruminated what I might say to him, but decided against telling him that, although I felt at peace in the sanctity of an empty church, I was not so at peace in a full one. On the other hand, I was tempted to put before him a suggestion about paying for the upkeep of churches but, again, decided to say nothing because no note of controversy should be introduced in such a short 'visitation'. The suggestion I had in mind was that local people should be invited to pay an annual subscription just for the pleasure of *looking* at their local church. After all a church, whether you are a churchgoer or not, gives comfort and represents to the eye of the beholder centuries of prayer. When, however, I once proposed this idea to a vicar I was put in my place. 'We want you in the church,' was the gist of his reply. 'We don't want you paying for the privilege of not coming.'

At twenty-five minutes past two on the appointed day I stationed myself on the bridge, just as on that night I had waited for George Brown, and stood so that I could see a car coming down the lane and see it turn a hundred yards on from Monty's Leap, thus giving me time to alert Jeannie that the 'visitation' was about to begin.

We had already discussed what we should offer the Bishop when he arrived; something which could be consumed within a quarter of an hour. Obviously he would have had lunch. Equally obviously it was too soon to offer him a Cornish cream tea. Thus we decided upon coffee and brandy; and in readiness Jeannie cleaned the silver and I, in my Martha capacity, cleaned the house.

'A Land Rover is coming down the lane!' I called out to Jeannie from the bridge.

I had expected a more formal vehicle.

'It's the Vicar's Land Rover!'

The Vicar's Land Rover resembled a farmer's second-hand Land Rover; well used, blurred paint and functional. The Vicar himself, John Friggens, is a charming person and much respected in St Buryan, whose inhabitants are half Protestant and half Methodist.

I hastened back to join Jeannie, then went to the

window to peer at the Land Rover's arrival. It pulled to a stop outside the barn and, a moment later, out stepped the Vicar, his curate, and the Bishop. Thereupon Jeannie and I raced round to the front to greet them.

'Welcome, my lord,' I said, and felt very unnatural in doing so, but had been told that this was how one first addressed a Bishop, and that thereafter it was 'sir'.

He looked resplendent. He wore a cerise robe with a gold Cross on a chain hanging from his neck; jewelled rings were on his fingers, and in his right hand he was holding, as if it were a walking stick, a tall crook. He was bareheaded, dark, of medium height and good looking and my first impression, with all due respect to my fellow Cornishmen, was to wonder why such an urbane cleric should have chosen to come to Cornwall.

'It is very nice of you to visit us,' said Jeannie, politely.

'Ah,' said the Bishop, looking around and gazing across the moorland to the sea, 'this is the kind of place where I would like to live.'

A remark which immediately endeared him to us.

We proceeded to walk up the path, and had turned the corner of the cottage to go into the porch when, from the donkeys' favourite watching point in the field above the small garden, came an enormous bellow.

Fred had seen the Bishop.

We could not hear ourselves speak. It was a bellow, up and down the scale in ever-increasing crescendo, as if trumpeters of the Brigade of Guards were hailing the Queen. It was the bellow which Fred reserves for the most special occasions, such as when the *QE2* visited Minack. It was Fred at his most excited. A Bishop! A Bishop has come to see me!

The Bishop was enchanted.

'A donkey!'

'Fred,' I said, 'and that's Penny behind him.' Poor Penny, with her strangled cry of a hee-haw, could not compete with her son.

'I must speak to him,' said the Bishop, charmingly, catching Fred's mood.

'If you'll follow me.'

I led the way past the fuchsia bush with its flowers hanging like miniature red Chinese lanterns, and across the small patch of ground to the wrought-iron gate through which the donkeys come in and out of the big field.

'Come on, Fred!' I called out. 'Come and meet the Bishop.'

The Bishop leaned his crook against the wall and bent over the gate, his gold Cross and chain dangling.

'Come on, Fred!' I called out again.

Suddenly the bellow died away, first to a sound like a flute, then to a whisper, then to silence. Total silence.

Fred had come to the gate and had turned his bottom to the Bishop. The dark brown lines along his spine and down each shoulder were clearly to be seen.

'Look, Bishop,' he seemed to be saying, 'I've got a Cross too.'

8

The sun was on the lintel, the massive rough granite lintel above the fireplace. It was no splash of sun. It was a shaft, the size of a fist.

'Summer has begun,' I said to Jeannie, who was in the kitchen preparing dinner.

The sun had moved far enough west for it to be setting below the hill of the donkey field; and as it dipped there came a moment when it filtered through the glass of the porch, through the open doorway, and touched the old stone. Each evening, each week, it moved across the lintel until high summer was over; and then back it would come, imperceptibly moving to the point where we had first seen it, and then it would vanish. Autumn, winter, spring would pass before we saw it again.

'A warning,' said Jeannie from the kitchen.

'How do you mean, a warning?'

The tiny kitchen is part of the sitting-room, although it is cunningly hidden; and you would not know it was there unless you looked round the corner over the stable-type door. It was over this door that Jeannie's face appeared. She was laughing.

'A warning,' she said, 'that the year is going by and the New Year resolutions are not being achieved.'

'That's not true.'

'Nearly six months of the year,' she said, 'and you haven't yet fried a sausage.'

'That was never a resolution.'

'Just a joke. I was thinking of the gourmet's dinner you promised; the exquisite cuisine I was going to enjoy after sitting back and watching you prepare it.'

'There was the onion soup.'

'Delicious, the best I've ever tasted, and such skill on your part and patience . . .'

'You're joking again.'

'No, seriously . . . I *am* looking forward to that dinner.'

'Don't worry, you'll have it. There's plenty of time.'

Then, I added: 'I've done well with the seeds anyhow. That's one resolution fulfilled!'

Rows of seedboxes, like soldiers on parade, lined the path below the rose garden. Some empty, the seedlings having already been planted out, most of them full. Four full boxes of Snowdrift alyssum, three of Rosie O'Day, a deep rose pink alyssum; four boxes of Blue Blazer ageratum; five boxes of Suttons Triumph antirrhinum, first introduced to flower growers in 1935; two boxes of balsam; four boxes of Sunshine Calceolaria Rugosa, catalogued as one of the most expensive flower seeds in the world, and promising to be a brilliant yellow and weather resisting; two boxes of cosmea, described as having fine, fern-like foliage and lovely tall flowers like single dahlias; a box of sunflowers; eight boxes of lobelia, Cambridge Blue and dark blue Crystal Palace; four boxes of nicotiana, the fragrant tobacco plant; seven boxes of Majestic Giant mixed pansies; four boxes of rudbeckia, late flowering and resembling huge coloured daisies; two boxes of salvia; and two of zinnia.

This sumptuous array of small plants fascinated me, fascinated me, in fact, so much that Jeannie used to explain to visitors who admired them that they were going to be there for ever. 'He doesn't seem to be thinking of the garden,' she would say. 'He just wants to keep them in the boxes and look at them.'

New growers of their own plants will understand how I felt. Always before I had collected boxes of plants from someone else who had done the work and it had been as easy, as impersonal, as buying goods at a supermarket. Now, at last, after the years of being a commercial grower of potatoes, daffodils, tomatoes and flowers of all sorts, I had grown plants for my own pleasure. Moreover, I reckoned that the total number of plants were worth nearly £50 against the cost of around £5 for seed and £5 for commercially prepared composts. Pride in achievement, therefore, was coupled with satisfaction in my economy; and so those who have experienced this small delight, will understand why I went on looking at the plants, watching them growing larger and larger in their boxes, rather than transplanting them into the rough world of the garden where I could not cosset them so easily against drying out, against slugs and snails, or against the wind.

I owed much to Percy Potter, who is in charge of the Sutton Trial Grounds at Gulval near Penzance, and to William Hocking, his assistant, for preliminary advice. They are born gardeners, growing by instinct and an inherent experience; and Percy speaks a Fred Streeter language.

'Look at them tractors,' Percy said to me the other day. 'Pounding the soil into concrete. How do they expect to get a decent crop? Then soon after they've planted whatever it is the tractors will be over the ground again spraying . . . killing the insects, killing the weeds. It's all very well, but were we ever intended to treat nature like this? My old man used to say that gentle steel manuring was the finest thing you could do to a crop in a field or a garden. Steel manuring, you know what I mean, a steady shifting of the soil with a hoe.'

He has his failures, seeds which mysteriously fail to germinate; and the year of my seedboxes gave me a chance to joke at him.

'Can I help you out, Percy?'

Or:

'Your alyssum isn't doing well . . . I've plenty to spare. You're welcome to some!'

And Percy would turn to Jeannie:

'Great gardener he thinks he is . . . I might as well go home and he can take over!'

'The snag is, Percy,' Jeannie said laughing, 'he doesn't know what is in his seedboxes.'

'Rubbish, Jeannie.'

She was, however, partly correct. I had failed to buy an indelible pencil and, after sowing the seeds, I had used an ordinary pen to write on each label. As a result of my stupid act, the ink inevitably faded away until, too late, I discovered that the writing on each label had become an indecipherable smudge. Thus Rosie O'Day could have been Snowdrift; Sunshine Calceolaria Rugosa could have been balsam; nicotiana could have been rudbeckia; Crystal Palace lobelia could have been Blue Blazer ageratum. Yet, confusing as this may have been, the little plants looked splendid; and I was proud of the way I had both sown them and transplanted them, first in seed compost, then in potting compost. The fact I didn't know what they were was incidental.

I had had my difficulties in growing them. The seedboxes had first been placed on the bench in the small greenhouse where we bunch daffodils and, as seed growing and daffodil bunching for a while coincided, the boxes were placed at one end close to the lemon tree. This position, perhaps because of the sweet smelling leaves of the lemon tree, was also much favoured by Oliver, and the presence of the seedboxes did not alter his wish to lie there. Hence I would come into the greenhouse and find him comfortably curled up on the Cambridge Blue lobelia and I would proceed to remove him. I think he was puzzled by my behaviour, for I showed no hasty irritation, no shouting at him . . . I just gently picked him up and took him out. The reason for my gentleness is easy to guess. Had I scared him, he would have churned up the seedbox compost in the manner of a dirt track rider.

I solved this problem in due course by laying wire netting over the seedboxes; and later, after the seedlings were transplanted, the potted boxes were placed in the larger greenhouse and the door kept shut. It was not until I first began to plant them in the garden that trouble began again. Ambrose joined Oliver in causing the trouble.

Ambrose's distrust of the human race had appeared to be diminishing now that summer had come. Perhaps the sun lulled him. Perhaps the young rabbits he caught fed him into being such a satisfied cat that he was too lazy to be temperamental. True, he went into a panic if a stranger approached him, and he continued to refuse to be picked up or to jump on my lap . . . but there were subtle signs that his character was changing. For instance, he would come for walks with us and Oliver, and occasionally on these walks he would stop close in front of me, look up with a beatific Pollyanna face, and wait for me to stroke him. There I would be on a path, waist high bracken on either side, foxgloves peering their purple spires towards the sky, young green brambles scraping my legs as I walked, and down below me would be Ambrose, hinting that he was prepared to show me affection. Inevitably I felt flattered. Inevitably I stooped, and responded.

These walks, however, had their hazards. One of them took us up the lane across Monty's Leap and on round the bend where we turned right up a grassy path through moorland. When we reached the top, we turned right again with a bramble hedge on our left and a stone hedge spattered with blackthorn bushes on our right. Then on through bracken land and past a large badger sett, the same sett where the beagle was caught in a snare, and then right again down a sloping path towards the sea and the Coastal Path. The Coastal Path led back to Minack land and up the hill of Fred's field, where at the top we left it and passed through the white gate leading home to the cottage. The walk, even if we took it at a meandering pace, did not last more than twenty minutes, and we always set off in the early morning before there was any threat of strangers walking the Coastal Path.

The Coastal Path is, of course, an admirable institution, and the long stretch from Mousehole around Land's End to St Ives is one of the most beautiful walks in the world. It was completed in 1973 but, before that, we always kept our own section open to the public with direction signs, apart from clearing the undergrowth at those times of the year when it was in danger of hiding the path. It is a walk for the solitary, those who can gain more from the steep climbs, from the rugged beauty of sea-lashed rocks and pocket meadows, than the mere pleasure of exercise. Most of the walkers realise this, but the path also attracts the urban hikers who walk in packs, heads down, their belongings heaped on their backs so that they remind one of snails; and they pause only when they have their sandwiches and cakes, scattering paper and empty beer cans as a memorial of their passing. There are, too, the vandals. The Cornwall County Council erected wooden direction signs instead of the crude and ugly metal ones which are usually used for footpaths; and because they are of wood they can be smashed, and thus many *have* been smashed. Such walkers, however, are in the minority, and only occasionally do I find debris on Minack land; and this is perhaps helped by a typewritten notice I put on a board where the Coastal Path begins on Minack land. The notice read: YOU ARE VERY WELCOME TO CROSS THIS PRIVATE PROPERTY ALONG THE PATH WHICH IS MARKED.

The other day I had a look at this notice, and scrawled

across it were the words: You own nothing . . . it belongs
to *us*.

One morning this early summer Jeannie and I, Oliver
and Ambrose, set off on the round walk, as we call it,
soon after breakfast, and had reached the point when we
were walking downhill towards the sea and the Coastal
Path, when I spied coming towards us but away on the
path in Fred's field, a man and a woman, a child and a
dog. At that moment they were in the distance, a mass
of bracken, blackthorn and a couple of stone hedges in
between . . . but I realised that if they continued on their
route, an unleashed dog along with them, we would meet
head on when we arrived at the Coastal Path. Such a
meeting would scatter Oliver and Ambrose; and so I sang
out across the narrow valley:

'Would you mind putting your dog on the lead?'

There was no response, and I called out again.

Still no response, but I saw them stop, have a word with
each other, the woman hatless, the man in a peaked cap
like that of a French fisherman; and then I heard the shout
of his reply:

'Mind your own business!'

This was unexpected.

'I've two cats here,' I yelled back, 'and I don't want the
dog to chase them!'

This was ridiculous. A lovely morning, two peaceful
cats, and here was I having a shouting argument on their
behalf across the valley.

'Cats!' I shouted, hands cupped to mouth. 'Two cats!'

An epithet came hurtling back in reply.

At this instant, the woman leashed the dog, but the man,
a tug at his cap, began to stride purposefully towards us.

'We had better turn back,' said Jeannie.

'Fine,' I said, 'if the cats do likewise.'

'Oliver . . . Ambrose,' Jeannie beseeched.

Thereupon Oliver bolted forwards, and Ambrose bolted
backwards.

'Now we've done it,' I said.

'Oliver! Ambrose!'

Both, but in opposite directions, had disappeared into the bracken.

'We must be sensible,' I said.

'That means you'll have to go forward to look for Oliver, and I'll go backwards to look for Ambrose.'

'The man!' I replied.

He had now jumped over our boundary hedge and was striding along the Coastal Path looking like a football fan on the rampage. The peaked cap gave him an arrogant, threatening air.

'Oliver! . . . Oliver!'

As I called, I walked on towards the Coastal Path and, just as I reached it, out of the undergrowth on my right dashed Oliver. He ran back towards Jeannie, and I faced the gentleman alone.

'Thank you,' I said to him, when he came within speaking distance, recalling the woman leashing the dog. 'Thank you for holding your dog.'

I was hoping my face displayed a friendly smile. I can never be sure how my face looks. I have passed people, believing I was smiling at them, and Jeannie has said: 'Why did you look so glum?'

We were now within a few yards of each other.

'I'm sure,' I said to him – he wore a trim black beard and this, with his French fisherman's cap, reminded me of a character in a Simenon story – 'I'm sure you will understand when I tell you that I was trying to protect my cats.'

'Bloody hell I do,' he replied in unmistakable English.

Reluctantly I felt my adrenalin rising.

Foxgloves galore around us, the first bursting of elderberry flower saucers, fragment of a white sail of a yacht seen through the branches of a blackthorn, swifts diving over Fred's field, a magpie coarsely cackling, all the wild, natural extravagance of nature, scents of the sea roaming from the rocks, glint of the sun on pink campion, an early honeysuckle, rich golden gorse, arenas of white stitchwort . . . and all at the innocent beginning of a day.

'I *do* want to explain,' I said and, as I spoke, I was growing more angry every second. 'You see, they are two very nervous cats, and they don't expect to meet anyone on this walk, and if they meet a dog . . .'

'A dog has as much right to be here as any damned cat.'

'Rights' . . . the most disturbing, contemporary word in the British language. The right to strike, the right to have a wage rise, the right to do this, or do that, the right to be equal without any effort to earn such equality . . . an arid word because it brings no satisfaction. One 'right' achieved only breeds another.

'Of course, dear fellow,' I said, controlling my rising adrenalin by adopting a patronising tone. 'Nobody is contesting the right of your dog to be here . . . it's just that I didn't think you would want it to chase my cats.'

He glared at me. No peacemaking on his part.

'Anyhow,' I went on, 'you are obviously a stranger around here. On beautiful mornings in this area people who love it do not lose their temper.'

I turned my back on him and returned up the path to Jeannie.

'Oliver is here,' she said, and there was Oliver crouching a yard away, 'but no sign of Ambrose.'

There was no sign of Ambrose for the rest of the morning; for the rest of the afternoon as well, in fact. We called and we called. The innocent morning walk had turned into one of strain and distress. A sea of green bracken and in it, somewhere, was Ambrose, listening to our anguished cries, amused by them, saying to himself that he would extract the maximum pleasure from them before he reappeared. It was, however, greed which retrieved him in the end. Jeannie cooked some fish and, while it was still hot and the aroma strong, she carried the saucepan at bracken height along the path. A clever move. Ambrose could not resist it.

Nor, unfortunately, could he resist my plants when I began to set them out in the garden. Nor could Oliver. They stalked around like sinister members of the Mafia, watching me as I grouped the little plants in various corners, waiting for me to turn my back, waiting to pounce on a plant, then treating it as a football, deftly digging it up with a paw and tossing it from one to another.

'Stop it!' I would shriek when I saw them and they would scurry away into the safety of the escallonia, the massive bush of felt-like green leaves and clusters of pink flowers opposite the path to the porch, which we call Escallonia Towers; and they would sit there, heads peeping among the leaves, unashamedly prepared to play football again as soon as the opportunity occurred.

Jeannie thought them funny.

'They're only trying to be a Georgie Best,' she said.

'And look what happened to him,' I replied.

'Oh, just watch them now!'

I watched, and saw an ageratum sailing into the air.

'Damn you . . . get away, get away!'

And this time they raced down the path, side by side, coming to a stop close to the wooden gate of the small yard in front of the barn where the donkeys were peering over the fence, observing the scene.

Of course, I was not as angry as I appeared to be. My emotions are stronger than my deeds, and the loss of my temper has never been of much significance. I understand, however, why cats sometimes enrage people. When I was a cat hater I was often enraged; and I recall a period when I lived in Manchester in Portsmouth Street, off Ackers Street then famed for its theatrical digs, and I was maddened by the caterwauling of cats in the neighbourhood of my bedroom window. Night after night I was kept awake by their noise, and I used to lie in my bed plotting methods for their destruction. The method I decided upon was the use of a water pistol.

I had been given this tip about a water pistol when I was a child at Glendorgal, which was then our family home near Newquay, and it was given me by the old gardener. A seedbed of his had recently been punctured by the activities of strange cats and he was telling me how he succeeded in stopping their vandalism.

'I kept a water pistol at the ready,' he explained, 'and I lay in wait for a cat and when I saw it coming over the hedge and across the garden towards this lovely seedbed of newly sown carrots, broccoli and lettuce, I aimed the water pistol at it, pressed the trigger . . . and away ran the cat. Cats don't like water, you know.'

The old gardener had no wish to harm his enemy. His object was to frighten him. He was not like a well-known comedian to whom I listened on a radio programme. He declared he shot up cats with an air gun when they came into his garden. He justified this cruelty on the grounds that he was protecting the birds in his garden and, of course, no one can deny that cats catch birds, although I know of many exceptions. Monty and Lama were exceptions, so also are Oliver and Ambrose. True, I have known Ambrose catch a dunnock, but a dunnock hopping on the ground resembles a mouse and so perhaps there is an excuse for Ambrose's action. I was on the same radio programme myself a little while later and, remembering the comedian's outburst, I set out the point of view that the catching of birds by cats was part of the cycle of nature. Hawks kill birds, magpies, jackdaws, carrion crows steal nestlings, foxes catch gulls . . . and so perhaps the distress of seeing a cat catch a bird can be eased by putting its act in this perspective.

I did not, as it happens, use a water pistol to scatter my Manchester caterwauling cats. Each morning when I awoke the annoyance they had caused me seemed unimportant. The midnight wake often ends in this way. The angry letter composed in the darkness is never written. The determination to follow a certain course is unfulfilled. Fine plans become muted. Cool sense dissipates wild ideas. Even unhappiness can be dispelled. The thoughts of a midnight wake are usually deceptive.

Cats, I have now learnt since my cat-hater times, offer subtleties of pleasure that earn them forgiveness for their irritations. They have grace and style and a sweetness of movement, a detached elegance, and a marvellous devotion to those they choose to love. Cats are not for the coarse. I cannot vision a militant besotted by his rights having the time to appreciate a cat. A cat would be far too subtle for him. A cat, in my young days, was too subtle for me.

Now, however, my edgy moments can be soothed by watching Oliver, without a care in the world, strolling up the lane from Monty's Leap, pausing at the sound of a rustle in the grass, investigating, then meandering onwards; and, when the news bulletins bellow their stories of envy and dissatisfaction I can find consolation in observing Ambrose spreading himself in abandonment under the syringa bush, just as Monty used to do under the syringa bush at Mortlake. Thus I am now educated to forgive them their antics. I forgive them for using an ageratum as a football, or for digging up my bed of mignonette, that old fashioned flower, the seeds of which are so loth to germinate, or for removing with a flurry of paws my patch of night-scented stock that has just broken green from the soil close to the porch door.

These are the hazards that gardeners must expect if they have cats around the house. Thus my loss of temper, my shouting at them, were mock gestures of annoyance. I had learnt to tolerate them in the garden. I was satisfied with the compensations I received. There was, however, one bastion which they had failed to conquer, and that was the bed. True to my resolution, I still kept them at bay. I would come into the bedroom from my bath and find

Oliver curled on the eiderdown; and I would ruthlessly pick him up and carry him to the porch and deposit him on the cane chair. I was adamant that I should not spend my nights cramped and immobile; and if Oliver were allowed to remain, would not Ambrose be soon to follow? And yet . . . each time I removed Oliver, I seemed to be doing so more gently.

Once again I found myself questioning my attitude towards animals; towards all creatures of nature. Was it, in fact, an indulgence on my part? Love, kindness, understanding, being a reflection of my mood at the time? And if I were not in that mood, if it did not suit me, did I not change my attitude?

The snails are a case in point. At the first shower of spring, the snails emerged from their hibernation hideouts, trailed their slimy marks over the rocks, the soil, and immediately small pansies disappeared, French marigolds became stumps and tobacco plants had large bites in their leaves. Snails are the murderers of a young garden; yet I am fascinated by their innate determination for survival and how they exist throughout the growing year despite the ceaseless attack on them by thrushes and blackbirds and humans. Thus, in an effort to preserve both them and the garden, I gathered the snails that were attacking my plants into a bucket and carried the bucket across the stable field, the stable field in front of the barn where the donkeys spend much of their time, and deposited the snails at the bottom of the far hedge.

I felt the better for doing so. I had removed the snails without hurting them. I had proved my affection for the living creatures of nature. I was, if I were to speak the truth, rather proud of myself that I had withstood the temptation of using a proprietary brand of slug and snail bait. I had given the snails a chance to eat elsewhere, nibble weeds instead of plants, enjoy a life away from any angry gardener.

The snails, unfortunately, did not appreciate my good

intentions. Jeannie, a day later, was standing in the stable field grooming Penny, when she noticed a concourse of snails around her feet.

'The snails are on their way back to you!' she called out, laughing.

It was funny in one way; sad in another. They did indeed seem to be on their way back, relations included, and any other snails who had heard the news about the man who put snails in a bucket when they annoyed him, then carried them away to live another day. This time, however, I was not so kind.

Each morning I saw the result of their munching, bare leaves, desiccated pansies, and my impatience grew. My mood became no longer one of loving all creatures of nature; my own personal activities were being affected; I was no longer a do-gooder observer; I was involved with the survival of my plants, and so my benevolent attitude changed. My plants were more precious to me than snails and so bait, I decided, had to be used to kill them.

I used a spray. Pellets, unless they are covered, are a menace. Birds pick them up believing they are edible, and dogs and cats eat them, believing they are broken biscuits. Just a few of the pellets being eaten will kill. As for the spray, there is one basic rule. Get up early the next morning after it has been used, and destroy the doped snails before the thrushes and blackbirds pounce upon them.

Thus my sentimental attitude towards snails was shown to be a vacuous one as soon as my interests were at stake . . . so many causes are pursued by people unaffected by the disadvantages of the causes they espouse.

It is the wind, however, not snails, which is the real enemy of the garden, and the salt which comes with it. It sears in from Mount's Bay, white waves wildly flinging foam at each other, crashing against the rocks and the cliff, sending a cloud of salt up into the sky. A sticky mist in the wind, killing the leaves of the elders and the blackthorn, biting into the corners of the garden, finding gaps between bushes, and rushing to where the vegetables are growing, bruising the foot-high runner beans and peas, bashing the raspberry canes . . . spring winds are the killers. For two years in succession they have scythed into Minack so that the elms along the lane have been bared, and the leafless blackthorn and elders have failed in many places to survive. The wind is always our enemy. Only the evergreen leaves of the escallonia are safe against it. They withstand the wind, accept the sticky salt, and remain green.

Cats are not omnipotent.

One night in early June, a night when such a wind was blasting the cottage, I felt a lump at the bottom of the bed; and I put out a hand and touched fur. Oliver, I said to myself, and prepared to get out of bed. Then I felt a second lump. The two of them were there. What should I do? I was sleepy. I was averse to disturbing myself. The noise of the gale lulled my intended determination to be free. Let them be, I dopily said to myself.

And I did.

The first night that Oliver and Ambrose slept on our bed.

A broken New Year's resolution which now brings cramp, night after night, to my legs.

9

Broadbent was on the roof. It was raining. It was raining so hard that the noise of it sounded as if pebbles were spraying the porch glass. A fortnight of fine weather had broken; and Broadbent was up there, a bunch of black feathers, squatting close to the apex of the roof, as if the sun were still shining.

'Silly jackdaw,' said Jeannie, looking up at him from the porch.

He was a timid jackdaw. He was not one of those jackdaws which, once they have accepted the attention of a human being, demand so much that they become tyrants. Nor could I boast, in the way that human beings like to boast when a wild animal or bird shows interest in them, that he was tame. He was attached to us because he no doubt instinctively remembered how we had nursed him back to health. We were friendly. We threw him scraps. We were useful, but he did not belong to us.

'This weather makes it a good day for Labour Warms,' I said.

Labour Warms, the massive teak cupboard once in my nursery, containing an accumulation of letters and notebooks over the years, and still displaying in blue letters across its top the exhortation: LABOUR WARMS SLOTH HARMS.

'I can spend the day,' I went on, 'with papers littering the floor.'

'And at the end of it, you'll be able to say that a resolution has been fulfilled,' smiled Jeannie.

'At least I'm proving that I am *trying* to fulfil my resolutions.'

'Very praiseworthy.'

'You're in a sceptical mood again.'

'Oh no, not really. I was just thinking . . .'

'*What* are you thinking?'

Oliver was sitting on the carpet in front of the bookcase, his twig of a tail curled round him, the tip tapping his front paws.

'I was just thinking how Oliver and Ambrose have triumphed.'

'You were always on their side. You're rubbing it in.'

'It *is* funny, isn't it? That fine New Year resolution to keep them off the bed, and they conquered you. Two cats filling the bed!'

'An act of God.'

Jeannie was laughing.

'Anyhow,' she said, 'sensible of you to be philosophical about it.'

'I'm just being a good loser.'

'Did you hear that, Oliver?' said Jeannie, still laughing. 'He accepts his defeat like a good loser.'

'Enough of this,' I said.

'I'm only teasing you.'

'Oh, I know that . . . but I think it is time to change the subject.'

'To the subject of Labour Warms?'

'Yes.'

'It should be interesting.'

'There's so much. I can only make a start.'

'You'll become full of nostalgia.'

'I'll enjoy that.'

'Some people disapprove of nostalgia. They class it as sentimental indulgence.'

'Do you understand that? I don't. I can never understand the theory that you should always look forward and never look back.'

'Nor do I.'

People who don't want to look back must have led such disturbing lives that they haven't anything they wish to remember. Thus they cling to the future as if it were a lifebelt. They feel safe in the future because it hasn't happened.

I was standing by my Regency kidney-shaped desk filling my pipe; and Jeannie was sitting on the side of the armchair, and Oliver had just jumped on her lap.

'I met a well-meaning social worker the other day,' Jeannie said, 'who told me she was a visitor to an old people's home, and that she had recently scored a great success in her work.'

'What was that?'

'She said that when she first went to the home all the inmates were docile, sat in their chairs dreaming of the past. Her great success was that she changed all that. She said that she had been able to wake them up to the problems that faced us all today, and that they were no longer sitting there remembering. Then she added, excitedly, "do you know what? I have got them arguing with each other, and having rows. I have made them come alive!"'

'I suppose your friend had a point.'

'Oh, rubbish,' said Jeannie. 'Surely arguments on present day problems are no substitute for the quiet those old people were having with their memories?'

'Psychiatrists would probably not agree.'

'Oh, psychiatrists . . .'

My pipe was filled; filled with tobacco which comes from H. Simmons, the old established tobacconists in Burlington Arcade off Piccadilly, and called Down the Road, but when I tried to light it the matchstick snapped as soon as it struck the side of the box.

'Damn these matches.'

'I'll buy you a lighter.'

'Lovely . . . next Christmas then.'

There was a knock on the door, and the cry: 'Post!' and Oliver leapt from Jeannie's lap.

A couple of letters, a bill, and a cunningly phrased circular announcing that I had been given a lucky number in a draw for fabulous prizes, provided I bought an album of records.

'I'll go off now,' I said.

'I'll bring you a cup of coffee later on.'

I am one of those who finds it difficult to separate the past from the present. Time, to me, is a plateau. There is no mountain range which hides from me the emotions I once felt; and when, to my joy, I meet again someone whom I knew long ago there is for me no interval between the parting and the reunion. Such an attitude can cause awkward moments. I am brimful of happy memories, but the mind of the other is blank. Or I anticipate a meeting with a friend of my youth, the youthful face still fresh in my thoughts and then, on seeing him, I am startled into remembering a sentence by Leopardi . . . 'seeing again after some years a person I have known young, always at first I seem to see one who has suffered a great calamity.'

I had no clear recall, however, of those who featured on the first piece of paper I extracted from Labour Warms; and for good reason. No one would wish to remember the faces behind the initials of the following school report. I was fourteen and at Harrow.

Latin: Has improved slightly.   R.W.F.

French: Weak, could do better. A nice boy but a bit idle.   E.D.L.

English: Poor. I am of the opinion he could try a great deal more if he exerted himself.   R.W.F.

Mathematics: Not very satisfactory – a hindrance to the progress of others. There is no vice – only childish exuberance out of place and time.   J.H.H.

House Master's Report: A very nice interesting boy but really lazy. I have had him on reports, if this does not make him work and stop playing the fool in class sterner methods must be used. I like him very much and I have no doubt he will alter his ways. He is a keen little cricketer.   B.M.

A couple of years later the keen little cricketer won a place in the House cricket eleven but, playing in a vital match, he dropped a catch. That evening B.M., my house-master, summoned me to his study.

'Tangye,' he said, censoriously, 'you're useless to society.'

I had no qualifications when I left Harrow. I had failed to pass any of the appropriate examinations and so I was not viewed upon by prospective employers as being employable. This, of course, has been a perennial problem for school-leavers. If they cannot shove in front of employers paper evidence of their scholastic achievements, they are passed by in favour of those who can. Intelligence, flair (a quality which has no place in any examination, but with a potential more exciting than any), enthusiasm . . . all these are indefinable virtues and valueless without certificates of examination passes. Thus it is that the imaginative young, especially those who are timid, are passed over by those who sail into an examination room without the inhibitions of the imaginative; and so pass, and win favour.

I was lucky. I lived in a period when it was possible to move into a job through a backdoor; and, using the influence of a friend of my father, I was enrolled as a clerk in Unilever. Once there, however, I again became controlled by examination standards and was informed, in due course, that as I possessed no certificates to prove my worth I had little hope of an executive future. This did not worry me. I had already come to the conclusion that, though happy in the company of my colleagues, I was not going to spend the rest of my life selling soap and margarine; and then came my second opportunity to pass through a backdoor. A friend of a girlfriend knew Max Aitken, Beaverbrook's son, and I was given an introduction. Half an hour after the interview began, a dream came true. I was given a month's trial on the *Daily Express* in Manchester.

Had it not been for that introduction, much of what I found in Labour Warms would not have been there. For, as the result of that interview, as the result of my joining the *Daily Express*, I was introduced into a world which would forever have been denied me had I devoted my life to soap and margarine. There is no method in choosing the items I am going to quote; no time sequence. I am just picking out odds and ends from Labour Warms . . . and, in my mind's eye, I see the small boy who looked apprehensively up at the great teak cupboard standing in his nursery.

There is Jeannie's verse about Suez. I remember the horror when, lying in bed with Monty at the bottom of it, I switched on the portable radio to the early morning news and heard that British paratroops had dropped on Egypt and that fighting was in full swing. I was appalled. The attack, at a time when the British Empire was petering into extinction, thanks largely to the attitude of boredom towards such an empire by the British public, seemed to me to be senseless. It was even embarrassing. After all, in comparison with the Soviet Union and the United States, the power Britain possessed was the equivalent of peanuts.

'Oh God,' I said to Jeannie, 'the whole thing is doomed to failure. *How* could it have been started?'

I am not sure when I began to have second thoughts, second thoughts not about the wisdom of the attack but about the reasons which prompted it. The reasons had not been created by the British and the French, I realised. The reasons had been provided by the American Secretary of State, John Foster Dulles. Dulles had refused to supply President Nasser with arms (as a gesture towards Israel) and Nasser turned to the Russians for his tanks and aircraft. In pique at the deal, Dulles cut off American financial backing for the High Dam at Aswan, a key part of Nasser's plan to bring irrigation to the desert and, in revenge, Nasser nationalised the Suez Canal; and then the British and French were alerted to the likelihood of the Russians usurping their influence in the Middle East and beyond. The Autherine Lucey in Jeannie's verse is the coloured teacher who, at the time, was being banned from teaching in a white American school:

> The foreign policy of Mr Dulles
> Only sullies
> Anglo-American relations.
> And Eisenhower
> Is sour
> And votes against us at United Nations.
> And I would like to do something juicy
> And shout
> What about
> Autherine Lucey?
> And anyway it all began
> With the Aswan Dam.

A pithy verse, appropriate to the mood at the time; and it won the approval of the legendary A. P. Herbert, wit and a mainstay of *Punch* for many years; instigator of the first major Divorce Reform Bill when he was the Independent Member for Oxford University, dramatist, author of musical comedies like *Bless The Bride* (with the glorious music of Vivian Ellis), authority on the stars whose names he wished to change into those of history's heroes, a frustrated follower of and writer about football pools (creator of the Curate's Perm, the Organist's Perm, the Wealthy Widow's Perm), a tenacious pursuer of lost causes, a wonderful companion, and one of the dozen or so honoured in Churchill's resignation list after the war, when he became Sir Alan (much to his surprise).

He often stayed with us at Minack and, one day, he wrote:

> Here come the storm-tossed and the tired
> And find balm for every bane;
> Body and soul refreshed and fired,
> They sadly put to sea again.

The verse is not one of his better ones. I prefer the lines he wrote about two young sisters, Anne and Mary, whom he met one day when he was with us. He wrote it in the family visiting book after a few second's pause:

> Be wary man
> Man be wary
> First of Anne
> And then of Mary.

Once we arranged to meet him in Plymouth, staying in the same hotel; and the occasion was a party for a consortium, of which he was a member, that sought the ITV franchise for the South West. The consortium failed to win it, but the occasion prompted A.P.H., who was adept in drawing up Bills for Parliament, real or imaginary, to draw up the following one:

INDUSTRIAL EFFICIENCY (TANGYE)

A
BILL

To secure and maintain the industrial efficiency and material prosperity of the realm, and for other purposes.

WHEREAS it is impossible, and indeed unworthy for any true Englishman to enjoy a sound, continuous and sufficient sleep under the same roof as JEAN EVERALD TANGYE, unless located in the same room, and accordingly, upon her visits to large centres of population, through the unrest and frustration of men of art, commerce and all lawful affairs much injury is done to the efficiency of the realm and the Queen's revenue.

And it is expedient that the presence of the said dangerous and disturbing influence should be kept secret.

Be it therefore enacted by the Queen's most Excellent Majesty by and with the advice of the Lords Temporal and Spiritual and Common, in this present Parliament assembled, and by the authority of the same as follows:—

1. (I) It shall be an offence to publish, reveal or disclose the presence of JEAN EVERALD TANGYE in any County Borough, Municipal Borough, or parish having a population exceeding ten persons.

(II) Not withstanding anything in the Hotels or Immigration Acts, no reference of the presence of JEAN EVERALD or DEREK ALAN TREVITHICK TANGYE shall be made in the books of any tavern, inn or hotel.

2. (I) This Act may be cited as the JEAN TANGYE ACT *1959*.

(II) This Act shall come into operation forthwith.

(III) This Act shall apply to England, Wales, Scotland and Northern Ireland.

There were many letters from A.P.H. in Labour Warms. Scrawly writing, sometimes only decipherable with the aid of a magnifying glass. One summer Gwen his wife, and as good a friend to us as A.P.H., wrote asking whether we could have him to stay as he was badly needing a quiet holiday. Soon after his arrival, we were having breakfast one morning when he mentioned that he had no idea what to write next, a book or a play.

'Why not turn *The Water Gipsies* into a musical?' said Jeannie.

His novel, *The Water Gipsies*, a story about the canals, had been hugely successful many years before.

'Ah yes—' he began . . . and then, at that moment, there was a great squawking from the roof, and it was Hubert the gull of *A Gull on the Roof* crying out, beak to the heavens.

'There you are,' I said, 'Hubert approves!'

A month later A.P.H. completed the play and nervously set off from Minack to show it to Vivian Ellis, whose home was at Minehead; and Vivian proceeded to compose a score which was as enchanting as the other scores he had written for *Big Ben, Tough at the Top* and *Bless the Bride*. A year later, we had this letter from A.P.H. at The County Hotel, Theatre Square, Nottingham:

August 4 – 1955

Jean, darling, and Derek,

Observe the date! It was August 4, 1954, that I wrote the first sketch of the scenes of W.G. and the fatal words 'Act One, Scene One.' And now, just a year later, I am writing to report that the little ship has been well and truly launched, thank God . . . and you! As you will see from the enclosed, it really did seem to please them on Tuesday, and I thought it was wonderful to get anyone there at all, as it is very hot and stuffy. Very many thanks for your letter and telegram. Gwen said: 'Who's Hubert?' I feel rather played out. After the first night Gwen gave a little party here but the blasted management insisted on having a 'conference' and broke it up. We argued about this and that till nearly 4 a.m. (whisky, etc. flowing pretty freely) but I get up feeling like H— at 8 a.m. and at 9 was writing more verses! I may get home tomorrow, but I've got to come up to Manchester on Sunday.

The ghastly thing about this sort of tour is that it's a first night every Monday – culminating in that hideous business in London.

Well, bless you, and again 1001 thanks for your inspiration and support.

Much love from your exhausted Alan.

Jeannie and I were at the Winter Garden Theatre for the London first night and, when the curtain came down at the end of the performance, the audience rose applauding from their seats.

He continued periodically to stay with us and he was here when *A Gull on the Roof* was in manuscript, and he gave us much encouragement. He was here, too, when Charles Pick, the publisher, came to see me and, years later, it was Charles Pick who asked us to use our influence with A.P.H. into persuading him to write his autobiography. He had written *Independent Member*, but that was an account of his parliamentary days, and Charles Pick wanted a book that would cover the whole expanse of his life. It proved to be a mammoth book, requiring much research and, every now and then, he would send us reports on its progress. He became weary of it and yet his final chapter *A Good Run* is one of the most evocative farewells I have ever read. His remarks in the Preamble of the book flattered Jeannie and me . . .

though he mischievously balanced them in the copy he
gave us. In red ink he wrote:

> To Jean and Derek
>   their 'bloody book'
>   With love from Alan.

We were, it doesn't need me to say, greatly touched to
be asked to his eightieth birthday party at the Savoy. It
was a family affair and the invitation came from John,
his son, a director of Christie's, his daughters Crystal,
Lavender, and Jocelyn, who first won fame as a stage
designer at the Royal Court Theatre in London; and
Gwen. A half dozen guests, outside those of the family,
were present, and one of them of course was Vivian Ellis,
who came with Hermione his sister. After the dinner, after
the speeches, Vivian sat at the piano and played the songs
which A.P.H. loved. An elegant party and, when it was
over, A.P.H. took the red rose which he wore in his lapel
and gave it to Jeannie. She still has the petals. In a glass
jar with a silver top.

One never felt any age gap with him. He was always
a contemporary, and this was because he never talked
ponderously about age. At any age, he knew, one can
be foolish. At any age, too, one can be wise. No age has
an exclusive right to wisdom; and thus, possessing this
attitude that all ages are equal, he was as much in tune
with the young as with those of his own time.

Football pools were always a common ground with
us and he would conduct correspondence with Jeannie
about his efforts to win the jackpot. He persevered in this
attempt with dogged devotion, and went to the trouble of
writing *Pools Pilot* which began with the introduction:

> Some shallow thinkers may call this work dangerous;
> but that would be jumping to most unfair conclusions.

True, we offer instructions to high and humble, peer and plumber, which may, or may not lead them to profits and gains, free of income tax . . .

Despite, however, his perseverence, his research, his patience, he never did succeed in winning that hefty sum which, he said, would enable him to say as he was handed the £500,000 cheque: 'Me and my missus are going on just as before.'

Nor, of course, has Jeannie ever won it, although she has enjoyed one moment of triumph. It occurred when she checked her coupon on the Sunday before we travelled to London for A.P.H.'s Memorial Service at St Martin-in-the-Fields. On the previous Tuesday, when she was about to fill in the coupon, she looked up into the sky and said: 'Come on, Alan, help me with my coupon. Which teams shall I choose?'

Her entry scored 22 points; and she won £92.

The Memorial Service included a song, accompanied on the organ by Vivian Ellis, which came from *The Water Gipsies*. I remember A.P.H. writing the verses one sunny afternoon, sitting on the white seat beside the verbena bush opposite the barn; and I remember that the sound of the bells of Paul Church above Mousehole were being carried by the wind to Minack. This was the song:

Peace and quiet, that's the thing.
Here we hear the church bells ring.
We can hear the lofty lark
And the birds that love the dark.
Water tumbling down the weir,
Water whisp'ring 'sleep is here'—

Then the cock our waking clock
Softly calls across the lock.
Bells that ring, birds that sing,
Peace and quiet – that's the thing.

> Ah little boat! One summer day
> My love and I will sail away,
> And hand in hand some better land discover.
> Away, away, the seagulls cry,
> The sail is set, the tide is high,
> The winds blow free,
> But where is he my lover.

The first verse is then repeated. It was a simple song with a haunting melody; and those of us who were present that morning at St Martin-in-the-Fields were deeply moved. The '*Good Run*' had ended. Not that the ghost of A.P.H. would have been sad himself. After the Service the ghost would have suggested a visit to Joe Gilmore at the Savoy Bar and then asked for a gin. A couple of gins later, he might remark that he was beginning to feel unseaworthy and, if asked, he might quote a verse he spontaneously brought forth on his arrival one time at Hobart, Tasmania. A reporter asked if he would write his own epitaph. A.P.H. light-heartedly replied:

> The demon gin what did me in
> But bless the Lord who gave us gin.

Quite untrue, of course. He was naturally gregarious and, because he 'gave', he was always fun to be with.

When my mother was ill I wrote a daily letter to her, not out of duty, but out of a selfish wish to do so. My mother was absorbed by the detail of our lives. Some of these letters came back to me after she had died. Here are two of them I found in Labour Warms. They concern the early days at Minack:

February 5th

Darling, well here we are again and the snow is still on the car and the lane impassable and the ground so hard that a pick-axe can't break it. A bitter North East near gale has been blowing and has been doing what the frost hasn't done already. The wallflowers have now gone beyond repair, the violets and the anemones are finished, and the marigolds, and I can scarcely believe that the forget-me-nots can recover.

One must look back eight months to last June to measure the tragedy. Then we were deciding where to put the anemones, the wallflowers, the violets and so on. In June we planted our first wallflower seed which within a month had disappeared as it had been eaten by flea beetle. So we toured the area trying to get plants, and calling on nurserymen at Camborne, Redruth, Helston, and we were very excited when we found them at a place at St Ives. We bought 2,500 which we carefully planted, kept weeded, watching over them like growing children until last week they were beginning to flower. In June we had planted the 20,000 anemone corms. In June we had planted the violets ... and ever since there has been weeding and weeding. Now they have all finished before their cropping time had hardly started.

Another letter dated August 21st, no year:

Darling, we are all set to go into town for the shopping and it is 8 a.m. We go early to escape the crowds and I am going in because we seem to have a holocaust of wireworms and leather jackets on one part of the anemones. It really is a battle. The anemones in this part haven't been looking too good and yesterday we were weeding them and found these little bastards. So I am going into town to find something to deal with them.

Good heavens, my wife, my dear wife, has just

come into the room in a new costume. A simple grey affair, with a white collar, and a woollen texture. So I have been able to say how lucky she is to have a husband who immediately notices such a purchase. She got it at Harrods: 'Just for a day like this . . .' which is cold and blustery like the beginning of November.

For myself I have on a pair of white linen trousers which I got in Fiji. I have had no alteration to them and they fit perfectly. With jacket they cost thirty bob.

In the same corner of Labour Warms I found the file of correspondence my father kept during a tour of the world I made just before the 1939 war. He had kept all the letters I had written to my family and copies of the letters he wrote to me. I was close to my father although he was a man who found it difficult to communicate his true feelings to others. He and I used to go fly fishing for trout together along the winding Fowey river which runs below the railway line either side of Bodmin Road station; and though at the end of the day we would vividly discuss our fishing experiences, during the day while we were fishing we kept well apart. Each of us enjoyed the pleasure of being alone.

The letter I quote is one of those he wrote to me while I was staying in Tahiti and other islands of the South Seas; and as he himself had been to Samoa in his youth, he intuitively sensed my emotions. He always began his letters to me: 'My dear Cur'. A curious form of endearment. He was writing the letter from the family home Glendorgal, near Newquay:

My dear Cur, Your stay in Tahiti is fast nearing its close, and I have been thinking so much of you, for I can well understand your feelings, mingled with intense regret and yet the desire to get on. I am sure that you and I are kindred souls as regards our sentiments towards the South Seas, and your heartstrings will be torn just as much as mine, and those of the Bounty mutineers, and that of Rupert Brooke who heard 'the calling of the moon, and the whispering scents that stray, about the idle warm lagoon'. What a wonderful trip you are having. I never went to Tahiti to my lasting regret, but possibly you will be able to get a trader to Apia which I knew well. If you get there have a drink at the Tivoli Hotel on the beach, and look out for my ghost and any relatives. Possibly you may meet a man named Gurr there. He was R.L. Stevenson's solicitor. I bought some of Stevenson's books from him, and they are still in the library here.

I got the book by Robert Keable. Curiously enough I had never heard of it, ravenous though I am for any literature about the islands. What a strange career – parson, missionary, a Chaplain in France during the Great War, and ending his life with a native girl in far away Tahiti. I have found all the places both he and you mention on my German map, and so I can visualise all the spots alluded to. No wonder, on hearing the news from 'civilisation', you made up your mind to stay on in a carefree world; you were indeed wise to do so. But I fear that your return to 'civilisation' will be much in the nature of an anti-climax, for everything will seem so petty and sordid.

Aloha, farewell

I found in a corner of the cupboard a fan letter addressed to Jeannie about her book *Meet me at the Savoy*. A rather special fan letter for it came from Lady Juliet Duff, a legend of the Society world, a close friend of many of those distinguished men and women who belonged to the first part of the twentieth century. Out of the blue came this letter:

Dear Mrs Tangye: I have only just read your book, and I want so much to write and tell you how enormously I enjoyed it. The Savoy has never lost its magic for me, since my childhood days in the nineties, when I used to hear of the De Reszkes, Melba, and Calvé staying there. (My mother and step father Lord and Lady De Grey were, with Harry Higgins, directors of the Covent Garden Opera.) I imagined it, I think, as a kind of fairy palace where only very special people stayed, and which if I were lucky I might someday see.

When, in later years, I first went there, it was to the Restaurant, *never* the Grill, for 'ladies' were not supposed to go to the Grill, and you will hardly believe it when I tell you, that in 1913, John Manners (killed alas very early in the War) was had up by his Colonel and sharply reproved for taking his twin sisters to supper there! Afterwards it was the place we loved best (in spite of the charm of Santarelli in the Restaurant), Manetta always made one feel as though one were a welcome guest at a private party, and I am sure that had one ever gone there to supper alone, he would have fixed one up, saying: 'Would you like to go to Lady Diana's table, or I'm sure Mr Kommer would like you to join his party.'

I *am* so glad you said what you did about the American correspondents and broadcasters – no one else that I can discover paid them the tribute which is their due. I've always felt that a monument as big as St Paul's ought to be put to them for what they did for us during those horrible days (as someone said, never were neutral correspondents less neutral). I didn't know them all, like you did, but I always think gratefully of Ed Murrow, Bill Stoneman, Helen Kirkpatrick, Walter Graebner, and of dear little Ben Robertson who was killed.

What fascinating years you had there, and I am

sure you miss it in a way, though your present life does sound delightful, and I'm sure you wouldn't change it. Thank you again for a great treat, and if ever you are motoring to London, *do* look in on me here.

                                   Juliet Duff.
                                   Burbridge House,
                                        Wilton, Salisbury.

We had several letters from her during the coming years, but we never met. It was a period when we never moved from Minack because we never had the funds to pay for a journey to London. After *A Cat in the Window* was published, she, a cat lover, wrote me a kind letter:

I hope you have another book in mind, for you must never stop writing. The other night at Noël's opening I found myself sitting next to A.P.H. and we talked a lot about you both.

A friend and I had already seen the play in Bristol on Whit Saturday, and brought Noël back here for the weekend, and he was as delightful as ever; and reminiscing, we realised it was just over forty years since we first met. The lady he wrote *The Vortex* about brought him over to see me in Kent, in a tiny house where I lived in those days, and we picked gooseberries, and he said 'you *do* think I'll be a success don't you?' He had already written *The Young Idea*, but of course *The Vortex* brought him right to the top; and the lady he'd written it about, a Mrs Foster, came to the opening, and was delighted with everything.

To return to *A Cat in the Window* – how I wish I had known him, and he must have been so much nicer than the Field Marshall. By the way, a few weeks ago he and I were both staying at Chartwell, and at dinner one night I asked him something, and called him Lord Montgomery. He said 'Oh don't call me Lord Montgomery, call me Field Marshall!'

Now can you help over this? In your first book you speak of the hotel your brother Nigel runs; would it do for Lady Churchill, or is it for the young and agile? Winston is going away, and she so terribly wants a rest, and she hates Brighton. She's coming here next week-end, then has to go back to Chartwell to deal with a large party of ladies from Winston's constituency, so it would be the following week. If you have a moment do write and tell me what you think, or if there is anywhere else that would do for her.

Juliet Duff.

Noël Coward usually sent telegrams to his friends, notes were comparatively rare. I was surprised to receive one after I had sent him a copy of *A Donkey in the Meadow*. There it was in Labour Warms, and I read it again:

My dear Derek,

I was entirely enchanted by *A Donkey in the Meadow*, and thank you so very much for sending it to me. Your writing is so lucid and gay, and I enjoyed every minute of it.

I love Fred and I love Lama, in fact I love the lot.

Thank you a million . . . love Noël.

He had such gusto. In an area of the world which has much insincerity, he himself never failed to prove his integrity. Gertrude Lawrence said to me that she had never understood him, but she loved him for just being Noël. I think she was a little scared of him, certainly she was anxious to have his approval of every part she played. But Gertie always needed boosting by someone. She was never secure.

A year before she died, she asked me to write her biography; and her letter was followed by one from her lawyer, Fanny Holtzmann, offering me trips to New York and Hollywood. Jeannie and I had just started our life at Minack and so I wrote back that we had made our decision to live here and we were not going to be deviated from it whatever the temptation to do so. 'Anyhow,' I added in my letter, 'you're too young for a biography.' A year later she died.

Now, having seen the movie *Star*, which had Julie Andrews playing Gertie, I wish I had written her biography; and perhaps my contract would have given me the chance to write the script of the movie. As it was, the movie seemed to me to be a disaster. There was no whisper of Gertie's devastating charm. No sign of her subtlety in singing a song. No hint of her wayward femininity. No evidence of the loyalty she gave to friends. No touch of the magic with which she entranced an audience. When watching the movie, I suddenly found myself thinking of Derby Day and, instead of the thoroughbreds racing into the straight from Tattenham Corner, I saw a trundling London bus.

I found several of her letters in Labour Warms, and here are extracts from two of them. The first is an example of a very insecure Gertie, full of wild hopes:

The Cape Playhouse,
Sept 17, 1949   Cape Cod

Darlings,

Please forgive me for not having written you before this, but things have certainly been on the jump since my return. What with rehearsals, problems, the heat, and suddenly finding myself extremely tired, I found there was no chance to write without falling asleep at the desk. Added to all this I was whisked off to New York after the play at Dennis on the Saturday night to make a test for Warner Brothers. Jack Warner sent his own car and chauffeur and I went off all alone in the dark. We drove for seven hours through the night, arrived at 7 a.m. in New York where I was ushered (very secretly) into the most fabulous suite at Hampshire House, 3 bedrooms, 3 baths, kitchen and vast living room, overlooking Central Park. There I stayed for exactly one hour, and was then taken to the studios where I found Irving Rapper, the director and Carl Foynd the cameraman (both flown in specially from the Coast) plus 4 costumes, make-up men and wardrobe women. We worked without stopping to breathe until 7.15 p.m., by which time I felt as though I had been beaten up by bandits and left for dead. At the time I kept saying to myself 'Why am I doing all this?' and 'It's bound to be a flop anyhow, so why all the fuss?' . . . I flew back to the Cape at 8 a.m. on the Monday morning in time to rehearse again for the 2nd week of *September Tide* . . . well, days went by, the test had to be flown back to the Coast to be 'processed', and meanwhile I was certain it had all been a lot of time wasted. Then the avalanche began, and now deals have been made, contracts signed, and tonight in Hollywood Warner Brothers are throwing an enormous party for Tennessee Williams at which I am to be launched nation wide, like Vivien Leigh in *Gone With the Wind*.

So my dears, you have another film star on your hands for future accommodation – star of *Glass Menagerie*. Jane Wyman is playing the crippled girl, Kirk Douglas the son, and it is going to be Warner Brothers' prestige picture of the year, and they hope for the Academy Award, so maybe if I try very hard, which I shall, little 'Gee' may come home with an Oscar?

Devotedly,
Gee.

She didn't win an Oscar, though she won much praise for her performance of Amanda . . . though the Amanda of *The Glass Menagerie* was never as enchanting as the Amanda of *Private Lives*.

The second letter is the one she wrote after the opening in New York of *The King and I*. It was her great ambition to star at Drury Lane, but this was never to be. She died too soon.

April 1, 1951

Hello Darlings,

This is no April Fool's Day to me . . . we have got *the most terrific hit*.

Nothing has ever been produced on Broadway by anyone else that has in any way touched the public and the critics as has 'Anna'. I am sending you all the notices, and though we have only been open 3 days, I am *longing* to get the play to London . . . but we shall have to wait at least 3 years, as it looks now.

I think of you both even in my busiest and most nerve-racking days, and during the rehearsals and the road tryout, and I often envied your peaceful meadows. I shall be sending you some more packages of surprises now that all is calm again. . . .

You will go wild about the play. It is simply beautiful, touching, and most engaging and enchanting in every way, and I have had notices for my *singing*!! Have been studying for about 4 years since *Lady in the Dark*.

My love always,

Gee.

Gertie made a habit of these enthusiastic outbursts. Over-generous, over-extravagant, aiming to turn every occasion into one of drama and fun; she could, even in her personal relationships, imagine a goose to be a swan. When she died, the lights both of Broadway and

Shaftesbury Avenue were dimmed . . . not even Gertie's enthusiasm could have expected such a tribute.

It proceeded to rain all day. A cup of coffee in the morning, sandwiches at lunch, a pot of tea in the afternoon, and I continued to delve into Labour Warms. Much of it was a waste of time, reading old newspapers, the reason for keeping which I couldn't remember, staring at photographs, tearing up long ago bills; and it was just when I was about to stop that I found a number of Jack Broadbent's letters.

He was an eccentric, a passionately loyal friend, and a newspaper correspondent who perceptively surveyed the world scene. Periodically he would suddenly appear at Minack after having flown from Washington, or Paris, or Rome; and I described in *Lama* the hilarious, though poignant as it turned out to be, time he came for Christmas. The last letter he wrote to me had vision, as well as humour. . . .

Want a bet? The Americans (as I told you years ago) will make a deal with the Russians before I lose the last of my hair, which won't be long. There is no such thing now as an Anglo-American alliance. They don't want to listen to us. Why should they? Our Empire has gone, and they have helped its destruction by their envy of it . . . but how mad I get about those who have been running the Empire. They have neglected that great prize year by year for a generation at least. The Tories are more to blame than anybody else though the real fault is fundamental. Whatever political party in power tried to rule the Empire on what were the domestic necessities of home politics. Yet it will not be a bad thing for us, if we keep our heads. It can compel our people to face the facts. We have still a big part in the new world if we face facts and we have big enough men to act. If there is any imagination left in our would be leaders we are in for a good time. But if they are going to be the same bunch of stuffed shirts and other kinds of stupid people we shall sink lower and lower. About you and Jeannie, however, I am certain as ever you are doing what you like best and enjoying it. The more I see of cities and capitals, aeroplanes and jets, ships and motor cars, restaurants and bars, idiots and cunning men, politicians and newspapermen, editors and newspaper pundits, columnists and criminals . . . you made the right decision at the right time. Timing, that's what's so important in life.

Three months after his Christmas stay with us, he was found dead in a Westminster flat he had temporarily rented. The two rooms were in disorder and a gilded mirror in the sitting-room was smashed. In January he had retired from the *Daily Mail* with a golden handshake and, in the company of an officer of a Guards regiment, haunted various fashionable gambling clubs. Towards the end of March he told a friend that the Guards officer owed him a great deal of money. Whether this was an excuse to cover up his own losses, I do not know. All I can say is that the barman at the block of flats wrote to me (I had never met him) saying that he had something important to tell me; and he wished to tell me personally.

The next time I went to London, I set off one lunch-time to see the barman. I never saw him. He had died the week before.

So I will never know what happened to Jack Broadbent . . . though he was up there on the roof when I finished my session with Labour Warms.

10

My resolution to withstand domination by the donkeys was a fiasco, I am afraid, from the beginning.

I would slip out of the back door if they were in a position to see me coming out of the front, and slip out of the front door if they could see me coming out of the back . . . and then set off on a walk of my own. Or, if they were in the stable field in front of the barn, thus barring my normal route to the cliff, I would go up the three steps to Lama's field, turn left past the corner where we have built a stone hedge topped with earth and full of flowers, and down another few steps into the *QE2* field. Then I would scurry or, more likely, Jeannie and I both would be scurrying along the top-side of the field until we reached the far end where we would slide down a steep bank into one of our top cliff meadows. We would then believe we were free.

Freedom would be brief. The donkeys' acute hearing would catch the sound of our hasty footsteps or, if they were placed in the right situation, they would catch a glimpse of us as we sneaked away; and thereupon they would set up a heartrending hullabaloo and the sound of it would make us feel sorry for them. After hesitation, and an urgent talk, we would retrace our steps, unlatch the gate, fasten on the halters, and start on our walk again . . . except now there were four of us.

I had also, on that New Year's Day, been determined to withstand another form of pressure which they regularly put on us. They had two main grazing grounds, the stable field in front of the barn and the donkey field above the cottage; and if they had become bored in one, they would make it plain that they wanted to move to the other. They would stand, heads side by side, looking over one or other of the gates, pawing occasionally at the ground and displaying their impatience, sometimes whinnying, sometimes hee-hawing, until at last I would say to Jeannie: 'We had better move them.'

Such a decision would seem to imply that there was now only the simple procedure of putting on their halters and leading them up the path from the stable field or down the path from the donkey field. This was not so. As soon as they realised they had successfully imposed their wishes upon us, as soon as we had reached the gate, halters in hand, one or other of them, or both, would play a maddening trick upon us. Instead of meekly standing, waiting for the halters to be fastened, they would turn their bottoms to us and walk away. Or, if Penny were compliant, pushing her head forward so that there was no problem in fixing the halter, Fred, perversely, would scamper away as I approached him.

'Fred!' I would shout. 'Fred! Come here!'

This, he thought, was hilariously funny; a quirky humour which I did not find funny at all. In disgust I would take Penny by the lead, walk out through the gate and shut it; and thereupon Fred would race across the field and slide to a stop at the gate, as if he were daring to say: 'Hey, you're leaving me behind!' This impression, however, was just a trick, a device to annoy me again . . . for when I had pulled back Penny to the gate and opened it, halter in my hand, Fred would dash away again, leaving me to fume. Penny also, from time to time, would make me fume. Penny would behave in the same fashion. She would dance away when I approached her, kicking her heels, putting her head down as if she were laughing, while Fred with halter in place, lead in my hand, would tolerantly watch her antics. For both, such behaviour was a means of bringing spice to the day.

One might suppose that, once they had their halters in place, the act of leading them from field to field would also be a simple affair. Once again, one would be wrong. When, for instance, we led them from the stable field up past the cottage to the donkey field, there was always one particular point near a rock and a few yards from our bedroom window where each would anchor their four feet. It was a ritual. Without fail, every time they reached this point, they would come to a full stop.

'Come on! Come on!'

And they would refuse to move.

Perhaps they acted in this way as a joke, although their faces did not suggest this. When they were joking it was easy to see they were doing so by their manner, but when they came to a full stop on the path, they seemed to be adopting a bolshy attitude. As if they were saying: 'We're as good as them. They may feed us and look after us, and without them we don't know where we would be . . . but we are going to prove that we have the power. If we don't want to move, they can't make us.'

If these were their thoughts, they fortunately did not persist with them. We would tug, cajole, shout a few epithets, and they would proceed; but there was now another hazard. We had to steer them between the flower beds which bordered the path, steer them from taking a mouthful of nicotiana, or of antirrhinums, or of marigolds, or alyssum, or pansies, or rudbeckia, or any other of the flowers I had grown so hopefully in the spring. Then, when they had reached the corner of the cottage which leads to the porch there was the huge escallonia on the one side and, on the other, the fragrant tree-like bush with feathery green leaves and tiny white flowers, the name of which I do not know. These flowers and bushes were nectar to the donkeys. They lunged at them as we passed. We pulled them away. They lunged again. The short walk from stable field to donkey field and back was always an adventure.

The flowers they lunged at, however, had not bloomed as successfully as I had hoped. It was easy to find excuses . . . there had been a persistent cold wind soon after I had planted them out from the seedboxes, and then came a hot spell that dried our shallow soil into the texture of sand. We watered and watered, pumping from the small reservoir whose main purpose was to supply the greenhouses, but as I stood, hose in hand, splashing the small plants, I knew there was no body in the soil to hold it. Hence I realised that the trouble was largely of my own making. Back in the winter, long before I became excited about my seedlings, I should have first prepared the soil and put heart in it. They were all small beds around the cottage of the rockery type, and so I should have treated each one as a flower pot.

Many of the plants, therefore, disappeared without any aid from Penny and Fred; and all the cosseting I provided did not save the Sunshine Calceolaria Rugosa. Splendid, firm little plants in the box, they began to wilt as soon as I put them out. I fussed over them like a nanny. I watered them, fed them with liquid manure and, when they continued to show no signs of recovering, I regretfully found myself becoming angry. Only too late did I realise what was the real trouble. Leather jackets, those squishy inch-long grubs which turn into daddy-long-legs, were eating the roots.

I am not, therefore, a good gardener. I should have

foreseen all these problems; though there were successes to report. The cosmea, the balsam and the salvia were failures because the slugs ate them, but the Crystal Palace lobelia were a glorious dark blue; and the Suttons Triumph antirrhinums gave a wonderful first display and, when this was finished, I gave the dead blooms a haircut, and so prepared the way for a second, even better, display. Little sign of the Cambridge Blue lobelia, however, and no sign at all of Rosie O'Day, the deep rose pink alyssum. The Snowdrift alyssum became brown patches during the hot spell but, when the rains came, it soon burst into white and this was a lesson. Alyssum needs continuous drenching if it is to flower.

The nicotiana were a success so long as one looked at them in the evening, in the early morning, or on a very dull day. Their scent then was gorgeous, and so were the pink and white flowers, but when the sun shone the petals withered and the plants became bedraggled, looking as if they should have been thrown on the compost heap; and I would apologise for them: 'You should see them at night!' I would say brightly to anyone who seemed to be gazing at them in disapproval.

The sunflowers, too, were a success and so were the Blue Blazer ageratum. The sunflowers were such a success that they grew tall enough for a child to be hoisted on to my shoulders in order to look at the great dinner plates of the flowers; and they were much admired until a September gale blew them down. I salvaged the dinner plates and brought them into the greenhouse because, from the beginning, I had hoped they would provide seeds for the wild birds. Not a hope. It was to be a wet autumn and there was no sun to ripen them.

The Blue Blazer ageratum was a modest little flower, and it edged the border of a new bed we had made, siding the lane close to Monty's Leap; and there were clusters of it elsewhere, and it gave pleasure all through the summer. But the seed of my New Year resolution which proved to be my triumph was rudbeckia. Wherever I had put out the plants they blossomed into great daisy-type flowers of orange with mahogany centres and they brought colour to the garden when, I have to confess, my own contribution had, for the most part, failed.

As for Jeannie, my efforts helped to confirm her distrust of annuals. She is a perennial believer. She accepts that certain annuals are well worth growing, but believes that anyone with a small garden who relies on them is asking for trouble. Hence, although she showed sympathy, she also felt self-justified; and the blank corners of the garden supported her. Perennials, she argued, dig their roots deep into the ground and are immune to droughts and strong enough to withstand early spring cold winds.

My complaint about perennials is that they spread, smothering everything around them. Hence a Michaelmas daisy, for instance, will envelop a corner of our garden, produce its flowers at the appropriate time, but be a great chunk of non-flowering plant for the rest of the year. A tidy gardener would, no doubt, keep it under control, but Jeannie has such a love for all plants, suitable or unsuitable, that she can never bring herself to be ruthless enough to deal with them. Jeannie can never throw anything away. Our strawberry plants had a virus, but she wanted to keep the remnants of them. I once had a ton of bulbs which the Ministry of Agriculture Advisory Officer advised me, because of their condition, to throw into the sea. Not a chance. Jeannie was determined to keep them. She was convinced that, in some miraculous way, they would recover. They didn't.

Her particular success this summer lay in her nurturing of the geranium cuttings which she had planted out in the greenhouse the previous autumn. Along one side of the Orlyt in front of the cottage was a splendid bed of geraniums, deep red ones and pink ones. They had all so enjoyed their winter quarters that they had grown long stalks, thus becoming elongated geraniums.

Nonetheless, they had already earned their occupation of the greenhouse by providing cut blooms for the cottage and now, suddenly, they were available for another role; and this was to fill the vacant places caused by the failure of my cosseted annuals.

Giraffe-like geraniums, therefore, were now dug up from the Orlyt by Jeannie and transported to various barren spots in the garden, and carefully planted and watered in. A splash of red, or pink, now lit up the barren spots and so it remained until the geranium realised what had happened ... that it was no longer leading a sheltered life in the greenhouse and that, in middle age, it had been suddenly thrust into reality. The leaves would then yellow, the blooms droop, and I would say to Jeannie that it would have been much better if she had left the geraniums where they were happy. In time, though, I was to be proved wrong. The giraffe-like geraniums acclimatised themselves to their new, tough situation; and colourfully filled the gaps my annuals had created.

We have, of course, always to be on guard against plants, bushes or trees which are poisonous for donkeys. Yew is a killer, and rhubarb, and Russell lupins. We once had a kind person give us two small eucalyptus trees and we planted them in the wood close to the hut where Boris, our Muscovy drake, had lived. Penny and Fred were once allowed to wander in this small wood, but were stopped when we realised that they were treating the bark of the trees as a delicacy and that, therefore, the trees were in danger.

The 'Verboten' sign, however, which we put up, our refusal to let them go anywhere near the small wood, both annoyed and intrigued them. Fred, in particular, was fascinated as to why the one-time access was now denied him. Whenever we went with him on an aimless stroll, halter around his head, the lead in my hand, and we neared the gap which led to the wood, he would strain to go there. One day he *did* go there, and it was my fault that he did so.

I had been giving rides on Fred and Penny to two children and, after these were over, the two children asked if they could see Oliver and Ambrose. I said of course if we could find them, and I immediately began to wonder where they might be and, thereupon, I forgot the donkeys. When I ushered the children out of the gate in the donkey field above the cottage, I foolishly left it ajar behind me. The donkeys did not notice my mistake for an hour or more. The children had gone and I was weeding the roses, when Jeannie called out the news that the donkeys were in the wood. The wood where the donkeys were banned; where there was my mythical 'Verboten' sign; where the two eucalyptus trees were, unfortunately, planted. Fred, in his excitement to be where he shouldn't be, proceeded to gulp them.

We have all been in such a situation at some time in our lives when we have been tempted to indulge in some pleasure which should either have been totally ignored or treated with moderation. We have learnt from such experiences out of the misery of the after-effects. Fred learnt the same way.

The two eucalyptus trees gave him a hangover that he will remember for ever.

Donkeys, of course, are always pitting their wits against their owners; always, like long-term prisoners, plotting to escape. The donkeys mean no harm, nor are they wishing to prove they are hard done by. It is a kind of chess game they want to win. Penny and Fred, therefore, would contemplate as they stood motionless in a corner of a field as to how they could defeat our methods of incarcerating them.

Fred, for instance, would heave his bottom against the gate which led down towards the cliff in an attempt to open it; and so I countered by stringing barbed wire across it so that the next time he heaved, it hurt. Then there was the small white-painted gate close to the barn. The gate was made of stakes from a wreck, as was the fence either side of it, and the gate was fastened by a conventional bolt with a knob which was dropped into a slot when we closed the gate.

Fred must have watched us drop the knob on many occasions . . . until at last the idea dawned on him that if he were able to lift the knob upwards with his teeth and then shift the bolt until it was free of the catch on the fence, the gate would open for him. This trick, in due course, he perfected; and the day he achieved it, there was very nearly a disaster.

One morning I looked out of the bedroom window and saw the gate was open.

'We shut the gate last night, didn't we?'

'I saw you fasten it.'

'Well, it's open now!'

'Oh heavens, that means they're out!'

'Come on, hurry, we have to find them!'

This is never easy. I have seen them careering along the Coastal Path towards Carn Barges and, though thankful to have seen them, have wondered how to catch them. I have known them join the cows of Jack Cockram, my neighbour, and then find them heading the parade of cows as they were called in for milking. I have found them hiding in one of our small cliff meadows, or I have discovered them in the moorland on the other side of the shallow valley. There are any number of places they can escape to, where they can munch strange grass, where they can relish the devilment of their escape, where, in their opinion, they can enjoy freedom, be amused by our shouts as we look for them, knowing all the time that, in due course, we would find them and take them back to the comfort of their normal surroundings.

We have, however, one dominating fear when they escape. It may be irritating to find them on Carn Barges or, after a period of searching, in a cliff meadow, or somewhere on the moorland, but it also produces a sense of great relief. Our dominating fear is that they might, once they have made their escape, gallop down our mile-long lane to the main road. The thought of this horrifies us; and thus we have a plan that, whenever the alarm is raised of their escape, one of us always hastens to search up the lane, while the other sets off around the moorland.

On this occasion, it was I who went up the lane and, from past experience, I expected that if they had gone this way I would find them mooching around the farm buildings at the top of the hill; or, if Jack Cockram, or Walter Grose, or Bill Trevorrow had seen them, I would expect to find them corralled in a field. These three were always ready to break off from their farm work to stop the donkeys from going any further, but when I reached the farm buildings I saw neither donkeys nor human beings. All was quiet. Everyone was out, and so there had been no one to see the donkeys pass by; and that is what had happened. I walked on a few yards until I was at the spot where I could look down the farm-to-main-road part of the lane and saw, in the far distance, Penny and Fred.

I had no time to go back and fetch Jeannie and clearly there was no one around to help me cut them off; and cut them off I had to do, or else within a few minutes they would be on the road. 'Dear Derek,' I said to myself, 'keep calm, work out a plan, control your panic . . .' – and I was in a panic, because I knew that if I ran down the lane after them they would only rush onwards. In fact, I would only be a means of hurrying them into danger.

I had, therefore, to be stealthy. I observed from a distance that they had paused by some tasty hedge greenery at a point where the lane zig-zagged out of view. It was late May time, pleasant juices were in leaves and stalks, and this, I realised, was in my favour. If they did not see me, if I were so inconspicuous that they continued to nibble and chew the hedge delights, I could cut them off from the main road; and so it seemed that the best thing I could do was to run through the fields parallel to the lane, my head low, silent, a guerrilla in action, though on a peaceful mission instead of one bred on hate.

I let myself into the first field, knowing that I had six hundred yards and two further fields before I would be able to be between the donkeys and the main road; and I immediately ran into trouble when I reached the second field. It was waist-high in fine grass, all ready to be cut for hay. I dared not run along the narrow gap between the grass and the hedge for fear that the donkeys might hear me, and set off again; and so I had to risk being seen, being shouted at by the irate owner of the field, as I floundered through the grass, leaving a flattened trail behind me.

I reached the far hedge, climbed over it, and now found myself in a field of growing corn; and as I knew that I had reached a position which was nearly parallel to where the donkeys had paused, I stopped running and began to creep. I aimed to climb over the hedge siding the lane about twenty yards below the donkeys, but when I arrived at my chosen spot I found the hedge was topped by a mass of blackthorn. Any moment, I realised, the donkeys would be moving on. Penny would lead, I guessed. She was always the bold one on these safaris. Fred organised the break-out, Penny took over thereafter, and I had to get through the blackthorn before she set off again at the gallop.

A minute later I was on top of the hedge with blackthorn scratching my legs, scratching my face, scratching my hands and arms . . . and down below me, a few yards to my left, was an artful Penny and behind her an astonished Fred. What was *he* doing there? Ears pricked, a hee-haw at the ready, but Fred was not prepared for the reaction of Penny. His attitude seemed to be one of 'all is discovered', and he appeared willing to accept an unconditional surrender. Not so Penny.

Penny, sensing my entangled predicament amongst the blackthorn, was watching me carefully, wondering whether to make a dash. At that instant, if she had so acted, she would have won. She would have had a free run to her destiny on the main road . . . but, for a second, she hesitated and that was enough time for me. I made one last bleeding scramble through the blackthorn, took a flying leap to the lane, and held up my arms wide like a policeman on traffic duty. The wild adventure was over. Two donkeys who had chased danger were meekly on their way home . . . and to a new latch on the gate which, I hope, will for ever defeat the intelligence of Fred.

I was unable to keep my resolution to be free of donkey domination for the same reason that I was unable to keep my resolution to be free of cat domination. Every day I was involved in them. Every day, despite their often independent moods, I was made aware that they were a part of our lives. They were not pets. They did not belong to that category of unfortunate animal or bird or exotic snake which are bought by people as if they were manufactured toys and then discarded. We were all at one. It is not a kind of attitude that some people can appreciate. Magic does not exist for them; and it is magic which brings an animal and a human being together in mutual understanding. The animal trusts; and the human being sees in the animal the qualities he would like to see in his fellow human beings.

A consequence of such a relationship can be over-imaginative concern about the welfare of the animal, a form of hypochondria; and if I am in a certain mood, if I am tired or something has distressed me, I can suffer from over-imaginative concern. On the other hand, I am glad I feel as I do because I am constantly amazed by the casualness of others. I do not understand, for instance, those who allow a dog to wander the streets on its own, or a man I often see taking his dog for a walk along a busy country road where there is no pavement, without the dog being on a lead. Nor do I understand those who are so insensitive as to allow a dog to bark incessantly, thus ruining the peace of others. I am not blaming the dog for these things. I am blaming the owners.

Then there are the strange breed of people who indulge in dogs and cats as presents at Christmas-time. We all know examples of what happens. A puppy or a kitten is given as a present, producing ecstatic cries around the Christmas tree, games are played all through the holiday and into the New Year, and the puppy believes he has found his heaven. By the end of the month, however, the novelty has worn off, the puppy or kitten becomes more and more inconvenient, its owners have no space in their lives to love it, and so they begin to plan how to be rid of it . . . dump it at a stranger's door? Take it on a car ride and drop it in some faraway countryside? Drown it perhaps, or leave it at night outside an Animal Home without leaving any money for its upkeep? Is such callousness the result of a society so obsessed by materialistic doctrines that it is blind and deaf to the magical pleasures? It seems so.

Penny causes me over-imaginative concern from time to time. She once nearly died from an attack of laminitis, a severe inflammation of the feet, and as this affliction can always recur, I am constantly on the watch for it. She has, however, a habit of giving me false alarms. She will stand still for an hour or more in the middle of the donkey field above the cottage, shifting her feet as if in discomfort, head down, looking lugubrious, until at last I am compelled, because of my anxiety, to walk over to her and murmur sweet nothings to her. She enjoys this attention and when, in order to test her true condition, I give her a gentle slap on the bottom to make her walk and so see whether she has difficulty in doing so, she replies to my solicitude by setting off at a gallop: 'I've fooled you again!' she seems to be inferring. Of course I am delighted . . . except on one occasion, of which I will soon tell.

Fred, however, startled me one day when I saw him standing in a corner of the field holding the right front leg off the ground; and it dangled as if a fetlock had been broken. It was lunch-time. After breakfast, we had led him and Penny up from the stable field, where they had spent the night, and I had noticed nothing wrong. I had, therefore, no reason to guess why he was behaving so oddly, and when I crossed the field to him I gained no clue. He was looking sorrowful enough, let me rub his ears, his head down so that his white nose was touching the grass, allowed me to feel his dangling foot without objection, giving me the impression all the time that he wanted me to realise that he was a brave but very sick donkey. The impression, however, could also have been a ploy. In the past it was Penny who had always received the vet's attention; and I had often observed that Fred, while the attention was in progress, would shuffle round a few yards away making token bites at the grass, eyeing Penny and the vet a little jealously. He would like the vet's attention too. He was to receive it.

An hour after lunch I was saying to Jeannie that I was really worried. Fred had not moved a pace since I had been with him. He just stood close to the wood with his bottom to the trees, head lowered, right foot dangling.

'I'm going to 'phone the vet,' I said.

This is not a simple task. I have to drive the car, because we have no wish to be on the telephone, three miles to the nearest telephone box; and the vet has to drive six miles from his headquarters in Penzance. Thus one does not want to telephone unless the matter is truly serious, for vets, like doctors, are busy enough without being called out for trivial reasons.

'I'm sure you're right *this* time,' said Jeannie.

She was referring to the occasion, a few weeks before, when I was *not* delighted that Penny had fooled me.

She had been for a day or so in what we call her

Connemara mood, as if she were spending the day dreaming of her younger days in the Connemara hills amid bogs and tinkers, and a colleen or two who had put their arms around her neck before she set off in a cattle truck for her travels across the Irish Sea to Exeter where she was auctioned, and to Wadebridge, and to the Plume of Feathers at Scorrier, and to Minack. In such a mood, she was desultory. In such a mood, she would stand at the far end of the field ignoring us while we stood at the gate calling her, offering her chocolate biscuits, or carrots, or potato crisps. Fred did not mind this mood. He ate the chocolate biscuits, the carrots, the potato crisps all by himself.

This particular morning, Jeannie had driven into Penzance early. We had already, of course, been to see Penny and she seemed to be in a deeper Connemara mood than ever, standing at the far end of the field and not bothering to move as we came towards her. This worried us. Fred was capering around, but Penny was still.

An hour after Jeannie had left, I had a look at her again, and there she was lying down on the ground, head on the grass, and the sight gave me a twinge of anxiety. When I reached her, however, she began to move, began to struggle to get up . . . front legs straightened, a heave of the body propelled by the back legs, and then a slow unwieldy effort to be upright. I put my arm round her neck and talked to her. Then I said: 'Come on, Penny, let's go for a walk across the field.' She did not move. I gave her a gentle slap, and she still did not move. I gave her another one, and another one, and at last she hobbled a few feet. It was agony to watch. She could not put her back foot to the ground, it was as if she were half-paralysed; and she proceeded to make my distress even worse by turning her head, black ears lowered, and looking at me with such mournful eyes that it seemed she was saying goodbye to me. It was pitiful.

Clearly I had to get the vet to see her as soon as

possible but, since Jeannie had the car, I had to borrow the telephone of one of the farms at the top of the hill. I never liked doing so, but it was an emergency, and I knew they would not mind; and so I left Penny to be miserable on her own, and hastened up the lane.

I met Bill Trevorrow coming down, his old Flossie at his heels.

'Something seriously wrong with Penny,' I said. 'Can I use your 'phone to ring the vet?'

'Go ahead. The missus is in . . . what's happened?'

'She can't walk.'

A few minutes later I passed Walter Grose. Walter, whose family of cats of all shapes and sizes, of all mixtures of colours gather around his van while he has his sandwiches. Walter has worked one of the farms most of his life though he lives in St Buryan.

'Penny poorly? I'm sorry about that.'

'I thought it best to get the vet as soon as possible.'

I was sorry in a way that I had seen either Bill or Walter. I prefer secrecy in illness, animal or human . . . but now I was broadcasting Penny's distress.

'It could be thrush,' said Walter. 'That's rot in her foot. It's a difficult job to cure.'

Soon I was at Mrs Trevorrow's and I rang the vet, and the girl said someone would come as soon as possible. I returned down the lane, passing no one this time, until I reached Minack and the field where I had left Penny.

She was grazing beside Fred; and I was surprised by her apparent normality.

An hour later, Jeannie returned, and I told her what had happened. I described the pain that Penny so clearly demonstrated she was suffering from. Then I added, puzzled: 'She seems to be better. She seems to be able to walk.'

Occasions sometimes occur when a sector of oneself would like a bad thing to happen. You have, for instance, rung the police to report you have seen a suspicious

character around, and when the police arrive you hope
that your suspicions are confirmed; or you ring the fire
brigade because of a frying pan blaze in the kitchen, then
find yourself, against your will, hoping that it won't go
out before the fire brigade arrives; or you see a holiday
maker in difficulties in the sea, race to give a 999 call,
then reluctantly hope that the helicopter which is soon
on the scene has not wasted its time.

Thus with the vet and Penny.

As hour by hour went by and the vet did not come, I
watched Penny apprehensively as she became more and
more normal.

Then at last a small white car came hurrying down the
lane, stuttered to a pause at Monty's Leap, then revved
up again to rush to a full stop by the barn.

Out jumped not one vet, but three.

'Sorry I'm late,' said the vet I knew. 'We've been
operating on a cow.'

He was fair-haired and eager, and he had a natural
kindness which gave confidence. He was also making me
feel how grateful I would be if there were a hole in the
ground I could hide in. I had seen Penny. My apprehension
had been confirmed. She was in the stable field looking
alert; looking as if she were the healthiest donkey in the
district.

She had fooled me again. A major fooling; and I was
not amused.

The visit of the vet to Fred, however, was a different story.

THE LESSER or PIGMY SHREW

11

Fred had an abscess in his hoof, the hoof of his right foreleg; and it was so painful that he could not even take pleasure in the fuss that was made of him.

'What's up with him?'

Bill Trevorrow had come down the lane and was standing by the wall adjoining the barn.

'A flint from the chippings got wedged in his foot,' I said, 'and the vet says it's like having an abscess under the nail of your finger.'

'He looks bad.'

'Sometimes when I'm moving the two of them from the top field down here I don't put a halter on Fred. I put one on Penny, lead her down here, and then a minute or so later Fred follows at speed, travelling so fast that he slides to a stop. That's how he collected the flint.'

Fred was standing dejected a few yards away.

'Saw him when I was with the steers,' said Bill, 'and I could see something was wrong. That's why I came down.'

The steers were in the fields on the other side of the shallow valley. We kept an eye on them, just as Bill kept an eye on the donkeys; and when, on one occasion, we noticed a steer had lain still in the middle of a field for an hour or more while his companions had roamed off elsewhere, Jeannie hastened up to the farm to tell Bill. A false alarm, as it turned out, but Bill was grateful that we had troubled. And now I was grateful that he had troubled about Fred.

'The abscess will have to burst,' I said, 'before he gets better.'

'It'll have to do that all right.'

'Meanwhile, the vet's told us to bathe it twice a day in warm water and Dettol.'

'How does Fred take to that?'

'He doesn't.'

The vet had said that we should fill a bucket with the Dettol and warm water, then persuade Fred to stand his leg in it. The vet had spoken as if the deed were as easy as giving Fred a carrot. Fred, however, when he saw the bucket, reared like a bronco.

'Tell you what,' said Bill. 'Get Geoffrey to catch hold of his foot and then pour the Dettol into the hoof . . . and if you want any help, let me know.'

There were other offers of help. A small girl on holiday from Birmingham said she would come every day and stroke him, saying the stroking might take his mind off the pain. Leslie, who keeps the post office at St Buryan and who, when Fred had birthday parties, provided the ice-cream, sent him a carton of vanilla ice-cream. Our friend the Vicar of Marazion called and commiserated and, no doubt, offered a prayer. And all the while Fred remained miserable.

Penny, too, fussed over him, keeping him company, never straying far away from his lugubrious figure; and Oliver and Ambrose showed their interest, if not concern, by regularly sitting on the wall watching the treatment of Dettol and warm water.

After a week, and two further visits from the vet, there were signs of improvement. A wellwisher brought him a bunch of carrots, and after a first doubtful nibble he ate the lot. Chocolate biscuits were next day on the menu, then a packet of potato crisps and, finally, as a signal that his suffering was over, came the sudden colossal hee-haw from the centre of the field.

A sock, however, played an important part in his recovery. After the first treatment of Dettol and warm water, it became obvious that his foot had to be protected or else it would be sure to collect dirt. A bandage was out of the question, and I didn't care for another suggestion of wrapping polythene around it, for fear that Fred might bite it and swallow the pieces. It was then I had my idea about the sock. I was wearing a garish yellow pair which I had been given, and the thought suddenly occurred to me that here was the answer.

'Fred!' I said, though at that time he was too sick to respond. 'I'm going to give you a sock.' And I promptly took one off and a few minutes later it was on his foot.

It was at first just a useful covering but later, as he improved, he began to take a fancy to it. A garish yellow sock gave him a distinction. It was as if he knew that such a sight on a donkey was unusual and was certain to cause comment; and it *did* cause comment. Mirth too. A donkey wearing a yellow sock was a reason for laughter.

Meanwhile, Oliver and Ambrose had been consolidating their places on the bed and, since my resolution banning them from such comfort was now in tatters, I was wise enough to accept my defeat with grace. I was also influenced by the fact that Ambrose was prepared to offer such a sign of affection, because in daytime he continued to be often on edge and elusive. If I saw him outside and went to pick him up, he would still, more often than not, dart away from me; and when sometimes he copied Oliver, turning on his back, displaying his tummy to the skies and apparently inviting me to touch him, he would jump to his feet and run as soon as I was close to him. It was maddening . . . and yet the moments were increasing when he tantalisingly gave me hope that he was changing into a normal loving cat like Monty or Lama or Oliver. One morning after breakfast, for instance, he jumped on to my lap uninvited for the very first time in his life. I was astonished. I sat there immobile, Ambrose overflowing across my lap from cushion to cushion, and called for Jeannie to come and witness such a unique occasion.

Nevertheless, although there were such signs that he was improving his daylight manners, it was at night on the bed that he relaxed in our company. I would be awakened by Oliver purring on my chest, a whisker length away from my face, while Ambrose, also purring loudly, was spreadeagled across my feet pinioning them to the mattress; and, because I was accepting my defeat with good grace, I did nothing to disturb either of them.

I recognised the fact that I was their prisoner; and I refrained from shifting my leg just a little bit in order to give it relief because I feared that in retaliation they might both jump off the bed and I did not want that. I preferred the purring chains. I preferred to accept the compliment that they had chosen me as the site for sleep rather than the hay in the barn, the sofa in the sitting-room, or the expanse of the spare bed. Thus I would lie there in the dark, yearning to bend my knees, stretch, turn to one side or the other, kick my legs in freedom; and foolishly choosing not to do so for fear of interrupting the purring pleasures of two cats who had broken my New Year resolution.

The purrs of Ambrose were more prolonged than those of Oliver. Oliver was inclined to purr in short bursts, sudden moments of love of great intensity; while Ambrose was a long distance purrer; and indeed his purrs were of such duration that I would go to sleep listening to them, wake up perhaps a couple of hours later, and still be listening to them. Purring on the bed at night was for him as natural as breathing.

This persistence, however, sometimes irritated Oliver. It kept him awake, as a distant barking dog might keep me awake. Thus, at some stage, he would lose patience and I would be startled from my slumber by an explosion of cat temper. Oliver had hit Ambrose with a paw; and I would then hear a sleepy voice beside me: 'Stop it, you two. Stop those fisticuffs!' There would then be silence for a while as they settled down again . . . only for Ambrose in due course to start purring again.

Occasionally they would both act as if they were the guardians of our bedroom. The window which served as their entrance faced the lane running down to Monty's Leap; and in Monty's and Lama's time we used to fix a wire contraption in the open window to prevent them from going out at night . . . because Monty was a Londoner without experience of foxes and badgers, while Lama was small and vulnerable and we were happier knowing she was safe indoors.

Oliver and Ambrose, on the other hand, could look after themselves and, in any case, on the two occasions we did put up the contraption, Oliver knocked it down from the outside when wanting to come in, and made such a noise in doing so that we decided to give up the idea, and the contraption now lies on the floor under the bed.

One night I was lying awake while Ambrose was purring away at the the bottom of the bed and Oliver lying close enough for me to put my hand on him, and I was wondering about certain *oughts* with which we were faced. *Ought* is the word we use for those things we have an irking sense we ought to do, but don't want to do. They cover a wide area of activities.

'I *ought* to write to so-and-so.'

'We *ought* to accept the invitation.'

'As I'm going nearby, I *ought* to go and see them.'

'This is a function we really *ought* to go to.'

'We haven't seen them for so long, we *ought* to ask them.'

The maddening thing about *oughts* is that they often operate both ways without those concerned being aware of it. Thus the person you felt you *ought* to invite only accepts, did you but know it, because he feels he *ought* to accept. Or, if you go to a party, are tired and want to go home, but do not do so because you feel you *ought* to stay longer, this is equalled by the behaviour of your host and hostess, who are only remaining with you because they feel they *ought* to.

I was thinking about certain of my current *oughts* when suddenly there was a commotion on the bed and the two cats, deep in slumber at one moment, had catapulted themselves on to the window-sill at the next. There was a full moon and it was very still; no noise except the perpetual murmur of the sea.

'I bet it's a fox,' I whispered to Jeannie, who was also awake.

Periodically a fox will investigate our dustbins, pushing off the lids so that they clatter noisily when they hit the ground. I lay waiting for the clatter. Not a sound.

But at the window Oliver and Ambrose were frozen, like two sentries, guns at the ready. This was a crisis. Clearly there was danger outside, or a threatening mystery, otherwise they would not have stayed so still. They would have jumped out of the window.

'Do you hear that strange noise?' I said softly.

Silence. Then there it was again. A crackly crunching.

'I'm going to have a look,' I whispered to Jeannie, and stealthily got out of bed and went to the window. I knelt there, Oliver on one side of me, Ambrose on the other, all three of us staring out of the window into the moonlight.

A crackly crunch.

The grey rocks and the old stones of the barn are ethereal in moonlight. It is a fairyland where pixies might suddenly appear; and the lane leading to Monty's Leap is touched with silver and, if you are in the mood to do so, you see the ghosts of past inhabitants of Minack, of old horses and cattle, of carts and haywains, and you regain in your imagination the leisurely pace of other ages.

'Can you see anything?' I heard Jeannie whisper behind me.

I dared not speak. I made a gesture with my hand which meant: 'Yes, I can . . . come and join us.'

It was a young badger just below in the rockery, and oblivious to our gaze he was pushing his black and white striped head into the plants, picking off the clinging snails, and eating them as if he were a small boy eating boiled sweets. He was having a feast; crunch, crunch, crunch . . . there were scores of snails awaiting him, and I watched him move from the waterbutt on my right through a cluster of rudbeckia into a cluster of pansies, then between two of Jeannie's long-legged geraniums into a clump of nicotiana. Perhaps he was the same badger who ate the carrots; the carrots scheduled for Penny and Fred during the winter. He was just as greedy. He did not miss a snail . . . and Oliver and Ambrose, Jeannie and I were fascinated. And the badger himself might have been fascinated had he looked up . . . two cats and two humans observing his indulgence.

Such an incident is of small importance. Some will say that it is pointless even to recall it. Such people are the busy ones who are so active talking about how to improve the world we live in that they have no time for the detail which can make living enjoyable. They proclaim grandiose ideas at Conferences, discuss problems as if they can be solved by computers, and avoid advocating the basic solutions because these can only be reached by the effort of each individual; and individualism is out of fashion.

Thus the busy ones carry on with their Reports, their Campaigns, and their Solutions of all our problems in a haze of generalities which disregard the basic truths. One of the basic truths awaits anyone who has the ears and eyes and sense to recognise it. It requires no law, no Report, no

Campaign, no ranting speech read at the Conference rostrum. It lies in gaining pleasure from small, unimportant matters which are everywhere around us waiting to enrich our lives . . . like watching, in the company of Oliver and Ambrose, the activities of a young badger gobbling snails in the moonlight.

I do not, however, consider chasing a mouse in the early hours of the morning a means of gaining pleasure; and this is a task that we have to endure from time to time. They are not mice which come voluntarily into the bedroom. They are the victims of a pounce by Ambrose in some corner of the land outside and are brought in by him in a misguided mood of generosity. Cats everywhere, of course, often have the misconception that a mouse is a welcome present. It is brought into the house with a glad cry and, if dead, deposited on the carpet where it can easily be seen; and when it is removed, thrown with distressing disgust by the recipient into a far section of undergrowth, the donor stalks around in puzzlement. Where has it gone? Why has my present disappeared?

Ambrose, on the other hand, was in favour of live presents. I would be woken up from a sleep by a tally-ho call as he came in through the open window, followed by a thump when he jumped down to the floor. It was a distinctive thump. If he came in minus a present, he jumped to the floor so silently that one might not suspect he had come in . . . but, if he had a present, he chose to behave like a clumsy heavyweight. Thus, when I heard the thump, I would become nervously on guard.

'Do you hear anything?' I murmured on one such occasion, and I had no answer because Jeannie was still asleep, so I lay there and listened.

A rustle to my right in the direction of Jeannie's little walnut desk, and I remembered she had left on the floor a Harrod's box in which was tissue paper.

'Jeannie,' I said again, nudging her. 'Wake up. There's a mouse in the room.'

A convulsion.

'What? What did you say? I'm asleep. I don't want to wake up.'

'It's a mouse. There's a mouse on the floor just beside you . . . can't you hear it?'

Silence for a second, then the rustle again.

'I was having such a lovely sleep.'

We lay still for a while. Perhaps I had been wrong. Perhaps it was just a fluttering moth. This is the customary optimism when you hear the scratch of a mouse. You cannot bear the prospect of dealing with it, so you pretend you have made a mistake . . . and then the noise of it starts up again. The moment of decision has arrived. You either spend the rest of the night half awake, or you go on the attack immediately. We decided to attack.

'Switch on the light and fetch the torch,' said Jeannie. She was always in charge on these occasions. She was a mouse-catching expert. She hated the task, but she followed a method which, although it often took time to be successful, was infallible. The primary aim of this method was to remove the mouse *alive* from the bedroom and deposit it outside into the garden.

The method, needless to say, did not require the aid of Oliver and Ambrose. Cats, in any case, are reluctant to help in such a situation. Mouse catching, in their view, is an outdoor activity or, at any rate, this was the attitude adopted by Monty and Lama in the past, and Oliver and Ambrose in the present. Face them with a mouse on the carpet and they turned away. Push them under a chest of drawers where the mouse was hiding, and they wriggled free and ran. Indoor mouse catching was apparently unfair. The job had better be left to Jeannie.

I shone the torch into a corner.

'There it is! . . . Quick!'

The mouse darted under the bed.

'Damn!'

Jeannie was holding her own particular trap. A cloth.

Her object was to manoeuvre the mouse into a position where she could throw the cloth over it, then bravely pick it up, and drop it out of the window.

I heaved the bed to one side, and the mouse disappeared under the William and Mary chest of drawers. I flushed it out from there with a feather duster, and back it scampered under the bed. I was becoming impatient. Another heave of the bed, and away it ran to the Harrod's box.

'I've got it,' cried Jeannie. 'No, I haven't.'

A slippery mouse, it kept us floundering around the small bedroom for twenty minutes or more, making us more and more angry with Ambrose for being the cause of it all. Then, at last, the cry of triumph. Jeannie had caught it and was leaning out of the window, dropping cloth and mouse gently into the nicotiana.

Lights out. Peace again. Then another sound.

Oliver and Ambrose were purring. The chase over, they had come back to bed.

Oliver himself was also the victim of Ambrose's thump. One night Oliver was lying curled up close to me in bed when Ambrose woke me up with a menacing heavyweight thump as he landed on the floor from the window. He stayed a few minutes indoors, then I saw the silhouette of his figure at the window, and he jumped out again, leaving me uncomfortably suspicious that he had left a present behind. However, hearing no scratching noise to disturb me, I soon dozed off.

A while later I was awake again. I had been startled from dreaming by a painful sensation on my face, as if barbed wire had been pulled across it; and it took me only a second to realise that Oliver had dashed over me. No harm, as it turned out, had been done, but it was obvious to me that Oliver had acted in panic. Something had frightened him out of his wits. I switched on the light and, there to my dismay, just at the spot where Oliver had lain curled in slumber was a tiny mouse, the tiniest mouse I had ever seen. No wonder Oliver acted in panic.

We also acted in panic. Jeannie cried out in horror, and I pulled the blanket so violently that the mouse flew to the floor. It was not, however, a mouse. It was, as I learnt later when I looked it up in *Thorburn's Mammals*, a shrew, the lesser or Pigmy shrew to be exact; and Thorburn wrote that 'though hardy as regards severe cold under natural conditions, the constitution of this little animal is extremely frail and sensitive to any kind of shock or untoward circumstances.' Its length from snout to tail was barely two inches.

Naturally, after reading this account, we looked back on the episode with disquiet. If Oliver had been scared into a panic, what about the shrew? It was certainly an untoward circumstance to find itself terrorising a cat, and it was certainly a shock to be chased by Jeannie and myself. Once again, however, Jeannie had shown her skill. True, the chase was prolonged because to catch a two-inch object travelling at speed is bound to be a difficult task . . . but Jeannie, in due course, achieved it. And the Pigmy shrew was carefully deposited out of the window into the garden.

As for Oliver, he had lost his nerve. Not for a fortnight did he return to sleep on the bed.

Oliver was an endearing cat. He endeared himself to us, of course, by the manner he had come into our lives, his patiently conducted conquest of us, the way that Sunday morning he suddenly produced Ambrose as I stood at Monty's Leap. His beginning with us at Minack had become a kind of folk story in our minds, unbelievable unless we had seen it to be real, and a story to hold on to. The impossible *does* occur. Miracles, using the jargon, *do* happen. No need ever to give up hope.

Oliver had a habit which I sometimes found was very touching. I would be sitting or standing at some spot not far from the cottage and enduring a mood of sadness, or inadequacy, or regret, any of those disquieting emotions which inevitably upset one from time to time . . . and

Oliver would always appear. He would come up to me and roll upside down, or put his paw on my feet showing that he wanted to jump up, or he would just sit looking at me, yapping. He had become a very talkative cat, and the language varied from tenor-like growls to a sound like someone tuning up on a mouth organ, to the yap. Jeannie was rude about this yap, and the coarse vowel noises which followed. She said that he should take elocution lessons on how to speak.

Oliver had, however, this sense when I needed him, or when Jeannie needed him, an ESP which has never failed us. This black cat which infiltrated into our lives against our wishes was sure that he had a special role to play.

Every few weeks, his namesake would come to see us: Mike Oliver, wartime colonel in the Royal Garhwall Rifles, one of the famous regiments of the British Raj, and who now was in charge of the St Francis Cat and Dog Home at Porth on the outskirts of Newquay. This old friend was a weaver of tweed when we first knew him, living at Mitchell on the noisy A30, alone with a Siamese cat called Ny Ling. He wove beautiful tweed, and many of our friends bought it from him, as we did ourselves . . . but, as a past regular officer of the Royal Garhwall Rifles, he did not possess the ruthless panache of a salesman and, although the tweed was beautiful, the sales were not.

He married a pretty girl called Ruby, who came from Mitchell. As tweed sales fell, he became a life insurance agent and persuasively sold policies to both Jeannie and me; and then, around this time, he was offered the Wardenship of the St Francis Home, which provided him with a bungalow overlooking the Trevelgue Valley at Porth, dog kennels and cattery on the premises, and away from the roar of the A30. They now had a family of two girls and a boy and they decided to accept the offer. Ny Ling went too.

The money for the Home comes from a Trust created by an old Newquay lady in her Will. It is a modest Trust,

providing no salary for the Warden other than the benefit
of a free home and so, like other such animal homes, the
upkeep is largely dependent on charity contributions and
the fees obtained for the boarding of cats and dogs when
their owners were away.

But such charity contributions and fees never balance
the cost of maintaining the stray cats and dogs which come
to the Home; and since Mike Oliver never turns a stray
away, goes to great trouble and expense to find a home for
each one, looks after and feeds them sometimes for months
on end before a suitable home is found, it is inevitable that
he has to pay out from his own pocket. It is the penalty for
being soft-hearted, for having a natural love for animals.

He is, however, a disciplinarian.

'Cats!'

He calls them at meal times as if he were summoning the
battalion to the parade ground.

'Cats!'

Ny Ling has gone, and there are thirty cats in his place;
cats for whom a home could not be found; cats who, in any
case, do not want to leave; straight-haired cats, fluffy cats,
tabby cats, elegant cats.

'Cats!'

They come hurrying up the valley field where Dougal
and Tufty, the donkeys, are munching grass, out of the
armchairs in the bungalow, from various corners around
the outhouses. They must not be late. The colonel does not
like them to be late.

'Cats!'

They arrive at the assembly point, line up at thirty
saucers, and are counted. One is missing.

'Tito! Where's Tito?'

A scurry, and Tito appears. Everything is in order.
Dinner begins.

All the family share in the work; Louise, Caroline,
John and, of course, Ruby. She is undismayed by animal
crises, discovery of kittens left by someone at the door

in a box, howling of a dog deserted by a holidaymaker, heartbreak sight of a puppy rescued from drowning after being thrown into the sea by the owner who did not want it . . . she takes such things in her stride and gets on with the practical aspect of looking after the inhabitants of the Home. Others, like the Olivers, in many parts of the country, care for such Homes in the same way. On my own doorstep there is the Mousehole Bird Hospital founded by the famous Yglesias sisters and which, after being abandoned by the RSPCA, is now struggling for survival, through the efforts of a local committee. In all these Homes, those engaged in running them are doing so for the reward of personal achievement rather than one of money, as in voluntary organisations of any kind. They are the givers. They do not count the hours they work, or belly-ache about their rights. They have a job to do, and set out to do it well.

Caroline Oliver is our god-daughter. She is a slight, fey girl, a Barrie child, and she has a serene confidence in the company of animals which makes her fearless. She is a donkey jockey in the weekly summer races at Newquay, calms temperamental dogs which come to the Home, breaks up a fight however savage, is accepted by any strange cat, and is always acquiring new pets. She arrived one day at Minack in the back of her father's car, a dog sitting in the front seat, nursing a wild baby rabbit and a tiny kitten both sitting on her lap; and quite unself-consciously she carried the kitten into the cottage, sat down on a chair, and proceeded to feed the kitten with milk from an old fashioned fountain pen filler. Then she returned the kitten to the car, where it proceeded to cuddle up with the rabbit.

The dog, a black and white mongrel, meanwhile remained in the car.

'He's a bit odd,' explained Mike. 'It's a pity, but there you are. I've only had him a week.'

'What's wrong?'

'He runs round in circles, brain damage perhaps. It was found running loose on Goss Moor and somebody told the police. Hit by a car no doubt.' Then he added: 'I'll get him better, you'll see.'

The police always notify him when they have an abandoned dog. They rely on him for his help.

'You can take him for a walk,' I said.

Oliver and Ambrose were lying curled on a patch of hay I had put in the greenhouse specially for them. They were safe because I knew that Mike would put the dog on a lead until he was away from the cottage. He always did so when he brought a dog. A few people, however, advance up the lane with their dog running at random, only to reply, when I gently suggest they control them, that the dog doesn't chase cats or that, if they do, they won't hurt them. I am sure they speak the truth, but I prefer to play safe. Thus I quickly find that the dog is put on the lead when I warn: 'Watch out for Fred! . . . If a dog comes close to him he might kick it over the hedge!'

The dog who went in circles had his walk. He set off in excitement, and returned wishing, no doubt, the walk could have gone on for ever. Once away on his walk he had run hither and thither quite naturally and then, as soon as he returned, he began running in circles again.

The colonel was disappointed, but he had an answer to this setback. A sharp order would bring the dog to his senses. Discipline was a necessity if full capabilities, animal or human, were to be obtained. Flabby attitudes gained nothing. Only encouraged the weak to become weaker.

'Dog!' he commanded. 'Get in the car!'

And the dog immediately jumped in.

A month later I saw Mike again. The dog no longer ran round in circles. He had cured it.

12

The sun on the lintel was returning to the point where it first shone at the beginning of summer. Each evening it moved another inch across the rough surface of the granite, inch by inch until at last it vanished. The sun was no longer setting above the donkey field. Autumn had come.

'I'm still waiting.'

'Waiting for what?' I asked.

Jeannie was pottering in the kitchen, and I was sitting on the sofa, staring up at the lintel.

'You know perfectly well,' she said, coming out of the kitchen, smiling, holding a saucepan in her hand.

I thought, as I looked at her, how lucky I was to have married a girl who was as slim and pretty and feminine as when I first met her, as when the great Cochran had asked her to become one of his Young Ladies and she had refused because she thought it more fun to be Press Officer at the Savoy. Since then, since that moment when she sensed that a life dependent upon mixing with the famous and the ambitious could be over-prolonged, becoming a frivolous vacuum, she had been a peasant, working with her hands in the soil, coping with the primitive life, and never questioning the wisdom of the change. She had learnt the true values; and so she was unaffected by the fact that her book *Meet me at the Savoy* turned her into a legend, and that her novels *Hotel Regina* and *Home is the Hotel* had been mentioned in the same category as Arnold Bennett's *Imperial Palace* and Vicki Baum's *Grand Hotel*; and that her paintings and drawings of Minack had been sold all over the world. Her femininity and child-like impetuosity remained, and her contentment.

'Have patience,' I said.

'I've had patience all the year,' she said gently. 'Ever since New Year's Day.'

'Have a little more patience.'

'Doubt in your voice.'

'No, there isn't any doubt . . . I've been thinking about the menu for a long time.'

'A very long time.'

'You could put me off altogether if you make a joke of it.'

'Perhaps that's what you want me to do,' she said, laughing.

'I've even decided upon the first course.'

'What's it to be?'

'Cold cucumber soup.'

She looked at me in astonishment.

'But *I* made the cucumber soup,' she said, 'and it's in the freezer!'

'Ah,' I replied. '*I* grew the cucumbers, and *I* found the recipe.'

'I don't know,' she said, returning to the galley of the kitchen. 'I just don't dare think what the rest of the menu will be like.'

'Nor do I. I'm still thinking it up.'

'Don't strain yourself.'

I continued to sit in my corner of the sofa, staring up at the lintel.

I was thinking of the other inhabitants of Minack who had watched the sun come and go on the lintel. Mystery people who had spent their lives here, leaving no record of their time except the old stone hedges in the fields around us, the carved out meadows on the cliffs, the ancient barn with its granite slabs bound together by clay, the little well beside the lane, the trees they had planted for shelter, the great rocks they had touched, and the cottage with its solid chimney and its arm length thick walls, the dome of the bread oven perfectly built with its small stones, and the lintel above the fireplace where burning furze kept them warm when the gales blew.

Perhaps it was sparks from one furze which set the thatched roof alight many years ago. It was a fire, one would have thought, that would have stayed in the minds of those who lived in St Buryan parish; a story that would have been handed on by parents to their children. Yet, until recently, I never could discover what had happened. Old men of the village, always ready to tell a story, could tell me nothing of the details, only contradictory dates of when it happened . . . 1916 said one, 1922 said another. 'Another world down Minack,' I would be told. 'I've lived in the village all my life and never been down Minack.' They pronounce Minack as Mynack, and it is the local shortened version of Dorminack, the formal name for the cottage. It has always been thus. No one in the parish ever calls the cottage by any name but Minack.

This summer, however, I discovered the truth about the fire at the cottage, but there is still a question mark as to how it started. I had a visit from an elderly lady who had been away from the area for many years, and she had come on a pilgrimage to see the playground of her youth. She had been brought up in one of the three cottages which face the sea a mile or so westwards along the coast, hidden from us by a hill, and where Jane Wyllie of *A Drake at the Door* used to live.

She told me that as a child she used to play games with her friends around Minack and she pointed to a great slab of a rock which juts out from the cottage and said they used to dance barefoot upon it; and years, years later it was the same rock that A. P. Herbert used to romance upon, saying that he was sure it was a rock of magic.

Then she went on to tell us that in 1912 the cottage was empty except that it was used as a store for furniture belonging to the Trewern family who, at that time, farmed Rosemodress, the farm at the top of the hill. Old man Trewern, who was blind, I had often been told about, and he had caught my imagination. He used to come down the curving lane from Rosemodress guided by his stick and, when he reached Minack, crossing Monty's Leap, then up the lane towards the cottage, he stopped when he reached the barn where the old horse of the farm was stabled. He would then go into the stable, and sit down on a stool which was kept there, and listen. Listen to the shifting of the old horse's hooves, listen to him munching the hay in a trough, listen in his mind to the days when the horse led the plough around Minack.

It was in 1912, apparently, that the cottage caught fire and the thatched roof and all the contents were gutted. Obviously there had been no fire-fighting equipment available, mechanised or horse drawn, and so there was no hope for the cottage. Yet it did not char into oblivion. One might even say that, except for the thatched roof, little damage was done. The walls were too thick to be affected, and the lintel too massive.

Massive enough to be there fifty, a hundred, two hundred years into the future; and I wonder whose eyes and what kind of people will be looking at it then.

I have ideas as to what kind of people I would like them to be. I would like people to live here who do not adopt a façade, acting as if effect is of greater value than reality. I would like them to believe that life is a mystery and not an organisation ruled by human beings. I would not like them to be people who are envious of others, who spend more time looking for faults than appreciating virtues; and I would not like them to be social butterflies who prefer chatter to silence. I would like them to be aware of the past, relish the present, and be not too concerned about the future. I would not like them to have orderly minds, because orderly minds would object to the inconvenience of living far from the routine of a housing centre. I would like them to be dreamers, irrational people who are not enslaved by conventional attitudes and contemporary fads; and, as a result, they would be so immersed in the magic of Minack that they would find themselves believing that they had lived here before. They would be stayers, therefore. They would not run away when winter came. They would belong.

Our predecessors, however, never had reason to romance in this way. They lived in the age of innocence. They believed in King and Country, in God, and weather signs in the sky. They were free to be themselves, came slowly to conclusions without being brainwashed by television pundits, or hemmed in by a multitude of laws they did not understand, or by ever-increasing taxes which forced them to give up their pleasures. Life may have been hard for them in many ways, but at least it was simple.

It was simple, for instance, for Harry Ladner. Harry Ladner, who had died some years previously, was the last long-time resident of the cottage before our arrival. Captain Harry he was called; a courtesy title, a title of fun, for he had never been a captain of any sort. He was, too, a man of fun and in between scratching a livelihood from catching rabbits, growing early potatoes, having a few pigs, a cow or two, and daffodils, he would spend much time at the Wink, the pub at Lamorna. There he would regale the customers, those who were strangers, with unlikely stories of the Cornish countryside so colourfully that his glass was never empty. His was an art, a dying art, of entertaining visitors, holding them enthralled with splendid local stories of wreckers and highwaymen and ghosts and stirring stories of the sea. The visitors were delighted, the locals smiled; and when time was called Captain Harry would set out to stagger back to Minack. It was a rough walk, up and down, boulders to trip him up, hedges to climb, and so often, if the weather were fine, he would take a rest amongst the bracken and sleep the night away.

'Ah, Harry Ladner,' I have heard old men say. 'He was a case!'

He was, however, a happy man. He was also, in his own small way, an impresario. He had good timing. He sensed when the occasion was correct to tell this story or that; and he only brought forth his special blockbuster at rare intervals and, only then, if he were sure that no one present had been present at any previous occasion. Had I heard him tell it, I do not think I would have believed him, but I am told that so convincing was he, such a natural con man in fact, that I would have joined every other listener in breathlessly awaiting the outcome of this particular blockbuster.

He would ask his listeners whether they had ever known five rabbits being shot with one bullet from a rifle; and, of course, they would reply that such a deed was impossible. Thereupon he would hold up a bullet in his hand and tell his audience that, if they came back the following evening, he would show them five rabbits all shot by the one bullet. Couldn't he easily cheat? Oh no, he had never cheated, and he promised faithfully that only the one bullet would be fired. His glass was filled again and again, and then he staggered back to Minack.

Next evening at the Wink the customers waited. Seven o'clock, eight o'clock, no sign of Captain Harry . . . and then triumphantly he arrived, carrying five shot rabbits attached to a stick.

'There you are,' he said. 'All five shot by a single bullet.'

'How can you prove it?'

'Ah,' he snorted and, in my mind, I imagine that he was talking like Chris Gittins as the immortal Walter Gabriel of *The Archers*, 'I don't have to prove it. They are there. I just waited until the five of them was lined up in a row.'

More glasses, many more glasses were filled, and once more he returned unsteadily to Minack.

The rumbustious charm of such people is disappearing, partly because television is smoothing away the rough edges of those who live in isolated hamlets, and partly because bureaucratic and commercial forces are determined to eliminate the elusive quality of Cornwall. This elusive quality has its roots in a mysticism which is foreign to a materialistic society and is difficult to defend. Why, for instance, should a desolate moorland, home of foxes, badgers, rabbits and wild birds, be treated as sacred when a housing estate on the site would provide hundreds of homes? Why should a caravan on a headland be considered unsightly when the farming community are allowed to erect vast hangers of barns wherever they wish without official consent? Why shouldn't there be chalets close to a beach, providing holidays for factory workers and others? Why shouldn't it be allowed to build a house on the coast?

Logical answers to such questions are a problem to find. Anything to do with subtlety, sensitivity and taste, is difficult to explain to those who are conditioned into believing that economic indexes provide the criterion for happiness; and it is made the more difficult when one realises that in this age of mania of equality the comparative few appreciate beauty. The majority are happy crowded on Blackpool sands or the Costa Brava. The majority like noise, queueing, wearing funny hats, and simple foods like fish and chips. Nothing wrong in that. But it is sad, I feel, when they move out of their established enclaves and proceed to uproot those who do not share their standards; and are encouraged to do so, for gain, both by bureaucratic and commercial forces.

West Cornwall at the present time, for instance, is under siege. The developers and the roadmakers have been creeping down the spine of Cornwall for the past few years, employing their earth-moving machines to gouge away the countryside, building zombie housing estates around ancient villages, and erecting monstrous edifices in old town centres like that of Truro, where the beautiful cathedral is squashed against a multi-storey car park. Nothing that the developers produce can be admired. All is functional . . . the hideous multiple stores, carbon copies of those in Birmingham, Streatham or Derby; the squat, massive insurance and building society offices which sprout like mushrooms in every High Street, and even the hoardings which advertise the housing estates. There is one such hoarding on the top of Paul Hill above Newlyn, which has been there for five years . . . suitable for commuter belt country, but a running sore for those who prefer to forget the existence of developers in the wild land of the far west.

The Road, however, offers the biggest menace. The Road is the brainchild of the Department of the Environment and its offshoot, the Western Road Construction Unit. The Unit has been responsible for the motorways of the West Country and, despite there being several really necessary routes to develop, such as from Truro to Falmouth and from Falmouth to Helston, it has fixed its attention upon creating the Road to Penzance.

One stretch requiring two hundred acres of farmland will run from Camborne to St Erth where the present A30 turns off to St Ives; and the second stretch will run from St Erth to the Heliport at the entrance of Penzance, requiring another one hundred acres of farmland. One suspects that the main purpose of the Road is to provide jobs for the Unit and the contractors involved . . . for no one in the area has any wish for it.

After all, the Road can only lead to Land's End and the sea . . . and, except in the short period of peak August holiday traffic, the present road is a motorist's paradise, so sparse is the traffic. Hence millions of taxpayers' money is about to be wasted, at the same time as bringing to a stop the kind of tourist who is so vital to the economy of West Cornwall.

But if there are those outside Cornwall who are determined to destroy the beauty of Cornwall, there are many people within the county who are equally determined to stop them. These are not just Canute-minded members of Conservation Groups . . . they are local councillors, county councillors and members of the public, who are becoming ever increasingly aware that the mystical charm of Cornwall could vanish in a decade if the developers have their way. The control of caravan sites, for instance, is an example of what has been achieved.

The long-established caravan sites, those that sprawl like fungi on various coastal stretches, will, unfortunately, have to remain . . . but any new caravan site, even if it is permitted, is subject to very stringent planning control. Often this means that the site has a dual purpose, being a home for touring caravans in the summer, but reverting to grazing pasture for cattle during the rest of the year. Hence there is no permanent disfigurement of the landscape. I am thinking, at this moment, of two recently established caravan sites, that of Treverven a few miles from Minack, and of Trelowarren, ancient home of the Vyvyan family near the Helford River. Neither of these gives offence; and there are other smaller ones, attached to farms, like the one at Boleigh which we pass on the way to Penzance, that are inconspicuous.

Thus, although once I was a critic of the caravan holiday, I am now in favour. The only snag about such a holiday affects the holidaymakers themselves. They swop household chores for caravan chores, and the Jeannies of this world have to continue with their cooking.

That sentence reminds me of my own self-indulgent behaviour. I have taken Jeannie's efforts in the kitchen too long for granted. I sit ruminating on the sofa while she is fussing over pots and pans and preparing delicacies to delight me. It is time I fulfilled the last of my New Year resolutions. I must cook a meal she will remember.

Postscript

I wish I could say that the meal was a complete success. It was nearly so, but I made a stupid mistake at the end. The menu I chose was as follows:–

Cucumber Soup
Sole Miroton with Pommes de Terre Duchesse.
Cape Gooseberry Flan.

The cucumber soup, I have already admitted, came from the freezer. The choice of *Sole Miroton* was a matter of luck. I took from the bookshelf a copy of Madame Prunier's Fish Cookery Book, the same copy that inspired me years before at Mortlake, opened a page at random, shut my eyes, and dabbed my finger on the recipe for *Sole Miroton*. It read:

Poach the fillets flat with white wine and fish fumet. Dish them on a rather creamy mushroom purée, and scatter on the fillets some roughly chopped *fines herbes*

(Parsley, chervil, chives and tarragon). Cover with highly seasoned Bercy Sauce, and brown quickly.

The Cape Gooseberry flan I chose because I had grown a number of Cape Gooseberry plants from seed and each plant had grown into a mammoth size in the greenhouse and had a proliferation of fruit. We had not expected such a proliferation. We had grown them because Jeannie has a particular liking for the Cape Gooseberry coated in sugar which is served with Friandises in restaurants. We did not, however, realise until we grew them, that they were also a winter fruit, a delicious, sweet gooseberry which needed no cooking and was ideal for tarts and flans.

Thus the menu was set, a Sunday lunchtime was chosen as the occasion, and the necessary materials obtained. Soon after breakfast on the appointed day, I persuaded Jeannie to disappear from the cottage for the morning; and she went away in a state of apprehension. She could not believe that my *Sole Miroton* could be anything but a disaster.

I too, as I stood alone in the kitchen, was in a state of apprehension. My high-sounding promises had reached the moment of action. I had to prepare a fish fumet, and a fish velouté for the Bercy Sauce.

Put four tablespoonfuls of white wine and the same of fish fumet in a saucepan [read the recipe for Bercy Sauce] with a dessertspoonful of chopped shallot, and reduce it by a third. Add not quite half a pint of fish velouté, bring to the boil, and finish with two ounces of butter and a teaspoonful of chopped parsley.

Keep calm, I said to myself, read the instructions carefully, don't hurry, and above all don't lose your nerve. Your character is being put to the test.

At that moment there was a miaow at my feet.

'Oliver!'

There was another miaow, a squeak of a miaow.

'Ambrose!'

I greeted them as one greets old friends in a moment of crisis. The rush of warmth, the sudden easing of tension. It did not matter to me that they had ulterior motives. I just felt grateful for their presence.

Thus, as I cooked, they watched my progress . . . the stewing of the fish bones, the sieving through a strainer, the making of a *roux* (flour and butter), the simmering, the preparation of the mushroom purée and the potatoes and, finally, after Jeannie had returned, the poaching of the sole.

'And now,' I said, when I had finished. 'You can be the official tasters.'

And they gobbled a fillet.

Jeannie did not gobble. She slowly savoured my delicacy. She even declared it a triumph of *haute cuisine*. She declared that *Sole Miroton* was one of the great fish dishes of the world . . . and such was her praise that I doffed my imaginary chef's hat again and again after our plates were empty.

Then came the Cape Gooseberry flan.

And this *was* a disaster.

I set it down confidently on the table, produced a bowl of Cornish cream, and cut two slices. They were uneatable.

In cooking the pastry I had made a fundamental mistake. I had mixed the pastry and fashioned it into the circular tin, then failed to pre-heat the oven. Thus my flan went into a cold oven; and the consequence was pastry with the consistency of cardboard.

Jeannie's only comment was to suggest that the gulls on the roof would enjoy it; and the donkeys if there were still some to spare; and Broadbent.